Analyzing Syntax

Analyzing syntax: a lexical-functional approach is a comprehensive and accessible textbook on syntactic analysis, designed for students of linguistics at advanced undergraduate or graduate level. Working within the 'Lexical Functional Grammar' (LFG) approach, it provides students with a framework for analyzing and describing grammatical structure, using extensive examples from both European and non-European languages.

As well as building on what linguists have learned about language in general, particular attention is paid to the unique features of individual languages. While its primary focus is on syntactic structure, the book also deals with aspects of meaning, function, and word structure that are directly relevant to syntax.

Clearly organized into topics, this textbook is ideal for one-semester courses in syntax and grammatical analysis.

PAUL R. KROEGER is Associate Professor and Head of Department at the Graduate Institute of Applied Linguistics, Dallas. He has previously published *Phrase structure and grammatical relations in Tagalog* (1993). He has also carried out linguistic fieldwork in East Malaysia, and has written for many journals including *Pacific Linguistics, Oceanic Linguistics*, and the *Philippine Journal of Linguistics*.

Analyzing Syntax
A Lexical-Functional Approach

PAUL R. KROEGER

Graduate Institute of Applied Linguistics, Dallas

 CAMBRIDGE
UNIVERSITY PRESS

PUBLISHED BY THE PRESS SYNDICATE OF THE UNIVERSITY OF CAMBRIDGE
The Pitt Building, Trumpington Street, Cambridge, United Kingdom

CAMBRIDGE UNIVERSITY PRESS
The Edinburgh Building, Cambridge, CB2 2RU, UK
40 West 20th Street, New York, NY 10011–4211, USA
477 Williamstown Road, Port Melbourne, VIC 3207, Australia
Ruiz de Alarcón 13, 28014 Madrid, Spain
Dock House, The Waterfront, Cape Town 8001, South Africa

http://www.cambridge.org

First published 2004
Reprinted 2006

Printed in the United Kingdom at the University Press, Cambridge

Typeface Times 10.5/13 pt.   *System* LATEX 2$_\varepsilon$ [TB]

A catalogue record for this book is available from the British Library

Library of Congress Cataloging in Publication data
Kroeger, Paul, 1952–
Analyzing syntax : a lexical-functional approach / Paul R. Kroeger.
   p.   cm.
Includes bibliographical references and index.
ISBN 0 521 81623 8   ISBN 0 521 01654 1 (pb.)
1. Grammar, Comparative and general – Syntax.   2. Lexical-functional grammar.
I. Title.
P291.K76   2004
415 – dc21   2003055382

ISBN 0 521 81623 8 hardback
ISBN 0 521 01654 1 paperback

For my parents, Dick and Cathie

Contents

Preface and acknowledgments

This book provides a framework for analyzing and describing grammatical structure, building on what linguists have learned about language in general while paying careful attention to the unique features of each particular language. Its primary focus is on syntax (sentence structure), but it also deals with aspects of meaning, function, and word structure that are directly relevant to syntax.

This is a book about syntactic analysis, rather than syntactic theory. I have adopted a simplified version of Lexical Functional Grammar (LFG) as the analytical framework for the book, but I have tried in each chapter to emphasize linguistic phenomena over formal notation. The analyses presented here are very much in the spirit of LFG, but the notation employed is modified and simplified compared to that of standard LFG. Those readers who want a more complete introduction to LFG as a formal system are encouraged to consult Bresnan (2001), Dalrymple (2001), or Falk (2001).

This book is written at a level which should be appropriate for advanced undergraduate or beginning graduate students. It presupposes some familiarity with basic linguistic concepts and terminology, but no previous background in formal syntax. The contents can be covered fairly easily in a typical semester-length course. The book does not assume that its readers have native-speaker intuitions about English. So, for example, in some places the meanings of English idioms are explained, alternative possible interpretations of certain constructions are explicitly spelled out, etc.

Only a few exercises are included in this volume, and they are clustered in the first five chapters of the book. Most of these exercises focus more on the interpretation of linguistic evidence than on the primary analysis of unfamiliar language data. Many teachers will want to supplement these with other, more analytical, data problems, depending on the needs and background of the students. In teaching this material, I have also found it extremely helpful to have students write a short research paper about some aspect of the syntax of their own language, or another language that they know well. Exploring one particular issue in greater depth helps to solidify their grasp of the framework as a whole. This project also gives students a small taste of what it feels like to do original research, and gets them reading some of the relevant linguistic literature.

It would be only a slight exaggeration to say that every linguist I know has helped me with this project in one way or another, and it is impossible for me to list them all by name. But, in addition to specific contributions mentioned in the footnotes, special thanks are due to the following people for linguistic and editorial advice: Wayan Arka, Dorothee Beerman, Joan Bresnan, Don Burquest, Mary Dalrymple, Yo Matsumoto, Sam Mchombo, Brian O'Herin, Jane Simpson, Fu Tan, and Janet Watkins. Thanks also to the faculty, staff, and students of the Linguistics Department at Stanford University, who did so much to make my sabbatical there in 2000–01 enjoyable and productive. Finally, thanks to my wife, Chaw-Nen, for her patience with this very time-consuming process.

Abbreviations

1	1st person
2	2nd person
3	3rd person
A	agent (trans. subject)
ABS	absolutive
ACC	accusative
ACCOMP	accompaniment
ADNOM	adnominal
ADVBL	adverbializer
ANTIPASS	antipassive
APPL	applicative
ART	article
ASP	aspect
ASSOC	associative
AUX	auxiliary
AV	active voice (Austronesian: Actor voice)
BEN	benefactive
CAUS	causative
CLASS	classifier
COMP	complementizer
COP	copula
DAT	dative
DEF	definite
DS	different subject
DU(AL)	dual
DV	dative voice (Austronesian)
EMPH	emphatic
ERG	ergative
EX(CL)	exclusive
F(EM)	feminine
FOC	focus
FUT	future tense
GEN	genitive
HABIT	habitual
HON	honorific

IMPERF	imperfective
INCHOAT	inchoative
INCL	inclusive
INDIC	indicative
INF	infinitive
INSTR	instrumental
INTERROG	interrogative
intr.	intransitive
INVOL	involuntary/non-volitional
IRR	irrealis
IV	instrumental voice (Austronesian)
LNK	linker
LOC	locative
M(ASC)	masculine
MOD	modality
N(EUT)	neuter
NEG	negative
NMLZR	nominalizer
NOM	nominative
NON.FIN	non-finite
NONPAST	nonpast tense
O.agr	object agreement
OBJ	primary object
OBJ$_2$	secondary object
OBL	oblique argument
OV	objective voice (Austronesian)
P	patient (trans. object)
p.c.	personal communication
PASS	passive
PAST	past tense
PERF	perfective
PFCT	perfect
PERS	person; personal name
pl / PL	plural
POL	politeness
POSS	possessor
POTENT	potential
PRES	present tense
PRO	pronoun
PROG	progressive
PRTCPL	participle
PTCLE	particle
PURP	purpose
Q(UES)	question

REAL	realis
REC.PAST	recent past tense
REL	relativizer
REM.PAST	remote past tense
S(UBJ)	subject
S.agr	subject agreement
S-ADJ	sentential adjunct
S-COMP	sentential complement
SBJNCT	subjunctive
SEQ	sequential
sg /SG	singular
SIMUL	simultaneous
SS	same subject
TOP	topic
tr./TRANS	transitive
UV	Undergoer voice (Austronesian)
XADJ	open adjunct
XCOMP	open complement (or predicate complement)

1   Three aspects of syntactic structure

Probably no one has ever before said or heard the following sentence, yet any normal adult speaker of English will understand it:

(1)   John Adams could have been elected to a fourth term as President, if his step-sister had not been so ugly.

In the same way, a speaker of any language will say and hear many sentences during the course of a normal day which he has never said or heard before. Moreover, other speakers of the same language will not only recognize these original creations as being well-formed sentences but will also (usually) understand what they mean.

These observations tell us something important about the nature of language. A person who knows how to speak a language does not have to memorize every possible sentence in that language. Rather, speakers produce sentences CREATIVELY. Some common phrases and sentences may be repeated so often that they are memorized as a single unit, e.g., idioms and proverbs. But, for the most part, we do not memorize sentences; rather, we construct them when we need them, to express a particular idea.

This creative use of language is possible because the patterns of a language are determined by a set of RULES. A speaker who (unconsciously) "knows" these rules can use them to create and understand any number of new sentences. Linguists use the term GRAMMAR to refer to the set of rules needed to produce well-formed utterances in a particular language. The chief concern of this book will be to help you analyze and describe the kinds of grammatical patterns commonly found in human languages, in particular those aspects of the grammar that are relevant to SYNTAX, i.e., the arrangement of words in a sentence.

1.1   Grammar and grammaticality

Our ultimate goal, as linguists, is to understand the speaker's "internal grammar," i.e., the system of rules which a speaker unconsciously uses in speaking and listening. Since speakers are not aware of using these rules, they cannot simply tell us what the rules are. (As noted below, we are not speaking here of PRESCRIPTIVE rules, like those commonly taught in school. Those would be easier for speakers to describe, because they are consciously learned.) We begin by making observations about what people say, what they do not say, how they interpret what other speakers say, etc. Our description of the grammar, based on careful analysis of these observations, will involve formulating explicit rules that can model (i.e., produce the same grammatical patterns as) the speaker's internal grammar.

Of course, in order to speak and understand a language we must know not only rules but also words. Linguists use the term LEXICON to refer to the set of all the words (or, more generally, meaningful elements) in the language. We can think of the lexicon as the speaker's "mental dictionary." Much of the information in the lexicon is unpredictable, such as the fact that the pronunciation /kæt/ refers (in English) to a small carnivorous mammal with whiskers. But the lexicon contains a number of regularities as well. Precisely how much regularity is a hotly debated question; we will return to this issue in chapter 3. In this chapter, we introduce some basic concepts needed for discussing grammatical systems.

1.1.1   "Grammaticality" and variation

In claiming that sentence (1) is a well-formed English sentence we do not imply that it is either true or sensible. In fact, it is stunningly illogical and historically inaccurate on several counts. (That is why no one else is likely ever to have said it before.) This distinction between the form of a sentence and its meaning is an important one. In some cases we might consider a sentence to be well-formed even when it has no sensible meaning at all. Chomsky (1957) used the following pair of sentences, which have become famous through countless repetitions, to illustrate this point:

(2) a   Colorless green ideas sleep furiously.
    b   Furiously sleep ideas green colorless.

Chomsky claimed: "Sentences [2a] and [2b] are equally nonsensical, but any speaker of English will recognize that only the former is grammatical." The second part of this claim has sometimes been disputed, but the essential point is that speakers have an intuitive sense of "grammaticality," or correctness of form, which does not depend on our ability to interpret the meaning of the sentence.

Chomsky argued that any speaker of English would consider sentence (2a) to be "grammatical," even though it makes no sense. (More specifically, the meanings of the individual words in this sentence are not compatible with each other, and so this combination of word-meanings produces contradictory information.) Conversely, as the following sentences show, we can often understand a sentence perfectly well even if it is not "grammatical":

(3) a   Me Tarzan, you Jane.
    b   Those guys was trying to kill me.
    c   When he came here?

When speakers reject the sentences in (3) as being "ungrammatical" or "bad English," they mean that one (or more) of the rules of their internal grammar has been violated. One way in which a linguist tries to understand this internal grammar is to formulate a set of rules which will model the judgments of a native speaker: a set of rules which will produce all of the sentences that speakers consider to be grammatical but none of the sentences that speakers consider to be ungrammatical.

This may sound like a fairly straightforward goal, but there are a number of factors which complicate the process. For one thing, speakers of a given language do not always agree about the grammaticality of particular sentences. Each of the sentences in (4a, b, c), for example, would be perfectly acceptable to English speakers from certain geographical areas, but sound quite odd to English speakers from other areas. This kind of variation among regional dialects is found at least to some extent in most of the world's languages. Sentence (4d) involves a different kind of variation, namely variation among individual speakers. It is not associated with a particular region; even speakers from the same dialect area may differ as to whether they would say such sentences, or accept them as being grammatical.[1]

(4) a   I might could be persuaded to try that.
   b   My back door needs fixed.
   c   The ship is arriving Monday week.
   d   They have come visited us every day this month.

Of course language is a means of communication, and if two speakers have radically different internal grammars, communication will be extremely difficult if not impossible. For many purposes, we can speak of "the grammar" of a language as if it were a body of knowledge which all speakers of that language must share; and to a very large extent this is true. But we must always be aware of the variation among dialects and individuals which this over-simplified view ignores. Indeed, the variation itself is also something that linguists seek to document and explain.

Another challenge to the linguist who wants to describe and model the rule system of a language is that languages are always changing. Moreover, community attitudes about language often change more slowly than the actual practice of the community in speaking the language. Consider the examples in (5).

(5) a   With two things hath God man's soul endowed.
   b   I know not what course others may take, but as for me . . .
   c   The problem is, is that no one wants this job.
   d   The mission of the *Enterprise* is to boldly go where no man has gone before.

The word order of (5a) was perfectly normal in Old English (before 1100 A D), but most speakers of modern English will probably consider it extremely odd, if not actually ungrammatical. Example (5b) is taken from a famous speech by Patrick Henry (1775 A D). Similar examples are very common in Shakespeare and the King James Bible (1611 A D), but today they are regarded as archaic or (in modern usage) unnatural.

The construction in (5c) is a much more recent innovation. It is now very widely used in informal speech, at least in American English, but most educated speakers would probably reject it in formal written styles. Moreover, standard reference books on English grammar, school textbooks, etc. do not recognize it as an acceptable way of speaking.

Sentence (5d) is an example of a "split infinitive," because the adverb *boldly* appears in the middle of the infinitive *to go*. This pattern emerged in the fourteenth century due to a cluster of morphological and syntactic changes in Middle English, and has been used quite commonly ever since (Hall, 1882; Kiparsky, 1997). However in the nineteenth century, as part of a growing concern for defining "correct" usage in English, influential authorities began to assert that the split infinitive was "bad English" (i.e., ungrammatical), apparently because no such pattern exists in Latin. This judgment is maintained in school textbooks to the present day.

The case of the split infinitive is a notorious example of a PRESCRIPTIVE approach to grammar: grammarians telling other people how to talk. Of course, there are many contexts where a prescriptive approach is appropriate and indeed necessary: e.g., in planning and developing the standard form of a new national language, in teaching adult language learners to speak correctly, in teaching high school students to write acceptable essays, etc. But these areas of "applied linguistics" will not be our primary focus.

The approach we adopt in this book will be DESCRIPTIVE rather than prescriptive. This means that we take it as our goal to observe, describe, and analyze what speakers of a language actually say, rather than trying to tell them what they should or should not say. Most of our examples will come from published sources. As a result, these examples often represent a standardized or high-prestige variety of the language.[2] But the same approach can be applied to data from non-standard dialects, or even languages which have no written form at all. Indeed, one of the goals of this book is to equip you to undertake this kind of research.

Our approach will be primarily SYNCHRONIC; that is, we will be primarily interested in describing the structure of a particular language or dialect at a particular time (normally the present), rather than comparing it with related dialects or investigating how the language has changed over time.

As we noted in the introduction to this chapter, SYNTAX is the branch of linguistics which seeks to describe and account for the arrangement of words in a sentence. In order to do this we will often need to look at the structure of the words themselves, i.e., at certain aspects of the MORPHOLOGY. For example, in some languages the presence of a certain prefix or suffix on the verb determines where other words in the sentence may or may not occur. Moreover, even though form and meaning are partially independent of each other, as we have seen, they are also intimately connected. So in studying the form of sentences we will often be led to consider their SEMANTICS (i.e., meaning) as well.

Finally, in addition to the form and meaning of individual sentences, we will sometimes need to consider connections between one sentence and another, or the function of a particular sentence in a specific context. (The study of these aspects of language use is called PRAGMATICS.) And we may occasionally mention stylistic or social factors which influence the kind of sentence patterns a speaker might use; but our primary focus will be on the sentence patterns themselves. Morphology, semantics, pragmatics, and sociolinguistics are major fields of study in their own right, but in this book we will touch on them only where they are directly relevant to the syntactic issues that we consider.

1.1.2   Sentence structure

A sentence is not simply a string of words, one after another. An overwhelming body of linguistic and psycho-linguistic evidence shows that speakers think of sentences as having a fairly complex structure, with certain words grouped together to function as units, larger groups formed from smaller groups, and important relationships defined between one group and another.

Of course, these structural relationships are "invisible," because all we hear is the string of words. In some ways the task of the linguist is similar to that of early chemists. By observing changes in the physical properties of substances when they were combined in various ways, these chemists were able to develop theories about the unseen structures of atoms and molecules which could account for their observations. In the same way, the linguist tries to understand unseen linguistic structures based on observations about what can be heard.

One reason for thinking that sentences do in fact have this kind of abstract structure is that a given string of words may be AMBIGUOUS, i.e., allow two different interpretations, even when none of the individual words in the string is itself ambiguous. Consider the following examples (adapted from Huddleston, 1984).

(6) a   Liz attacked the man with a knife.
   b   Ed likes Sue more than Jill.
   c   The proposal that Hitler was advancing seemed preposterous.

The meaning of example (6a) depends on the structural relationships of the phrase *with a knife*. This sentence could be used to answer two different questions: *Who did Liz attack? The man with a knife* or *What did Liz attack the man with? With a knife*.

The meaning of example (6b) depends on the relationship of the word *Jill* to the verb *like*: is *Jill* to be understood as the subject of *like* (as in *Ed likes Sue more than Jill likes Sue*), or as the object of *like* (as in *Ed likes Sue more than Ed likes Jill*)? The meaning of example (6c) depends on the relationship between the word *proposal* and the phrase *that Hitler was advancing*. Is the proposal something which is being advanced by Hitler? Or is Hitler himself supposedly advancing, and the proposal merely a report (by some other person) of this event?[3] Such examples of STRUCTURAL AMBIGUITY can provide important evidence about the structures which speakers assign to sentences.

Languages show great variety in terms of the strings of words that they use; that is one of the reasons why word-by-word translation fails so miserably. But when we compare abstract structural properties, languages turn out to be much more similar to each other than we might have guessed. In some respects the variation among languages is surprisingly limited. For this reason, studying data from a wide range of languages can be a great help to us in knowing what to look for when we tackle a new language, particularly if that language has not been analyzed before.

1.2   Outline of a framework

The job of the syntactician can be divided into two main steps: first, determine the correct structure(s) for each grammatical sentence; and second, formulate a set of rules which will distinguish between grammatical and ungrammatical structures for that language (i.e., allow us to predict which structures will be grammatical and which ungrammatical). Of course, the two tasks are closely related, and we will be concerned with both. But we will devote most of our attention in this book to the first of these issues, in particular to the kinds of evidence that are relevant for determining linguistic structure.

In order to discuss the details of syntactic structure with any kind of precision we will need to develop (i) a technical vocabulary; (ii) a system for representing structural relations; and (iii) a set of concepts which are relevant to this task. Such an inventory of vocabulary, notation and concepts is called a syntactic FRAMEWORK.

A good framework must do at least three things. First, it should make it easy to describe the syntactic patterns found in any particular language. Second, it should make it easy to compare syntactic patterns between languages. Third, it should allow us to make generalizations about human language in general, i.e., to state THEORIES (factual claims about how language works).

In the remainder of this chapter, we will sketch out the beginnings of a framework for syntactic analysis. As a way of introducing some of the concepts which we will need to use in talking about syntactic structure, let us first think about structural complexity. What makes a sentence "complex"? Which of the following Malay sentences is the most complex? Try to rank them, from simplest to most complex.

(7) a   Dia mandi.
        3sg bathe
        'He is bathing.'

   b   Saya makan nasi.
        1sg   eat   cooked.rice
        'I eat/am eating rice.'

   c   Orang tua itu makan nasi goreng setiap hari.
        person old that eat   rice fry   each day
        'That old person eats fried rice every day.'

   d   Dia belajar untuk   menjadi pensyarah.[4]
        3sg study   in.order become lecturer
        'He is studying to become a lecturer.'

One way to measure complexity, though perhaps not the most revealing way, is by absolute length (number of words). On this basis, (7a) is clearly the simplest and (7c) the most complex. Of course, there are other, and more persuasive, reasons for considering (7a) to be the simplest. Semantically it names a single event, 'bathe', which involves just one participant. Sentence (7b), on the other hand, names an event which involves two participants, the "eater" and the "eaten."

Sentence (7c) names an event of exactly the same type as (7b). It uses the same verb (*makan* 'eat') and involves the same number of participants playing the same roles. So in this respect we might evaluate them as being equally simple. But (7c) also contains an additional piece of information, namely the fact that this event occurs 'every day.' This time phrase is, in a sense, added on to the basic description of the event.

In discussing the meaning of a clause, we will use the term PREDICATE to refer to the word which names the action, event, or state described by that clause. Typically this word will be a verb.

Now any event named by the predicate 'eat' must involve at least two participants, the "eater" and the "eaten." (This is true even though one or the other of these participants may not be mentioned in a particular description of the event, e.g., *John is still eating* or *The fish was eaten*.) For this reason we say that the predicate 'eat' takes two ARGUMENTS. But a time phrase like 'every day' is not an inherent part of the meaning of 'eat.' This kind of phrase can be added freely to virtually any clause that describes an event. An extra piece of information of this kind, something that is not an argument of the predicate, is called an ADJUNCT.

The ARGUMENT STRUCTURE of a predicate is a representation of the number and type of arguments associated with that predicate, as illustrated in (8). We will use the general term AGENT to represent the participant who performs a certain action, and the term PATIENT for the participant that something happens to; see section 1.2.1 for further discussion and examples.

(8)   *bathe* < agent >
             eat < agent, patient >

Argument structure is important to the syntax, because it determines many of the basic grammatical properties of the clause in which the predicate occurs. Argument structure is closely related to meaning, but it is obviously not intended to represent the full meaning of a sentence, or even of a predicate. For example, it is true that (7b) and (7c) have the same argument structure; but that does not mean that the meaning of the two sentences is equivalent. One reason for this is that adjuncts are not a part of the argument structure. Another reason is that the argument structure indicates only the role which each argument plays in the event, but does not give any information about the inherent properties of the arguments themselves, e.g., the fact that the agent in (7c) is an old person.

This last point brings us back to another important difference between (7b) and (7c). Sentence (7b), repeated below as (9a), consists of three basic elements: a subject, a verb, and a direct object. (What we mean by "subject" and "direct object" will be discussed in section 1.2.3.) Each of these elements is named by a single word. Sentence (7c) (ignoring the adjunct phrase) has the same three basic elements; but here the subject and object are each expressed by a phrase containing more than one word, as shown by the brackets in (9b).

(9) a   [Saya] makan [nasi].
          1sg   eat   cooked.rice
          'I eat/am eating rice.'

    b   [Orang tua itu] makan [nasi goreng].
          person old that eat   rice fry
          'That old person eats fried rice.'

The fact that groups of words can function as units (or CONSTITUENTS) within sentences is an important aspect of the grammar of every human language. In analyzing the structure of a sentence, it is very important to identify the constituent boundaries (i.e., to determine which words group together as units), to specify the linear order of constituents in the sentence, and to specify the ordering of the words within each constituent. The aspect of syntactic structure which represents these kinds of information is called CONSTITUENT STRUCTURE (or PHRASE STRUCTURE).

Now let us return to sentence (7d), repeated below as (10). This sentence is shorter than (7c), in that it contains fewer words; and it involves only a single participant (the one who is studying). So at first glance it may look simpler than (7c). But the meaning is more complex. This sentence actually describes two events, 'studying' and 'becoming a lecturer.' The two events have a certain logical relationship to each other: the agent does X in order to achieve Y. Each of these events is named by a distinct predicate, *belajar* 'study' and *menjadi* 'become,' and each predicate has its own argument structure.

(10)   Dia belajar untuk   menjadi pensyarah. (= 7d)
          3sg study   in.order become lecturer
          'He is studying to become a lecturer.'

Corresponding to this semantic complexity, the grammatical structure of (7d) is considerably more complex than that of (7c). This kind of sentence structure will be discussed in some detail in chapter 5. For now we will just observe that in (7d) we find one CLAUSE (or simple sentence) embedded within another. That is, one clause functions as a constituent of another, specifically in this case as an adjunct. Moreover, the subject of the embedded clause is understood to be identical with the subject of the main clause. The function of the embedded clause within the larger sentence, and the relationship between the subject of the embedded clause and the subject of the main clause, are part of the FUNCTIONAL STRUCTURE of the sentence.

We have mentioned three aspects of the structural complexity of sentence (7d): argument structure, constituent structure, and functional structure. These three aspects of syntactic structure will be important for our analysis of a wide variety of constructions; so in the remainder of this chapter we will briefly review some of the basic features of each.

1.2.1   Argument structure

As stated above, argument structure is a representation of the number and type of arguments associated with a particular predicate. Determining the number of arguments is not always as easy as one might expect; but identifying the "type" of these arguments may seem even more difficult. What exactly do we mean by this?

In fact this question has been a hotly debated issue among linguists. The approach which we will adopt here is to assign participants to broad semantic or conceptual categories according to the role they play in the described event or situation: "agent" for participants that do something; "patient" for participants to whom something is done; "experiencer" for participants who think or feel something, etc. Unfortunately (but not surprisingly) there is no one set of semantic role labels which all linguists agree on, and different linguists sometimes use the same labels in different ways. But in this book we will refer to (at least) the following semantic roles:

(11)   INVENTORY OF SEMANTIC ROLES:
        AGENT: causer or initiator of events
        EXPERIENCER: animate entity which perceives a stimulus or registers a
            particular mental or emotional process or state
        RECIPIENT: animate entity which receives or acquires something
        BENEFICIARY: entity (usually animate) for whose benefit an action is
            performed
        INSTRUMENT: inanimate entity used by an agent to perform some action
        THEME: entity which undergoes a change of location or possession, or
            whose location is being specified
        PATIENT: entity which is acted upon, affected, or created; or of which a
            state or change of state is predicated
        STIMULUS: object of perception, cognition, or emotion; entity which is
            seen, heard, known, remembered, loved, hated, etc.
        LOCATION: spatial reference point of the event. The LOCATION role
            includes the sub-types SOURCE, GOAL, and PATH, which respectively
            describe the origin (or beginning-point), destination (or end-point), and
            pathway of a motion
        ACCOMPANIMENT (or COMITATIVE): entity which accompanies or is
            associated with the performance of an action

Some examples of the most common of these roles are given in (12):

(12) a   *John   gave Mary   a bouquet of roses.*
          AGENT   RECIPIENT THEME

     b   *John   baked Mary   a chocolate cake.*
          AGENT   BENEFICIARY PATIENT

c   *John   opened the lock   with a key.*
    AGENT   PATIENT INSTRUMENT

d   *The key   opened the lock.*
    INSTRUMENT   PATIENT

e   *Sherlock Holmes heard a piercing scream.*
    EXPERIENCER   STIMULUS

For many verbs, it is not too difficult to identify the arguments with one or another of these roles; some examples are given in (13). But in other cases a particular argument may not seem to fit naturally into any of these categories; for example, what is the semantic role of *mother* in *Susan resembles her mother*? Or an argument may appear to bear two roles; for example, *John* seems to be both an agent and a theme in *John jumped into the well*.

(13)   *dance* <agent>
    eat <agent, patient>
    love <experiencer, stimulus>
    give <agent, theme, recipient>

These kinds of issues have been discussed at considerable length, but for our purposes they do not represent a major problem. The primary function of these role labels is to allow us to distinguish among the arguments of a particular predicate.[5] Thus some linguists prefer to use unique labels for each predicate, as we did above in referring to the arguments of *eat* as the "eater" and the "eaten." But it is also true that the categories in (11) are quite useful for describing a wide variety of grammatical patterns. That is why the use of these labels remains so popular, in spite of certain well-known problems.

Notice that the list in (11) is restricted to ARGUMENT roles. Some other commonly expressed types of semantic information, e.g., time, manner, purpose, etc. are not included here, because the elements which express these concepts are almost always ADJUNCTS rather than arguments. This distinction between arguments and adjuncts is important, but not always easy to make. The basic difference is that arguments are closely associated with the meaning of the predicate itself, while adjuncts are not.

Adjuncts contribute to the meaning of the sentence as a whole, but are never necessary to complete the meaning of the predicate. Thus adjuncts are always optional, whereas arguments are frequently obligatory. Sentence (14a) shows that the object of *use* is obligatory, and therefore an argument. As (14b) illustrates, even when an argument is grammatically optional it may be semantically obligatory; for example, even when the patient of *eat* is not expressed, we know that something gets eaten. But adjuncts can always be omitted without creating this kind of implication, as seen in (15).

(14)   ARGUMENTS
    a   Mary used <u>my shirt</u> for a hand towel.
       *Mary used for a hand towel.

b   John ate <u>an apple</u>.
     John ate.   (implies that John ate <u>something</u>)

(15)   ADJUNCTS
 a   George fell down the stairs <u>last night</u>.
      George fell down the stairs.   (no implied time reference)

 b   My daughter <u>intentionally</u> swallowed a penny.
      My daughter swallowed a penny.   (neutral with respect to volitionality)

A second important difference is that arguments must be unique within their clause, but adjuncts may be freely multiplied. For example, the third sentence in (16a) is ungrammatical because it contains two recipient phrases; this shows that the recipient of *give* is an argument. On the other hand, the grammaticality of (16b–c) shows that time and manner phrases are adjuncts, rather than arguments.

(16) a   John gave <u>Susan</u> a bouquet of roses.
          John gave a bouquet of roses <u>to his mother</u>.
          *John gave <u>Susan</u> a bouquet of roses <u>to his mother</u>.

 b   TIME ADJUNCTS
      George fell down the stairs <u>last night</u> <u>at 3:00 AM</u> <u>during the typhoon</u>.

 c   MANNER ADJUNCTS
      My daughter <u>suddenly</u>, <u>impulsively</u>, <u>without thinking</u>, swallowed a penny.

A third difference is that verbs may place SELECTIONAL RESTRICTIONS on their arguments, but not on adjuncts. For example, the patient of *drink* must be a liquid. The patient of *assassinate* must be an important political figure. German has two words for 'eat': *essen*, which requires a human agent; and *fressen*, which requires a non-human agent. Restrictions of this kind, which are associated with a specific verb, are never imposed on adjuncts.

Notice that selectional restrictions of this kind must be stated in terms of semantic roles (agent, patient, etc.) rather than grammatical relations (subject, object, etc.). This is illustrated in (17–19). The examples in (17) show that the patient of *drink* must be a liquid, whether it appears as object or subject. The examples in (18) show that the verb *love* requires an animate experiencer, not an animate subject; (18b), which has an animate subject, is extremely odd, whereas (18a), which has an inanimate subject, is perfectly sensible. And (19) shows that the experiencer of *teach* must be animate, whether it appears as a direct object (19a) or the object of a preposition (19b).

(17) a   #John drank his sandwich.
     b   #The sandwich was drunk by John.

(18) a   That book is loved by children around the world.
     b   #Children around the world are loved by that book.

(19) a   #Mary taught her motorcycle classical Chinese.
     b   #Mary taught classical Chinese to her motorcycle.

A number of other criteria for distinguishing arguments from adjuncts have been proposed, but this is a complex issue and we will not pursue it further here.

1.2.2   Constituent structure

The CONSTITUENT STRUCTURE of a sentence contains information about constituent boundaries, linear order and syntactic categories (parts of speech). The most commonly used notation for representing constituent structure is the phrase structure tree diagram. A very simple tree diagram is shown in (20):

(20)

This tree contains three NODES. The top-most node, *A*, is the MOTHER of the two lower nodes, *B* and *C*. *B* and *C* are DAUGHTERS of the same mother, and so we refer to them as SISTER nodes. The simple tree in (20) represents a constituent of category *A* which is composed of two parts, one of category *B* and the other of category *C*, occurring in that order.

When a tree diagram is used to represent the constituent structure of a grammatical unit (e.g., a phrase or sentence), syntactic categories are used to label the nodes; the most common of these are listed in (21).

(21)
Word-level		**Phrasal**	
N	= noun	NP	= noun phrase
A	= adjective	AP	= adjective phrase
V	= verb	VP	= verb phrase
P	= preposition	PP	= preposition phrase
Det	= determiner	S	= sentence or clause
Adv	= adverb		
Conj	= conjunction		

A CONSTITUENT within a sentence corresponds to all and only the material which is dominated by a single node (i.e., all the daughters, granddaughters, great-granddaughters, etc. of that node). The linear order of constituents is shown by the left-to-right order of the corresponding nodes, and the linear order of words in the sentence is shown by the left-to-right order of the TERMINAL NODES (i.e., the lowest nodes in the tree).

To give a concrete example, the constituent structure for a simple preposition phrase (PP) in English (omitting the terminal nodes) is shown in (22a). This diagram shows that the preposition P must precede its object NP; and that within NP, the determiner Det will precede the head noun N. This tree represents the structure of phrases such as *on the beach*, *under the table*, etc. Figure (22b) shows the structure of the Malay sentence in (9b), which is repeated below. Note that the tree in (22b) assumes a "flat" clause structure, lacking any VP node, because we have not presented any evidence for the existence of a VP constituent in Malay.

(22) a

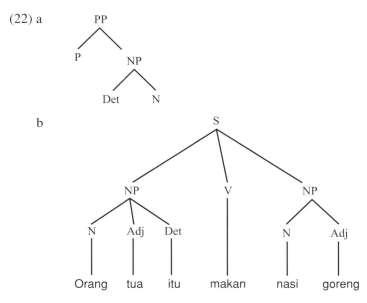

(9) b   [Orang tua itu] makan [nasi goreng].
             person old that eat   rice fry
             'That old person eats fried rice.'

In order to specify which tree structures are grammatical in a particular language, the grammar of the language must contain (i) a set of PHRASE STRUCTURE RULES, and (ii) a LEXICON. A phrase structure (PS) rule is a simple, context-free rule (i.e., no conditioning environment is stated) which defines a possible combination of mother and daughter nodes. The simple PS rule in (23) says that the tree fragment in (20) is a valid combination, i.e., a grammatical structure.

(23)   A   →   B   C

In order for a larger tree to be considered grammatical, each node in the tree must be LICENSED in this way by some phrase structure rule in the grammar of the language. To license (or "generate") the PP structure in (22a), the grammar of English must contain the rules in (24a). To generate the tree structure in (22b), the grammar of Malay must contain rules like those in (24b); the parentheses in this rule are used to mark optional elements.[6]

(24) a   **English**
            PP   →   P   NP
            NP   →   Det   N

      b   **Malay**
            S   →   NP   V   NP
            NP   →   N   (Adj)   (Det)

Phrase sructure rules of this kind determine possible tree structures, but the actual words of a sentence (terminal nodes of the tree) are provided by the lexicon. The lexicon can be thought of as the speaker's "mental dictionary." It is more than just a list of all the words in the language. Each word must have a LEXICAL ENTRY which contains information about the meaning, pronunciation, and grammatical features of that particular word. The grammatical information contained in the lexical entry will determine the contexts in which this word may occur. An important part of this information is the word's syntactic category (part of speech). While general phrase structure rules like those in (24) license possible combinations of mother and daughter nodes in the tree, a special rule of LEXICAL INSERTION licenses a node whose label is a word-level category (e.g., N, A, V, etc.) to have as its only daughter a word belonging to that same category.

In the next chapter we will discuss linguistic criteria for identifying constituents and categories in a particular language; but first we need to review a few basic facts about functional structure.

1.2.3   Functional structure

GRAMMATICAL RELATIONS like subject and object are an important part of the grammatical structure of a sentence, in particular of that aspect which we referred to above as FUNCTIONAL STRUCTURE. The terms "subject" and "object" are very familiar, of course, but it may be helpful to clarify what they actually mean. Some traditional grammars define the subject as the "doer of the action", and the object as the "person or thing acted upon by the doer." This definition seems to work for sentences like (25a–b), but is clearly wrong in examples like (25c–d).

(25) a   Mary slapped John.
   b   A dog bit John.
   c   John was bitten by a dog.
   d   John underwent major heart surgery.

John is "acted upon" in all four of these sentences; but the NP *John* bears the object relation in (25a–b) and the subject relation in (25c–d). Phrases like "the doer of the action" or "the person or thing acted upon" identify particular semantic roles, namely agent and patient. But, as these examples illustrate, the subject is not always an agent, and the patient is not always an object.

Another traditional definition of the subject is "what the sentence is about." Again, this definition seems to work for many sentences, but fails in others. All three of the sentences in (26) seem to be "about" Bill (i.e., *Bill* is the topic); but *Bill* is the subject in (26a), the object in (26b), and neither subject nor object in (26c). These examples show that we cannot reliably identify the subject of a sentence with either the agent or the topic. Rather, we must define subjects and other grammatical relations on the basis of their syntactic properties. We will return to this issue frequently in later chapters; see especially chapters 10 and 11.

(26) a   Bill is a very crafty fellow.
   b   (Jack is pretty reliable, but) Bill I don't trust.
   c   As for Bill, I wouldn't take his promises very seriously.

Subjects and objects are often referred to as TERMS, or DIRECT ARGU-MENTS. Arguments which are not subjects or objects are called INDIRECT or OBLIQUE ARGUMENTS. These labels reflect the idea that the relationship be-tween a verb and its subject or object is "closer," or has greater syntactic signif-icance, than the relationship with other elements in the clause. One indicator of the special status of subjects and objects in English is that subjects and objects are expressed by bare noun phrases, whereas oblique arguments (as well as many adjuncts) are marked with prepositions. Some examples of oblique argument phrases are presented in the following sentences:

(27) a   Michael Jackson donated his sunglasses <u>to the National Museum</u>. (RECIPIENT)
   b   Samson killed the Philistines <u>with a jawbone</u>.   (INSTRUMENT)
   c   The Raja constructed a beautiful palace <u>for his wife</u>.   (BENEFICIARY)
   d   The Prime Minister deposited his money <u>in a Swiss bank</u>. (LOCATION)

We will use the abbreviations SUBJ, OBJ, and OBL to refer to subjects, objects and oblique arguments, respectively. Some sentences, like those in (28), seem to have more than one object NP. In this case we will refer to the object which is closest to the verb (marked with a single underline in these examples) as the DIRECT or PRIMARY OBJECT (abbreviated OBJ). We will refer to the object which is farther from the verb (marked here with a double underline) as the SECONDARY OBJECT, using the abbreviation OBJ$_2$.

(28) a   Mary gave <u>her son</u> <u>a new bicycle</u>.
   b   Reluctantly, Henry showed <u>Susan</u> <u>his manuscript</u>.
   c   Uncle George told <u>the children</u> <u>a story</u>.

Notice that the secondary object relation does not correspond to the tradi-tional notion "indirect object."[7] In traditional grammar, *Mary* would be called the "indirect object" of both sentences (29a) and (29b). But in this usage the term "indirect object" actually refers to a semantic role (recipient, goal, or beneficiary) rather than to a grammatical relation. The grammatical relation of *Mary* is dif-ferent in these two sentences: *Mary* is the primary object in (29a) but an oblique argument in (29b).

(29) a   John gave Mary his old radio.
   b   John gave his old radio to Mary.

To summarize, then, we can classify the elements of a simple clause (aside from the predicate itself) as either arguments or adjuncts. In order to be expressed grammatically, arguments must be assigned a grammatical relation within the clause. We have identified two basic classes of argument relations, obliques vs. terms (or direct arguments). Terms (i.e., SUBJ, OBJ, OBJ₂) play an active role in a wide variety of syntactic constructions, while oblique arguments are relatively "inert." This classification of clausal elements is summarized in the following diagram:

(30)

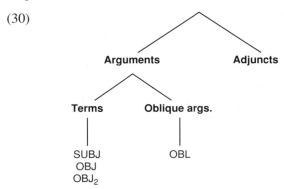

It is sometimes helpful to ignore (temporarily) details of word order and constituent structure within a sentence, and to focus exclusively on the assignment of grammatical relations. On such occasions we will use a simple network diagram to represent this information.[8] For example, the relational structure of the simple sentence *John loves Mary* could be represented as follows:

(31)

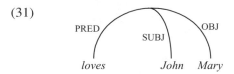

Each arc of the diagram represents a major element of the clause. The PRED(icate), i.e., the verb in this case, is the head of the clause; the other arcs represent either arguments or (in more complex examples) adjuncts. Note that the order of elements here is arbitrary; the diagram is an abstract representation of grammatical relations, and carries no information about word order and constituency.

1.2.4   Correspondences

We have introduced three different representations, each corresponding to a different aspect of syntactic structure: argument structure, constituent structure, and functional structure. Each representation provides a partial description of the structure of a sentence. In one sense, these three representations are independent of each other. None of the three is derived from the others. Rather, all three descriptions are true simultaneously, each containing a different type of information.

On the other hand, it is important for us to be able to specify the mappings, or correspondences, between elements of these three structures. For example, we need to be able to show who did what to whom; that is, which NP in the constituent structure corresponds to which semantic role in argument structure. Grammatical relations play a crucial role in defining these correspondences.

The mapping between semantic roles and grammatical relations is often referred to as LINKING. One way of representing this mapping is shown in (32). As discussed in chapter 3, section 3.2.1, a number of different theories have been proposed concerning how these correspondences are determined. But for now we will simply assume that all of this information is contained in the lexical entry of the verb.

(32)   a   *sing* <agent>
                          |
                        SUBJ

       b   *hit*   <agent, patient>
                          | |
                        SUBJ   OBJ

       c   *put*   <agent, theme, goal>
                          | | |
                        SUBJ   OBJ   OBL

We will used the term SUBCATEGORIZATION to refer to the set of grammatical relations which are specified in a verb's lexical entry. As the name implies, we can use this information to divide the lexical category Verb into a number of subcategories: verbs which take only a subject, verbs which take a subject and an object, etc. The subcategorization of a verb plays a major role in determining what syntactic environments that verb may occur in. To see why, let us consider the mapping between constituent structure and functional structure.

We can use an annotated tree structure like that in (33a) to show the grammatical relation which is assigned to each phrasal constituent in the tree. (Most syntacticians posit a VP constituent for English which includes the verb, its objects, and oblique arguments but not the subject. The evidence supporting this hypothesis will be discussed in chapter 2, but for the purposes of this chapter we will temporarily assume the "flat" structure shown in [33a].)

How is the assignment of grammatical relations determined? In many languages, this mapping is largely determined on the basis of case and/or agreement morphology. But in English, which has very little of that kind of morphology but relatively fixed word order, the mapping is determined by position: each grammatical relation can be associated with a particular position in the phrase structure.

These associations can be stated using annotated phrase structure rules like the one in (33b).

(33) a

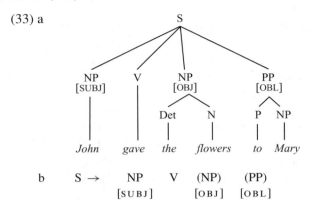

b   S →   NP   V   (NP)   (PP)
        [SUBJ]   [OBJ] [OBL]

The rule in (33b) will correctly generate the tree in (33a). Unfortunately, it would also allow the ungrammatical sentences in (34) to be generated:

(34) a   *John likes.
    b   ??Mary gives the young boy.
    c   *The girl yawns Mary.

These sentences are bad because the number of NPs in the clause does not match the number of arguments which the verb requires. More precisely, the sub-categorization requirements of the verbs are not satisfied: the set of grammatical relations which the verb must assign does not match the number of NPs available to bear those relations. *Like* is a transitive verb which requires an object; *yawn* is an intransitive verb which does not take an object; and *give* requires three arguments, while only two NPs are present in (34b). Obviously the grammar of the language must include some mechanism for rejecting such sentences as being ungrammatical.

1.2.5   Well-formedness conditions

The mismatch between the structure of the clause and the subcat-egorization requirements of the verb becomes obvious when we compare the functional structure of the clause with the verb's argument structure. The functional structure of (34b) is shown in (35a). As this diagram indicates, the clause is INCOMPLETE: the verb *give* requires an oblique argument (the recipient) but the clause does not contain any obliques. The problem with (34c) is just the opposite: the clause contains too many arguments, rather than too few. Specifically, as shown in (35b), the clause contains an OBJ; but no OBJ appears in the subcategorization of the verb *yawn*. In such a case we say that the clause is INCOHERENT.

(35) a   *Mary gives the young boy.

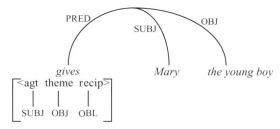

b   *The girl yawns Mary.

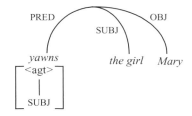

In order to prevent sentences like those in (34) from being produced, our rule system must include a general constraint which requires that the functional structure of each clause matches the subcategorization of its PRED. If a clause does not contain a grammatical relation which is required by the verb's subcategorization, we say that the clause is not COMPLETE. If a clause does contain a grammatical relation which is not allowed by the verb's subcategorization, we say that the clause is not COHERENT. In either case, the functional structure of the clause is not well-formed, and therefore the sentence is ungrammatical.

To these two conditions (Completeness and Coherence) we may add a third, namely that each grammatical relation must be uniquely assigned within its clause. In other words, there cannot be two subjects, two primary objects, etc. in a single clause. This explains why the sentences in (36) are ungrammatical. But it is important to remember that this Uniqueness condition applies only to argument relations (refer to the classification in (30) above), and not to adjuncts.

(36) a   *Mary Mrs. Thatcher John's brother made a fortune trading cattle futures.
     b   *John loves Mary Mrs. Thatcher his brother.

However, there is one type of argument relation that does not seem to obey the Uniqueness condition, namely OBL (oblique arguments). As illustrated in (37), it is often possible for a fully grammatical clause to contain more than one oblique argument:[9]

(37) a   John transferred his legal residence from California to Arkansas.
     b   Mary threw bread-crumbs into the water for the fish.
     c   The farmer drew water from the well with a wooden bucket.

But not every combination of oblique arguments is allowed, as demonstrated in (38). Those examples are ungrammatical because they contain two oblique arguments of the same kind, i.e., marked by the same prepositions and bearing identical semantic roles. The grammatical sentences in (37), however, contain two oblique arguments which bear distinct semantic roles.

(38) a   *John gave a bouquet of roses <u>to his mother</u> <u>to Susan</u>.
   b   *Mary was cheated <u>by a salesman</u> <u>by her broker</u>.
   c   *The farmer drew water <u>with a hand pump</u> <u>with a bucket</u>.

These facts suggest that the Uniqueness constraint applies to oblique arguments as well, provided that we recognize more than one Oblique grammatical relation. The grammatical relations of the various oblique arguments in (37) can be differentiated by reference to their semantic roles: OBL_{INST} for instrument phrases, OBL_{BEN} for beneficiary phrases, OBL_{GOAL} for goal phrases, etc. These various OBL relations are said to be SEMANTICALLY RESTRICTED, since each relation can only be associated with a particular semantic role.[10]

Now that we have clarified the Uniqueness constraint, our three WELL-FORMEDNESS CONDITIONS can be stated (somewhat informally) as in (39); see Kaplan and Bresnan (1982) for a more rigorous formulation.

(39)   WELL-FORMEDNESS CONDITIONS[11]
   a   COMPLETENESS: the functional structure of a clause must contain every grammatical relation which is obligatory in the subcategorization of its PRED.
   b   COHERENCE: the functional structure of a clause may not contain any argument relation which is not permitted by the subcategorization of its PRED.
   c   UNIQUENESS: no argument relation may be assigned more than once within a single functional structure.

We define a grammatical (or WELL-FORMED) clause structure as being one in which (a) every local combination of mother and daughters is licensed by a PS-rule, and (b) the well-formedness conditions are met as well. That is, in order to be considered grammatical, a sentence must conform not only to the PS-rules of that particular language but also to these three well-formedness conditions, which are assumed to hold for all languages.

Notes

1. Pullum (1990); A. Zwicky (p.c.).
2. But note that dialect variation is likely even within large standardized languages like English, Mandarin, or Indonesian.
3. More precisely, the clause may be interpreted as either a modifier or a complement of the head noun.
4. This example is from Asmah and Rama (1968).

5. In this sense it might be helpful to think of a role label as an index, or pointer, to a particular variable in the full semantic representation of the situation or event being described.

6. The fact that the adjective is an optional element of NP in Malay is not evident from (9b) alone, but can be seen in (9a) and in other sentences which we will discuss in chapter 2.

7. In languages like German, which have overt dative case marking, "indirect objects" may bear the OBJ_2 relation.

8. This type of relational network diagram is used by Avery Andrews in an unpublished 1992 draft of his *Syntax textbook* (pp. 194 ff.).

9. As noted in (11), we assume here that instruments and beneficiaries can be optional arguments.

10. In some languages, a single clause can contain more than one secondary object. In such languages several different secondary object relations can be identified, which are again semantically restricted.

11. As the well-formedness conditions are stated here, a possible ambiguity arises when applying them to complex sentences, i.e., sentences which contain one or more sub-ordinate clauses. In order to avoid this problem, we need to ensure that grammatical relations which are subcategorized by a particular verb V should be assigned to "clause-mates" of V, i.e., constituents of the clause headed by V, rather than to arguments of any lower subordinate clause. For the time being we will simply assume that the constraints in (39) are applied in this way.

2   Identifying constituents and categories

As we saw in chapter 1, phrase structure diagrams are used to represent several different kinds of information about the structure of a sentence: (i) word order; (ii) constituent boundaries; and (iii) the category of each word and constituent in the sentence. It is important to remember that these tree diagrams are just pictures which are supposed to represent certain linguistic properties of real sentences. Before we can draw the pictures, we first have to understand the linguistic reality which they are intended to represent.

For example, we stated that a CONSTITUENT within a tree structure corresponds to "all and only the material which is dominated by a single node." But this is primarily a statement about how we draw trees. In order to apply this definition, we first need to be able to find constituents in real language data, i.e., to determine which groups of words function as a "unit" in a particular sentence. Our decisions about how to draw the tree are based on observable facts about the language.

This is a specific instance of a general point which seems obvious, but is nevertheless worth emphasizing: our analysis of the grammatical structure of a language must be based on linguistic evidence. In this chapter we will discuss various kinds of evidence which can help us answer basic analytical questions about constituent structure. How do we identify constituent boundaries within a sentence? How do we determine the category of a particular word or phrase?

Sometimes these questions are relatively easy to answer, but in other cases the issues involved may be quite complex. One of our goals in this discussion is, of course, to develop the skills and concepts needed to analyze the phrase structure of a given sentence in a particular language. But a second and equally important goal is to illustrate the role of evidence in linguistic analysis, to show how language data can be used to argue for or against a particular hypothesis.

In section 2.1, we will introduce the discussion of constituency tests with some very simple Malay data. But in the rest of this chapter we will deal primarily with English, because some of the evidence which we need to discuss is relatively complex. We will have to assume a significant amount of knowledge about the basic grammatical patterns of the language, something we could not assume if we chose another language. As a result, some of the tests we use and the specific structures and categories that we identify may be valid only for English. But the general methodology, the process by which we identify these structures and categories, can be used for a wide variety of languages.

2.1   Tests for constituency in Malay

In chapter 1 we proposed, without offering any evidence, some constituent boundaries for the simple Malay sentence repeated in (1a). What was the
basis for identifying these groups of words as constituents?

(1) a   [Orang tua itu] makan [nasi goreng].
           person old that eat   rice fry
           'That old person eats fried rice.'

    b   [Ahmad] makan [nasi].
           Ahmad   eat   cooked.rice
           'Ahmad eats rice.'

In the last chapter we pointed out one reason, namely the fact that both of these
phrases can be replaced by a single word, as illustrated in (1b). Since a single
word is clearly a "unit" of some kind, it seems reasonable to suspect that groups
of words which can occur in the same position must also be units, and probably
units of the same kind. But, given the complex ways in which word order can vary
in most languages, this kind of "substitution test" alone is not enough to support
our claim about constituent boundaries.

A second (but clearly related) reason for accepting this claim is that each of
these phrases forms a semantic unit. *Orang tua itu* refers to a single, specific
individual. Because of this, the whole phrase can function as the antecedent of a
pronoun, as shown in (2).

(2) a   [Orang tua itu] biasa   datang ke kedai ini.
           person old that usually come to shop this
           'That old person usually comes to this shop.'

    b   [Dia] selalu makan nasi goreng.
           he/she always eat   rice fry
           'He always eats fried rice.'

And although the phrase *orang tua itu* consists of three words, it bears only
one semantic role (agent) and one grammatical relation (subject) in (1a). But
we must be careful here. In some languages, a group of words which forms a
semantic and functional unit need not form a unit for purposes of word order (i.e.,
a constituent). For example, the sentences in (3) contain functional units ('small
child' and 'new methods') which are not constituents in phrase structure, because
the adjectives are widely separated from the nouns that they modify. Functional
units of this kind are often referred to as DISCONTINUOUS CONSTITUENTS.

(3) a   **Warlpiri** (Simpson and Bresnan, 1983)
           Kurdu-ngku ka   wajili-pi-nyi   maliki-Ø wita-ngku.
           child-ERG   ASPECT running-do-NONPAST dog-ABS small-ERG
           'The small child is chasing the dog.'

b   **Latin** (Matthews, 1981:106; patterned after Caesar, *Civil Wars*)
         Novae   ab utrisque rationes   reperiebantur.
         new-F.NOM.PL by both   method-NOM.PL were.being.found
         'New methods were found by both sides.'

Such languages are the exception rather than the rule; but in all languages there are many contexts where semantics and grammatical relations alone will not enable us to determine the constituent boundaries. We need other kinds of evidence, in particular evidence which is more directly related to the linear arrangement of words in the sentence.

Another reason for believing that *orang tua itu* is a syntactic constituent is that the same string of words can occur in a variety of positions within the sentence: subject (4a), object (4b), oblique argument (4c), etc. By treating this and similar strings as constituents, we can greatly simplify our analysis of Malay word-order patterns, eliminating the massive redundancy which would be needed to generate a particular string in each position where it might occur.

(4) a   [Orang tua itu] makan nasi goreng.
         person old that eat   rice fry
         'That old person eats fried rice.'

    b   Saya belum kenal [orang tua itu].
         I   not.yet know person old that
         'I am not yet acquainted with that old person.'

    c   Ibu   memberikan wang   kepada [orang tua itu].
         mother give   money to   person old that
         'Mother gives money to that old person.'

    d   Ibu   belanja [orang tua itu] minum teh.
         mother treat   person old that drink   tea
         'Mother bought a cup of tea for that old person.'

We noted above that strings of words which can replace a single word in a particular position must be "units" (i.e., constituents) of the appropriate type. This conclusion is supported by the discovery that only one such unit can occur in subject or object position, as demonstrated in (5). Therefore, where several words occur together in these positions, those words must form a single constituent.

(5) a   *[Perempuan ini] [orang tua itu] makan nasi.
         woman   this person old that eat   rice
         *'This woman that old person is eating rice.'

    b   *Fauzi makan [ikan itu] [nasi goreng].
         Fauzi eat   fish   that rice fry
         *'Fauzi is eating that fish some fried rice.'

Malay, like most other languages, has various ways of changing the word order of a sentence. When a group of words can be "moved" as a unit, we can normally assume that the group forms a syntactic constituent. So examples like (6b–d) support the claim that the direct object phrase in (6a) is a constituent.

(6) a   Saya makan [ikan besar itu].
          I   eat   fish big   that
          'I ate/am eating that big fish.'

    b   [Ikan besar itu] saya makan.
          fish big   that I   eat
          'That big fish I ate/am eating.'

    c   [Ikan besar itu]=lah   yang saya makan.
          fish big   that =FOC REL I   eat
          'It was that big fish that I ate.'

    d   [Ikan besar itu] di-makan oleh anjing saya.
          fish big   that PASS-eat by   dog   my
          'That big fish was eaten by my dog.'

Another reason for identifying the phrases we have been discussing here as constituents is that they can be replaced by question words to form a content question (sometimes called a CONSTITUENT QUESTION). This is illustrated in (7).

(7) a   [Orang tua itu] makan [ikan besar itu].
          person old that eat   fish big   that
          'That old person ate the big fish.'

    b   Siapa yang makan [ikan besar itu]?
          who   REL eat   fish big   that
          'Who ate that big fish?'

    c   [Orang tua itu] makan apa?
          person old that eat   what
          'What did that old person eat?'

Similarly, constituents can form the answer to a content question, whereas a string of words which is not a syntactic constituent is not a possible answer, as illustrated in (8c).

(8) a   Q: Siapa yang makan ikan besar itu?   A: Orang tua itu.
             who   REL eat   fish big   that   person old that
             'Who ate that big fish?'   'That old person.'

    b   Q: Orang tua itu makan apa?   A: Ikan besar itu.
             person old that eat   what   fish big   that
             'What did that old person eat?'   'That big fish.'

    c   Q: Orang tua itu makan apa?   A: *Besar itu.
             person old that eat   what   big   that
             'What did that old person eat?'   *'That big.'

Let us briefly summarize the kinds of evidence we have mentioned. We have claimed that certain strings of Malay words form a syntactic constituent because these strings:

a   can replace, or be replaced by, a single word
b   correspond to a single semantic unit
c   can function as the antecedent of a pronoun
d   occur in a variety of positions within the sentence
e   occur in positions which must be unique
f   can be "moved" (or re-ordered) as a unit
g   can be replaced by a question word
h   can function as the answer to a content question

We noted that the semantic evidence is helpful in many languages, but must be used with caution. In section 2.2 we will examine these and other criteria as they apply to English. In section 2.3 we will use these criteria to test the hypothesis that a verb and its direct object form a constituent in English. In section 2.4 we will briefly review the difference between coordination and subordination. In section 2.5 we will review some of the criteria for identifying syntactic categories, and discuss one particular case where the evidence seems at first glance to be contradictory.

2.2   Tests for constituency in English

A wide variety of constructions have been cited as providing evidence for constituent boundaries in English: see, for example, the discussions in Radford (1988:69–105), McCawley (1988:47–66), and Tallerman (1998:116–138). In this section we will illustrate how some of these tests work by using them to examine the behavior of certain prepositional elements. We will be investigating the structure of strings which consist of a verb, a preposition, and a noun phrase (V-P-NP). As we will see, there are (at least) two very different kinds of strings which match this pattern.

Let us begin by comparing (9a) with (9b), both of which end with the sequence V-P-NP. These two sentences are identical except for the last word. How then can we explain the contrast in (10)?

(9) a   John ran up a big hill.
    b   John ran up a big bill.

(10) a   Up a big hill John ran.[1]
     b   *Up a big bill John ran.

Most English speakers would intuitively say that the function of *up* in the (a) sentences is different from its function in the (b) sentences. But what exactly is the difference? The phrase *run up* in (9b) is an example of a PHRASAL VERB, or "verb-particle" construction. Phrasal verbs in English involve fixed combinations

of a verb plus a prepositional particle. One way of identifying phrasal
that the particle may occur either before or after the object NP, unlike
prepositions which always precede their object. Note the contrast betw
phrasal verb in (11) and the normal preposition phrase in (12):

(11) a   Peter blew *out* the candle.
    b   Peter blew the candle *out*.

(12) a   Peter flew *out* the window.
    b   *Peter flew the window *out*.

In fact, when the object of a phrasal verb is a pronoun, the particle must follow
the object as in (13b). But with true PPs, the preposition always precedes its
object, whether the object is a pronoun (as in 14a) or a full NP.

(13) a   I want to look *over* the contract before I sign.
    b   Before I sign the contract, I want to look it *over*.
    c   *?Before I sign the contract, I want to look *over* it.

(14) a   Since the gate was locked, John climbed *over* it.
    b   *Since the gate was locked, John climbed it *over*.

There is often a semantic difference as well. A normal preposition is generally used in its basic, literal meaning, whereas the particle in a phrasal verb
generally has a metaphorical or idiomatic meaning. For example, sentence (9b)
John ran up a big bill does not mean that either John or the bill were literally moving up to a higher location, or that John was literally running. The
meaning of the verb plus particle combination is often quite unpredictable, e.g.,
put off 'to offend'; *turn down* 'to reject'; *knock back* 'to reject' (Australian
English).

However, for our present purposes we are most interested in looking for structural differences between (9a) and (9b). Specifically, we will use some familiar constituency tests to look for constituent boundaries within these V-P-NP
strings.

2.2.1   Clefting

The two constructions illustrated in (15) and (16) are used to focus,
or place special emphasis on, a constituent that conveys new information (see
chapter 6). In a CLEFT SENTENCE (15) the focused constituent comes first,
while in the PSEUDO-CLEFT construction (16), the focused constituent appears
at the end of the sentence.

(15)   **Cleft sentences:**
    a   It was [your big brother] who built this house.
    b   It is [her artificial smile] that I can't stand.
    c   It was [for Mary] that John bought the flowers (not for Susan).
    d   It was [just last week] that Mary offered me the job.

Pseudo-Clefts:

a   What I can't stand is [her artificial smile].

b   What John said to Mary was [that he intended to run for parliament].

c   What I like for breakfast is [fried noodles].

In both constructions, the material that occurs in the focused position must be a complete constituent, and only one constituent may appear in this position at a time.

(17)   **Cleft sentences:**

a   *It was [a book] [to Mary] that John gave.

b   *It was [last week] [your brother] that I arrested.

c   *It was [your big] who built this house brother.

(18)   **Pseudo-Clefts:**

a   *What John gave was [a book] [to Mary].

b   *?What Bill stole was [my diary] [from my desk drawer].

c   *What I can't stand smile is [her artificial].

As McCawley (1988) points out, the Pseudo-Cleft construction cannot generally be used to focus preposition phrases; but we can use clefting to test the structure of the sentences in (9). As (19) demonstrates, the sequence [P+NP] can be clefted in (9a), but not in (9b). This contrast suggests that the clefted material forms a constituent (a PP) in (9a), but not in (9b). Applying the same test to the sentences in (13) and (14), we again find that the sequence [P+NP] forms a constituent in the prepositional example (20a) but not in the phrasal verb example (20b).

(19) a   According to tradition, it was [up this hill] that Napoleon and his 500 soldiers ran.

b   *According to the head waiter, it was [up this bill] that John ran.

(20) a   If my hypothesis is correct, it was [over this fence] that the prisoners climbed.

b   *If my hypothesis is correct, it was [over this contract] that my lawyer looked.

2.2.2   Topicalization

The next test involves a sentence pattern which is generally called TOPICALIZATION. In this construction, a constituent which normally follows the verb is moved to the front of the sentence, preceding the subject NP. Constituents of various categories can be topicalized, as illustrated in (21).

(21) a   [Your elder sister]$_{NP}$ I can't stand.

b   [That you sincerely wanted to help]$_{S'}$ I do not doubt.[2]

c   [Out of his pocket]$_{PP}$ John pulled a crumpled $100 bill.

d   John arrived 15 minutes late, and [very sorry indeed]$_{AdjP}$ he appeared.

Only one constituent can be topicalized in any given clause, as shown in (22). Moreover, as the examples in (23)[3] show, nothing less than a whole constituent (in this case an NP) can be topicalized. This means not only that the fronted elements must form a single constituent, but also that no "fragments" (i.e., words which do not form a constituent) can be left behind in post-verbal position.

(22) a I gave that book to Mary last Christmas.
      b *[That book] [to Mary] I gave last Christmas.
      c *[Last Christmas] [that book] I gave to Mary.
      d *[Last Christmas] [to Mary] I gave that book.

(23) a *[Your elder] I can't stand sister.
      b *[Elder sister] I can't stand your.
      c *[Sister] I can't stand your elder.
      d *[Your] I can't stand elder sister.

The examples in (10) involve the topicalization of a sequence [P+NP]. The fact that (10a) is grammatical indicates that the sequence forms a constituent in (9a), which we identified as a normal preposition phrase. The fact that (10b) is ungrammatical indicates that the sequence [P+NP] does not form a constituent in (9b), the phrasal verb example. The same result holds for examples (11)–(14): topicalization is impossible with the phrasal verb examples (24a and 25a), but fine for the normal preposition phrase (24b and 25b). Thus the topicalization patterns lead us to the same conclusion as the clefting data we examined in the previous section.

(24) a *[Out the candle] Peter blew.
      b   [Out the window] Peter flew.

(25) a *[Over the contract] John looked.
      b   [Over the gate] John climbed.

2.2.3   Sentence fragments

In school students are usually urged to write in "complete" sentences; but in informal spoken language, speakers do not always follow this rule. One type of utterance which may be less than a complete sentence is the "short form" answer to a content question. As the examples in (26) through (28) illustrate, these sentence fragments must normally form a single, complete constituent.

(26) A: What did you throw just now?
      B: *?A rock into the water.

(27) A: What did you buy at the flea market?
      B: An old Swedish wineskin./ *An old Swedish.

(28) A: Which sister gave you that florescent green necktie?
      B: My second sister./ *My second.

However, this test must be applied carefully, since there are various contexts in which an element which is normally obligatory can be omitted from a constituent. For example, in many languages adjectives can be used without any head noun to name classes of people, as in (29). Head nouns can also be omitted in certain other contexts, e.g., (30) and (31). Other types of omissions will be discussed in section 2.3.

(29) a   [the good], [the bad], and [the ugly]
     b   [The rich] get richer and [the poor] get children.

(30)   Would you like [white wine] or [red]?

(31) A   Which of these sentences sounds more natural to you?
     B   The second.

So the fact that a string of words can occur as a sentence fragment does not always mean that the string forms a complete constituent. But the converse appears to be true: if a given string cannot occur as a sentence fragment, that generally means that the string is not a constituent. With this qualification in mind, let us try to apply this test to our [P+NP] sequences.

As the following examples show, a normal PP can be used as a sentence fragment (32 and 34), but this does not work for the phrasal verb examples (33 and 35). This contrast provides additional evidence that the combination of preposition plus NP in the phrasal verb construction does not form a constituent.

(32) A   Where did John run?
     B   Up a big hill.

(33) A   (?)What did John run?
     B   *Up a big bill.

(34) A   Where did Peter fly?
     B   Out the window.

(35) a   What did Peter blow?
     b   *Out the candle.

2.2.4   Coordination

Coordination is often used to provide evidence about constituent boundaries, but, as with sentence fragments, this test needs to be used with caution. A general constraint on coordinate structures is that only constituents can be conjoined. This is illustrated in (36).

(36) a   [John's video camera] and [Mary's digital camera] were stolen by bandits.
     b   *[John's video] and [Mary's digital] camera were stolen by bandits.

However, the comments in the preceding section concerning elliptical constructions apply here as well. Sentence (30) above is an example of coordination involving one elliptical conjunct. So the fact that coordination is possible does not necessarily mean that both conjuncts are complete constituents. But it does seem safe to say that if a string cannot be conjoined, it is not a constituent.

This generalization can be used to test the constituent structure of phrasal verb constructions. True PPs can be freely conjoined, as illustrated in (37). But the combination of preposition plus NP in the phrasal verb construction cannot be conjoined, as illustrated in (38–39). This fact again indicates that the sequence of words does not form a constituent.

(37) a   Peter flew [out the window] and [across the river].
     b   John ran [up a big hill] and [through a grassy meadow].

(38) a   Peter blew out the candle and blew up the balloon.
     b   *Peter blew [out the candle] and [up the balloon].

(39) a   John turned off the lights and turned on the radio.
     b   *John turned [off the lights] and [on the radio].

Examples like (40)[4] and (41) are sometimes cited as evidence for the claim that only constituents of the same category can be conjoined. Certainly this is the normal pattern; and virtually any category can be conjoined with itself, as illustrated in (42).

(40) a   John wrote [a letter] and [a postcard].   [NP with NP]
     b   John wrote [to Mary] and [to Fred].   [PP with PP]
     c   *John wrote [to Mary] and [a postcard].   [PP with NP]

(41)   *Mary knows [the truth] and [that you are innocent].   [NP with S′]

(42) a   My true love gave me [four calling birds] and
          [three French hens].   [NP with NP]
     b   I found ants [in the sugar bowl] and
          [under the bread box].   [PP with PP]
     c   You have a [very beautiful] but
          [slightly crazy] daughter.   [AdjP with AdjP]
     d   Mary knows [that the police made a mistake]
          and [that you are innocent].   [S′ with S′]

However, this preference for same-category coordination is not an absolute requirement. One of the best-known exceptions to the general pattern involves predicate complements with the copular verb *be*. Phrases which can function as complements to *be* can often be conjoined even if they belong to different syntactic categories:

(43) a   Gen. Lee was [a rebel to the core] and [proud of it].   [NP with AP]
     b   John hasn't returned my calls;
          he must be either [out of town] or [extremely busy].   [PP with AP]
     c   Mary is [a dedicated professional] and [under a binding
          contract]; she will perform as scheduled.   [NP with PP]

In addition to the regular coordinate structures discussed thus far, English permits a second type of coordination called Shared Constituent Coordination or "Right Node Raising." This construction, which is only used in relatively formal speaking or writing, is illustrated in (44b) and (45b):

(44) a   John walked up the hill, and Mary ran up the hill.
     b   John walked, and Mary ran, [up the hill].

(45) a   The CIA admitted responsibility for the incident, but the KGB denied responsibility for the incident.
     b   The CIA admitted, but the KGB denied, [responsibility for the incident].

This construction actually involves the coordination of two truncated sentences, each of which would be completed by the same final phrase. This final, "shared" group of words must normally form a constituent, as shown by examples like (46):[5]

(46) a   John handed bananas to the monkeys, but Peter threw bananas to the monkeys.
     b   ?*John handed, but Peter threw, [bananas to the monkeys].

As expected, we find that Right Node Raising is possible with normal PPs, as in (44), but not with the sequence of particle plus NP in the phrasal verb construction, as seen in (47) and (48):

(47) a   John crossed out the best answer, and Mary figured out the best answer.
     b   *John crossed, and Mary figured, [out the best answer].

(48) a   Peter picked up the telephone, and Wendy hung up the telephone.
     b   *Peter picked, and Wendy hung, [up the telephone].

2.3   Evidence for a VP constituent in English

In the preceding section we used a number of tests for constituency to examine the structure of the phrasal verb construction. In each case, we concluded that the prepositional "particle" which is a part of the phrasal verb does not form a constituent with the object NP.

In this section we will consider another aspect of English phrase structure which has been a topic of some debate. In chapter 1, example (34), we presented an annotated phrase structure diagram for a simple English clause which assumed that the subject and object NPs were both immediate sisters of the verb. (We made the same assumption about oblique argument PPs as well.) However, many syntacticians have claimed that this is not the case: they argue that the object NP in English is a sister of V, but the subject is not. More precisely, they claim that a verb and its non-subject complements form a constituent which excludes the subject. This constituent is usually labeled "VP," as in (49b). In this section we will look at evidence which can help us choose between this VP analysis and the "flat" clause structure shown in (49a).

(49) a

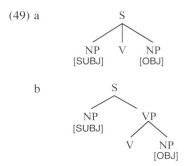

2.3.1   **Sentence fragments**

In section 2.2.3 we saw that the answer to a content question need not be a complete sentence, but generally it must be a complete constituent. Example (50) contains a Wh-question followed by two possible answers. The first answer consists of a verb plus its primary and secondary object NPs; while the second answer consists of a verb, an object NP, and an oblique benefactive phrase. The fact that these sentence fragments are grammatical provides evidence that the verb and its non-subject complements form a constituent.

(50) A   What are you going to do now?
     B   Give my dog a bath.
     B′   Buy a birthday card for my mother.

2.3.2   **Coordination**

In section 2.2.4 we noted only constituents may be conjoined. Thus examples like those in (51) provide evidence that the verb and its non-subject complements form a constituent.

(51) a   You can either [surrender these documents to the police] or [move to Mexico].
     b   When I retire I am going to [grow a beard] and [paint abstract watercolors].
     c   All parents should, in case of a cyclone, [pack some food] and [bring their children to the storm shelter].

Moreover, aside from certain restricted environments, only constituents of the same category can be conjoined. For this reason, the examples in (52) show not only that a transitive verb and its object form a complete constituent, but also that a bare intransitive verb can function as a constituent of the same category, i.e., a VP.

(52) a   Would you rather [swim] or [build sand castles]?
     b   He loves to [play the guitar] and [sing].

In section 2.2.4 we also discussed a second type of coordination called Shared Constituent Coordination, or "Right Node Raising." The basic generalization which we observed for this construction was that the final, "shared" group of words normally forms a constituent.[6] In light of this generalization, examples like (53) provide further evidence that a verb and its non-subject complements form a constituent.

(53) a   Mary certainly will, though her husband probably will not, *give buns to the elephant.*

b   My father occasionally, and my mother regularly, *lets the cat into the bedroom.*

2.3.3   Pseudo-Clefts

In section 2.2.2 we saw that only a complete constituent may appear in the focus position of a Cleft or Pseudo-Cleft sentence. Clefting cannot be applied to the constituents we are examining here, but the Pseudo-Cleft construction does work. Example (54) shows that a verb and its non-subject complements can occur in the focus position of a Pseudo-Cleft, providing further evidence that they form a constituent.

(54) a   What Mary does with her money is *keep it under the mattress.*

b   What you need to do now is *surrender these documents to the police.*

2.3.4   Preposing and postposing

The two sentences in (55) contain strings of words (shown in italics) which have been preposed for special emphasis, occurring before the subject of their clause. In both cases, the preposed string consists of a verb plus its object NP. Whether these sentences are examples of topicalization or some other similar construction, the fact that they are grammatical provides evidence that the verb and its object form a constituent.

(55) a   I will dance with your mother, if I must, but *kiss your elder sister* I will not.

b   John promised that he will finish the assignment, and *finish the assignment* he will.[7]

The examples in (56) show that a verb plus its complements can also be post-posed to the end of the sentence, occurring after adverbial time phrases, etc. This provides further evidence that the verb and its non-subject complements form a constituent, i.e., a VP.

(56) a   Mary will, for the next 21 days, *submit a daily report on your activities.*

b   I try, whenever circumstances allow it, *to give Helen the benefit of the doubt.*

c   The guilty party can at any time *return the watch to its rightful owner*, and no further action will be taken.

2.3.5   VP-Ellipsis

The tests discussed in the preceding sections have all been relatively "general," in the sense that they can be applied to constituents of many different categories. However, the VP constituent in English has some syntactic properties which are unique, not shared by any other type of constituent. These unique properties can also be used to provide evidence for constituency. We will consider here a construction which is generally referred to as VP-ELLIPSIS (or VP-DELETION).

ELLIPSIS is a general term referring to the omission (or deletion) of some element in a sentence which can be understood from the immediate context. The type of ellipsis we are concerned with here, VP-Ellipsis, is illustrated in (57):

(57) a   Max didn't [help me with the dishes], but his brother did ___.
  b   If Mary [gives buns to the elephant], then John will ___ too.
  c   I could never have [formulated the argument] as clearly as Susan has ___.
  d   Bill agreed to [kiss the Russian ambassador on both cheeks], but Al wouldn't ___.

As the name implies, the omitted elements in this construction must constitute a VP. However, it is important to distinguish this pattern from other types of ellipsis which are also allowed in English. GAPPING, for example, is a kind of ellipsis in which the omitted material need not be a constituent at all, as illustrated in (58):

(58) a   Ernie loves the French girl, Bert ___ the Russian ___.
  b   John borrowed a novel from the library, Mary ___ a German phrase book ___.

McCawley (1988:48–49) points out two important differences between VP-Ellipsis and Gapping. First, Gapping can only apply in coordinate sentences in which two clauses with parallel grammatical structure are conjoined. Gapping is ungrammatical in subordinating sentence patterns, as illustrated in (59). VP-Ellipsis, on the contrary, is equally grammatical in either coordinate or subordinate sentences, as we saw in (57); and can even apply across sentence boundaries, as in (60):

(59) a   *If Ernie marries the French girl, then Bert (will) ___ the Russian ___.
  b   *John borrowed a novel from the library before Mary ___ a German phrase book ___.
(60)   A: I don't believe Mary will [give buns to the elephant].
    B: No, but John will ___.

Second, with VP-Ellipsis at least one auxiliary verb must be "left behind"; that is, at least one auxiliary verb must occur just before the position of the omitted VP. If there is no auxiliary verb, as in (61), the sentence is ungrammatical. When

ıitted in the Gapping construction, however, all auxiliary verbs must
ed. The presence of an auxiliary verb makes the whole sentence
ıl, as seen in (62).[8]

x didn't [help me with the dishes], but his brother ___.
b   *If Mary [gives buns to the elephant], then John ___ too.

(62) a   *Ernie has been courting the French girl, Bert has been ___ the Russian ___.
   b   *John will borrow a novel from the library, Mary will ___ a German phrase
      book ___.

Obviously this description of the VP-Ellipsis construction assumes that there
is a VP constituent in English. But that is exactly what we have been trying to
prove; are we guilty of circular reasoning here? Actually, we are not. What we are
doing is appealing to a basic methodological principle in linguistics which states
that a simple analysis is normally preferred over a more complex analysis. The
logic of the present argument is roughly as follows. If we assume that there is a
VP constituent, we can give a very simple analysis of the data. If there were no
such constituent, then it would be much more difficult to specify precisely what
the omitted elements in this construction must be. The analysis which assumes
the existence of the VP is preferred because it provides a much simpler grammar
for the language.

Based on our analysis of VP-Ellipsis, together with the other evidence discussed
above, we conclude that there is indeed a VP constituent, and it is a sister of the
NP[SUBJ]. So, for example, a sentence like *Mary keeps her money under the
mattress* would have the structure shown in (63).

(63)

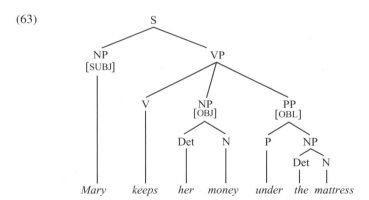

2.3.6   **Adverb placement**

Another piece of evidence which is relevant to VPs but not relevant to most other constituents comes from the placement of certain types of
adverbs. Contrast the distribution of *probably* with *violently* in the following
examples:

(64) a   *Probably* Morris will disagree with your theory.

    b   Morris *probably* will disagree with your theory.

    c   Morris will *probably* disagree with your theory.

    d   *Morris will disagree *probably* with your theory.

    e   *Morris will disagree with *probably* your theory.

    f   *Morris will disagree with your *probably* theory.

    g   Morris will disagree with your theory *probably*.

(65) a   *Violently* Morris will disagree with your theory.

    b   *Morris *violently* will disagree with your theory.

    c   Morris will *violently* disagree with your theory.

    d   Morris will disagree *violently* with your theory.

    e   *Morris will disagree with *violently* your theory.

    f   *Morris will disagree with your *violently* theory.

    g   Morris will disagree with your theory *violently*.

At first glance the distribution of these adverbs seems quite complex, and it may not be clear how to explain the differences between the two. But constituent structure does seem to be relevant. For example, neither adverb can come between the modifier *your* and its head noun *theory* (as in the [f] sentences), or between the preposition *with* and its object NP (as in the [e] sentences). In other words, no adverb can occur inside the NP or PP constituents.

Now, if we assume that the main verb and its PP complement (*disagree with your theory*) form a VP constituent, then we can make a further generalization about the data: the adverb *probably* never occurs inside the VP, while the adverb *violently* can never be separated from the VP. To be more precise, let us assume (for the moment) that the basic sentence has the phrase structure shown in (66). Then we can account for all the data in (64) and (65) with two simple statements: (i) *probably* must be an immediate daughter of the S node; and (ii) *violently* must be an immediate daughter of the VP node.

(66)

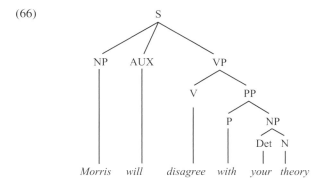

Once again it may appear that we have assumed the very thing we were trying to prove, namely the existence of a VP constituent. However, as in the discussion of VP-Ellipsis, we are really developing an argument on the basis of simplicity. If we assume that there is a VP constituent, we can describe the contrasting

s of the adverbs in a very simple way: adverbs of one type (which we
NTENCE ADVERBS) must be daughters of S, while those of another
ƆVERBS) must be daughters of VP. If there were no VP constituent,
much more difficult to specify the distribution of adverbs within the
.... :e again, the simplest analysis of the facts is one which posits the
existence of VP.

We should point out that the syntax of English adverbs is actually fairly
complex.[9] Adverbs which describe the speaker's evaluation of the proposition
(e.g., *fortunately, tragically, surprisingly*, etc.), epistemic comments relating to
truth or probability (e.g., *certainly, obviously, possibly, definitely*, etc.), and certain
time and place expressions modify the sentence as a whole. They are elements
of S, and so do not normally occur within the VP. Adverbs of manner (e.g.,
completely, carefully, quickly, etc.) are generally elements of the VP; but they
can sometimes be topicalized, or fronted, to the beginning of the sentence. The
position of both types of adverbs can be influenced by a wide variety of semantic
and pragmatic factors. And some adverbs do not seem to fit neatly into either
type.

But in spite of these complexities, which we will not attempt to deal with
here, it is clear that constituent structure is an important factor in determining
the placement of adverbs in English, and that the simplest analysis of the data
requires us to posit the existence of a VP.

2.3.7   Conclusion

We have discussed a fairly wide variety of tests for constituency in
English, and many others have been proposed which we cannot consider here.
We should, however, point out that any given test may not be usable for certain
examples. The grammar of a language is a very complex system, and the grammaticality of a particular example may depend on many factors besides constituent
structure. Radford (1988:101) expresses this principle in the following words:

> On occasions, a test may fail to yield the anticipated results, simply because
> some independent factor is "interfering" with the test and making it inappli-
> cable in some particular context.

For example, we noted that certain adverbs (e.g., *violently*) must be immediate
daughters of the VP node. But nothing in this statement explains why (67b)
should be ungrammatical. The contrast between that example and the grammatical
(67a, c) is due to an independent principle of English grammar[10] which states that
nothing can separate a verb from its direct object.

(67) a   Morris will *violently* attack your theory.
   b   *Morris will attack *violently* your theory.
   c   Morris will attack your theory *violently*.

For this reason it is important to consider several different tests, and to choose the analysis which provides the simplest and most natural account for the full range of data.

2.4   Coordination, subordination, and recursion

Before we turn to the issue of syntactic categories, it will be helpful to review a few more basic concepts related to constituency. Let us begin with the concept of RECURSION. Essentially, recursion simply means that a phrasal constituent can be embedded within (i.e., be dominated by) another constituent having the same category. Such a structure may be licensed by a single phrase structure rule, or by a combination of several rules.

A RECURSIVE phrase structure rule is one which allows a mother node of some phrasal category to have a daughter of that same category. For example, if we assume (following Nevis, 1988) that the English possessive marker - 's is a genitive case marker, the recursive rule in (68) could generate NPs which contain any number of successively embedded NPs, as illustrated in (69). The phrase structure configuration of one such example is shown in (70).

(68)   NP → NP[CASE gen]   N

(69) a   John's sister
     b   John's sister's husband
     c   John's sister's husband's uncle
     d   John's sister's husband's uncle's daughter (etc.)

(70)

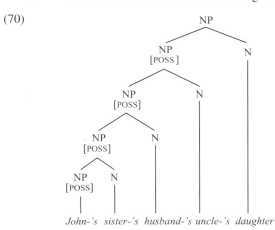

John-'s sister-'s husband-'s uncle-'s daughter

Recursive structures can also be generated when there are two phrasal categories such that each of them can dominate the other. For example, as indicated by the rules in (71), a PP must normally have a daughter of category NP, and an NP may optionally contain a PP complement. These rules allow repeated embedding of PP within NP within PP within NP etc., as illustrated in (72) and (73).

(71)   PP → P   NP
            NP → Det   N   (PP)

(72) a   that house in Penang
     b   the garden of [that house in Penang]
     c   the tree in [the garden of [that house in Penang]]
     d   a durian on [the tree in [the garden of [that house in Penang]]]

(73)

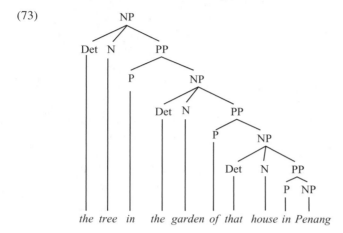

A particularly interesting type of recursion arises when one clause (category S or S′) is embedded inside another. There are two basic configurations which this embedding may produce; we refer to them as COORDINATION vs. SUBORDINATION. Coordination may involve constituents of any category, but the term "subordination" is normally reserved for clausal or sentential categories.

In a COORDINATE structure, two constituents belonging to the same category are joined as sisters to form another constituent of that category. Such a structure is "doubly headed," since both of the conjoined elements function as heads of the larger unit. Some simple examples of coordinate phrases are shown in (74):

(74) a   [[Snow White]$_{NP}$ and [the seven dwarfs]$_{NP}$]$_{NP}$
     b   [[quite brilliant]$_{AP}$ but [totally mad]$_{AP}$]$_{AP}$
     c   [[by hook]$_{PP}$ or [by crook]$_{PP}$]$_{PP}$
     d   [[the lady]$_{NP}$ or [the tiger]$_{NP}$]$_{NP}$
     e

                    NP
              ┌────┼────┐
          NP   Conj   NP
        ┌──┴──┐ │ ┌──┴──┐
      Det   N   Det   N
       │   │   │   │   │
     the lady   or   the tiger

In a coordinate sentence, two (or more) S constituents occur as daughters and co-heads of a higher S. Each of the daughter clauses has the internal structure of an independent sentence, and neither is embedded in the other. Coordinate sentences in English are normally linked by conjunctions such as *and, but*, and *or*, as in the examples in (75). In other languages, coordinate sentences may be formed by simply juxtaposing two independent clauses, with only the second receiving final intonation.

(75) a   [[The Archduke was murdered by a Serb nationalist]ₛ and [the whole world was plunged into a terrible war]ₛ]ₛ

   b   [[Give me liberty]ₛ or [give me death]ₛ]ₛ

   c   [[The spirit is willing]ₛ but [the flesh is weak]ₛ]ₛ

   d

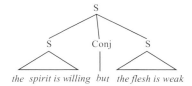

A SUBORDINATE clause is one which functions as a dependent, rather than a co-head. We can identify three basic types of subordinate clause:

a   Complement clauses
b   Adjunct (or Adverbial) clauses
c   Relative clauses

RELATIVE CLAUSES are clauses which function as modifiers within a noun phrase; these will be discussed in detail in chapter 7. ADJUNCT CLAUSES, as their name suggests, are clauses which function as an adjunct or adverbial element of another clause; some examples are given in (76).

(76) a   [Before John could finish his dinner], a group of reporters arrived demanding an interview.

   b   The elephant's child was spanked [because he asked too many questions].

   c   [In order for your client to win this case], you need to find a more reliable witness.

COMPLEMENT CLAUSES are clauses which occur as arguments of a verb; in other words, they are required or licensed by the subcategorization features of the verb. The larger clause, which contains the complement clause, is referred to as the MATRIX clause. Some examples of complement clauses are given in (77).

(77) a   John believes [that the airplane was invented by an Irishman].

   b   Mary planned [for John to arrive in Dallas on New Year's Day].

   c   [That anyone believes Mary's story] surprises me.

   d   [For the President to be re-elected] would cause panic on Wall Street.

The element which introduces a complement clause, e.g., *that* or *for* in (77), is called a COMPLEMENTIZER (abbreviated COMP). The complementizer and the clause which it introduces together form a constituent which is normally labeled S′ or S̄ (pronounced "S-bar"). This structure is illustrated in (78).

(78)

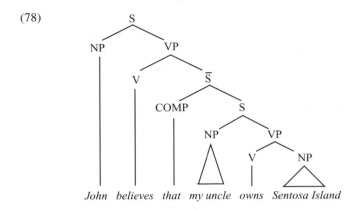

John   believes   that   my uncle   owns   Sentosa Island

Subordinate clauses of various kinds will figure prominently in many of the chapters which follow, so we will not discuss them further here. We turn instead to the issue of identifying syntactic categories.

2.5   "Mixed" categories

There is an old saying to the effect that "any noun in English can be verbed." While this is a slight exaggeration, it is true that a very large number of English common nouns can also be used as verbs; some examples are given in (79). Conversely, many verbs can also be used as nouns, as illustrated in (80).

(79) a   Help me *crate* these apples.
  b   Don't forget to *lock* the door.
  c   I need to *shoe* that horse before you ride him.
  d   Don't *tape* the envelopes, it makes them harder to open.
  e   Stephen was *stoned* by an angry mob.

(80) a   the long *march*
  b   a good *run*
  c   May I have the next *dance*?

In most if not all languages, there are a number of words whose category (part of speech) is ambiguous in this way. Such words can be used in more than one way, e.g., as either a noun or a verb in this case; but each use of the word has the normal properties associated with that category. So, for example, all of the potentially ambiguous words in (79) are clearly verbs in those sentences, while the potentially ambiguous words in (80) are clearly nouns. Such cases do not pose a major analytical problem; both uses will be listed in the lexicon.

A more difficult problem arises in some languages with forms which simultaneously exhibit properties of two different categories. Two well-known examples in English are GERUNDS and PARTICIPLES. A gerund is sometimes described as a "verbal noun," or "a verb which is used as a noun." In the same way, a participle is often described as a "verbal adjective," or "an adjective derived from a verb." English gerunds are formed by adding the suffix *–ing* to the verb root (e.g., *Smoking is not allowed*). Present participles are also formed by adding *–ing*, as in *a smiling face*; while past participles are (for most verbs) formed by adding *–ed* or *–en*, as in *a broken promise*.

Sentence (81) illustrates why it can be difficult to assign these forms to a particular category. The word *reading* is a gerund. It has some properties which are characteristic of verbs, such as taking a direct object and being modified by an adverb. On the other hand, the phrase which it heads in this example clearly functions as an NP, being the subject of the sentence. Notice that this "mixed" status is not a special or accidental property of that particular verb. Rather, it is a systematic part of English grammar; virtually any verb stem in the language can be expressed as a gerund.

(81)   [Carefully *reading* the instructions]$_{NP}$ will help you avoid mistakes.

In section 2.5.1 we will review the criteria used for determining syntactic categories. In section 2.5.2 we will use these criteria to examine the categorial status of gerunds in more detail. We will see that, in addressing a puzzle of this kind, it is extremely important to distinguish ambiguous category membership of the kind illustrated in (79) and (80) from "mixed" properties of the kind illustrated in (81).

2.5.1   Identifying syntactic categories

Traditional definitions for syntactic categories (parts of speech) were based on characteristics of meaning or semantic types. Some familiar examples are given in (82).

(82)   A NOUN is a word that names a person, place, or thing.
            An VERB is a word that names an action or event.
            An ADJECTIVE is a word that describes a state.

These definitions are useful in certain ways, but they would fail to identify abstract nouns like *destruction, theft, beauty, heaviness*. They cannot distinguish between the verb *love* and the adjective *fond (of)*; nor between the noun *fool* and the adjective *foolish*, since there is very little semantic difference between the two.

(83)   They are fools.
            They are foolish.

For this reason, the lexical categories (or word classes) in a particular language must be defined in terms of language-specific grammatical criteria, rather than semantic properties. There are actually two separate problems facing us here, which need to be addressed separately. First we must ask the question, "Which words belong together in the same class?" Only then can we ask the second question, "What name (or label) should we assign to each word class?"

The first question must be answered on the basis of specific grammatical features in a particular language. The second question must be answered on the basis of general semantic patterns which apply to all languages. That is, the category of a particular word must be determined on the basis of grammatical properties such as distribution, syntactic functions, and morphological features. Once the word classes in a language have been defined in this way, they can be assigned a label (Noun, Verb, etc.) based on universal notional patterns, e.g., "the category which contains basic terms denoting people, places and things is called NOUN."[11]

To return to our previous example, the noun *fool* and the adjective *foolish* can be distinguished by properties like the following:

(84) a   Modification by adverb vs. adjective:
         They are utter fools. *They are very fools.
         *They are utter foolish. They are very foolish.

    b   Inflection for number
         fool   fools
         foolish *foolishes

    c   Comparative forms
         fool   *fooler/*more fool
         foolish   more foolish

    d   Occurrence as subject of a clause
         Fools rush in where angels fear to tread.
         *Foolish rush in where angels fear to tread.

Thus *fool* belongs to the class of words which can be modified by adjectives and inflected for number, have no comparative form, and can occur as subjects. Other words which share these properties, and so belong to the same category, include *man, house*, and *tree*. But *foolish* belongs to the class of words which can be modified by adverbs, do have a comparative form, cannot be inflected for number, and cannot occur as subjects. Other words which share these properties include *big, green*, and *angry*. Based on the semantic class of the prototypical elements in each category, we would label the first category "Noun" and the second "Adjective."

As examples of the kinds of grammatical criteria (or tests) that can be used to determine which class a word belongs to, consider the following partial characterizations of nouns, verbs, and adjectives in English:

> Class 1 (labeled NOUN) consists of words which can be inflected for number (*dog, dogs; child, children; goose, geese*); can be modified by determiners and adjectives; and can function as subject, direct object, or object of a preposition. These words may take prepositional complements (e.g., *father of the bride, letter to my children*).

Class 2 (labeled VERB) consists of words which can be inflected for tense and aspect (*sing, sang, sung, singing; take, took, taken, taking; weave, wove, woven, weaving*); can be inflected for subject-person agreement in simple present tense (*I sing, he sings; I take, he takes*, etc.); can be modified by adverbs but not adjectives; and can function as the head of a clause. Some words of this class can take NP objects, and/or AdjP or VP complements.

Class 3 (labeled ADJECTIVE) consists of words which can be inflected for degree (*big, bigger, biggest; good, better, best*); and can be modified by adverbs of degree but not by other adjectives (*really big, truly great*; but not **real big, *true great*). They can modify nouns but no other category. Some words of this class can take prepositional complements (e.g., *angry at his father, afraid of his shadow*).

These descriptions are, of course, far from complete. Even so, we notice at once that not all nouns can be inflected for number: the MASS NOUNS (*air, music, sunshine, moonlight*, etc.) are normally used only in the singular, and some other nouns (*scissors, trousers*) occur only in the plural. Similarly, not all adjectives have comparative or superlative forms. So these descriptions are lists of properties associated with the class as a whole, and not of each individual member.

On the whole, this approach works fairly well. But sometimes we encounter word forms in a particular language which exhibit "mixed" properties. The tests which are used to determine class membership in that language may give ambiguous results for such a form, suggesting that the word belongs to two classes at once, or to neither class properly.

In the following section we will focus on the English gerunds. First we will illustrate the "mixed" grammatical properties which make it difficult to determine whether gerunds should be classified as nouns or verbs, or even whether they can be assigned to any category at all. Then we will examine the distribution of these properties more closely, trying to resolve this apparent ambiguity.

2.5.2   English gerunds

Examples (85) through (90) (adapted from Wasow and Roeper, 1972) contain pairs of sentences which use the same *V-ing* form. In each pair, the *V-ing* form in the (a) sentence has certain grammatical features which are characteristic of nouns, while the same form in the (b) sentence has grammatical features which are characteristic of verbs.

(85) a   I detest loud singing.
     b   I detest singing loudly.

(86) a   John enjoyed a reading of *The Bald Soprano*.
     b   John enjoyed reading *The Bald Soprano*.

(87) a   The killing of his dog upset John.
     b   Killing his dog upset John.

(88) a   Sightings of UFOs make Mary nervous.
     b   Sighting UFOs makes Mary nervous.

(89) a   I enjoy graceful diving.
     b   I enjoy having dived gracefully.

(90) a   No cooking is good enough for John.
     b   Not cooking is a rare treat for his wife.

Let us list some of the grammatical differences which make the (a) sentences look more nominal, while the (b) sentences look more verbal:

a   **articles:** used as determiners only with nouns, not with verbs. Note the use of articles to modify the *V-ing* form in (86a) and (87a).

b   **modifiers:** nouns may be modified by adjectives, as in (85a) and (89a); but verbs must be modified by adverbs, is in (85b) and (89b).

c   **number:** nouns may be pluralized, as in (88a); but verbs never take the plural suffix.

d   **object marking:** the direct objects of verbs appear as bare NPs, as in (86b), (87b), and (88b). Nouns do not take direct objects but may take prepositional complements, as in (86a), (87a), and (88a) where the complements are marked with the preposition *of*.

e   **negation:** nouns may be negated with *no* (90a), while verbs must be negated with *not* (90b).

f   **tense/aspect:** verbs may appear in the perfect tense (89b), whereas this is impossible for nouns.

These seemingly contradictory characteristics have led some linguists to state that gerunds are neither nouns nor verbs, but exhibit properties of both categories in varying proportions. However, the evidence presented above does not support this claim. It is true that we see the same *V-ing* form occurring in one sentence as a noun and in another sentence as a verb. But what we do not find is a mixture of nominal and verbal features in the same example. In other words, each individual use of a *V-ing* form can be unambiguously classified as either a noun or a verb.

What this pattern suggests is that the suffix *-ing* itself is ambiguous: it can either be used as a nominalizer, deriving nouns from verb roots as in the (a) sentences; or it can be used to mark a special type of verb, as in the (b) sentences. The term GERUND should properly be applied only to the verbal forms, though for clarity these are sometimes referred to as VERBAL GERUNDS.

So we are suggesting that the examples above illustrate two distinct uses of the same suffix, or perhaps two homophonous suffixes. This claim is supported by a difference in the productivity of these two uses. It is quite normal for derivational processes like nominalization to have lexical exceptions. As (91) illustrates, there are many verb roots which cannot be nominalized by the *-ing* suffix. However, virtually any verb root can be used to form a "true" (i.e., verbal) gerund, as illustrated in (92).

(91) a   *careful considering (cf. consideration) of the alternatives
     b   *a denying (cf. denial) of the charges
     c   *Henry's false accusing (cf. accusation) of his rival
     d   *the late arriving (cf. arrival) of Mrs. Thatcher

(92) a   carefully considering the alternatives
     b   denying the charges
     c   Henry's falsely accusing his rival
     d   Mrs. Thatcher's arriving late

Further evidence of the derivational nature of -*ing* nominalization is that the resulting nouns often have special and unpredictable meanings, as in (93a). The corresponding verbal gerunds, however, are semantically regular, as in (93b). Other examples of -*ing* nominalizations which have specialized meanings include *fillings, clippings, findings, droppings, bearings* (two meanings), *heading, rigging, binding, setting, building*, etc.

(93) a   [NOMINALIZATION] I can think of several different *readings* for that
           sentence, but this must be the preferred *reading*.
     b   [GERUND] Students should not begin this project without carefully *reading*
           the instructions.

In addition to these diagnostic features, there are several other systematic differences between -*ing* nominalizations and verbal gerunds. We will mention a few of these differences briefly.

Interpretation of missing subjects: Look back at example (86) and ask, "Who is doing the reading?" In (86b), *John* himself is the reader; but in (86a), *John* is listening to someone else reading out loud. Similarly, in (85b) the speaker (*I*) is also the singer; but in (85a), the singer is someone else. All of the examples in (85) – (90) exhibit this same pattern: the missing subject of the gerunds (the [b] sentences) is interpreted as being co-referential with some other NP in the same sentence; but the missing subject of the nominalizations (the [a] sentences) is normally interpreted as referring to some other participant.

Marking of overt subjects: In light of the preceding generalization, we might ask: what does the subject look like when it is not missing? How is it marked? Some examples are given in (94) and (95). In both examples, the (b) and (c) sentences involve verbal gerunds, as shown by the adverbial modifiers and (in [95]) a direct object NP; while the (a) sentences involve nominalizations, as shown by the adjective modifiers and (in [95]) a PP complement. As these examples illustrate, the NP corresponding to the "subject" of a nominalization always appears in the possessive or genitive form (e.g., *his*); but the subject of a verbal gerund may appear in either the accusative form (e.g., *him*) or the genitive.

(94) a   [NOMINALIZATION] Bill's loud singing annoyed me.
     b   [GERUND] Bill's singing loudly annoyed me.
     c   [GERUND] Bill singing loudly is enough to wake the dead.

(95) a   [NOMINALIZATION] People resent his secret buying of shares in a rival
            company.
     b   [GERUND] People resent his secretly buying shares in a rival company.
     c   [GERUND] People resent him secretly buying shares in a rival company.

Semantic interpretation: In many contexts, a gerund and its corresponding nominalization will have essentially the same meaning. However, in some examples there is a subtle difference in interpretation between the two. When such a difference is encountered, the gerund typically refers to the fact that a particular action took place (the FACTIVE interpretation), while the nominalization may refer to something else, such as the manner in which it was done. This contrast is illustrated in (96): the most natural interpretation of the gerund (96a) is "the fact that John was driving a Mercedes," whereas the most natural interpretation of the nominalization (96b) is "the manner in which John was driving the Mercedes." A similar contrast may occur with other types of nominalizations as well, as illustrated in (97): the gerund in (97a) has the factive interpretation, while the nominalization in (97b) has the manner interpretation.

(96) a   [GERUND] John's driving a Mercedes astonished his creditors.
     b   [NOMINALIZATION] John's driving of the Mercedes terrified his
            passengers.

(97) a   [GERUND] The landlord complained about John managing the apartments.
     b   [NOMINALIZATION] The landlord complained about John's management
            of the apartments.

Sentence (98a) is a famous example of ambiguity involving a nominalization with -*ing*. In this sentence *the hunters* can be interpreted either as the patient of *shooting* (the factive interpretation), or as the agent (the manner interpretation). But, as (98b) illustrates, the corresponding gerund is unambiguous. It allows only the factive interpretation, and not the manner interpretation.

(98) a   [NOMINALIZATION] The shooting of the hunters was awful.
     b   [GERUND] Shooting the hunters was a tragic mistake/#pathetically
            inaccurate.

To summarize, then, in terms of the category of the *V-ing* forms themselves the situation is fairly simple. Nominalizations ending in -*ing* (the [a] forms in examples [85] – [88]) are simply nouns, while true gerunds (the [b] forms) are verbs. But while the *V-ing* nominalizations seem to have all the properties we would expect of nouns, gerunds provide a greater challenge.

What is puzzling about gerunds is not primarily their category but their distribution, or rather the distribution of the phrases which they head. Internally the phrase looks like a VP, since the gerund takes NP objects, adverbial modifiers, etc.[12] But externally (within the wider sentence), the phrase has the distribution of an NP, typically occurring in subject and object positions as in examples (85) – (90). This is why gerunds are sometimes referred to as a "mixed category."

We can sum up this discussion by saying that a gerund is a verb with a special property, namely that the VP which it "projects" (i.e., heads) functions as an NP. This suggests that the VP node is embedded under an NP node. Exactly how this should be represented is beyond the scope of this book; see Haspelmath (1996) and Bresnan (1997) for a summary of various proposals that have been made, as well as examples of mixed categories in a number of other languages.

2.5.3   Conclusion

Gerunds pose an interesting challenge to the claim that each word belongs to a single syntactic category. At first glance, it appears that the *V-ing* forms have some properties which are characteristic of nouns and other properties which are characteristic of verbs. Such cases have led some linguists to deny that categories like NOUN and VERB can be defined as discrete classes, i.e., that we can define clear boundaries between one category and the other with no overlap in membership.

However, what emerges from a closer examination of the data is an "either–or" pattern: in terms of the phrase-internal syntax, any particular *V-ing* example may have properties of either nouns or verbs, but not both. While there is (as usual) some variation in the number of diagnostic tests which work for any particular example, we have seen no examples of a single form having characteristic properties of both word classes at the same time. In other words, it does in fact seem to be possible to classify each *V-ing* form unambiguously as either a noun or a verb.

We can draw two lessons from this case study. First, it is important to distinguish ambiguous category membership (words which may belong to two or more categories) from a truly "mixed" category. Apparent cases of "gradient" (i.e., non-discrete) category membership may in fact be due to multiple functions of a single affix, or to homophonous affixes. And, of course, many languages have words (or roots) which can be used either as nouns or verbs, etc. But the fact that different senses of a particular word may belong to different categories does not mean that the categories themselves are ill-defined.

Second, in analyzing true mixed categories, it is important to specify precisely which properties the problematic forms share with each of the basic categories. In the case of gerunds, for example, we found that the phrase-internal syntax is verbal while the external distribution is nominal. In every example of a mixed category which has been carefully studied to date, the mixture of features is not arbitrary or random. Rather, it follows a clear pattern which suggests that a phrase of one category is embedded within a phrase of some other category.

Mixed categories constitute a significant challenge to the approach outlined above for defining syntactic categories, but on the whole this approach has proven to be quite effective. No linguist would deny that some words in any language may be difficult to assign to a category, or that defining the syntactic categories of a given language may be a very complex business. For example, professional linguists have argued for at least a hundred years, without reaching a consensus, over the question of whether or not the Philippine languages have verbs. What is important is that such thorny issues must be decided on the basis of grammatical evidence.

Exercise 2A: English participles

English verbs may appear in two different participial forms: present participles (*sinking, taking, painting*) and past participles (*sunk, taken, painted*). In this chapter we have discussed the apparent ambiguity of gerunds, which seem to have grammatical properties of both nouns and verbs. In the same way, participles in English appear to be ambiguous between the categories Adjective and Verb. In this exercise we will examine various uses of participial forms to see whether they can be unambiguously classified as either adjectives or verbs, or whether there are some instances where a single form seems to have characteristic features of both categories. For your convenience, some of the characteristic grammatical properties of adjectives and verbs are summarized below:

Summary of criteria for class membership:
VERBS:

a   five inflectional forms, marking tense, aspect, and agreement
b   verbs function as the head of a clause
c   may take NP, PP, AdjP, or clausal complements (depending on subcategorization)

ADJECTIVES:

a   can be marked for comparative and superlative forms (*bigger, biggest; more beautiful, most beautiful*)
b   can function as modifier of nouns, and as the predicate complement of verbs like *be, seem, become, consider, find*, etc., e.g.
   John seems nice/hungry/Italian/*sing/*eat/*fell.
   I find her stories funny/dull/sad.
c   can be modified by adverbs of degree (*too, very, quite, rather, less*, etc.); note the following contrast:
   (i) *That is a very nice picture.*
   (ii) *John really/*very works when he is facing a deadline.*

Task 1: For each of the following examples, state whether the underlined participial form should be assigned to category V or Adj. Briefly indicate the reason for each decision.

(A1) a John fixed the <u>squeaking</u> hinge.
   b The captain's <u>laughing</u> daughter was a favorite with all the soldiers.
   c Mary found a <u>broken</u> guitar in the attic.
   d The king's <u>pampered</u> daughter kept her toys in a brightly <u>painted</u> box.
   e Peter is the most <u>respected</u> economist in his department.

(A2) a Those noisy motorcycles are extremely <u>annoying</u>.
   b John considers cold showers <u>invigorating</u>.
   c I found the proposal very <u>appealing</u>.

(A3) a   The winner looked <u>elated</u>.
      b   John seems quite <u>annoyed</u> at his mother.
      c   The president did not sound <u>convinced</u>.

(A4) a   That child has the most <u>charming</u> smile I have ever seen.
      b   Max is (*very) <u>charming</u> a snake.

(A5) a   He made me a very <u>tempting</u> offer.
      b   Mary is (*very) <u>tempting</u> the child with a piece of chocolate.

(A6) a   The queen was <u>riding</u> a bicycle.
      b   Christopher Robin is <u>feeding</u> buns to the elephant.
      c   Yeltsin's statements are <u>alarming</u> American officials.

Task 2: Each of the following examples involves a participle used as the complement of a verb of perception. Based on this data, or any other examples that you can find, state whether the participial form in this construction belongs to category V or Adj. Briefly state the reasons for your decision.

(A7) a   I saw the Prime Minister <u>riding</u> a bicycle.
      b   I saw a young child (*very) <u>appealing</u> for help.
      c   No one heard the serpent (*very) <u>tempting</u> Eve to eat the apple.
      d   I heard the ambassador (*very) <u>insulting</u> his interpreter.
             (cf. *He made a very insulting gesture.*)

(A8) a   I have seen suspects much/*very <u>abused</u> by the police.
      b   John heard his wife (*very) <u>insulted</u> by a policeman.
      c   King Louis saw his palace (*very) <u>destroyed</u> by the mob.
      d   I saw Kissinger <u>awarded</u> the Nobel Peace Prize.

Task 3: The following examples contain participial relative clauses, which immediately follow the modified noun. Based on this data, or any other examples that you can find, state whether the participial forms in this construction belong to category V or Adj. Briefly state the reasons for your decision.

(A9) a   The child <u>riding</u> a bicycle is my nephew.
      b   The woman (*very) <u>tempting</u> the governor is a former Miss America.
      c   The statements currently (*very) <u>alarming</u> American officials are not coming from the Kremlin.
             (cf. *Yeltsin holds some very alarming views.*)

(A10) a   A person (*very) <u>bitten</u> by a snake should get medical help immediately.
      b   Any politician <u>given</u> money by a foreign power should resign from office.
      c   The candidate unanimously (*very) <u>expected</u> to win was disqualified under suspicious circumstances.
      d   The man <u>elected</u> president in 1968 was driven from office in 1974.
      e   The police have identified the group (widely/*very) <u>considered</u> responsible for the bombing.

Notes

1. Without some discourse context, this sentence would be more natural with a definite article: *Up the big hill John ran.* We retain the indefinite article here in order to preserve the parallelism with (10b).
2. As explained in section 2.4, the category label S' (pronounced "S-bar") is commonly used for the constituent formed by a complementizer plus the complement clause which it marks, e.g., *that* + S.
3. Radford (1988), ex. (54).
4. Radford (1988), ex. (77).
5. Abbott (1976) and Grosu (1976) show that the acceptability of Right Node Raising examples is influenced by pragmatic factors, and subject to variation across speakers. For these reasons it may be less reliable than the other tests for constituency discussed in this section.
6. But see n. 5.
7. Radford's ex. 168a, p. 101.
8. Another difference is that Gapping is used primarily in formal styles, whereas VP-Ellipsis is common in all styles of English (Rick Nivens, p.c.).
9. See McCawley (1988, vol. 2, ch. 19) for a detailed discussion.
10. Radford (p. 102) refers to this as the Strict Adjacency Principle.
11. See Lyons (1966); Schachter (1985).
12. The main VP-internal feature which distinguishes gerunds from other verbs is that the subject NP takes genitive or accusative case, as in (95), rather than nominative case.

3 Passives, applicatives, and "Dative Shift"

Consider the following pair of Japanese sentences (from Tsujimura, 1996):

(1) a   Sensei=ga   Taroo=o   sikat-ta.
            teacher=NOM Taroo=ACC scold-PAST
            'The teacher scolded Taroo.'

    b   Taroo=ga   sensei=ni   sikar-are-ta.
            Taroo=NOM teacher=OBL[1] scold-PASSIVE-PAST
            'Taroo was scolded by the teacher.'

Clearly the two sentences are quite similar. They appear to mean the same thing, the word order is essentially the same (subject first, verb last), the same basic words are used. In fact, there seem to be only two significant differences. First, the verb in (1b) contains an additional morpheme, the suffix -*(r)are*, which does not occur in (1a). Second, while the same participants appear filling the same semantic roles in both sentences, there is a shift in the assignment of grammatical relations. The patient *Taroo* is the direct object in (1a), but the subject in (1b); and the agent *Sensei* is the subject in (1a), but an oblique argument in (1b).

Obviously the correlation between these two differences is not accidental. The function of the suffix -*(r)are* is to signal precisely the shift in grammatical relations observed in (1b). Sentence (1a) is called the ACTIVE form, while (1b) is called the PASSIVE form; and -*(r)are* is identified as the passive suffix.

As the English translations of (1a) and (1b) illustrate, a very similar alternation occurs in English. Some further examples of active sentences are given in (2), the corresponding passive sentences in (3).

(2) a   A snake bit John's dog.
    b   Ali bought this bicycle for his son.
    c   The allies quickly forgot Churchill's advice.
    d   Jill hit Jack on the head with an umbrella.

(3) a   John's dog was bitten by a snake.
    b   This bicycle was bought by Ali for his son.
    c   Churchill's advice was quickly forgotten (by the allies).
    d   Jack was hit on the head with an umbrella (by Jill).

In comparing the active and passive forms, we find that the same basic pattern holds in English which we observed in Japanese. Again, the two forms have the same basic meaning, the same participants filling the same semantic roles, and the same basic (SVX) word order. We also find the same shift in grammatical relations: the object of the active sentence appears as the subject of the passive sentence; and the subject of the active sentence appears as an oblique argument in the passive sentence, optionally omitted but marked with the preposition *by* when present.

The main difference we can observe between Japanese and English is that in Japanese the passive is marked only by adding an affix to the verb, while the English passive requires both a special participial form of the main verb and a special auxiliary (*be*). Japanese can be said to have a purely MORPHOLOGICAL PASSIVE, while a language like English, in which the passive requires the addition of extra words (with or without special morphology on the main verb) is said to have a PERIPHRASTIC PASSIVE.

The opposition (or alternation) between active and passive is by far the most common type of VOICE system among the world's languages. We will examine some others in chapter 11. The term VOICE refers to a system of oppositions involving a change in the semantic role which is associated with the subject relation.

We will begin this chapter by discussing some of the typical features of a passive construction. Then we will try to formulate a rule which expresses how passive sentences are formed. Finally we will extend the same approach to account for other morpho-syntactic alternations which do not affect the subject relation, but which change the assignment of other grammatical relations.

3.1   Some typological features of passives

Passives are normally formed from transitive (or ditransitive) verbs.[2] The most typical passive constructions are based on agent–patient activity verbs: actions that one participant does to another. In some languages, passivization may be restricted or impossible with other types of verbs, e.g., non-volitional experiencer verbs like *see, hear,* and *know*, or other statives (*own, resemble, contain,* etc.).

In comparing the active and passive sentences above we noted two changes in the assignment of grammatical relations: the "promotion" of the patient from direct object to subject; and the "demotion" of the agent from subject to oblique. The second of these changes (the demotion of the agent) is a feature of all passive constructions; but the first (the promotion of the patient) need not occur in some languages under certain conditions. If the patient is not promoted, then the resulting passive sentence will have no grammatical subject, as illustrated in example (4b). This type of sentence is called an IMPERSONAL PASSIVE.

(4)   **Finnish** (Comrie, 1977; Ida Toivonen, p.c.)

a   Äiti   jätti hänet   kotiin.
        mother left him(ACC) to.home
        'Mother left him at home.'

b   Hänet   jätettiin kotiin.
   him(ACC) was.left to.home
   'He was left at home.'

Since the impersonal passive construction does not involve the promotion of a patient, it can often be applied to verbs which lack patients, e.g., intransitive verbs. Examples (5) and (6), adapted from Comrie (1977), illustrate this. In each example the (a) sentence shows a basic active intransitive clause, while the (b) sentence shows a corresponding impersonal passive construction. The (c) sentence presents a normal (personal) passive, based on a transitive verb, for comparison. Notice that the agent phrase of the impersonal passive, if it is mentioned at all, is marked in the same way as the agent phrase of a personal passive. As these examples illustrate, an impersonal passive construction may have no subject at all, as in Latin and Finnish, or it may have a dummy subject, as in German.

(5)   **Latin**

a   Milites   acriter pugnaverunt.
   soldier.NOM.PL fiercely fight-PAST.3pl
   'The soldiers fought fiercely.'

b   Acriter (a.militibus)   pugnatum   est.
   fiercely by.soldier.ABL.PL fight-PFCT.PASS.SG.NEUT is
   Lit: 'It was fought fiercely (by the soldiers).'
   i.e., 'There was fierce fighting (by the soldiers).'

c   Dareus   ab.Alexandro   victus   est.
   Darius.NOM by.Alexander.ABL conquer-PFCT.PASS.SG.MASC is
   'Darius was conquered by Alexander.'

(6)   **German**

a   Die   Frauen tanzten   gestern.
   the.FEM.NOM.PL women dance-PAST.PL yesterday
   'The women danced yesterday.'

b   Es wurde gestern (von den   Frauen) getanzt.
   It became yesterday by the.DAT.PL women dance.PRTCPL
   Lit: 'It was danced yesterday (by the women).'
   i.e., 'There was dancing yesterday (by the women).'

c   Hans wurde von der   Frau geküsst.
   Hans became by the.DAT.SG woman kiss.PRTCPL
   'Hans was kissed by the woman.'

We saw in (3) that the demoted (i.e., oblique) agent phrase is optional in English passives, and this turns out to be true in most other languages as well. But in some languages, such as Latvian and Classical Arabic, the passive agent is not even optional; it cannot be expressed at all. Thus (according to Keenan, 1985a) all languages which have a passive construction allow the agentless passive. Some of these languages have only agentless passives; and in a number of others, while

gent phrase is allowed, the agentless passive is far more common in
ech.[3]

concluding this section, let us briefly mention one specialized use of the
hich is particularly common among Southeast Asian languages. Many
of these languages have a passive construction which is used only for unpleasant
or unfortunate events. A Vietnamese example[4] is given in (7). Passives of this
type are called ADVERSATIVE PASSIVES.

(7)   Quang bi   Bao ghet.
           Quang suffer Bao hate
           'Quang is hated by Bao.'

Aside from the semantic restrictions on the use of this construction, it looks
very much like the personal passives described above. But there is another type of
construction found in some languages which is also called an adversative passive,
but which differs from a "normal" passive in some very significant ways. Two
Japanese examples of this type of adversative passive are presented in (8) and
(9):[5]

(8) a   Kodomo=ga sinda.
         child=NOM died
         'A child died.'

    b   Taroo=ga   kodomo=ni sin-are-ta.
         Taroo=NOM child=OBL die-PASSIVE-PAST
         'Taroo was adversely affected by the death of his child.'

(9) a   Ame=ga   hutta.
         rain=NOM fell
         'It rained.'

    b   Ziroo=ga   ame=ni   hur-are-ta.
         Ziroo=NOM rain=OBL fall-PASSIVE-PAST
         'Ziroo was rained on.'

Comparing these examples to the normal Japanese passive in (1), we notice a
number of similarities. The same passive suffix is used in both constructions, and
the demoted subject of the active sentence is marked, in the passive form, with the
clitic =ni. But there are some important differences as well. In discussing example
(1) we noted that passivization does not affect the argument structure of the clause:
the same participants fill the same semantic roles in both active and passive. But in
(8) and (9) we see that the adversative passive sentence actually contains an extra
argument which is not found in the corresponding active sentence. Both of these
examples are based on intransitive verbs. The intransitive subject (not an agent
in these examples) is demoted in the passive form, as expected. But there is no
object which can be promoted to subject of the passive. Instead, a new participant
is introduced as the subject of the passive, and this new participant is the one who
is adversely affected by the action described in the basic intransitive clause.

really interesting than unfortunate or unpleasant events
are marked differently

The adversative passive in Japanese can also be formed with transitive verbs, as illustrated in (10). Here the agent is demoted to oblique status in the passive, as expected; but the patient is not promoted. Rather, a new participant is once again introduced as the subject of the passive, and this new participant is interpreted as being the one who is adversely affected by the action.

(10) a   Sensei=ga   kodomo=o sikat-ta.
            teacher=NOM child=ACC scold-PAST
            'The teacher scolded the child.'

    b   Taroo=ga   sensei=ni   kodomo=o sikar-are-ta.
            Taroo=NOM teacher=OBL child=ACC scold-PASSIVE-PAST
            'Taroo was adversely affected by the teacher's scolding his child.'

Tsujimura (1996) notes another significant difference between the adversative and normal passives in Japanese: the adversative passive must always contain an oblique *ni* phrase expressing the agent (or, more generally, the most prominent semantic role); but in normal passives, the *ni* phrase is optional.

3.2   Passive as a lexical rule

Let us summarize our conclusions to this point about the structure of a typical personal passive construction. Passivization does not affect the argument structure of the clause, either by changing the number of semantic arguments[6] (though, of course, the passive agent need not be overtly expressed in the syntax), or by changing the semantic roles which they fill. Passivization is primarily a realignment of grammatical relations, always involving the demotion of the agent from active subject to passive oblique, and normally involving the promotion of the patient from active object to passive subject. These changes are reflected in the argument structure diagrams in (11a–b).

(11) a   *beat*   < agent,   patient   > **Active**
                     | |
                  SUBJ   OBJ

    b   *be beaten* < agent,   patient   > **Passive**
                     | |
                 (OBL)   SUBJ

The question we want to consider now is, how does the grammar produce these changes? What kind of rule(s) are needed to derive passive sentences? The basic intuition which we will try to capture is that passive sentences are special simply because they contain a passive verb. We will treat passivization as a process that derives passive verbs.

Aside from the form of the verb itself (and, in English, the presence of the auxiliary), the syntactic structure of a passive sentence is quite similar to that of its active counterpart. In particular, the passive sentence exhibits normal, basic

· phrase structure and word-order patterns. The grammar of English must include phrase structure (PS) rules something like those in (12) in order to account for the active sentences in (2) above. But these same rules will also allow us to generate the corresponding passive sentences in (3).[7] This is illustrated in (13), which gives the PS diagrams for examples (2b) and (3b).

(12)   S → NP   VP
                    [SUBJ]

           VP →   V   (NP)   (PP)*
                      [OBJ]   [OBL]

(13) a

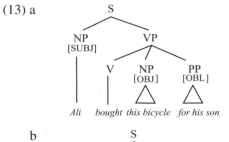

Ali   bought this bicycle for his son

   b

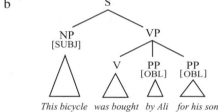

This bicycle was bought by Ali for his son

These observations, together with further evidence discussed in the appendix to this chapter, suggest that it would be wrong to treat passive constructions as a special type of sentence. Rather, we will treat them as normal sentences which contain a special type of verb.

As we have seen, a typical passive verb is "special" (i.e., different from the corresponding active form) in at least two respects: (i) its morphological shape; and (ii) its subcategorization, i.e., the grammatical relations which it assigns. In chapter 1 we saw that the verb's subcategorization determines the structure of the clause as a whole, because of the Completeness and Coherence conditions. Since no special PS rules are needed, passive sentences will be generated "automatically" if passive verbs are available in the lexicon. The crucial issue then is how passive verbs are formed. But before we procede with the details of the analysis, let us consider briefly the nature of the mapping between grammatical relations (GRs) and semantic roles.

3.2.1   The linking of arguments to GRs

In chapter 1 we stated that the LEXICAL ENTRY of a word (representing the information which a speaker holds in his "mental dictionary") must contain all the phonological, semantic, and grammatical information which is unpredictable or specific to that word. In the case of a verb, a crucial part of the lexical entry must be the argument structure and subcategorization features (i.e., assignment of grammatical relations), as illustrated in (11).

But notice that much of the information in (11a) is in fact predictable. Even if no information about GRs were included in that figure, we could predict that the agent should be the subject and the patient should be the direct object. In fact, for virtually any active verb in English that takes an agent and a patient, the same pattern holds: the agent will be the subject and the patient the direct object; and the same pattern is found in most other languages of the world. For English, we can go even further: we can predict that beneficiaries, instruments, and locatives will normally be expressed as oblique arguments in a basic active clause. Again, this is a very widespread pattern cross-linguistically.

These observations suggest that the alignment of GRs need not be included in the verb's lexical entry at all. Normally we try to exclude as much redundant information as possible from our analysis of the grammar, and especially from our lexical entries. The standard approach is to express regular patterns which apply to a large number of words by grammatical rules, using the lexical entry to represent only the information which is specific to a particular word, as mentioned above.

If we could formulate a set of rules (often called LINKING RULES) which would determine the GR assignment for each semantic role in the verb's argument structure, we could eliminate a large amount of redundant information from the lexicon. Moreover, instead of formulating a passive rule which would change (11a) into (11b), we could express passivization as a process which modifies the application of the linking rules themselves, resulting in a different alignment of GRs. In fact, this same approach could be used for the other constructions to be described later in this chapter.

A number of different theories of linking have in fact been proposed;[8] and this is probably the right direction in which to look for a satisfying analysis of the issues we are discussing. Unfortunately, the technical details of these proposals are quite complex, and beyond the scope of the present book. One reason for this complexity is the fact that, as we examine a broader range of data, we discover that linking patterns are not quite as regular as we may have imagined at first glance.

For example, a few languages (e.g., those which have been described as SYNTACTICALLY ERGATIVE; see chapter 11) seem to follow very different linking principles from those of English. Moreover, even in the more familiar languages, in which the linking patterns for agent–patient type verbs are fairly predictable, the situation with experiencer verbs and other non-agentive verbs is often far more complex. And in most, if not all, languages, there are a certain number of specific verbs which are simply irregular, or unpredictable in their assignment of GRs. For these irregular verbs, the linking patterns will need to be specified in the lexical entry, even if regular rules can be formulated for most other verbs in the language.

To take a concrete example, the English verbs *like* and *please* have very similar meanings and assign the same semantic roles: both verbs take an experiencer and a stimulus. Yet they exhibit opposite linking patterns: with *like*, the experiencer is subject (as in *I like it*); but with *please*, the stimulus is subject (as in *It pleases me*). Moreover, in Old English the verb *like* followed the opposite pattern from what it does today (e.g., *It liketh me not* 'I do not like it'). Clearly for these verbs the assignment of GRs is not predictable on the basis of semantic roles, and will need to be lexically specified.

For the sake of simplicity, we will continue to assume that the assignment of grammatical relations to semantic roles is fully specified in the lexical entry of each verb. We recognize that this approach leaves us with some predictable information in our lexical entries; but it also gives us a way of dealing with the constructions we are interested in, without getting bogged down in too many formal details.

3.2.2   Lexical entries and lexical rules

We sometimes speak of the lexicon as being the speaker's "mental dictionary." This phrase may give the impression that the lexicon is simply a list of words, or a static list of lexical entries containing various kinds of information about each word in the language. But many linguists now believe that the structure of the lexicon is considerably more complex than that.

Any speaker of a language like English knows a large number of "basic" words (e.g., those which consist of a single morpheme) as well as many derived words (those formed by some kind of derivational process). For example, there are various suffixes which derive nouns from adjectives. Two of these are illustrated in (14).

(14)

SUFFIX	ADJECTIVE	NOUN
-ity	*insane*	*insan-ity*
	trivial	*trivial-ity*
	obese	*obes-ity*
	scarce	*scarc-ity*
	profound	*profund-ity*
	local	*local-ity*
	special	*special-ity*
	lax	*lax-ity*
-ness	*strange*	*strange-ness*
	polite	*polite-ness*
	happy	*happi-ness*
	bold	*bold-ness*
	black	*black-ness*
	good	*good-ness*

Obviously there is a systematic relationship between the basic adjectives and the derived nouns in this table. This relationship can be expressed as a rule which

derives one from the other by adding the appropriate suffix. (Rules of this ty
are called WORD FORMATION RULES.) But notice that the pattern express
by these rules is only partly regular. For example, the suffix *–ity* applies on
to certain adjectives and not to others (**strange-ity*, **black-ity*, **good-ity*, etc
The suffix *–ness* is much more productive, but there are some adjectives to whic
it does not normally apply (?**superiorness* vs. *superiority*; ?**possibleness* vs.
possibility; ?*longness* vs. *length*; ?*freeness* vs. *freedom*).

So each of these rules applies to certain adjectives but not to others. But how
do we know which adjectives take which nominalizer? Forms like ?*freeness* and
?*longness* are not grammatically impossible in the way that **eat-ness* or **dog-ity*
would be.[9] These latter forms would violate the word formation rules involved,
since the suffix *–ness* can never be attached to a verb, nor can *–ity* be attached to a
noun. But without studying the history of each individual word, it is not so easy to
explain why **good-ity* and ?**possibleness* are not real English words. Speakers
of English simply have to memorize which word formation rule applies to which
words.

 sittingness +

To give another example, since we use the term *rubber-ize* meaning 'to cover
something with rubber,' there seems to be no grammatical constraint which would
prevent the formation of ??*chocolat-ize* or ??*sugar-ize*, meaning to cover something with chocolate or sugar. These words seem possible (unlike **sing-ize* or
**much-ize*), but they are not part of the English lexicon.

So it appears that the lexicon must specify not only all of the basic words in
the language but also all of the derived words. That is, out of all the possible
words which could be derived using the word formation rules of the language,
the lexicon must specify which ones are "real" words. In many cases, both the
input and the output of some word formation rule will be listed in the lexicon.
For example, any speaker of English knows that not only the basic words *black*
and *good* but also the corresponding derived words *blackness* and *goodness* are
real English words; both the basic and the derived forms exist as entries in the
lexicon. But we have seen other cases where a possible output form is not an actual
word; *possible* is, but ?**possibleness* is not, a part of the lexicon of English. There
are even a few cases where what looks like a derived (or output) form does not
correspond to any actual input form. For example, words like *ostracize* and *levity*
seem to end in derivational suffixes, but there are no corresponding basic forms
in English (**ostrac*, **lev*).

A word-formation rule (such as the rule which derives abstract nouns by adding
the suffix *–ness* to adjectives) is a special type of LEXICAL RULE, that is, a rule
which derives one lexical entry from another. The lexicon is not a simple word
list, but is actually part of the rule system of the grammar, since it includes not
only the words (lexical entries) of the language but also a set of lexical rules.
As we have seen, these lexical rules do not in general apply to every possible
input form. Rather, they apply on a case-by-case basis. Both input and output
forms will be listed as separate entries in the lexicon, if they are both actual
words. But, if that is true, what use is the rule? Is it really part of the grammar
at all?

A lexical rule expresses a systematic relationship between two sets of words like those illustrated in (14). This systematic pattern is part of the speaker's knowledge about the structure of the language. In a sense the rule may be "redundant," since both input and output forms are listed separately. But the speaker's knowledge of this rule may facilitate the tasks of speaking, listening, and learning language. These rules are often a source of new words entering the language by analogy. For example, some English speakers now use *obeseness* in place of *obesity*. Other more famous examples include *Spoonerism* and *bowdlerize*, both derived from proper names. The rules can even be manipulated by the speaker for comic effect, as in the following quote from the novel *Gaudy Night*, by Dorothy Sayers (the hero is discussing the architecture of Balliol College in Oxford University):

> We are mortified in nineteenth-century Gothic, lest in our overweening *Balliolity* we forget God. (1936: 335)

In the next section, we will apply this concept of lexical rules to develop an analysis of the passive construction.

3.2.3　The passive rule

Obviously there is a close and systematic relationship between corresponding active and passive sentences like those illustrated in (1)–(3), and this relationship should be reflected in our analysis of the grammar. We have suggested that the relationship between such pairs of sentences can be reduced to a relationship between corresponding active and passive verbs. Ignoring for now the morphological details, which are irregular for many English verbs, the crucial difference between active and passive verbs is the alignment of grammatical relations to arguments. This difference was illustrated in (11), repeated below. Thus the rule of passivization which we wish to formulate must be one which expresses the systematic relationship between (11a) and (11b).

(11) a　*beat*　< agent, patient > **Active**
　　　　　　　　　|　　　|
　　　　　　　　SUBJ　OBJ

　　 b　*be beaten* < agent, patient > **Passive**
　　　　　　　　　|　　　|
　　　　　　　　(OBL)　SUBJ

We have described a lexical rule as a rule which derives one lexical entry from another, expressing a regular pattern of relationships between words. By analyzing the passive as a lexical rule, we are claiming that both the active verb and its passive counterpart are listed as separate lexical entries. The passive rule will express the systematic relationship between these entries.

Taking the active as the basic form, we need a rule which will derive passive verbs from active verbs. For the moment, we will ignore the morphological effects of passivization and focus only on the changes in grammatical relations. In our formal statement of the lexical rule, we will indicate only changes to the lexical entry. In other words, we will assume that any information not explicitly referred to in the rule remains the same. Under this assumption, the passive rule stated in (15) would act on the basic (active) form in (11a) to produce the passive form in (11b):

(15)   **Passive rule:**
$$\begin{bmatrix} \text{SUBJ} & \rightarrow & \text{OBL}_{\text{agt}} \\ \text{OBJ} & \rightarrow & \text{SUBJ} \end{bmatrix}$$

This rule is interpreted in the following way: every reference to the OBJ relation in the original lexical entry is to be replaced by SUBJ in the derived lexical entry; and (simultaneously) every reference to SUBJ in the original lexical entry is to be replaced by OBL$_{\text{agt}}$ in the derived lexical entry. These changes will derive (11b) from (11a).

As noted above, a characteristic property of lexical rules is that they have lexical exceptions; that is, they may apply to some possible input forms, but not to others. Of course, some rules are more productive than others. Even though passivization is quite productive, our lexical treatment of this process is supported by the fact that certain transitive verbs must be lexically marked as exceptions to the rule, i.e., they cannot be passivized. Some examples are given in (16)–(20).[10]

(16) a   John resembles Mr. Nixon.
     b   *Mr. Nixon is resembled by John.

(17) a   Our committee lacks the necessary resources.
     b   *The necessary resources are lacked by our committee.

(18) a   Anyone can afford a Proton Saga.
     b   *?A Proton Saga can be afforded by anyone.
     c   *A new car can't be afforded by me.

(19) a   This box contains 24 pencils.
     b   *24 pencils are contained *by/in this box.

(20) a   Your humor eludes me.
     b   *I am eluded by your humor.

Further evidence which supports treating passivization as a lexical rule is presented in the appendix to this chapter.

3.3   Applicative in Bantu languages

Passivization is a prototypical example of a "relation-changing process"; that is, a process which changes the grammatical relation of one or more arguments. In the previous section we introduced a simple notation for representing passivization as a lexical process. The same kind of approach can be applied to various other relation-changing processes, two of which will be discussed in this section and the next.

3.3.1   Chichewa

Let us begin by considering some data from Chichewa, a Bantu language of eastern Africa. Based on the following sentences, can you identify the function of the Chichewa suffix *-ir* ∼ *-er*,[11] (glossed as APPL in these examples)?[12]

(21) a   Mbidzi   zi-na-perek-a   msampha kwa nkhandwe.
            zebras(10) SUBJ(10)-PAST-hand-ASP trap   to   fox
            'The zebras handed the trap to the fox.'

     b   Mbidzi   zi-na-perek-er-a   nkhandwe msampha.
            zebras(10) SUBJ(10)-PAST-hand-APPL-ASP fox   trap
            'The zebras handed the fox the trap.'

(22) a   Ndi-na-tumiz-a   kalata kwa mfumu.
            1sg.SUBJ-PAST-send-ASP letter to   chief
            'I sent a letter to the chief.'

     b   Ndi-na-tumiz-ir-a   mfumu kalata.
            1sg.SUBJ-PAST-send-APPL-ASP chief   letter
            'I sent the chief a letter.'

(23) a   Fisi   a-na-dul-a   chingwe ndi   mpeni.
            hyena(1) SUBJ(1)-PAST-cut-ASP rope   with knife
            'The hyena cut the rope with a knife.'

     b   Fisi   a-na-dul-ir-a   mpeni chingwe.
            hyena(1) SUBJ(1)-PAST-cut-APPL-ASP knife rope
            'The hyena cut the rope with a knife.'

(24) a   Msangalatsi a-ku-yend-a   ndi ndodo.
            entertainer(1) SUBJ(1)-PRES-walk-ASP with stick
            'The entertainer is walking with a stick.'

     b   Msangalatsi a-ku-yend-er-a   ndodo.
            entertainer(1) SUBJ(1)-PRES-walk-APPL-ASP stick
            'The entertainer is walking with a stick.'

These pairs of sentences have certain properties in common with the active–passive pairs which we examined at the beginning of this chapter. Once again the same verb root is used in both, and the verb in the (b) sentence bears a special morphological marker not found in the (a) sentence. Once again, the same participants occur with the same semantic roles; the main difference seems to involve the subcategorization frame of the verb, i.e., the assignment of grammatical relations. But unlike the passive examples, in these data the same argument appears as subject in both sentences. So these examples do not involve a voice alternation.

Now let us examine the data in greater detail. In each example, the (a) sentence contains a prepositional object (an oblique argument) which appears as a bare NP in the (b) sentence. Along with this change of category (PP to NP), there is a corresponding change of word order in examples (21–23): in the (a) sentences, the prepositional object follows an NP object; whereas in the (b) sentence it immediately follows the verb. These two changes together suggest that the prepositional argument of the (a) sentence has become the direct object of the (b) sentence. Since this alternation correlates perfectly with the distribution of the suffix -*ir*, we are led to suspect that it is the presence of the suffix which triggers this change.

Obviously we need to look for more evidence before we can accept this hypothesis; but first, let us introduce some useful terminology. An APPLICATIVE affix is one which increases the valence (transitivity) of the verb by changing an oblique argument into a direct object. The direct object which is created in this way is sometimes referred to as the APPLIED OBJECT. The hypothesis we wish to examine, then, is that the suffix –*ir* in these data is functioning as an applicative.

3.3.1.1   The semantic role of the applied object
Before addressing this hypothesis directly, notice that the applied objects bear different semantic roles in different examples: recipient in (21–22), instrument in (23–24). In the (a) sentences, the semantic roles of the oblique arguments are distinguished by the use of an appropriate preposition: *kwa* for recipient, *ndi* for instrument. But in the applicative form, there is no overt marking for the semantic role of the applied object.

It turns out that the suffix –*ir* can also be used with benefactive applied objects, as illustrated in (25). However, in the case of benefactives there is no corresponding prepositional form. Chichewa apparently lacks a preposition to mark beneficiaries; they can only be expressed using the applicative construction.

(25) a   Mtsikana a-na-phik-ir-a   ana   nsima.
          girl(1)   SUBJ(1)-PAST-cook-APPL-ASP children cornmeal
          'The girl cooked cornmeal for the children.'

     b   Atsikana a-na-vin-ir-a   mfumu.
          girls(2) SUBJ(2)-PAST-dance-APPL-ASP chief
          'The girls danced for the chief.'

     c   Kalulu a-na-gul-ir-a   mbidzi nsapato.
          hare(1) SUBJ(1)-PAST-buy-APPL-ASP zebras shoes
          'The hare bought shoes for the zebras.'

3.3.1.2   Evidence for objecthood
In order to test the hypothesis that the suffix –*ir* functions as an applicative marker, and to formulate a rule which accurately expresses this function, we need

to examine the grammatical relation of the applied object. It was suggested above that the change in category, from PP to NP, reflected a change in grammatical relation, from oblique argument to object. The word-order facts seem to support this idea. Notice that when there are two NP objects in a single clause, the applied object comes first, immediately following the verb. In most languages which have a double object construction, i.e., two unmarked NP objects in the same clause, the primary object appears adjacent to the verb while the secondary object is more distant from the verb. This is true in Chichewa as well.

Another kind of evidence which suggests that the applied object is the primary object is found in the agreement system. Chichewa has a complex system of eighteen gender classes, similar to that of most other Bantu languages. Modifiers are marked for the gender class of their head noun, and the verb agrees with the gender class of its subject.

While subject agreement is obligatory, object agreement is optional. With a basic transitive verb, the direct object must immediately follow the verb if the verb does not bear an object agreement marker. But if the verb is marked for object agreement, then the object does not need to be adjacent to the verb; in fact, it may occur anywhere outside the VP, and may even be optionally deleted.[13]

Baker (1988) states that there is only one basic (i.e., underived) ditransitive verb in Chichewa, namely the verb -pats- meaning 'to give.' This verb takes two NP objects, but only the primary object (the recipient) can trigger object agreement, as illustrated in (26).[14] Example (26c) is ungrammatical because the object agreement marker reflects the gender class of the secondary object (the theme).[15]

(26) a   Amayi   [a-na-pats-a   mwana mtsuko]$_{VP}$
             woman(1) SUBJ(1)-PAST-give-ASP child(1) waterpot (3)
             'The woman gave the child a waterpot.'

      b   Amayi   [a-na-*mu*-pats-a   mtsuko]$_{VP}$ (*mwana*).
             woman(1) SUBJ(1)-PAST-OBJ(1)-give-ASP waterpot(3) child(1)
             'The woman gave him (the child) a waterpot.'

      c   *Amayi   [a-na-*u*-pats-a   mwana]$_{VP}$ (*mtsuko*).
             woman(1) SUBJ(1)-PAST-OBJ(3)-give-ASP child(1)   waterpot(3)
             'The woman gave it (a waterpot) to the child.'

Note that the secondary object is part of the VP. When object agreement is marked, as in (26b), the primary object must occur outside the VP, and so must follow the secondary object. One way that the VP boundary can be demonstrated is by observing constraints on word-order variation. Bresnan and Mchombo (1987:745–747) show that the OBJ NP must immediately follow the verb when there is no object agreement marker. If and only if the verb is marked for object agreement, the SUBJ NP may occur between the verb and the OBJ NP, either at the beginning of the sentence (OBJ-SUBJ-V) or at the end of the sentence (V-SUBJ-OBJ).

In the applicative construction, the applied object can always trigger object
agreement, as illustrated in (27).[16] This fact shows that the applied object is the
primary object.

(27) a   Anyani   [a-ku-*u*-phwany-ir-a   dengu]$_{VP}$ (*mwala*).
            baboons(2) SUBJ(2)-PRES-OBJ(3)-break-APPL-ASP basket   stone(3)
            'The baboons are breaking the basket with it (the stone).'

     b   Amayi   [a-ku-*mu*-tumb-ir-a   mtsuko]$_{VP}$ (*mwana*).
            woman(1) SUBJ(1)-PRES-OBJ(1)-mold-APPL-ASP waterpot(3) child(1)
            'The woman is molding him (the child) a waterpot.'

Further evidence for objecthood comes from the passive construction. The
basic pattern of passivization in Chichewa is shown in (28). As this example
shows, the passive verb in Chichewa is marked with the suffix –*idw*, and the
agent is optionally expressed as the object of the instrumental preposition *ndi*.

(28) a   Mtsikana a-na-phik-a   nsima.
            girl(1) SUBJ(1)-PAST-cook-ASP cornmeal(9)
            'The girl cooked cornmeal.'

     b   Nsima   i-na-phik-idw-a   (ndi mtsikana).
            cornmeal(9) SUBJ(9)-PAST-cook-PASS-ASP (by girl)
            'The cornmeal was cooked (by the girl).'

With the basic ditransitive verb -*pats*- 'give', only the primary object
(the recipient) can become the subject of the passive, as illustrated in (29).

(29) a   Ngombe zi-na-pats-a   mbuzi   nsima.
            cows(10) SUBJ(10)-PAST-give-ASP goats(10) cornmeal(9)
            'The cows gave the goats cornmeal.'

     b   mbuzi   zi-na-pats-idw-a   nsima   (ndi ngombe).
            goats(10) SUBJ(10)-PAST-give-PASS-ASP cornmeal(9) (by cows)
            'The goats were given cornmeal (by the cows).'

     c   *Nsima   i-na-pats-idw-a   mbuzi   (ndi ngombe).
            cornmeal(9) SUBJ(9)-PAST-give-PASS-ASP goats(10) (by cows)
            'The cornmeal was given the goats (by the cows).'

Now English sometimes allows the object of a preposition to appear as the
subject of a passive sentence, e.g., *This bed has obviously been slept in*. This
construction is sometimes called the PREPOSITIONAL PASSIVE (or PSEUDO-
PASSIVE), and is only grammatical when certain fairly complex semantic conditions are met. Chichewa has no prepositional passive, as demonstrated in (30b),
the passive version of (30a); this example is bad, with or without the preposition.
However, it is possible for a "prepositional object" to appear as the subject of a
passive sentence if the verb also carries the applicative suffix, as in (30c). But
notice that no preposition appears in this example.

(30) a   Msangalatsi a-ku-yend-a   ndi   ndodo.
          entertainer(1) SUBJ(1)-PRES-walk-ASP with stick(9)
          'The entertainer is walking with a stick.'

     b   *Ndodo i-ku-yend-edw-a   (ndi).
          stick(9) SUBJ(9)-PRES-walk-PASS-ASP with
          (for: 'The stick is being walked with.')

     c   Ndodo i-ku-yend-er-edw-a.
          stick(9) SUBJ(9)-PRES-walk-APPL-PASS-ASP
          'The stick is being walked with.'

It is easy to explain the grammaticality of (30c) once we recognize it as the
passive version of the applicative construction in (24b). The function of the applicative is to change an oblique argument (in this case, the instrument marked by
ndi) into a direct object. The function of the passive is to change a direct object
into a subject. So we can see (30c) as being derived by a two-step process: first
applicative; then passive. But the fact that the passive rule will change the applied
object in (24b) into the subject of (30c) provides strong evidence that the applied
object does in fact bear the grammatical relation OBJ.

In example (24b), the applied object is the only object in a clause. When the
applicative involves a double object construction, as in (21–23) and (25), it is the
applied object which becomes the subject of a passive (31a). The "underlying
object," i.e., the patient or theme argument, cannot be promoted to subject of the
passive, as illustrated in (31b). This fact gives strong support to the hypothesis
that the applied object is the primary object.[17]

(31) a   Kalulu a-na-gul-ir-a   mbidzi   nsapato.
          hare(1a) SUBJ(1)-PAST-buy-APPL-ASP zebras(10) shoes(10)
          'The hare bought shoes for the zebras.'

     b   Mbidzi   zi-na-gul-ir-idw-a   nsapato   (ndi kalulu).
          zebras(10) SUBJ(10)-PAST-buy-APPL-PASS-ASP shoes(10) (by hare)
          'The zebras were bought shoes (by the hare).'

     c   *Nsapato   zi-na-gul-ir-idw-a   mbidzi   (ndi kalulu).
          shoes(10) SUBJ(10)-PAST-buy-APPL-PASS-ASP zebras(10) (by hare)
          'Shoes were bought for the zebras (by the hare).'

3.3.1.3   The applicative rule

As we noted at the beginning of this section, the effect of the applicative affix
is in some ways similar to passivization: it preserves semantic roles but changes
grammatical relations. For this reason, we can use the same basic kind of rule to
represent the process of applicative formation that we used for the passive.

Consider for example the pair of sentences in (22), repeated below. The lexical
entries for the verbs in these two examples must include the argument structure
representations in (32). Comparing these two structures, we see that the recipient
is an oblique argument in (32a) but the primary object in (32b); the theme is the
(primary) object in (32a) but the secondary object in (32b).

(22) a   Ndi-na-tumiz-a   kalata kwa mfumu.
           1sg.SUBJ-PAST-send-ASP letter to   chief
           'I sent a letter to the chief.'

    b   Ndi-na-tumiz-ir-a   mfumu kalata.
           1sg.SUBJ-PAST-send-APPL-ASP chief   letter
           'I sent the chief a letter.'

(32) a   *tumiz*   < agent,   theme,   recipient   > **Prepositional form**
                     | | |
                   SUBJ OBJ   OBL$_{rec}$

    b   *tumiz-ir* < agent,   theme,   recipient   > **Applied object**
                   | | |
                 SUBJ OBJ$_2$ OBJ

What is needed then is a lexical rule to derive the structure in (32b) from that in (32a). Once again, the rule mentions only the changes to the lexical entry: the OBL of (32a) becomes OBJ in (32b); the OBJ of (32a) becomes OBJ$_2$ in (32b). Obviously the grammar must also specify the morphological process which is used to signal (or trigger) this change. There are many different ways in which this could be done, but for convenience we will simply include that information in the same rule (33). The "X" here stands for the phonological shape of the base form, which in this case is the verb root. (Recall that the changes of GR which are specified by this rule occur simultaneously, so the order in which they are listed does not matter.)

(33)   **Applicative rule:**

$$
\begin{bmatrix}
[X]_v & \rightarrow & [X\text{-}ir]_v \\
OBL & \rightarrow & OBJ \\
OBJ & \rightarrow & OBJ_2
\end{bmatrix}
$$

This rule is typical of applicative constructions in many languages, and it accounts very well for the recipient and benefactive applicatives in Chichewa. Chichewa instrumental applicatives follow the same basic pattern, as illustrated in the examples above; but they exhibit certain special features which this simple rule as it stands cannot account for. An adequate analysis of this problem is beyond the scope of the present book; see Alsina and Mchombo (1993) for details.

3.3.1.4   Interaction with passive

We suggested above that sentences like (30b) and (31a) are derived by a two-step process: first applicative; then passive. Let us look more closely at how this process would work. Remember that we are treating applicative and passive as lexical rules, which operate on the lexical entries of verbs to produce new verbs. In order to demonstrate the effect of each rule on the arguments of the verb, we will use complete sentences in our examples. This does not mean that the rules are changing one sentence into another. Rather, the changes to the verb itself are reflected in the kind of sentence it appears in.

Let us begin with a basic transitive clause involving a prepositional object such as (21a), repeated below as (34a). Adding the applicative suffix to the verb will trigger the changes discussed above (OBL becomes OBJ, OBJ becomes OBJ$_2$); the resulting form would be (21b), repeated below as (34b). As we have seen, the applied object can become the subject of a passive, as in (34c); but the secondary object (in this case the theme) cannot, as shown in (34d). In order to make the theme appear as subject we would need to apply the passive rule to the basic form in (34a); the resulting passive sentence is shown in (34e).[18]

(34) a   Mbidzi   zi-na-perek-a   msampha kwa nkhandwe.
         zebras(10) SUBJ(10)-PAST-hand-ASP trap(3)   to   fox(9)
         'The zebras handed the trap to the fox.'

     b   Mbidzi   zi-na-perek-er-a   nkhandwe msampha.
         zebras(10) SUBJ(10)-PAST-hand-APPL-ASP fox(9)   trap(3)
         'The zebras handed the fox the trap.'

     c   Nkhandwe i-na-perek-er-edw-a   msampha (ndi mbidzi).
         fox(9)   SUBJ(9)-PAST-hand-APPL-PASS-ASP trap(3)   by   zebras
         'The fox was handed a trap (by the zebras).'

     d   *Msampha u-na-perek-er-edw-a   nkhandwe (ndi mbidzi).
         trap(3)   SUBJ(3)-PAST-hand-APPL-PASS-ASP fox(9)   by   zebras
         'The trap was handed to the fox (by the zebras).'

     e   Msampha u-na-perek-edw-a   kwa nkhandwe (ndi mbidzi).
         trap(3)   SUBJ(3)-PAST-hand-PASS-ASP to   fox(9)   by   zebras
         'The trap was handed to the fox (by the zebras).'

Now let us abstract from this data the changes to the lexical entry of the verb. The argument structure and subcategorization of the verb root *perek* are given in (35a). Adding the suffix *–er* changes the recipient to primary object and the theme to secondary object, as in (35b). Let us assume that Chichewa has a passive rule much like that proposed in (15) above. Applying this rule to (35b) would produce the structure shown in (35c).

(35)   **Correct derivation:**

     a   *perek*   <   agt,   thm,   rec   > (=34a) **Basic form**
                              | | |
                            SUBJ   OBJ   OBL$_{rec}$

     b   *perek-er*   <   agt,   thm,   rec   > (=34b) **Applicative**
                              | | |
                            SUBJ   OBJ$_2$ OBJ

     c   *perek-er-edw* <   agt,   thm,   rec   > (=34c) **Passive**
                              | | |
                          (OBL$_{agt}$) OBJ$_2$ SUBJ

Notice that the order of application of these rules is important. What would happen if we applied the rules in the opposite order, i.e., passive before applicative? This process is illustrated in (36). Adding the passive suffix to the basic form of the verb produces the structure in (36b), which corresponds to sentence (34e). Since this sentence still contains an oblique recipient argument, we might expect that the applicative rule could be used to promote this oblique argument to OBJ, as in (36c).[19] But this structure cannot be allowed by the grammar, because it corresponds to an ungrammatical sentence (34d).

(36)   **Incorrect order (Passive before Applicative):**

a   *perek*   <   agt,   thm,   rec   >   (=34a) **Basic form**

                          | | |

                     SUBJ   OBJ OBL$_{rec}$

b   *perek-edw*   <   agt,   thm,   rec   >   (=34e) **Passive**

                          | | |

              (OBL$_{agt}$) SUBJ OBL$_{rec}$

c   **perek-edw-er* <   agt,   thm,   rec   >   (=34d) **Applicative**

                          | | |

              (OBL$_{agt}$) SUBJ OBJ

The derivation shown in (36) must be prohibited because it leads to ungrammatical results. That is, the grammar of Chichewa must ensure that the passive and applicative rules can only apply in a particular order: applicative can apply before the passive, but never after the passive.

Notice that the order of rules in the grammatical derivation (35) corresponds to the order of affixes in the verb: the applicative suffix must be added first, and only then the passive suffix. In other words, the applicative suffix attaches closer to the root than the passive suffix. This correlation between morphological structure and the order of application of derivational processes is no accident. It reflects a very widespread pattern across languages, which Baker (1985) has referred to as the "Mirror Principle." We might reformulate Baker's principle in the following way:

(37)   **Mirror Principle**
       The order of affixation (from the inside out) reflects the order of derivation.
       That is, if one derivational process must apply before some other
       derivational process, then the affix which marks the first process will not
       occur in a position farther from the root than the affix which marks the
       second.

This principle probably does not hold as an absolute universal, but it is a very strong tendency across languages. Notice that it relates specifically to derivational morphology; it makes no predictions about the relative position of inflectional affixes.

3.3.2   Kinyarwanda

Kinyarwanda, another Bantu language, has several different applicative suffixes. As in Chichewa, the suffix *-ir* ~ *-er* has a benefactive use (38), and this is the only way of expressing a benefactive. The same suffix can be used (as in 39b) when the applied object expresses the reason for doing something, or the "goal" of the action (Kimenyi, 1980), e.g., 'singing for money,' 'working for food,' etc. Example (39a) shows that the preposition *ku=* can also be used for this function.

(38)   Benefactive (Kimenyi, 1980:32)
            umkoobwa a-ra-som-**er**-a   umuhuungu igitabo.
            girl   she-PRES-read-BEN-ASP boy   book
            'The girl is reading a book for the boy.'

(39)   Reason/"Goal" (Kimenyi, 1980:87)
        a   Karooli y-a-fash-ije   abaantu **ku**=busa.
            Charles he-PAST-help-ASP people   **for**=nothing
            'Charles helped the people for nothing.'

        b   Karooli y-a-fash-**ir**-ije   ubusa   abaantu.
            Charles he-PAST-help-GOAL-ASP nothing people
            'Charles for nothing helped the people.'

Instruments may be marked with the preposition *n(a)=*, as in (40a), or with applicative suffix *-iish* ∼ *-eesh* (40b).

(40)   Instrument (Kimenyi, 1980:81; Givón, 1984:178)
        a   Umualimu a-ra-andika   ibaruwa **n**=ikaramu.
            teacher   he-ASP-write letter   **with**=pen
            'The teacher is writing the letter with a pen.'

        b   Umualimu a-ra-andik-**iish**-a   ikarumu ibaruwa.
            teacher   he-ASP-write-INSTR pen   letter
            'The teacher is using the pen to write the letter.'

Another use for the preposition *n(a)=* is to express manner, as in (41a), and also to mark secondary props which are associated in some way with the action, e.g., 'he danced with a hat on.' However, a different applicative suffix (*-an*) is used when these elements are promoted to OBJ, as in (41b).

(41)   Associative/Manner (Givón, 1984:178)
        a   Mariya y-a-tets-e   inkoko **n**=agahiinda.
            Mary   she-PAST-cook-ASP chicken **with**=sorrow
            'Mary cooked the chicken with regret.'

        b   Mariya y-a-tek-**an**-ye   agahiinda inkoko.
            Mary   she-PAST-cook-ASSOC-ASP sorrow   chicken
            'Mary regretfully cooked the chicken.'

Another use of the *-an* suffix is for animate participants who accompany the agent, as in (42b). The preposition used in the corresponding non-applicative clause (42a) is *n(i)=*.

(42)   Accompaniment (Givón, 1984:178)
   a   Mariya y-a-tets-e   inkoko **ni**=Yohani
         Mary   she-PAST-cook-ASP chicken **with**=John
         'Mary cooked the chicken with John.'

   b   Mariya y-a-tek-**an-**ye   Yohani inkoko.
         Mary   she-PAST-cook-ACCOMP-ASP John   chicken
         'Mary together with John cooked the chicken.'

The chart in (43) summarizes the prepositions and applicative suffixes which are used for these various semantic roles:

(43)   SEMANTIC ROLE   PREPOSITION   APPLICATIVE SUFFIX
          Beneficiary   –   *-ir ~ -er*
          Reason/"Goal"   *ku*=   *-ir ~ -er*
          Instrument   *n(a)*=   *-iish~ -eesh*
          Associative/Manner *n(a)*=   *-an*
          Accompaniment   *n(i)*=   *-an*

As with Chichewa, both passive and applicative may apply to the same verb. An example (from Kimenyi, 1980:81) is presented in (44).

(44) a   Umagabo a-ra-andika   ibaruwa n=iikaramu.   (BASIC FORM)
          man   he-ASP-write letter   with=pen
          'The man is writing a letter with the pen.'

   b   *ikarumu i-ra-andik-w-a   ibaruwa n=umagabo.   ("PSEUDO-PASSIVE")
          pen   it-ASP-write-PASS letter   by=man
          (*'The pen is being written a letter with by the man.')

   c   Umagabo a-ra-andik-iish-ya   ikarumu ibaruwa.   (APPLICATIVE)
          man   he-ASP-write-INSTR pen   letter
          'The man is using the pen to write a letter.'

   d   ikarumu i-ra-andik-iish-w-a   ibaruwa n=umagabo. (APPLICATIVE
          pen   it-ASP-write-INSTR-PASS letter   by=man   + PASSIVE)
          'The pen is being used by the man to write a letter.'

Exercise 3A: "Dative Shift" in English

The pairs of sentences in (A1)–(A4) illustrate two different subcategorization patterns which a number of agent-theme-recipient verbs allow. This pattern is often referred to as "Dative Shift," because it involves an alternation in the marking of the recipient (or "dative") argument. In this exercise you are asked to provide a partial analysis of this alternation.

Task 1: Formulate a lexical rule to account for the relationship between the following pairs of sentences.

(A1) a   King John gave a beautiful palace to his daughter.
    b   King John gave his daughter a beautiful palace.

(A2) a   Uncle George left $50,000 to his nephew.
    b   Uncle George left his nephew $50,000.

(A3) a   Grandfather told a story to the children before they went to bed.
    b   Grandfather told the children a story before they went to bed.

(A4) a   The socialist candidate sent a letter to every voter.
    b   The socialist candidate sent every voter a letter.

Task 2: The following data reflect standard American usage. How must the rule you proposed above interact with the passive rule to account for these examples? Illustrate this by giving sample derivations for (A5b–c).

(A5) a   A beautiful palace was given to the princess.
    b   The princess was given a beautiful palace.
    c   *A beautiful palace was given the princess.

(A6) a $50,000 was left to his nephew.
    b   His nephew was left $50,000.
    c   *$50,000 was left his nephew.

(A7) a   A story was told to the children before they went to bed.
    b   The children were told a story before they went to bed.
    c   *A story was told the children before they went to bed.

(A8) a   A letter was sent to every voter.
    b   Every voter was sent a letter.
    c   *A letter was sent every voter.

Task 3: Speakers of some British dialects find most of the (c) sentences in these examples (as well as the [b] sentences) acceptable. How could you use your analysis to account for this dialect difference?
(This is the end of the exercise.)

3.4   Further notes on the English dative alternation

(Note: this section assumes that the reader has already worked through Exercise 3A.)

3.4.1   "Benefactive shift" and the "Possessor Effect"

The "Dative Shift" rule also applies to many benefactive constructions, as illustrated in the following examples:

(45) a   John baked a cake for his daughter.
    b   John baked his daughter a cake.

(46) a   Ali bought a bicycle for his son.
    b   Ali bought his son a bicycle.

(47) a   Alice knitted a sweater for Uncle George.
    b   Alice knitted Uncle George a sweater.

However, in other quite similar cases it does not apply. How can we explain the failure of Dative Shift to apply in the following examples?

(48) a   Mary drove the car for her father.
     b   *Mary drove her father the car.

(49) a   Aladdin polished the lamp for his mother.
     b   *Aladdin polished his mother the lamp.

(50) a   John pays the rent for his mother.
     b   #John pays his mother the rent. (not the same meaning!)

(51) a   Jack sold the cow for his mother.
     b   #Jack sold his mother the cow. (not the same meaning!)

In comparing the cases where Dative Shift "works," examples (45)–(47), with those where it is impossible, examples (48)–(51), we can observe an interesting pattern. The double object construction (the [b] form) is only possible where the beneficiary argument, marked with *for* in the (a) sentences, can be interpreted as receiving or acquiring possession of the patient or theme.

Let us take (47) as an example. Sentence (47a) is actually ambiguous: *Alice knitted a sweater for Uncle George*. The most natural interpretation is that Uncle George becomes the owner of the sweater; perhaps Alice knits it for him as a birthday or Christmas present. Let us call this the "recipient reading." But another interpretation is also possible. Suppose that Uncle George has promised to knit a sweater for the church bazaar, but then is given extra work to do at his office. He finds that he is too busy to knit the sweater, so he calls Alice and she agrees to do it for him. The finished sweater goes not to Uncle George but to the church bazaar. Let us call this the "on-behalf-of reading." But sentence (47b) (*Alice knitted Uncle George a sweater*) is not ambiguous. It allows only the recipient reading; Uncle George must gain possession of the sweater.

The situation in examples (48)–(51) is quite different. Even though these sentences contain a benefactive *for*-phrase, the beneficiary argument cannot be interpreted as acquiring ownership or possession of the patient. In (49), Aladdin's mother may or may not own the lamp, but the act of polishing does not change that fact one way or the other. The verbs in these examples do not allow the "recipient reading"; only the "on-behalf-of reading" is possible. For this reason, the beneficiary argument can only be expressed as an oblique *for*-phrase, and never as a bare NP object.

The general pattern then seems to be that oblique beneficiaries (*for* phrases) are potentially ambiguous, but beneficiary objects must always be interpreted as being recipients or possessors. Where this interpretation is not available, the double object form is ungrammatical. If we assume that the double object construction is derived from the prepositional form by the Dative rule which you formulated in Exercise A, then we have identified a semantic constraint on the application of this rule: Dative Shift applies only to recipient-type arguments.

This constraint does not relate only to benefactive constructions, where the oblique PP is marked with *for*. Even with some *to*-phrases, Dative Shift fails to apply for the same reason. Note the contrast between the following examples:

(52) a   Karl Marx wrote a letter to his wife.
   b   Karl Marx wrote his wife a letter.

(53) a   Karl Marx dedicated the book to his wife.
   b   *Karl Marx dedicated his wife the book.

The difference between these examples can be explained on semantic grounds. When I write a letter to someone, that person normally becomes the possessor of the letter. But when I dedicate a book to someone, that person does not become the possessor of the book. I may give one or more copies of the book to the person, but that is a separate action; the act of dedicating a book does not involve a transfer of ownership or possession.

Pinker (1989) refers to this constraint on the Dative rule in English as the "Possessor Effect." He states (p. 48) that the rule of Dative Shift can only apply to verbs which are "capable of denoting prospective possession of the referent of the second object by the referent of the first object." In other words, the double object construction implies that the primary object (the recipient) gains possession of the theme or patient. Where this interpretation is impossible, the Dative rule cannot apply. Pinker illustrates the Possessor Effect with the following example, which involves a contrast between the homophonous words *border* and *boarder*.

(54) a   John sent a package to the boarder/border.
   b   John sent the boarder/*border a package.

A *boarder* is a normally a person (e.g., someone who rents a room in someone else's house). Since people can easily be imagined as recipients, the verb *send* in this case can be interpreted as involving transfer of possession, and the double object construction is grammatical. But a *border* is an inanimate location. It cannot be said to possess or own anything. Therefore in this case the verb *send* can only be interpreted as involving a change of location, and the double object construction is impossible.

3.4.2   Lexical exceptions

We noted above that lexical rules typically have lexically specified exceptions. This is true of the Dative rule as well. In addition to the systematic exceptions illustrated in the preceding section, Dative Shift also fails to apply with certain verbs which do take a true recipient argument, verbs which we would expect (on semantic grounds) the rule to apply to. Some examples are given below:

(55) a   J. Paul Getty donated a famous painting to the museum.

    b   *J. Paul Getty donated the museum a famous painting.

(56) a   Uncle George contributed $50,000 to the building fund.

    b   *Uncle George contributed the building fund $50,000.

Even though the verbs *donate* and *contribute* are semantically very similar to *give*, they unexpectedly fail to alternate; they allow only the prepositional marking of the recipient. Thus it appears that they must simply be marked (lexically) as exceptions to the Dative rule; that is, the predicted output form is not listed in the lexicon.[20]

There have been various attempts to "explain" these exceptions on the basis of etymology, phonological shape, etc. There is a general tendency for Dative Shift to apply to native Germanic verbs (*give, send, throw, lend*, etc.) but not to Latin-derived verbs (*donate, contribute, dedicate, describe*, etc.). Latinate words which have assimilated to the "native" phonological pattern (e.g., those with word-initial stress, or beginning with an unstressed schwa) are more likely to undergo this rule (e.g., *promise, offer, assign, allow*, etc.). But none of these rules will allow us to make the correct prediction in every case. In general, we simply have to recognize that certain verbs are marked in the lexicon as exceptions to the Dative rule. Lexical exceptions of this kind are a normal feature of lexical rules.

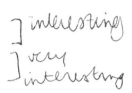
interesting
very interesting

Exercise 3B: Indonesian verbal affixes

Based on the following data, identify the function of the Indonesian verbal affixes *di-*, *-kan*, and *-i*, and write lexical rules for each affix. (Do not worry about the verbal prefixes *meN-* and *ber-*.) Do these rules need to be ordered? If so, state the correct ordering and give sample derivations contrasting the correct and incorrect orders. **Hint**: the two suffixes never co-occur. (**Note**: the agentive preposition *oleh* is optional when the agent phrase immediately follows the verb.)[21]

B1   Guru   kami duduk di ruang Pak rektor.
        teacher our   sit   in room Mr. rector
        'Our teacher is sitting in the rector's office.'

B2   Guru   kami menduduki ruang Pak rektor.
        teacher our   sit   room Mr. rector
        'Our teacher is occupying the rector's office.'

B3   Ruang Pak rektor diduduki oleh guru   kami.
        room Mr. rector sit   by   teacher our
        'The rector's office is occupied by our teacher.'

B4   Air   akan meresap ke-dalam tanah.
        water FUT seep   into   ground.
        'Water will seep into the ground.'
        (i.e., 'Water will be absorbed by the ground.')

B5   Air   meresapi tanah.
      water seep   ground
      'Water seeps into the ground.'

B6   Tanah   diresapi air.
      ground seep   water
      'The ground is seeped into by water.'
      (i.e., 'The ground is absorbing water.')

B7   *Tanah   diresap air.
      ground seep   water

B8   Dia sering menghindar dari teman-teman-nya.
      he often stay_away from friends-his
      'He often stays away from his friends.'

B9   Dia sering menghindari teman-teman-nya.
      He often stay_away   friends-his
      'He often avoids his friends.'

B10   Pesawat itu   sedang mendekat.
      plane   that PROG near
      'The plane is approaching.'

B11   Pesawat itu   sedang mendekati kota.
      airplane that PROG near   city
      'The plane is approaching the city.'

B12   Ayah membeli sepeda baru untuk adik.
      father buy   bicycle new for   yg_sib
      'Father bought a new bicycle for younger sibling.'

B13   Ayah membelikan adik   sepeda baru.
      father buy   yg_sib bicycle new
      'Father bought younger sibling a new bicycle.'

B14   Adik   dibelikan sepeda baru oleh Ayah.
      yg_sib buy   bicycle new by   father
      'Younger sibling was bought a new bicycle by Father.'

B15   Sepeda baru dibeli oleh Ayah untuk adik.
      bicycle new buy   by   father for   yg_sib
      'A new bicycle was bought by Father for younger sibling.'

B16   *Sepeda baru dibelikan adik   oleh Ayah.
      bicycle new buy   yg_sib by   Father

B17   Dia sedang membuat baju untuk adik.
      She PROG   make   shirt for   yg_sib
      'She is making a shirt for my younger sibling.'

B18   Baju sedang dibuat untuk adik.
      shirt PROG make   for   yg_sib
      'The shirt is being made for my younger sibling.'

B19   Dia sedang membuatkan adik   baju.
       She PROG make   yg_sib shirt
       'She is making my younger sibling a shirt.'

B20   Adik   sedang dibuatkan baju.
       yg_sib PROG   make   shirt
       'Younger sibling is being made a shirt.'

B21   *Baju sedang dibuatkan adik.
       shirt PROG   make   yg_sib
       (cannot mean 'A shirt is being made for younger sibling.')

B22   *Adik   sedang dibuat baju.
       yg_sib PROG   make   shirt
       (could only mean 'Younger sibling is being made by the shirt.')

B23   Ima memasak sate   untuk kami.
       Ima cook   satay for   us
       'Ima cooked satay for us.'

B24   Ima memasakkan kami sate.
       Ima cook   us   satay
       'Ima cooked satay for us.'

B25   Sate   dimasak untuk kami (oleh Ima).
       satay cook   for   us   by   Ima
       'Satay was cooked for us by Ima.'

B26   *Sate   dimasakkan kami.
       satay cook   us
       (cannot mean 'Satay was cooked for us.')

B27   Kami dimasakkan sate   oleh Ima.
       we   cook   satay by   Ima
       'We were cooked satay by Ima.'

B28   #Kami dimasak sate.
       we   cook   satay
       'We were cooked by the satay.'

B29   Anak-anak suka   melompat di halaman sekolah.
       children   enjoy jump   at yard   school
       'Children enjoy jumping in the school yard.'

B30   Anak-anak melompati pagar.
       children   jump   fence
       'Children jumped over the fence.'

B31   Pagar dilompati (oleh) anak-anak.
       fence jump   (by)   children
       'The fence was jumped by the children.'

3.5   Appendix: Evidence for a lexical analysis of passives

This appendix discusses in slightly greater detail some of the motivation for adopting a lexical approach to the passive construction. The first section expands on our earlier observation that passive sentences seem to be quite "normal" syntactically: they do not encode marked pragmatic functions (topic or focus); and they participate in a full range of syntactic processes. The second section considers morphological evidence, specifically the relationship of passivization to certain derivational processes which are generally agreed to apply within the lexicon.

3.5.1   Passivization vs. topicalization

It will be helpful, following the discussion in Keenan (1985a), to compare the English passive with the "marked topic" constructions illustrated in (57). (We will discuss these sentence types in greater detail in chapter 6.)

(57)	a	My friend John was bitten by a snake.	**(Passive)**
	b	My friend John, a snake bit him.	**(Left-Dislocation)**
	c	John we managed to rescue; his dog we never found.	**(Topicalization)**
	d	As for John, a python swallowed his dog.	**(External topic)**

Superficially, both the passive and the various marked topic sentence patterns seem to be used as a way of "foregrounding," or giving prominence to, the patient. But there are a number of important differences as well. For example, the marked topic sentences in (57b–d) contain normal (active) verb forms, whereas the passive sentence in (57a) requires a special form of the verb, together with a special auxiliary element.

Second, as noted in section 3.2 above, the passive sentence exhibits normal, basic phrase structure and word-order patterns. It could be generated by the same phrase structure rules which are needed independently to generate active sentences, e.g., those in (12) above. In contrast, the marked topic sentences in (57b–d) have structures which could not be generated by the basic PS rules in (12).

Third, a passive sentence can be topicalized. Normally it is impossible for an English sentence to contain more than one marked topic element, as illustrated in (58c–d). But in a passive sentence it is often possible for some element other than the subject to be topicalized, as in (59b–d). This indicates that the passive subject does not bear a marked pragmatic function. Rather, the patient as passive subject is more prominent than the patient as active object primarily because the subject relation itself has greater natural prominence than the direct object.

(58)	a	I saw the President in Chicago a few days ago.
	b	As for the President, I saw him in Chicago a few days ago.
	c	*As for the President, in Chicago I saw him a few days ago.
	d	*In Chicago as for the President, I saw him a few days ago.

(59) a   The President was invited to a Polish wedding in Chicago.
  b   In Chicago the President was invited to a Polish wedding.
  c   As for Chicago, the President was invited to a Polish wedding there.
  d   As for Polish weddings, the President was invited to one in Chicago.

Thus passives seem to be more neutral, or basic, in terms of both phrase structure and pragmatic force than the marked topic sentences in (57b–d). Passives are more "basic" in another sense as well: a number of syntactic processes, such as Yes–No question formation, relative clause formation, and nominalization (or gerund formation) can apply just as easily to passive clauses as to active clauses (60). But these processes cannot apply at all (or only apply in very unusual contexts) with pragmatically marked sentence types, as illustrated in (61).

(60) a   The President was attacked in the Rose Garden.
  b   Was the President attacked in the Rose Garden?
  c   the garden in which the President was attacked
  d   The nation was shocked at the President's being attacked in the Rose Garden.

(61) a   As for the President, a terrorist attacked him in the Rose Garden.
  b   *Did a terrorist as for the President, attack him in the Rose Garden?
  c   *the garden in which as for the President a terrorist attacked him
  d   *The nation was shocked at as for the President, a terrorist attacking him in the Rose Garden.

These considerations lead us to the conclusion that a passive is not a special type of sentence, in the way a Yes–No question or marked topic construction is. Passive sentences seem quite "normal" in terms of their syntactic structure and behavior. Rather, what is special about a typical passive construction is the kind of verb which it contains.

3.5.2   **Morphological evidence**

Bresnan (1982a) presents a variety of evidence which supports treating passivization as a lexical rule. One such piece of evidence, based on work by Wasow (1977) and a number of other writers, involves the derivation of adjectives from passive participles. We will briefly summarize the argument in this section. We begin with a discussion of the differences between verbal participles and adjectives derived from participles, which you examined in the exercise at the end of chapter 2.

In chapter 2 we saw that gerunds appear to have grammatical properties of both nouns and verbs. But, on closer inspection of the data, we found that each individual instance of the *V-ing* form can be classified as either a nominalization or a true (verbal) gerund. No examples showed features of both categories at the same time. In the same way, participles in English appear to be ambiguous between the categories Adjective and Verb. But, once again, a careful examination of the data leads to the conclusion that there are two different kinds of participles:

one adjectival and the other verbal. The two have the same phonological shape, but can be distinguished on the basis of grammatical properties.

For example, adjectives but not verbs can function as modifiers within a noun phrase. Thus the passive participles in (62) must be adjectives, not verbs. In the same way, as illustrated in (63a), adjectives but not verbs can function as predicate complements of verbs like *be, seem, become*, etc. Thus the passive participles in (63b–d) must be adjectives, not verbs.

(62) a   John found a *broken* guitar in the attic.
    b   The king's *cherished* daughter kept her letters in a *painted* box.

(63) a   John seems nice/hungry/Italian/*sing/*eat/*fell.
    b   The winner looked *elated*.
    c   John seems *annoyed* at his mother.
    d   The president did not sound *convinced*.

Adjectives but not verbs can be modified by adverbs of degree (*too, very, quite, rather*, etc.) or the comparative and superlative markers *more* and *most*, as illustrated in (64). Thus the passive participles in (65) must be adjectives, not verbs.

(64) a   That is a very nice picture.
    b   Susan gave the most beautiful performance I have ever heard of.
    c   John really/*very works when he is facing a deadline.
    d   *Arthur most ate of anyone at the dinner.

(65) a   Mary looks very *bored*.
    b   Bill seems rather *depressed* about the stock market.
    c   John is the most *respected* player on the team.

Turning now to distinctive properties of verbs, certain verbs can take NP and AdjP predicate complements, as in (66a–d). Some adjectives can take PP complements, e.g., *proud of her son, hungry for success, lucky at cards, crazy about you*; but adjectives never take NP or AdjP complements, as illustrated in (66e–f). This implies that the passive participles in (67) must be verbs, not adjectives.

(66) a   Susan seems/becomes more lovely every year.
    b   Alice became a member of the board.
    c   Boris considers Arthur untrustworthy.
    d   The people elected Nixon president in 1968.
    e   *Arthur is obvious untrustworthy.
    f   *Nixon was possible president in 1968.

(67) a   Arthur is *considered* untrustworthy.
    b   Nixon was *elected* president in 1968.
    c   Mary was *called* a reactionary.

So once again we find that the same form (or homophonous forms) may be used in two different ways, either as an adjective (68a) or as a verb (68b); but we do not find properties of both adjectives and verbs in a single example (68c).

Tests like those mentioned above provide a way to distinguish between the verbal and adjectival uses of the passive participle. These two constructions are often referred to as VERBAL PASSIVES and ADJECTIVAL PASSIVES, respectively.

(68) a   He gave a very *considered* statement.
   b   Nixon's statement was *considered* profound.
   c   *Nixon's statement was very *considered* profound.

Clearly the adjectival forms in the examples above must be produced by a derivational process which derives adjectives from verbs. There is very strong evidence indicating that this rule of ADJECTIVE FORMATION must apply in the lexicon, because the adjectival forms created by this rule can themselves undergo other morphological processes which are generally agreed to be lexical. Since all lexical operations are assumed to apply before any syntactic operation applies, any process which "feeds" a lexical rule must itself be lexical.

To consider a specific example, the prefix *un-* has two distinct uses in English. It can be added to verbs to create a new verb which means 'to reverse the action named by the base verb,' e.g., *untie, unzip, unwrap, unlearn*. But it can also be added to adjectives to create a new adjective with the meaning 'not X' (where 'X' is the meaning of the basic adjective); examples: *unlikely, unhappy, unsafe, unable, unaware, unclean, unhelpful, unthinkable*, etc.

This prefix can be attached to a very large number of passive participles, e.g., *unknown, unloved, unspoken, untouched, unexpected, unborn*. Such forms are sometimes ambiguous, since the prefix *un-* can attach both to verbs and to adjectives. For example, the *un*-Adj rule can apply to the adjectival passive *wrapped* in (69a) to produce the negated adjective *unwrapped* in (69b). On the other hand, the *un*-V rule can apply to the transitive verb *wrap*, as in (69c). This negated verb can then be passivized to produce the verbal passive *unwrapped* in (69d). This verbal passive can then undergo the rule of Adjective Formation to become an adjectival passive, creating one of the readings for (69e), namely the reading which implies that presents were once wrapped and have now been unwrapped. The other reading for (69e) is similar to (69b), namely that the presents were never wrapped in the first place, and involves the same derivation.

(69) a   John left the *wrapped* presents under the tree.
   b   When Mary returned home, she found the presents still *unwrapped*.
   c   The children could not wait to *unwrap* the presents.
   d   The presents were *unwrapped* by excited children.
   e   The children carried the *unwrapped* presents into the living room.

The derivations for these examples are sketched out in (70):

(70) a   Base form   [wrap]$_V$
         Adj. Formation   [wrapped]$_{Adj}$ (a)
         un-Adj rule   [un-wrapped]$_{Adj}$ (b)

b	Base form	[wrap]$_v$	
	un-Verb rule	[un-wrap]$_v$	(c)
	Verbal passive	[unwrapped]$_v$	(d)
	Adj. Formation	[unwrapped]$_{Adj}$	(e)

However, with some verbs the prefix *un-* can appear only on adjectival passive forms; there is no corresponding active verb with *un-*. Some examples are given in (71–72).

(71) a   Our products are *untouched* by human hands.
   b   The island was *uninhabited* by humans.
   c   All his claims have been *unsupported* by any credible evidence.
   d   Her whereabouts are still *unknown*.
   e   The story remains *untold*.

(72) a   *Human hands *untouch* our products.
   b   *Humans *uninhabit* the island.
   c   *The evidence has *unsupported* all his claims.
   d   *They still *unknow* her whereabouts.
   e   *Bill *untold* the story.

This contrast shows that the participial forms in (71) must be derived by adding *un-* to adjectival passives, since the *un*-V rule cannot apply to the corresponding verbal forms (**untouch*, **unknow*, **untell*, etc.). These participial forms with *un-* can only be used as adjectives, and never as verbs, as illustrated in (73–74).

(73) a   John is completely unknown.
   b   John is (*completely) known to be a communist.
   c   *John is unknown to be a communist.

(74) a   Ann bought an unpainted bookshelf.
   b   The bookshelf was painted red by her uncle.
   c   *Ann bought an unpainted red bookshelf.[22]

Now the word formation rule which adds the prefix *un-* to adjectives is generally agreed to be a lexical rule. Since it can apply to adjectival passives, the rule of adjectival passive formation must also be a lexical rule because, under normal assumptions, no non-lexical (i.e., purely syntactic) process can affect the input to a lexical rule. In other words, all lexical rules must apply before any non-lexical (syntactic) rule.

Bresnan (1982a) shows that adjectival passives can function as the base form for various other lexical processes as well, including compounding (e.g., a *hand-carved* figure, *stone-ground* flour, a *store-bought* dress, *sun-dried* raisins, a *flea-bitten* dog, a *moth-eaten* coat, etc.). Such examples provide further evidence that the rule which derives adjectival passives is a lexical process. But what about verbal passives?

There are several reasons to believe that adjectival passives must be derived from verbal passives. First, the two forms always have the same phonological shape, in spite of the very irregular allomorphy of the past participle with many verb roots. This identity of allomorphy is an indication that the same morphological process is involved.

Second, recall that the past participle of a transitive verb has both active and passive uses, as illustrated in (75a–b). But when it is used as an adjective, the past participle can only be interpreted in the passive sense, as illustrated in (75c–d). This strongly suggests that the rule of adjective formation can apply to passive verbs but not to active transitive verbs. Thus adjectival passives must be derived from verbal passives.

(75) a   The President has *vetoed* that legislation.
     b   That legislation was *vetoed* by the President.
     c   the *vetoed* legislation
     d   #the *vetoed* President

Third, transitive verbs which exceptionally fail to undergo the verbal passive rule also fail to form adjectival passives. Some examples of such verbs were listed in (16–20), which are repeated below.

(16) a   John resembles Mr. Nixon.
     b   *Mr. Nixon is resembled by John.

(17) a   Our committee lacks the necessary resources.
     b   *The necessary resources are lacked by our committee.

(18) a   Anyone can afford a Proton Saga.
     b   *?A Proton Saga can be afforded by anyone.
     c   *A new car can't be afforded by me.

(19) a   This box contains 24 pencils.
     b   24 pencils are contained *by/in this box.

(20) a   Your humor eludes me.
     b   *I am eluded by your humor.

None of these roots allows the formation of adjectival passives, as illustrated in example (76).

(76) a   ??a widely-resembled face
     b   *the lacked resources
     c   an easily *afforded (cf. affordable) car
     d   *the contained pencils
     e   *the humor-eluded audience

The verb *contain* is an interesting example, since it has a secondary sense meaning 'control' or 'restrain' which does allow passivization. For this secondary sense of the verb, adjectival passive formation seems much more acceptable than it does for the primary sense illustrated in (19).

(77) a   Mary struggled to contain her anger.
     b   Mary's anger could not be contained any longer.
     c   her barely-contained anger
     d   his uncontained enthusiasm

So transitive verbs which are lexically marked as exceptions to the verbal passive rule must also be exceptions to the rule of adjectival passive formation. If adjectival passives are derived from verbal passives, as we are suggesting, this fact is automatically explained. The shared pattern of allomorphy and the obligatory passive interpretation of participial adjectives is also accounted for. If, on the other hand, we were to assume that the two types of passives were formed by two distinct and independent processes, a great deal of redundancy would have to be built into the grammar.

In this section we have presented arguments for two claims: first, that adjectival passives are formed by a lexical rule; and second, that adjectival passives are derived from verbal passives. These two conclusions together imply that the verbal passive rule must also be a lexical process, since it "feeds" (i.e., creates the input to) a lexical rule.

Notes

1. The clitic =*ni* can also be used to mark dative case. This gloss follows the analysis adopted by Tsujimura.
2. Much of the discussion in this section is based on the survey in Keenan (1985a:243–270).
3. Comrie (1977) cites Spanish and Polish as examples of languages in which the agent phrase may be expressed with personal passives, but not with impersonal passives.
4. From Keenan (1985a).
5. Examples 8–10 are from Tsujimura (1996), who also refers to this construction as the INDIRECT PASSIVE. However, this term is likely to be confusing, since it is used by other writers to refer to a passive which promotes a recipient, or "indirect object," to subject.
6. Some linguists assume that passive morphology actually does alter the argument structure of the verb, by removing the agent (or most agent-like) semantic role entirely. Under this analysis, the agent is no longer an argument of the passive verb, and can only be expressed as a prepositional adjunct. We have adopted a different analysis, assuming that the passive agent remains as an oblique argument in the verb's argument structure. But it is possible that languages actually differ on this point, with some expressing the passive agent as an oblique argument, others as an adjunct.
7. We are ignoring for the moment the issue of where the auxiliary verb should attach to the tree.
8. For one specific example, see the discussions of LEXICAL MAPPING THEORY in Bresnan and Kanerva (1989); Alsina and Mchombo (1993). For examples of other approaches see Dik (1978); Foley and Van Valin (1984); and Jackendoff (1990).
9. Speakers do in fact produce words like ?*freeness* under special circumstances, e.g., to express some special shade of meaning not captured by *freedom*.
10. Several of these examples are adapted from Stageberg (1971:183).
11. The variant forms are purely morphophonemic, resulting from a rule of vowel harmony. This alternation can be ignored for present purposes.
12. Unless otherwise noted, all examples in this section are from Baker (1988). The numbers in the glosses of these examples refer to Bantu noun classes. Tone is contrastive but not marked in these data.

13. Bresnan and Mchombo (1987) show that the "object agreement marker" in Chichewa is actually an incorporated pronoun. See chapter 7, section 7.3.1 for more examples of these incorporated pronouns.
14. Data provided by Sam Mchombo (p.c.).
15. The sentence could be grammatical, though semantically bizarre, with the interpretation "The woman gave him (the child) to the waterpot."
16. Example (27a) is from Alsina and Mchombo (1993).
17. We should note that (31c) also provides additional support for our earlier claim that oblique arguments cannot passivize in Chichewa.
18. Examples (34c, d, e) provided by Sam Mchombo (p.c.).
19. Example (24) shows that the applicative rule can apply to at least some intransitive verbs, so in principle it could apply to passive verbs as well.
20. A few verbs, e.g., *envy* and *cost*, occur only with the double object pattern. These verbs would be lexically specified for the double object pattern, corresponding to the "output" of the Dative rule; but there is no corresponding "input" form in the lexicon.
21. Thanks to Lalani Wood for helping to design this problem.
22. (74c) is ungrammatical with the intended reading in which *red* is a complement of *unpainted*. It is grammatical but paradoxical with the reading in which *unpainted* and *red* are both modifiers of *bookshelf*.

4   Reflexives

Pronouns are nominal elements whose reference is determined by the context of use. There are two different ways in which this may be true. First, pronouns may refer to something in the immediate speech situation, i.e., the time and place where the speaker is talking to the hearer. Words which function in this way, such as *here* and *now*, are called DEICTIC elements. First and second person pronouns are always used in this way: *I* refers to the speaker, *you* to the hearer.

The other way in which the semantic interpretation of pronouns may depend on the context of use is called ANAPHORA (literally 'referring back'). ANAPHORIC expressions are words whose interpretation depends on the interpretation of some other expression (typically a noun phrase) in the same discourse. This other element is called the ANTECEDENT. So an anaphoric pronoun is interpreted as refering to the same person, place, or thing as its antecedent. Third person pronouns (*he, she*, etc.) may be used either as deictics or as anaphors.

REFLEXIVE PRONOUNS (*himself, myself, themselves*, etc.) are a special type of pronoun. What makes them special is that their antecedents must satisfy certain grammatical restrictions which do not apply to "regular" pronouns (*he, she, him, her*, etc.). These restrictions will be the major focus of this chapter. We will explore the rules that determine which NPs are eligible to serve as the antecedent of a reflexive pronoun, contrasting them with the rules which govern the behavior of regular pronouns. We will look first at English, then consider reflexives in some other languages which have quite different sets of restrictions.

In describing the grammatical relationship between a pronoun and its antecedent, there are three major issues to be considered: agreement, domain (the degree of "distance" which is permitted between pronoun and antecedent), and relative prominence (to be defined below).

A huge amount of research has been concentrated on the relationship between pronouns and their antecedents in English, and many thousands of pages have been written on this topic. We cannot attempt a detailed study of the subject here. The brief introduction presented in this chapter has two main purposes. First, we hope to provide a basis for comparison of English with other languages, and to highlight the critical issues which must be addressed in describing the behavior of reflexive pronouns in any given language. Second, a clear understanding of the properties of reflexives will help us to analyze other syntactic constructions in later chapters.

4.1   Antecedents of reflexive pronouns

Before we begin, it is important to recall the difference between reflexive and emphatic pronouns. Emphatic pronouns in English, as in a number
of other languages, have the same form as reflexive pronouns; but their function
and distribution are quite different. A reflexive pronoun, like those in (1), bears a
semantic role and grammatical relation which is distinct from the semantic role
and grammatical relation of its antecedent. But emphatic pronouns, like those in
(2), do not have this kind of independent status within the clause. Rather, they
stand in APPOSITION to their antecedents, and therefore share the same semantic
role and grammatical relation.

Emphatic never same form as reflexive pronouns

(1) a   John has bought *himself* a new Mercedes.
   b   I surprised *myself* by winning the dancing competition.
   c   Mary tried to control *herself*, but could not resist tickling the Governor.

(2) a   The Governor *himself* will appoint the new police chief.
   b   I gave that money to the Governor *myself*.
   c   I have just had dinner with the Governor *himself*.

There are also many languages in which emphatic pronouns are distinct from
reflexives, e.g., German *sich* (reflexive) vs. *selbst* (emphatic). In this chapter we
will have nothing further to say about emphatic pronouns, focusing instead on
the properties of reflexive pronouns.

4.1.1   Agreement

Pronominal forms always reflect some of the inherent semantic features of their antecedent. In English, all pronouns must agree with their antecedents in person, number, and gender. Thus the masculine subject in (3a)
requires a masculine reflexive, the feminine subject in (3b) requires a feminine
reflexive, and the third person plural subject in (3c) requires a third person plural reflexive. This obligatory pattern of agreement is quite straightforward, but
as we will see it provides a very powerful tool for investigating various other
grammatical phenomena.

(3) a   My brother admires himself/*herself.
   b   My sister admires *himself/herself.
   c   My parents admire *himself/*herself/themselves.

Now in all of the sentences in (1) and (3) the antecedent of the reflexive happens
to be the subject of the sentence. This observation might suggest that there is a
general requirement in English to the effect that antecedents of reflexives must
always be subjects. However, it is easy to find examples which disprove this
hypothesis. As illustrated in (4), objects and certain other arguments of the clause
may also function as antecedents. We will return to this issue in section 4.3.

(4) a   John described Mary to himself/herself.

    b   John wrote Mary a poem about himself/herself.

    c   John showed Mary pictures of himself/herself playing tennis.

4.1.2   Domain

The examples in (3) not only show that reflexives must agree with their antecedents, they illustrate something else as well: reflexive pronouns must find an eligible antecedent within their immediate sentence. The form *herself* would be ungrammatical in (3a) because that sentence does not contain a possible antecedent (i.e., a feminine singular NP). Even if a potential antecedent is available in the immediately preceding sentence, as in the example below, the form *herself* would still be ungrammatical:

(3a′)   We saw Mrs. Thatcher on television last night. *My brother admires herself greatly.

Such examples show that a reflexive pronoun may not be separated from its antecedent by a sentence boundary. In fact, even an internal clause boundary may not separate the two, as demonstrated by the examples in (5):

(5) a   *My uncle is not generous, but [I love himself anyway].

    b   Mary suspects that [John admires himself/*herself too much].

    c   Mary waited for [John to excuse himself/*herself].

    d   I told you that [Mary would blame *myself/*yourself/herself].

the smallest clause which contains one must contain the other

In other words, a reflexive and its antecedent must be elements of the same simple clause; the smallest clause which contains either one of them must also contain the other. For this reason, we say that the relationship between a reflexive and its antecedent in English is CLAUSE-BOUNDED.

4.2   Antecedents of regular pronouns

Non-reflexive pronouns must also agree with their antecedents in person, number, and gender. However, unlike reflexives, "regular" pronouns CANNOT take an antecedent within their same minimal clause. The examples in (6) and (7) show that the antecedent of a regular pronoun cannot be the subject or object of the same simple sentence. (The "#" sign is used here to indicate that a pronoun cannot refer to the same person as a preceding NP, as explained in the notes following each sentence.)

(6) a   My brother admires #him.   (*him* must refer to someone else)

    b   My sister admires #her.   (*her* must refer to someone else)

    c   My parents admire #them.   (*them* must refer to someone else)

(7) a   John described Mary to #him/#her.
         (pronoun cannot refer to John or Mary)
   b   John wrote Mary a poem about #him/#her.
         (pronoun cannot refer to John or Mary)

But, once again, clause boundaries turn out to be more significant than sentence boundaries. As the examples in (8) demonstrate, regular pronouns may take an antecedent within the same sentence provided it is not part of the same minimal clause. In other words, there must be a clause boundary between the pronoun and its antecedent.

(8) a   My uncle is not generous, but [I love him anyway].
         (*him* can refer to 'my uncle')
   b   Mary suspects that [John admires her/#him too much].
         (*her* can refer to Mary, but *him* cannot refer to John)
   c   Mary waited for [John to excuse #him/her].
         (*her* can refer to Mary, but *him* cannot refer to John)
   d   I told you that [Mary would blame me/you/#her].
         (*her* cannot refer to Mary)

When we compare these examples with the parallel reflexive examples in (3–5), we see that reflexive and non-reflexive pronouns appear to be in complementary distribution: if the reflexive form is grammatical, then the corresponding regular pronoun could not be used to refer to the same antecedent, and vice versa. If we were to examine a wider range of data, we would find certain contexts in which this pattern of complementary distribution breaks down. Nevertheless, there is a very strong tendency, not just in English but in all languages which have a contrast between reflexive and non-reflexive pronouns, for non-reflexive pronouns to be unacceptable in contexts where a reflexive pronoun could appear.

Let us summarize the principles which we have discussed so far concerning the possible antecedents of reflexive and non-reflexive pronouns in English. (These principles are sometimes referred to as BINDING principles, a label which derives from the Binding Theory of Chomsky [1981].) The principles as stated here should be viewed as a tentative working hypothesis, a first approximation to an adequate description of the facts. In the next section we will see that they need to be modified in order to account for a wider range of data.

(9)   **Reflexive binding:**
   a   Reflexive pronouns must agree with their antecedents in person, number, and gender.
   b   A reflexive pronoun must find an antecedent within its minimal clause.

(10)   **Pronoun binding:**
   a   Non-reflexive pronouns must agree with their antecedents in person, number, and gender.
   b   A non-reflexive pronoun may not take as its antecedent an NP which occurs within its minimal clause.

4.3   Prominence conditions

4.3.1   Argument vs. non-argument antecedents

In the preceding section we stated that a regular pronoun cannot take an antecedent within its minimal clause. This statement is too strong, as demonstrated by examples like the following:

(11) a   John's mother loves him.   (*him* could refer to John)

    b   John's mother described Mary to him.   (*him* could refer to John)

    c   John told Mary's parents the truth about her. (*her* could refer to Mary)

Once again, we find regular pronouns and reflexives in complementary distribution, since the corresponding reflexives would be ungrammatical in these contexts:

(12) a   *John's mother loves himself.

    c   *John's mother described Mary to himself.

    d   *John told Mary's parents the truth about herself.

How can we reconcile these examples with the generalizations we made in sections 4.1 and 4.2? Notice that all of the antecedents in examples (3–8) were either subjects or objects of their clauses. In contrast, the antecedents in examples (11–12) are possessor phrases, i.e., non-arguments. This observation suggests that, in addition to the position of the antecedent (inside or outside the minimal clause), the role or function of the antecedent (e.g., argument vs. non-argument) may also be significant.

Examples like those in (13) support this suggestion. In both of these sentences, an NP (*John* or *Lady Margaret*) functioning as a prepositional complement of another noun is eligible to be the antecedent of a regular pronoun within the same minimal clause, contrary to the principle stated in (10b). Moreover, these NPs are not possible antecedents of a reflexive within their clause, even though nothing in principle (9b) rules this out.

(13) a   The news reports about John horrified him/*himself.

    b   Vincent's portrait of Lady Margaret disappointed her/*herself.

Examples (11–13) demonstrate that a regular pronoun can in fact take an NP within its minimal clause as its antecedent, provided that the NP is not an argument of that clause; and that the antecedent of a reflexive MUST be an argument. We can account for examples (11–13), as well as all the previous examples, by adding these constraints to our tentative formulation of the Binding principles:

(14)   **Reflexive binding**:

    a   Reflexive pronouns must agree with their antecedents in person, number, and gender.

    b   A reflexive pronoun must find an antecedent within its minimal clause.

    c   The antecedent must be an argument of that clause.

(15)   **Pronoun binding**:
   a   Non-reflexive pronouns must agree with their antecedents in person, number, and gender.
   b   A non-reflexive pronoun cannot take as its antecedent an argument of its minimal clause.

One apparent exception to the generalization in (15b) involves possessive pronouns (*his, my, their*, etc.), as illustrated in (16). But English does not have any distinct reflexive form of the possessive pronouns. It appears that the same possessive forms can function either as reflexives or as regular pronouns.

(16) a   John loves his mother.   (*his* could refer to John)
    b   Mary gave her children their allowance. (*her* could refer to Mary)
                                           (*their* could refer to children)

In (14–15) we spoke of the "minimal clause" as the domain which is relevant for determining binding properties of an anaphoric element. But in the following examples the relevant domain is actually an NP:

(17) a   John resented [Mary's description of him/*himself]$_{NP}$.
    b   John appreciated [Mary's description of herself/#her]$_{NP}$.

Such examples often involve abstract nouns which function as semantic predicates and can take the same kind of semantic arguments as a verb. In order to account for these examples, we should restate the Binding principles so that they refer to "arguments of the same predicate" rather than "arguments of the minimal clause"; but we will not address these details here.

4.3.2   The Relational Hierarchy

The Binding principles as stated in (14–15) refer to a distinction between arguments vs. non-arguments; but they make no mention of specific grammatical relations, nor do they suggest any need to make a distinction between one argument and another. However, examples like (18) reveal an asymmetry between subjects and objects: a subject NP can be the antecedent of a reflexive object, as in (18a), but an object NP cannot be the antecedent of a reflexive subject, as in (18b).

(18) a   My brother admires himself.
    b   *Himself admires my brother.

Similar asymmetries are observed between objects vs. oblique arguments, as illustrated in (19); and between oblique arguments vs. non-arguments, as illustrated in (20). Thus we seem to have a ranking of grammatical relations in terms of their eligibility to function as antecedents of reflexives: SUBJ outranks OBJ, OBJ outranks OBL, OBL outranks non-arguments.

(19) a   John protected Mary from herself.
    b   *John protected herself from Mary.

(20) a   John concealed from Mary the truth about herself.
    b   *John concealed from herself the truth about Mary.

The pattern that seems to emerge from these and other similar examples is that
the antecedent must have a more "prominent" position in the clause than the
reflexive, where prominence is defined in terms of the ranking of grammatical
relations listed in the preceding paragraph. This ranking turns out to be relevant
to a number of other syntactic phenomena as well. It is sometimes referred to as
the RELATIONAL HIERARCHY:

(21)   **MOST PROMINENT**   **LEAST PROMINENT**   *re possessive*
        subject > object > oblique argument > non-argument

In English, this hierarchy of grammatical relations corresponds very closely
to normal word-order patterns. For this reason, it is often difficult to distinguish
between word-order constraints and restrictions based on grammatical relations.
So, rather than appealing to a ranking of grammatical relations, we might propose a
simpler hypothesis: a reflexive pronoun must not precede its antecedent. However,
examples like (22) show that this is not always true.[1]

(22) a   Himself my brother admires; the rest of us he only tolerates.
    b   To herself Mary assigned the most difficult task of all.
    c   The latest rumors about himself were vigorously denied by the President.

For English and a number of other languages, it might be possible to define
"prominence" in terms of phrase structure configuration; this is the approach
adopted by Chomsky (1981). But this approach does not work so well for "non-
configurational" languages. For this reason (among others) we choose to specify
prominence relations in terms of the relational hierarchy, even for languages like
English. The Binding conditions for reflexives can now be restated as follows:

(23)   **Reflexive Binding:**
    a   **Agreement**: Reflexive pronouns must agree with their antecedents in
        person, number, and gender.
    b   **Domain condition**: A reflexive pronoun must find an antecedent which is
        an argument of its minimal clause.
    c   **Prominence condition**: The antecedent must outrank the reflexive on the
        Relational Hierarchy.

The concept of "prominence" is also relevant to the behavior of regular pronouns. Word order is significant, too, as illustrated in (24). But, in addition to these
syntactic factors, the interpretation of regular pronouns is also affected by a number of other factors, including discourse and pragmatic effects. At this time there
is no general consensus among linguists regarding which specific facts should be
accounted for in purely syntactic terms, and which should be explained in terms
of semantics or pragmatics; and we will not pursue these issues any further in this
book.

(24) a   Mary returned all of John's old letters to him. (*him* could refer to John)

    b   Mary returned to #him all of John's old letters. (*him* cannot refer to John)

    c   Mary returned all of #his old letters to John. (*his* cannot refer to John)

    d   Mary returned to John all of his old letters. (*his* could refer to John)

Exercise 4A: Subjects of imperatives in English

Task 1: An imperative clause in English contains no subject NP. We might say either that such a clause simply lacks a subject, or that its subject is "invisible" in some sense (which would then have to be explained). Which hypothesis is supported by examples like the following? Why?

(A1) a   Behave yourself/*you!

    b   Tell me the truth about yourself/*you/*himself/him.

    c   Please don't trouble yourself/*you/*myself/me about that.

    d   Pour yourself/*you/*myself/me a cup of coffee.

Task 2: What is the rule which determines the identity of the subject in a Tag Question, illustrated in the examples in (A2)? With this rule in mind, what bearing do the examples in (A3) have on the hypothesis which you adopted in the previous task?

(A2) a   Your parents can speak French, can't they/*can't he?

    b   John gave you that picture, didn't he/*didn't you?

    c   You still won't tell me the truth about Mary, will you/*will I/*will she?

    d   John certainly admires your parents, doesn't he/*don't they?

(A3) a   Be quiet, won't you?

    b   Just leave that alone, will you?

    c   Greet Mary for me, will you/*will I/*will she?

4.4   Reflexives in other languages

4.4.1   Malayalam

In Malayalam (a Dravidian language from southern India), the reflexive pronoun *swa-* (genitive form *swaṇṭam*) differs from English reflexives in two important ways. First, the antecedent of this reflexive element must always be a grammatical subject. This fact is illustrated in (25–28) (all examples in this section are from Mohanan 1982, 1983a, p. c.).

At first glance we might expect (25) to be ambiguous, allowing either *Johnny* or *Mary* to be interpreted as the antecedent of the reflexive, because *swaṇṭam* is neutral between masculine and feminine gender. But, as the gloss reflects, only the SUBJ (*Johnny*) is eligible; the OBJ (*Mary*) cannot function as the antecedent.

(25)   jooṇi   meeřiye   swaṇṭam wiiṭṭil   wecca umma weccu.

          Johnny-NOM Mary-ACC self's   house-LOC at   kiss   put

          'Johnny kissed Mary at Johnny's/*Mary's house.'

Examples (26–27) show that it is the grammatical relation, and not the semantic role, which determines an NP's potential to function as an antecedent. In (26a) the agent (*king*) is the subject of the clause, and is therefore a possible antecedent. But in the corresponding passive form (26b) the agent is no longer a grammatical subject. There is no eligible antecedent in this sentence, and so the whole sentence is ungrammatical. In (27a), the only possible antecedent would be the patient (*king*), but since it is the object it cannot function as the antecedent and the sentence is ungrammatical. In the corresponding passive form (27b), the patient is promoted to grammatical subject. It is therefore eligible to be the antecedent, and the sentence is grammatical. These examples show that either an agent or a patient may serve as the antecedent, provided it is the subject of its clause.

(26) a   ṙaajaawə   swaṇtam bhaaṙyaye ṇuḷḷi.
          king-NOM self's   wife-ACC pinched
          'The king pinched his (i.e., self's) wife.'

     b   *ṙaajaawinaal swaṇtam bhaaṙya   ṇuḷḷappeṭṭu.
          king-INSTR self's   wife-NOM pinch-PASSIVE-PAST
          *'Self's wife was pinched by the king.'

(27) a   *ṙaajaawine swaṇtam bhaaṙya   ṇuḷḷi.
          king-ACC self's   wife-NOM pinched
          *'Self's wife pinched the king.'

     b   ṙaajaawə   swaṇtam bhaaṙyayaal ṇuḷḷappeṭṭu.
          king-NOM self's   wife-INSTR pinch-PASSIVE-PAST
          'The king was pinched by his (i.e., self's) wife.'

Notice also that the contrast in grammaticality in (26) and (27) is not related to any change in word order. Word order in Malayalam is quite free. There seems to be a preference for the antecedent to precede the reflexive, but this is not an absolute requirement, as demonstrated by the following example (see also example 29):

(28)   swaṇtam makante ṭettukaleppatti ṙaajaawə   aaloociccukoṇṭiruṇṇu.
         self's   son-GEN mistakes-about king-NOM think-IMPERF
         'The king was thinking about his (lit. self's) son's mistakes.'

The other important difference between *swa-* and English reflexives is that the Malayalam reflexive may find an antecedent which is outside of its minimal clause. This is illustrated in (29–30).

In (29), sentence (27a) is embedded as a complement clause within a larger sentence. Even though (27a) was ungrammatical on its own, it becomes grammatical in (29) because there is an available antecedent for the reflexive, namely the subject of the matrix clause (*the minister*). Sentence (30) is ambiguous because there are two eligible subjects, one in the matrix clause (*queen*) and another in the highest complement clause (*king*),[2] and either one of them can be interpreted as the antecedent of the reflexive. Both examples show that a clause boundary may separate the reflexive from its antecedent, something which is impossible in English.

(29)   [r̄aajaawine swan̪t̪am bhaar̄ya   nuḷḷi   enn̪ə] bhaṭane
        king-ACC   self's   wife-NOM pinched that   soldier-ACC
        man̪t̪ri   wišwasippiccu.
        minister-NOM   made.believe
        'The minister convinced the soldier that the minister's / *soldier's /
        *king's wife pinched the king.'

(30)   [[swan̪t̪am makan   buddhimaan aan̪ə enn̪ə] r̄aajaawin̪ə
        self's   son-NOM intelligent is   that king-DAT
        t̪oon̪n̪i enn̪ə] raan̪i   man̪t̪riye   wišwasippiccu.
        thought that   queen-NOM minister-ACC made.believe
        'The queen convinced the minister that the king thought that the
        king's / queen's / *minister's son was intelligent.'

4.4.2   "Long-distance" reflexives in other languages

Sentences (29–30) provide good examples of a "long-distance" re-flexive, i.e., a reflexive pronoun which can take an antecedent outside its minimal clause. The fact that this reflexive element in Malayalam can only take a grammatical subject as its antecedent is no accident. There seems to be a very strong tendency across languages for long-distance reflexives to be "subject-oriented" in this sense.

Some examples of long-distance reflexives from other languages are shown below (data from Cole and Sung, 1994). In each case a reflexive within a subordinate clause can take an antecedent in a higher clause, but the antecedent must be a grammatical subject.

(31)   **Korean *casin***
        Chelswu-nun [Yenghi-ka   casin-ul silheha-nun   kes]-ul   molunta.
        Chelswu-TOP Yenghi-NOM self-ACC hate-ADNOM fact-ACC not.know
        'Chelswu didn't believe that Yenghi hates self (=Chelswu/Yenghi).'

(32)   **Chinese *ziji***
        Wangwu shuo [Zhangsan zengsong gei Lisi
        Wangwu say   Zhangsan give   to Lisi
        yipian guanyu ziji de   wenzhang].
        one   about   self LNK article
        'Wangwu says that Zhangsan gave to Lisi an article about self (=Wangwu /
        Zhangsan / *Lisi).'

(33)   **Icelandic *sig***
        Jón   sagði Maríu [að þú elskaðir sig].
        John told Maria that you loved   3.self
        'John told Maria that you loved him/*her.'

Cole and Sung (1994) actually suggest that some principle(s) of Universal Grammar require that long-distance reflexives in every language must take only subjects as antecedents. However, this claim appears to be too strong. O'Grady (1987) shows that the Korean third person reflexive pronoun *caki*, which can take long-distance antecedents, will take a subject as antecedent if one is available, as in (34). But, under certain circumstances, if no subject is available it can also take a non-subject as antecedent. This is illustrated in (35).

(34)   **Korean** *caki* (O'Grady 1987:256, 261)
     John-i   [nay-ka caki-lul   piphanha-yess-ta-ko] malha-yess-ta.
     John-NOM I-NOM self-ACC criticized   said
     'John said that I criticized self (=John).'

(35)   Nay-ka Bob-eykey [John-i   caki-lul   coaha-n-ta-ko] malha-yess-ta.
     I-NOM Bob-DAT John-NOM self-ACC liked   said
     'I told Bob that John liked self (=John or Bob).'

4.4.3   Tagalog

The Tagalog reflexive pronoun *sarili* has properties which are different from the reflexives in any of the languages discussed above. Like English, the Tagalog reflexive is "clause-bounded." However, in contrast to all of the languages we have considered to this point, the grammatical relation of the antecedent is irrelevant. For Tagalog, the relevant notion of prominence is defined in terms of semantic roles rather than grammatical relations.

Tagalog pronouns are inflected for person, number, and case, but do not distinguish gender. The reflexive element *sarili* does not change form, but is normally accompanied by a possessive pronoun which agrees with the person and number of the antecedent. As the following examples show, *sarili* must find its antecedent within its minimal clause, while the non-reflexive pronoun *siya* cannot take an antecedent within its minimal clause.[3]

(36) a   Inasahan   ni=Linda=ng   [ma-halik-an   siya   ng=pangulo].[4]
        expected-DV GEN=Linda=COMP INVOL-kiss-DV 3sg.NOM GEN=principal
        'Linda expected that the principal would kiss her/*him(self).'

    b   Inasahan   ni=Linda=ng
        expected-DV GEN=Linda=COMP
        [ma-halik-an   ng=pangulo   ang=sarili niya].
        INVOL-kiss-DV GEN=principal NOM=self 3sg.GEN
        'Linda expected that the principal would kiss himself/*her(self).'

In (36a), the pronoun *siya* is an element (specifically the patient) of the complement clause. The agent of that clause (*the principal*) is not a possible antecedent, because it is a clause-mate (and in fact a co-argument) of the pronoun. The experiencer of the matrix verb (*Linda*) is eligible, however, because it is outside the minimal clause which contains the pronoun. In (36b) *siya* is replaced by the reflexive *sarili*, and the binding possibilities are reversed. Now *Linda* is ineligible, because it is outside the minimal clause of the reflexive; the only possible antecedent is *the principal*, because this is the only other NP within the minimal clause containing the reflexive.

In light of our discussion in the preceding sections, it may seem surprising that Tagalog allows examples like (37):

(37)   Sinisisi   ni=Maria   ang=kaniya=ng sarili.
           IMPERF-blame-OV GEN=Maria NOM=her=LNK self
           Lit.: 'Herself is blamed by Maria.' (i.e., 'Maria blames herself.')

What is surprising about this example is that the reflexive element itself is the grammatical subject, as indicated by the NOM case marker, and that it takes a non-subject argument of the same minimal clause as its antecedent. In most languages, this pattern would be impossible, since a reflexive cannot outrank its antecedent on the Relational Hierarchy. In Tagalog, however, such examples are quite common; we have already seen another in (36b).

The acceptability of examples like these may lead us to suppose that there is no prominence condition at all for Tagalog reflexives; but this is not true. As Schachter (1976, 1977) and other writers have pointed out, there is an asymmetry between the agent (or, more generally, the Actor) of the clause and all other elements.[5] The Actor is always a possible antecedent for a reflexive inside its minimal clause, regardless of the grammatical relations borne by either element; and the Actor itself can never be a reflexive element, regardless of its grammatical relation.

The following examples, from Schachter (1977), illustrate this point. Each example contains an active sentence followed by the corresponding passive sentence, with no change in semantic roles. In (38), *Grandfather* is the Actor of both sentences, and so is eligible to be the antecedent of the reflexive no matter which argument is chosen as grammatical subject. In (39), the reflexive phrase *sarili* is the Actor. This is never allowed in Tagalog, whether or not it is selected as grammatical subject.

(38) a   Nag-aalala   ang=lolo   sa=kaniya=ng sarili.
           AV-IMPERF-worry NOM=grandfather DAT=his=LNK self
           'Grandfather worries about himself.'

     b   Inaalala   ng=lolo   ang=kaniya=ng sarili.
           IMPERF-worry-OV GEN=grandfather NOM=his=LNK self
           'Himself is worried about by Grandfather.'

(39) a   *Nag-aalala   sa=lolo   ang=kaniya=ng sarili.
           AV-IMPERF-worry DAT=grandfather NOM=his=LNK self
           'Himself worries about Grandfather.'

     b   *Inaalala   ang=lolo   ng=kaniya=ng sarili.
           IMPERF-blame-OV NOM=grandfather GEN=his=LNK self
           'Grandfather is worried about by himself.'

As noted above, the Actor is always a possible antecedent. But it is not the case, as some writers have claimed, that the Actor is the <u>only</u> possible antecedent for a reflexive pronoun. Non-Actors can also be antecedents for reflexive pronouns, as in example (40). Thus sentences like those in (41) are just as ambiguous in Tagalog as in English.

(40)   (from Martin, 1990:22)
Bakit ba kailangan=ng itago   mo   sa   kaniya ang   kaniya=ng sarili?
why Q need=COMP IV-hide 2sg.GEN DAT 3sg   NOM 3sg=LNK self
'Why do you have to hide her from herself?' (figurative)

(41) a   Ipinagbili ng=hari   ang=alipin sa=sarili niya.
IV-sell   GEN=king NOM=slave DAT=self 3sg
'The king sold the slave to himself (=the king/the slave).'

    b   Sinabi ni=Juan   kay=Maria ang=katotohanan
tell-OV GEN=Juan DAT=Maria NOM=truth
tungkol sa=sarili niya.
about   DAT=self 3sg
'John told Mary the truth about himself/herself.'

    c   (adapted from Andrews, 1985:143)
Iniabot ni=Juan   sa=bata   ang=kaniya=ng sarili=ng larawan.
IV-hand GEN=Juan DAT=child NOM=3sg=LNK self=LNK picture
'Juan handed the child a picture of himself (=Juan/the child).'

Thus the behavior of reflexives in Tagalog seems to be determined by semantic roles rather than grammatical relations. The general rule seems to be that the reflexive element cannot "outrank" (or be more prominent than) its antecedent on the following scale:

(42)   MOST PROMINENT   LEAST PROMINENT
Actor > all other arguments > non-argument

The fact that arguments outrank non-arguments is illustrated by example (43). Even though the reflexive pronoun in this sentence is part of the Actor NP, the sentence is still grammatical because it is a possessor, and not an argument; therefore it does not outrank its antecedent *Maria*, which is an argument (specifically the patient).

(43)   Pinatay   si=Maria   ng=sarili=ng   anak.
killed-OV NOM=Maria GEN=self=LNK child
'Mary was killed by self's (i.e., her own) child.'

In addition to these semantic constraints, Bell (1979) has suggested that (at least for Cebuano) there is a restriction on word order as well: the antecedent must precede the reflexive in the sentence. This does seem to be the preferred order in Tagalog, but it is not an absolute requirement as demonstrated by examples like (44). Moreover, reflexives can be topicalized using the *ay*-inversion construction, as illustrated in (45):

(44)   Patuloy   na   nagsasalita   sa=sarili   ang=kanyang ama.
          continuously LNK   AV-converse   DAT=self   NOM=his   father
          'His father is always talking to himself.'

(45) a   Ang=kanila=ng sarili ay   pinupuri   ng=mga=kandidato.
          NOM=3pl=LNK   self   INV   IMPERF-praise-OV   GEN=PL=candidate
          'The candidates praised themselves.'

     b   Ang=sarili niya   ay   nakita   ni=Juan   sa=salamin.
          NOM=self   3sg.GEN   INV   PERF.NV-see-OV   GEN=Juan   DAT=mirror
          'Juan saw himself in the mirror.'

4.5   Conclusion

We noted at the beginning of this chapter that there is a strong tendency for reflexives to be in complementary distribution with regular pronouns: in contexts where a reflexive could be used, the corresponding regular pronoun is likely to be inappropriate for referring to the same antecedent. So defining the possible contexts where reflexives can occur is an important step in analyzing the system of participant reference for a given language.

We have seen that different languages impose different constraints on the relationship between reflexives and their antecedents, but some common patterns do emerge. First, the reflexive must not be "more prominent" than its antecedent. For most languages, prominence can be defined in terms of the Relational Hierarchy. For the Philippine languages, prominence must be defined in terms of semantic roles.[6]

A second major issue is the domain of the Binding relation. In many languages, including English and Tagalog, the reflexive and its antecedent must be elements of the same minimal clause. However, many other languages allow "long-distance" reflexive binding in which the antecedent lies outside the minimal clause of the reflexive. There is a strong tendency for long-distance reflexives to be subject-oriented, i.e., to require a grammatical subject as antecedent. But this pattern is not an absolute universal, as our Korean counter-example in (35) illustrates.

Notes

1. Dalrymple (1993) points out that linear precedence can sometimes have an effect on reflexive binding in English, as illustrated by the following contrast:

   Mary talked to John about himself.
   *Mary talked about himself to John.

2. *The king* is a grammatical subject here, even though it bears dative case. See ch. 10 for discussion.
3. More precisely, the non-reflexive pronoun *siya* may not take any of its co-arguments as its antecedent.

4. The verbs in these examples are glossed according to their voice categories: AV for 'Active Voice,' OV for 'Objective Voice,' DV for 'Dative Voice,' IV for 'Instrumental Voice.' For now, we can treat the non-Active voice categories as special types of passive constructions; see ch. 11.

5. The ACTOR can be loosely defined as the most agent-like argument of the clause: the agent for verbs like *hit, cut*, etc; the experiencer for verbs like *see, hear, know*; the recipient for *receive*. The term "logical subject" is almost equivalent.

6. Manning (1996) discusses a number of other languages in which this is also the case.

5   Control

Look at the examples in (1). Each of these sentences begins with a preposed adverbial clause (i.e., a clausal adjunct) which specifies the time of the event named in the main clause. What does the distribution of reflexive pronouns tell us about the structure of these clausal adjuncts?

(1) a   While shaving himself/*herself, John told his wife about his trip.
   b   Before excusing *himself/herself, Mary helped John arrange his books.
   c   After disgracing *himself/herself at school, Mary was punished by her father.
   d   While dressing himself/*herself for the party, John was tickled by his 4-year-old daughter.
   e   After being shown a picture of himself/*herself at the party, John told Mary the whole story.

The adverbial clauses in these examples have several features in common. First, they all lack an overt subject NP. Second, they all lack an eligible antecedent NP for the reflexive pronoun; yet the reflexive is grammatical. Third, in each case the reflexive must agree with, and be interpreted as referring to, the subject of the main clause. Fourth, the object of the main clause is not a possible antecedent of the reflexive in the adverbial clause.

These facts would be less puzzling if we could analyze the subject of the main clause as the antecedent of the reflexive. But this is impossible, because English reflexives are clause-bounded, as we saw in the last chapter; they cannot take an antecedent which is not an argument of their minimal clause. (Note that the ungrammaticality of *herself in [1a], *himself in [1b], etc. demonstrates clearly that there is a clause boundary between the adverbial clause and the main clause.)

We cannot resolve this paradox by looking at either the adverbial clause or the main clause in isolation. Rather, we must examine the relationship between the two clauses. This relationship provides an example of a very important type of grammatical structure, often referred to as the CONTROL relation, which is the focus of this chapter.

5.1   "Understood" subjects and the control relation

The grammaticality of the reflexives in (1) can be explained if we assume that the adverbial clauses contain an "understood" or implicit (i.e., invisible) subject which functions as the antecedent. This solution is (in some ways) similar to the traditional analysis of the English imperative sentences which you analyzed as an exercise in chapter 4. But in this case there is an additional fact that needs to be accounted for. We noted above that the reflexive must be interpreted as referring to the subject of the main clause. Since the interpretation of a reflexive depends on the interpretation of its antecedent, this means that the implicit subject of the adverbial clause must always be interpreted as referring to the subject of the main clause.

This conclusion is further supported by the interpretation of regular pronouns in examples like (2). The pronoun *her* in this sentence could refer to *his daughter*, but *him* cannot refer to *John*, even though both *John* and *his daughter* are separated from the pronoun by a clause boundary. This contrast indicates that the adverbial clause contains a potential antecedent which is invisible and must refer to *John*.

(2)   While dressing her/#him for the party, John was tickled by his daughter.

Note that it is grammatical subjecthood, and not semantic role, which is relevant to the interpretation of the implicit subject. In examples (1c–d), the main clause is passivized. But, as the distribution of reflexives indicates, the implicit subject of the adverbial clause must be identified with the SUBJ patient, rather than the OBL agent of the main clause. In example (1e) the adverbial clause is passivized, but it still contains an implicit SUBJ which must be identified with the main clause SUBJ.

As mentioned above, this identification of the implicit SUBJ of the adverbial clause with the overt SUBJ of the main clause is an example of a CONTROL relation. This term indicates two things: first, that a particular argument of one clause (generally a subordinate clause of some kind) is omitted; and second, that this missing argument is interpreted as referring to a particular argument of some other clause (generally the matrix clause). In describing the examples in (1), we can say that the subject of the adjunct time clause is CONTROLLED BY the subject of the main clause. The missing argument (i.e., the understood subject) is referred to as the CONTROLLEE, while the argument which it is interpreted as referring to (in this case the main clause subject) is called the CONTROLLER.

In this chapter we will discuss a number of constructions in various languages which involve a control relation. We will distinguish between lexically determined control, which arises from the properties of a particular predicate, and syntactically determined control, which is associated with a specific construction type rather than with any particular word. We will also begin to develop a system for representing the grammatical structure of these constructions.

5.2   Lexically determined control relations

5.2.1   *Persuade*

The adverbial clauses in (1) are clearly adjuncts, and do not appear in the argument structure of the main verb. They are not selected by a specific main verb; rather, they can be freely added to any number of different sentences. (Of course, there may be semantic or discourse restrictions which determine the specific contexts in which it is appropriate to use a particular time clause.)

On the other hand, there are some verbs in English which require a non-finite clausal complement, and these complement clauses also involve a control relation. One example is the verb *persuade*. Consider the following sentences:

(3) a   John persuaded Mary to behave *himself/herself.
   b   John persuaded Mary to give evidence about *himself/him/herself/#her.

As with the adverbial clauses discussed in the previous section, the distribution of reflexives and regular pronouns shows that the infinitival complement in these sentences constitutes a distinct clausal unit. In (3b), for example, if there were no internal clause boundary, then both reflexives should be acceptable and both non-reflexive pronouns impossible for referring to *John* or *Mary*. The contrast in acceptability between the masculine and feminine forms suggests that *Mary*, but not *John*, is an element of the complement clause. These data could be accounted for by assuming that *Mary* is simply the subject of the complement clause, as shown in (4):

(4)   John persuaded [Mary to behave *himself/herself].

However, further investigation very quickly reveals this analysis to be inadequate. There are several pieces of evidence which show that the NP immediately following *persuade* (i.e., *Mary* in [3], or *the doctor* in [5a]) is actually its direct object. First, the post-verbal NP becomes the subject when *persuade* is passivized; compare (5a) with (5b). Second, when the post-verbal NP is a personal pronoun, as in (5c), it appears in the accusative case. Third, when the post-verbal NP is a reflexive, as in (5d), it can take the subject of *persuade* as its antecedent. This shows that it must be a clause-mate of the subject, contrary to the hypothesis suggested in (4).[1] Finally, adverbial elements which are part of the matrix clause (e.g., *after hours of negotiation* in [5e]) can be inserted between the post-verbal NP and the complement verb.

(5) a   Mary persuaded the doctor to examine her son.
   b   The doctor was persuaded to examine Mary's son.
   c   Mary persuaded him to examine her son.
   d   Mary persuaded herself to enter the dance contest.
   e   Mary persuaded the governor after hours of negotiation to pardon her husband.

Thus we seem to be faced with a paradox. The data in (3) indicate that the post-verbal NP must be the subject of the complement clause, while the data in (5) indicate that it must be the object of *persuade*. We will propose the following solution: both of these conclusions are true, but there is no paradox. That is, *Mary* in (3a) is an argument of both the matrix verb and the complement verb, and is assigned a grammatical relation within both clauses. It is simultaneously the object of *persuade* and the subject of *behave*. It is this double assignment of grammatical relations which creates the control relation.

5.2.2   *Promise*

Before discussing this analysis in greater detail, let us compare the behavior of *persuade* with another verb which takes the same kind of infinitival complement, namely *promise*:

(6) a   John persuaded Mary to behave *himself/herself.
    b   John promised Mary to behave himself/*herself.

(7) a   John persuaded Mary to devote *himself/herself to the task of literacy promotion.
    b   John promised Mary to devote himself/*herself to the task of literacy promotion.

(8) a   John persuaded Mary to give evidence about *himself/him/herself/#her.
    b   John promised Mary to give evidence about himself/#him/*herself/her.

Once again, the contrast in acceptability between the masculine and feminine forms indicates the presence of a clause boundary. But with *promise*, the pattern of grammaticality is reversed: it is the matrix subject, rather than the object, which determines the antecedent of the reflexive in the complement clause.

As a result, the type of analysis proposed in (4) is not even a possibility for *promise*; the Binding facts in (6b), (7b), and (8b) clearly indicate that *Mary* is not part of the complement clause in those sentences. This implies that the complement clause does not contain any visible subject NP. But since the reflexive *himself* in (6b) must take a less oblique argument of the complement clause as its antecedent, the complement must contain an implicit subject; and this implicit subject must be coreferential with the matrix subject, *John*. So this construction has all of the features which we described in section 5.1 as being characteristic of the control relation.

There is no obvious structural difference between (6a) and (6b), aside from the difference in the matrix verb. In both sentences, the complement clause must contain an implicit (understood) subject which is controlled by an argument of the main verb. So the structure of these sentences must look something like (9), where (SUBJ) is used to indicate the presence of an invisible subject, i.e., the CONTROLLEE:

(9) a   John persuaded Mary [(SUBJ) to behave *himself/herself].
    b   John promised Mary [(SUBJ) to behave himself/*herself].

The difference between the two verbs, of course, lies in the identity of the CONTROLLER. With *promise*, the unexpressed subject of the complement clause is understood as referring to the subject of the main clause, whereas with *persuade* it is understood as referring to the object of the main clause. This difference will need to be represented in the lexical entries for these two verbs.

The controllee will not need to be specified in this way. In English and most other languages, the controllee in structures of this type is always the subject. As (10) illustrates, the controllee must be the grammatical subject; it cannot be identified with a particular semantic role. The controllee in (10a) is the agent, while the controllee in (10b) is the patient.

(10) a   Mary persuaded the doctor to examine her son.
     b   Mary persuaded her son to be examined by the doctor.

5.3   Representing the control relation

An important question which we must address is how the control properties of *promise* and *persuade* can be represented in their respective lexical entries. But an even more basic question is, what is the nature of the control relation itself? What kind of linkage exists between the controller and the controllee?

Many linguists treat the controllee as a kind of invisible anaphoric element, a phonologically empty pronoun (usually labeled PRO), whose antecedent can be determined by the lexical entry of the main verb or by the grammatical requirements of the particular construction it appears in. A different view is proposed by Bresnan (1982b). She states that some kinds of control are indeed anaphoric in nature (see section 5.6). However, she argues that the constructions we have been discussing in sections 5.1 and 5.2 are not of this type. Rather, they are examples of what she calls FUNCTIONAL CONTROL. Functional control involves a dual assignment of grammatical relations: a single NP functions as an argument of both the subordinate clause and the matrix clause, and bears a grammatical relation in both clauses.

Before addressing these issues directly, let us review some basic facts about subordinate clauses.

5.3.1   Sentential complements (S-COMP)

In chapter 2 we defined a CLAUSAL COMPLEMENT as a subordinate clause which functions as an argument of the verb. This clause may be either finite (i.e., tense-bearing) or non-finite. The choice of verb form depends on which complementizer is used to introduce the dependent clause: *that* requires a finite complement, while *for* requires a non-finite complement.

Each verb selects the type of complement(s) which it can take. Many verbs of cognition (*think, know, doubt, believe*, etc.) require a finite sentential complement (a *that* clause) which expresses a proposition. One way in which this could be represented in the lexical entry for the verb *believe* is shown in (11). (The label S-COMP stands for "sentential complement.")

(11)   *believe* < experiencer, Proposition >
                              | |
                          S U B J   S - C O M P$_{that}$

The phrase structure for a sample sentence is shown in (12a); the corresponding functional structure is shown in (12b).

(12) a   PHRASE STRUCTURE

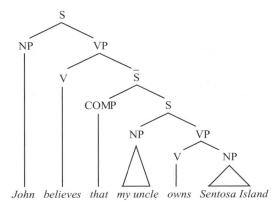

John believes that my uncle owns Sentosa Island

    b   FUNCTIONAL STRUCTURE

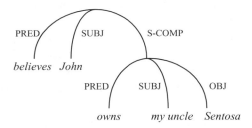

Other cognition predicates (e.g., *prefer, hate, long, eager*, etc.)[2] take a non-finite sentential complement (a *for-to* clause), which typically expresses a potential event or state. A possible lexical entry for the verb *prefer* is shown in (13):

(13)   *prefer* < experiencer, Proposition >
                              | |
                          S U B J   S - C O M P$_{for-to}$

The phrase structure for a sample sentence is shown in (14a); the corresponding functional structure is shown in (14b). (We will not discuss the analysis of *to* here, but simply assume it to be a marker of the infinitive.)

(14) a   PHRASE STRUCTURE

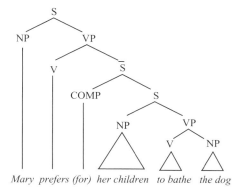

    Mary prefers (for) her children   to bathe   the dog

    b   FUNCTIONAL STRUCTURE

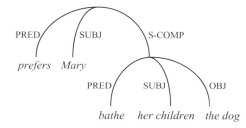

5.3.2   Open complements (XCOMP)

Now let us return to the primary focus of this section, which is how to represent the control relation. We will begin with lexically determined control structures of the type discussed in section 5.2.

There is an important difference between the complement of a verb like *promise* or *persuade* vs. the complement of *think* or *prefer*: complement clauses of the latter type contain an overt subject NP, while those of the former type do not. We have used the term SENTENTIAL COMPLEMENT (S-COMP) for complement clauses which do contain an overt subject. We will refer to a complement clause which lacks an overt subject as an OPEN COMPLEMENT, abbreviated XCOMP.[3]

The defining feature of functional control is the assignment of two grammatical relations to a single nominal element. For example, in sentence (3a) (*John persuaded Mary to behave herself*), *Mary* is simultaneously the subject of the complement clause and the object of the matrix clause. Another way to express this is to say that the subject of the complement clause is FUNCTIONALLY IDENTIFIED with the object of the matrix clause. This pattern can be seen clearly in the network diagram in (15): the OBJ arc of the matrix clause and the SUBJ arc of the complement clause lead to the same element, namely *Mary*.

(15)

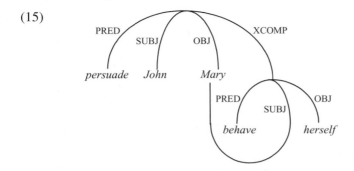

As this diagram shows, the XCOMP is a distinct clausal unit in terms of the functional structure of the sentence. But what about the phrase structure? The complement clause has no overt subject NP, and there is no direct evidence to indicate the presence of an "empty" NP position within the complement. In other words, there is no reason to identify the complement as an S rather than a VP constituent. In this book we will avoid the use of "invisible" elements or empty positions in phrase structure, unless there is positive evidence for the presence of such an element. We will therefore assume that the category of the complement is VP, as shown in (16), and not S.

(16)

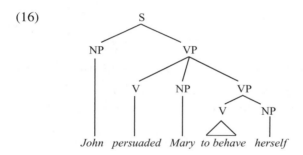

Sentence (6b), *John promised Mary to behave himself*, would have exactly the same phrase structure as that shown in (16). The only difference is in the functional structure, specifically in the identity of the controller as indicated in (17).

(17)

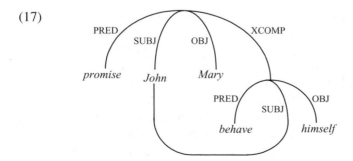

5.3.3   Lexical entries of control predicates

As noted in section 5.2, the most important difference between the control relation of the adverbial clauses in (1) vs. that of the complement clauses in (5–10) is that in the latter case, but not the former, control is LEXICALLY GOVERNED. This means that the open complement (XCOMP) construction occurs only where it is specified in the lexical entry of the matrix verb. Matrix verbs which require this kind of complement are sometimes called CONTROL PREDICATES.

As we have seen, verbs of this type (e.g., *promise* and *persuade*) do not all have the same control properties. Therefore something in the lexical entry of the verb must specify not only the existence but also nature of the control relation, specifically the identity of the controller. One way of representing this is with a CONTROL EQUATION, as in (18). These lexical entries will license the types of functional structures illustrated in (15) and (17).

(18) a   *persuade* < agent, experiencer, Action >
                   | | |
             SUBJ   OBJ   XCOMP
      [OBJ = XCOMP SUBJ]

   b   *promise* < agent, experiencer, Action >
                   | | |
             SUBJ   OBJ   XCOMP
      [SUBJ = XCOMP SUBJ]

Both of these verbs are three-place predicates, i.e., predicates which take three semantic arguments. In each case the third argument is itself a predicate of the appropriate semantic type, namely an ACTION, which is expressed as an open complement clause (XCOMP). The control equation in (18a) states that the object of *persuade* is functionally identified with the subject of its complement clause. In other words, the OBJ of the matrix clause also bears the SUBJ relation within the XCOMP. The equation in (18b) states that the subject of *promise* is functionally identified with the subject of its complement clause. In other words, the SUBJ of the matrix clause also bears the SUBJ relation within the XCOMP.

The control equations in (18) can also be thought of as defining pathways through the functional structure diagram. For example, the control equation in (18a) says that we arrive at the same argument by following the OBJ arc from the top of figure (15) as we would by following the top XCOMP arc and then the subordinate SUBJ arc.

5.3.4   Participial clauses (XADJ)

An adjunct (or adverbial) clause is a subordinate clause that is not a complement, i.e., is not an argument of the matrix verb. Just as we distinguish sentential complements (those that contain an overt subject NP) from open complements (those that do not), so too we can distinguish sentential adjuncts

(S-ADJ) from OPEN ADJUNCTS (XADJ). The sentences in (19) contain examples of sentential adjuncts, each containing an independent SUBJ, while the examples in (20) contain open adjuncts which lack an overt SUBJ:

(19) a   [While Mary was making him/*himself a cup of tea], John told her the whole story.

b   [While Susan was strapping herself/*himself into the cockpit], Henry gave her the instructions from HQ.

(20) a   [Making himself/*herself/her a cup of tea], John told Mary the whole story.

b   [While checking himself/*herself/her for injuries], the policeman asked Alice for her driver's license.

c   Henry gave Susan her instructions [while strapping himself/*herself/her into the cockpit].

The distribution of reflexives and regular pronouns in (20) shows that in this kind of adverbial clause, the subject of the participle (*making, dangling, strapping*) is controlled by the subject of the main clause. Since adjuncts are not lexically governed, the control relation must be defined by the rules which generate the construction itself. The structure of (20c) is shown in (21).

(21) a   PHRASE STRUCTURE

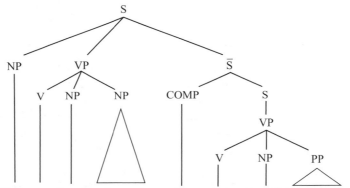

Henry gave Susan her instructions while strapping himself into the cockpit

b   FUNCTIONAL STRUCTURE

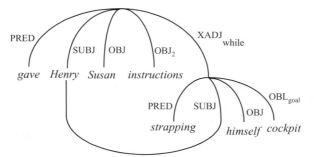

5.4   Control structures in other languages

5.4.1   *while* clauses in Malayalam

We will begin our survey of other languages with an open adjunct (XADJ) construction in Malayalam, a Dravidian language of southern India. When the subject of a 'while'-clause (formed with the post-position *koṇʈə* 'while; with') is omitted, it must be interpreted as being controlled by the subject of the matrix clause. Consider the following examples from Mohanan (1982:568–569, 585):

(22) a   meešameel iṛuṇṇu=koṇʈə, kuʈʈiye   pooliissukaar   ikkiḷiyaakki.
table-LOC sitting=while child-ACC policemen-NOM tickled
'While sitting on the table, the policemen tickled the child.'

b   meešameel iṛuṇṇu=koṇʈə, kuʈʈi   pooliissukaaṛaal ikkiḷiyaakkappeʈʈu.
table-LOC sitting=while child-NOM policemen-INSTR tickle-PASS-PAST
'While sitting on the table, the child was tickled by the policemen.'

In the Malayalam sentence (22a), as in its English translation, the only possible interpretation is that the policemen are sitting on the table; it cannot be taken to mean that the child is sitting on the table. Thus the understood subject of the adverbial clause must be controlled by the matrix subject. In the passive version (22b), both in Malayalam and in English, the interpretation is reversed: it must be the child who is sitting on the table. The contrast in the Malayalam examples shows quite clearly that it is the change of grammatical relation, specifically the identity of the main clause SUBJ, which causes the change of controller, since both word order and semantic roles remain constant. A similar contrast is found in (23):

(23) a   [__ kaʈʈil-il kiʈaṇṇu=koṇʈə] acchanə   amma   kaašə koʈuttu.
bed-LOC lay=while   father-DAT mother-NOM money gave
'Mother gave the money to Father while she/*he lay on the bed.'

b   *[__ amma   kaašə koʈuttu=koṇʈə] acchan   sukhamaayi iṛuṇṇu.
mother-NOM money gave=while   father-NOM happily   sat
'Father lived happily, while Mother gave him money.'

Example (23a) shows that the understood subject of the adverbial clause must refer to the matrix subject, and not to the secondary object. In other words, only the matrix SUBJ can be the controller. Example (23b) shows that the missing argument of the adverbial clause (i.e., the controllee) must be the subject, and not the secondary object.

5.4.2   Time clauses in Warlpiri

A similar construction is found in the Australian language Warlpiri (data from Hale, 1982). Example (24) illustrates the contrast between two complementizers. Both of these introduce an adverbial time clause with an understood subject (an XADJ), but the control relation (specifically the identity of the controller) varies depending on which complementizer is used.

(24) a   Napurrula ka-ju ngaju-ku wangka-mi,   ngurlu kipi-rninja=<u>karra</u>.
           Napurrula AUX me-DAT speak-NONPAST seed   winnow-INF=COMP
           'Napurrula is speaking to me, while winnowing mulga seed.'

    b   Karnta ka-rla wangka-mi   ngarrka-ku, karli   jarnti-rninja=<u>kurra</u>-ku.
           woman AUX   speak-NONPAST man-DAT   boomerang trim-INF=COMP-DAT
           'The woman is speaking to the man, while (the man) is trimming the boomerang.'

Example (24a) contains an adverbial clause marked with the complementizer =*karra*. When this complementizer is used, the only interpretation is that the winnowing is being done by the subject of the main clause ('Napurrula'). However, when the complementizer =*kurra* is used, as in (24b), a different interpretation is required: here the one doing the trimming cannot be the subject, but must be some other argument of the main clause (in this example 'the man'). The case marking of the controller (dative case in this example) is copied onto the end of the adverbial clause.

5.4.3   Purpose clauses vs. Equi complements in Warlpiri

Hale (1982) reports that the complementizer -*ku* in Warlpiri has two different uses. The examples in (25) below show how -*ku* is used to mark clausal adjuncts (adverbial clauses) expressing purpose. Note that the purpose clause may have its own subject NP, as in (25a), or it may lack an overt subject. In the latter case, the subject of the adverbial clause may be identified with an element of the main clause: often the main clause subject, as in (25b–c), but sometimes another element, e.g., the secondary object as in (25d). The interpretation of the missing subject in an adverbial purpose clause seems to be determined by semantic plausibility, rather than grammatical constraints. This fact suggests that we are dealing with some kind of anaphoric relationship, e.g., a null (silent) pronominal element, rather than functional control.

(25) a   Pangkarra=rna ka-ngu-rnu,   kurdu jarda nguna-nja=<u>ku</u>.
           blanket=I   carry-PAST-hither child sleep lie-INF=PURP
           'I have brought a blanket in order for the child to sleep.'

    b   Yapa   ka-lu ya-ni-rni   miyi ma-ninja=<u>ku</u>.
           people PRES go-NONPAST-hither   food get-INF=PURP
           'The people are coming in order to get food.'

    c   Ngarrka-jarra-rlu ka-pala parlku pangi-rni   marlu   purra-nja=<u>ku</u>.
           man-DUAL-ERG PRES   trench dig-NONPAST kangaroo cook-INF=PURP
           'The two men are digging a cooking trench in order to cook the kangaroo.'

d   Karnta-ngku ka-rla kurdu-ku   pangkarra yi-nyi   jarda nguna-nja=ku.
         woman-ERG PRES child-DAT blanket   give-NONPAST sleep lie-INF=PURP
         'The woman is giving the child a blanket in order (for the child) to sleep.'

Certain verbs (which we will refer to as Equi predicates; see section 5.5 below) select a complement clause which is also marked with the complementizer -ku. There are two important differences between this type of complement clause and the adverbial purpose clauses illustrated above. First, the complement clauses never contain an overt subject. Second, the identity of the complement subject is grammatically determined. Hale states that with transitive Equi verbs, such as *order, teach, prevent, tell, enlist, send*, etc. the complement subject is always controlled by the object of the main clause, as in (26a–b). With intransitive Equi verbs, such as *fail to, learn to, develop a desire to, lose desire to*, etc. the controller is always the subject of the main clause, as in (26c).

(26) a   Jakamarra-rlu=ju   jinjinyi-ma-nu warlu   yarrpi-rninja=ku.
          Jakamarra-ERG=me order-PAST   firewood kindle-INF=PURP
          'Jakamarra ordered me to build a fire.'

     b   Ngarrka-ngku ka-palangu kurdu-jarra ngarri-rni   maliki yampi-nja=ku.
          man-ERG   PRES   child-DUAL tell-NONPAST dog   leave-INF=PURP
          'The man is telling the two children to leave the dog alone.'

     c   Walya kiji-rninja=ku   ka-rna   kapakapa-jarri-mi   (ngaju).
          earth throw-INF=PURP PRES=I fail-INCHOAT-NONPAST (I)
          'I am failing to throw the dirt out (of the well); (it keeps caving back in on me.).'

The fact that the control relation in this construction is obligatory and is defined (for any particular matrix predicate) in terms of a specific grammatical relation are characteristic features of functional control.

5.4.4   Purpose clauses vs. Equi complements in Indonesian

In Indonesian, as in Warlpiri, we find a contrast between two types of complementizer. One complementizer, *untuk*, is used to indicate a functional control relation, whether in XCOMP or XADJ. The other type (*agar* or *supaya*) is used to introduce a sentential complement (S-COMP) or sentential adjunct (S-ADJ). We will begin by comparing the use of these complementizers with adjunct clauses. (The analysis and most of the examples in this section are based on Sneddon, 1996.)

Examples (27) and (29) illustrate two different types of adverbial purpose clauses. One type is introduced by the complementizer *untuk* 'for,' as in (27). In this construction, the adverbial clause never contains an overt subject NP.[4] Its subject is understood to be the same as (i.e., is controlled by) some argument of the main clause. This is the type of adverbial clause we refer to as an "open" adjunct (XADJ).

(27)   Saya pergi ke kantor pos <u>untuk</u> membeli perangko.
              I   go   to office post for   buy   stamp
              'I am going to the post office to buy stamps.'

The controller in this construction must be the matrix SUBJ (28a) or OBJ (28b). Example (28c) illustrates the fact that an oblique argument cannot be the controller.[5]

(28)   (adapted from Chung, 1976:89)
      a   (controller = SUBJ)
              Kami   membuka senjata itu   untuk [__ memperbaiki=nya].
              we(EXCL) AV-open rifle   that for   repair=3sg
              'We took the rifle apart in order to repair it.'

      b   (controller = OBJ)
              Kami   membawa senjata itu   ke toko untuk [__ di-perbaiki].
              we(EXCL) AV-take rifle   that to shop for   PASS-repair
              'We took the rifle to the shop to be repaired.'

      c   (controller = OBL)
              *Senjata itu di-buka   oleh tukang untuk [__ memperbaiki=nya].
              rifle   that PASS-open by   smith for   repair=3sg
              (for: 'The rifle was taken apart by the gun-smith in order to repair it.')

The other type of purpose clause is introduced by the complementizers *agar* or *supaya*, both meaning 'so that.' When these complementizers are used, the adverbial clause normally contains an overt subject NP; thus we identify it as a sentential adjunct (S-ADJ). The subject of the adverbial clause is often (but not always) different from the subject of the main clause, indicating that there is no obligatory control relation in this construction. If the two clauses have the same subject, the subject of the adverbial clause may optionally be deleted as shown in (29c).

(29) a   Dia jual sayur   <u>supaya</u> anak=nya dapat bersekolah.
              3sg sell vegetable so   child=3sg get   attend.school
              'She sells vegetables so that her son can go to school.'

      b   Kami berangkat pagi-pagi   <u>agar</u> kami   tidak terlambat.
              1pl.EX depart   early.morning so   1pl.EX not   late
              'We set off early in the morning so we wouldn't be late.'

      c   Dia pergi ke perpustakaan <u>supaya</u> (dia) dapat membaca buku.
              3sg go   to library   so   (3sg) get   read   book
              'He went to the library so that (he) could read a book.'

d   <u>Agar</u> kami   tidak terlambat kami   berangkat pagi-pagi.
       so   1pl.EX not   late   1pl.EX depart   early.morning
       'So that we wouldn't be late we set off early in the morning.'

An important difference between adjunct clauses and complements in Indonesian is that, while complement clauses must always follow the main verb, many adjunct clauses (including those introduced by *agar* or *supaya*) can be preposed to sentence-initial position, as in (29d).

The two types of complementizer exhibit a similar contrast when they are used in complement clauses: *untuk* introduces XCOMP, while *agar* and *supaya* introduce S-COMP. We will begin with the XCOMP construction. Certain control verbs select a complement clause introduced by the complementizer *untuk* 'for.' These complements never contain an overt subject NP; rather, the complement SUBJ is controlled by an argument of the matrix clause. (30a) illustrates that the OBJ cannot be the controllee.

(30) a   *Dia menolak <u>untuk</u> polis   memeriksa.
            3sg refuse   for   police AV-investigate
            (*'He refused for the police to investigate him.')

     b   Dia menolak <u>untuk</u> di-periksa   oleh polis.
            3sg refuse   for   PASS-investigate by   police
            'He refused to be investigated by the police.'

The choice of controller is determined by the matrix verb. If, as in (30b) and (31a), the main verb does not subcategorize for an OBJ, then the controller is the matrix SUBJ. In this case the complement clause is interpreted as having the same subject as the main clause. If the main verb does take an OBJ, the controller is the matrix patient. This means that the subject of the complement clause is controlled by the OBJ if the matrix verb is active, as in (31b); and by the SUBJ if the matrix verb is passive, as in (31c). With certain main verbs the complementizer may optionally be omitted, as in (31b). With some control predicates the complementizer is rarely if ever used; an example is given in (31d).

(31) a   Saya memutuskan <u>untuk</u> menolong mereka.
            I   decide   for   help   them
            'I decided to help them.'

     b   Pemerintah mengizinkan dia (<u>untuk</u>) menghadiri sidang.
            government permit   3sg for   attend   session
            'The government permitted him to attend the session.'

     c   Mereka di-panggil <u>untuk</u> mengambil bahagian.
            they   PASS-call   for   take   part
            'They were called to take part.'

     d   Suwono menyuruh anak=nya pergi ke sekolah.
            Suwono order   child=his go   to school
            'Suwono ordered his children to go to school.'

Indonesian has no morphologically distinct infinitive form of the verb, but Sneddon notes that these complement clauses cannot contain aspectual or modal auxiliaries. In other words, the complement clause cannot have independent specification of tense, aspect, or modality. The same appears to be true of complement clauses marked with *agar* or *supaya*.

Complement clauses marked with *agar* or *supaya* can have independent subject NPs. Once again, if the complement subject is coreferential with some argument of the main clause, it may optionally be deleted, as in (32d); or, alternatively, the coreferential NP may be omitted from the main clause (32e). If the main verb is a transitive verb meaning something like *order* or *request*, the complement subject is usually (but not always) omitted (32f).

(32) a   Bung Karno ingin <u>supaya</u> kami   menolong dia.
    Bung Karno want so   1pl.EX help   3sg
    'Bung Karno wants us to help him.'

    b   Dia bercita-cita <u>agar</u> anak=nya di-lamar   oleh orang kaya saja.
    3sg desire   so   child=3sg PASS-propose by person rich only
    'He desires that his daughter be proposed to by no one but a rich man.'

    c   Saya minta <u>supaya</u> saudara jangan pergi.
    I   request so   cousin don't go
    'I request that you don't go.'

    d   Saya dapat mengusulkan kepada pimpinan <u>supaya</u> (mereka) menerima saudara.
    I   get suggest   to   leadership so   (they) receive cousin
    'I can suggest to the leaders to accept you.'

    e   Rukman mengingatkan <u>agar</u> anak buah=nya tidak menembak.
    Rukman remind   so   child fruit=3sg not   shoot
    'Rukman warned his men not to shoot.'

    f   Muso mangajak Indonesia <u>supaya</u> bergandengan tangan dengan Moskow.
    Muso urge   Indonesia so   join   hand with   Moscow
    'Muso urged Indonesia to go hand-in-hand with Moscow.'

In summary, then, we have seen that the complementizer *untuk* is used to introduce adjunct and complement clauses which involve a functional control relation (XADJ and XCOMP). The complementizers *agar* and *supaya* are used to introduce sentential adjuncts and sentential complements (S-ADJ and S-COMP), which have independent subjects and do not involve any control relation.

5.4.5   "Object Raising" (*tough*-movement)

In all the constructions we have examined thus far, the controllee has been a grammatical subject. This is by far the most common situation. But there are a few constructions in which some other argument of the subordinate clause can be a controllee. One such construction, found in English and a number of other languages, involves a small class of adjectives which take infinitival complements. A very famous contrast which illustrates this pattern is seen in (33):

(33) a   John is easy to please.
     b   John is eager to please.

The crucial difference between (33a) and (33b) involves the semantic role of *John* with respect to the complement verb *please*: in (33a) *John* is interpreted as the patient; while in (33b) *John* is interpreted as the agent. Example (33b) involves a control relation similar to those illustrated in section 5.2; the complement subject is controlled by the subject of the main clause. The pattern we are interested in now is that illustrated in (33a), in which the complement object is controlled by the main clause subject.

Some further examples are given in (34), showing that the controllee may also be a prepositional object. This pattern is sometimes called "*tough*-movement," because *tough* is one of the adjectives which selects for complements of this type.

(34) a   This medicine is <u>tough</u> to swallow.
     b   That sonata is <u>easy</u> to play.
     c   That fruit is <u>ripe enough</u> to eat.
     d   This coffee is <u>too bitter</u> to drink.
     e   Mary is <u>hard</u> (for me) to talk to.
     f   John is <u>easy</u> to believe in/depend on/work for.
     g   That violin is <u>easy</u> to play sonatas on.

This construction has a number of unusual properties, which distinguish it from "normal" control constructions involving a subject controllee. We will not pursue a detailed analysis in this book, but it is interesting to notice that Indonesian has an equivalent construction. However, in Indonesian the complement verbs must be passives, i.e., the controllee must still be a grammatical subject.

(35)   **Indonesian** (Sneddon, 1996)
     a   Tulisan saudara sulit   (untuk) di-baca.
          writing cousin difficult (for)   PASS-read
          'Your writing is hard to read.'

     b   Jawaban=nya tidak mudah di-mengerti.
          answer=3sg not   easy PASS-understand
          'His answer is not easy to understand.'

     c   Papaya ini sudah cukup masak untuk di-makan.
          papaya this already enough ripe for   PASS-eat
          'This papaya is already ripe enough to eat.'

     d   Sepatu ini terlalu   mahal   untuk kami=beli.
          shoe   this too.much expensive for   1pl.EX(PASS)=buy
          'These shoes are too expensive for us to buy.'

5.5   Equi vs. Raising in English

5.5.1   Two classes of predicates

In this section we will discuss two classes of control predicates in English. Members of the first class, including verbs and adjectives like *try, plan, pretend, intend, refuse, agree, hope, eager, reluctant*, are often referred to as EQUI PREDICATES. Members of the second class, verbs and adjectives like *seem, appear, likely, certain, happen, tend, begin*, etc., are often referred to as RAISING PREDICATES. (Both of these labels derive from the early Transformational Grammar analyses of these constructions; even though our analysis has changed, the names are still widely used.)

Predicates in both classes take an infinitival open complement (XCOMP), whose subject is controlled by an element of the matrix clause. However, there are several systematic differences between the two classes which require an explanation. We will begin by listing some of these differences, then attempt to develop an analysis which will account for the data. We will suggest that the two classes of predicates are essentially identical in terms of assignment of grammatical relations and phrase structure configuration. The crucial difference between the two concerns the assignment of semantic roles.

5.5.1.1   Dummy subjects

Certain verbs in English allow the pro-forms *it* or *there* to appear as "dummy" subjects. This means that the pro-form appears in the subject position and bears the subject relation, but has no semantic content; it does not take an antecedent (in the usual sense) and is not assigned any semantic role by the verb. Predicates of the Raising type (36) allow dummy subjects to appear in their subject position, whereas predicates of the Equi type (37) do not:

(36) a   It seems to be raining.
   b   There are likely to be a lot of accidents if we get a snow-storm.
   c   It tends to get dark in the valley by mid-afternoon.
   d   There began to emerge a pattern in the criminal's behavior.

(37) a   *It tries to be raining.[6]
   b   *There are eager to be a lot of accidents if we get a snow-storm.
   c   *It intends to get dark in the valley by mid-afternoon.
   d   *There refused to emerge a pattern in the criminal's behavior.

5.5.1.2   Selectional restrictions

Predicates of the Equi type may impose selectional restrictions on their subjects. This is illustrated by the unacceptability of (38b) and (39b). However, predicates of the Raising type do not impose selectional restrictions on their subjects, as illustrated in (38a) and (39a):

(38) a   That brick appears to be cracked.
   b   #That brick tried to be cracked.

(39) a   Your radio is likely to be confiscated by the customs officers.
      b   #Your radio is eager to be confiscated by the customs officers.[7]

5.5.1.3   Passivization

When the complement of a predicate of the Equi type is passivized, the meaning
of the sentence as a whole is altered. This is illustrated in (41) and (43). But with
predicates of the Raising type, passivization does not affect the propositional
meaning in any significant way. That is, either form could be used to describe the
same situation, and if one sentence is true the other must be true as well. This is
illustrated in (40) and (42):

(40) a   Dr. Benson is likely to examine John.
      b   John is likely to be examined by Dr. Benson.
                 (no difference in meaning)

(41) a   Dr. Benson is reluctant to examine John.
      b   John is reluctant to be examined by Dr. Benson.
                 (clear difference in meaning)

(42) a   All the girls seem to like John.
      b   John seems to be liked by all the girls.
                 (no difference in meaning)

(43) a   All the girls try to like John.
      b   John tries to be liked by all the girls.
                 (clear difference in meaning)

5.5.1.4   Idiom chunks

Idiomatic phrases consist of several words, but the meaning of the phrase is
not predictable from the meanings of the individual words. The entire phrase
functions semantically as a single lexical unit. Predicates of the Raising type may
allow one part (or "chunk") of an idiomatic expression to appear in the subject
position, without losing the idiomatic meaning of the expression as a whole. This
is illustrated in the (a) sentences in (44–47). With predicates of the Equi type,
however, this is never possible, as illustrated in the corresponding (b) sentences.

(44) a   Tabs continue to be kept on the leading suspects.
      b   #Tabs intend to be kept on the leading suspects.
                 (*keep tabs on* = 'to watch or monitor someone's movements')

(45) a   John's goose seems to be cooked.
      b   #John's goose tries to be cooked.
                 (*his goose is cooked* = 'he is in serious trouble')

(46) a   The cat appears to be out of the bag.
      b   #The cat refuses to be out of the bag.
                 (*to let the cat out of the bag* = 'to reveal a secret')

(47) a   John's name is certain to be mud if anyone finds out about this.
      b   #John's name is reluctant to be mud if anyone finds out about this.
                 (*his name is mud* = 'he is disgraced/unpopular')

5.5.2   Explaining the contrasts

All of the differences illustrated in the preceding section relate in some way to semantic content rather than syntactic structure. We have no evidence that the contrast between these two classes correlates with a difference in grammatical relations or phrase structure. Predicates in both classes take an infinitival open complement (XCOMP), whose subject is controlled by the SUBJ of the matrix clause. Following our discussion in section 5.3, we could assign the structures shown in (48) to both the Raising example in (42a) and the Equi example in (43a).

(48) a

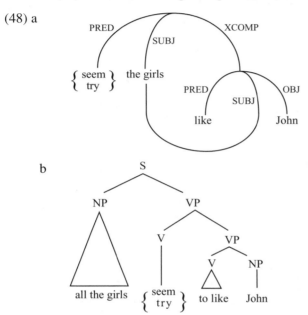

But if Raising and Equi constructions have the same basic syntactic structure, how can we explain the systematic differences between the two classes of predicates which were illustrated in section 5.5.1? Each of the contrasts noted above seems to point to the following conclusion: Raising predicates do not assign any semantic role to their subjects, and place no semantic restrictions on their subjects except the restrictions required by the embedded verb. Equi predicates, on the other hand, assign a semantic role to their subjects in the normal way. They may impose selectional restrictions etc. on their subjects like any other verb.

Let us first re-examine the data from the previous section to see how this basic intuition can help us account for the evidence. Then we will try to make this intuition more precise by formulating lexical entries for the two types of predicate.

5.5.2.1   Dummy subjects

The most basic fact about dummy subjects in English is that they cannot bear any semantic role. They can appear only in constructions in which the subject position is semantically vacuous (has no semantic content). Thus the fact that Equi predicates assign semantic roles to their subjects explains why they cannot take dummy subjects, as illustrated in (37). Dummy subjects are possible with Raising predicates, as in (36), because these predicates do not assign semantic roles to their subjects.

A second important fact about dummy subjects is that they are lexically specified. That is, certain specific verbs allow dummy *it*, others allow dummy *there*, while others do not allow dummy subjects at all. The prototypical verbs which take dummy subjects include verbs of existence and becoming, and weather verbs. But we cannot predict on the basis of semantics alone which verbs will and which will not take dummy subjects. This is something which must be specified in the lexical entry of the relevant verbs. For example, the verb *rain* can take dummy *it* as SUBJ (49a), but the verb *fall* cannot (49c). The verb *arrive* can take dummy *there* as SUBJ (50a), but the verb *return* cannot (50c).

(49) a   It is raining cats and dogs.
     b   It seems to be raining cats and dogs.
     c   *It is falling leaves.[8]
     d   *It seems to be falling leaves.

(50) a   There arrived a message from the front.
     b   There happened to arrive a message from the front.
     c   *There returned a messenger from the front.
     d   *There happened to return a messenger from the front.

The preceding examples demonstrate that, in order for a dummy subject to appear with a Raising predicate, the complement verb must be one which allows dummy subjects. The Raising predicate itself neither rejects nor licenses dummy subjects; the acceptability depends entirely on the properties of the complement verb. Thus we might say that Raising predicates are "transparent," in the sense that the lexical features of the complement verb determine what can appear in the matrix subject position.

5.5.2.2   Selectional restrictions

In chapter 1 we noted that the selectional restrictions which verbs impose must be stated in terms of semantic roles rather than grammatical relations. Examples (38) and (39) (repeated below) demonstrated that Equi predicates may impose selectional restrictions on their subjects, whereas Raising predicates do not. This contrast follows directly from our hypothesis about the difference in argument structure between the two. Since Equi predicates assign semantic roles to their subjects in the same way as any other verb, they may also impose similar kinds of selectional restrictions on them. Typically, Equi predicates involve agentive, volitional actions, so that inanimate subjects like those in (38b) and (39b) are often semantically unacceptable. Raising predicates, on the other hand, do not assign semantic roles to their subjects, and so cannot impose selectional restrictions on them.

(38) a   That brick appears to be cracked.
   b   #That brick tried to be cracked.

(39) a   Your radio is likely to be confiscated by the customs officers.
   b   #Your radio is eager to be confiscated by the customs officers.

Even though a Raising predicate does not itself impose any selectional restrictions on its subject, the complement verb in a Raising construction may impose such restrictions on the complement subject. For example, the verb *gush* (in its basic meaning) requires that its subject be a liquid, or at least a fluid, as illustrated in (51a–b). When this verb appears in the XCOMP of a Raising construction, this restriction is imposed on the XCOMP's subject, i.e., the controllee. But since the controllee is functionally identified with the controller, this same restriction must also apply to the controller, namely the subject of the Raising predicate, as illustrated in (51c–d). Thus, once again, Raising predicates are semantically "transparent" in the sense that any selectional restrictions imposed on the controllee by the complement verb apply equally to the controller (matrix subject).

(51) a   Oil gushed from the broken pipe.
   b   #The puppy gushed out of its basket.
   c   Oil seemed/is likely/began to gush from the broken pipe.
   d   #The puppy seemed/is likely/began to gush out of its basket.

5.5.2.3   Passivization

As illustrated in (40)–(43), passivizing the complement verb changes the meaning of an Equi construction, but not of a Raising construction. To see why this is so, let us re-examine (42) and (43), repeated below.

(42) a   All the girls seem to like John.
   b   John seems to be liked by all the girls.
        (no difference in meaning)

(43) a   All the girls try to like John.
   b   John tries to be liked by all the girls.
        (clear difference in meaning)

The complement verb in these examples, *like*, takes two arguments: an experiencer and a stimulus. We know that passivization changes the alignment of grammatical relations to semantic roles. But the controllee must always be the SUBJ of the complement clause, since the control relation is defined in terms of grammatical relations. So in the active form (the [a] sentences), the controllee is the experiencer; while in the passive form (the [b] sentences), the controllee is the stimulus.

Now the Equi predicate *try* also assigns a semantic role (namely agent) to its subject, i.e., the controller. But since the controller and controllee are functionally identified, the same participant must bear both semantic roles. The passivization of the complement verb changes the association between these roles, and so gives rise to a different interpretation concerning which participant in the situation is the volitional agent (who is doing the trying). In example (43a), the agent of *try* is identified with the experiencer of *like*; the girls make an effort to feel a particular emotion. But in (43b), the agent of *try* is identified with the stimulus of *like*. In this case it is John who must make an effort to be likeable. The diagrams in (52) are intended to represent these alignments, without as yet going into further details concerning the lexical entries involved:

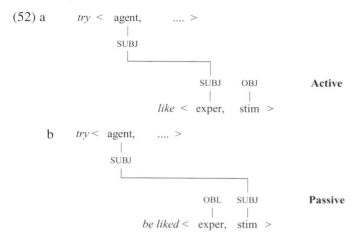

(52) a   *try* < agent, ... >
                        |
                     SUBJ

                              SUBJ   OBJ   **Active**
                               | |
                         like < exper,   stim >

   b   *try* < agent, ... >
                        |
                     SUBJ

                              OBL   SUBJ   **Passive**
                               | |
                   be liked < exper,   stim >

Since Raising predicates do not assign semantic roles to their subjects, the only role which the subject in (42) carries is the role assigned by the complement verb. Passivization of this verb does not alter the semantic roles which it assigns, and therefore does not affect the meaning of the sentence in any significant way. Clearly (42a) and (42b) describe the same kind of situation, as do (40a) and (40b).

5.5.2.4   Idiom chunks

An idiomatic phrase functions semantically as a single lexical unit. Its meaning cannot be analyzed COMPOSITIONALLY, i.e., as the sum of the meanings of its constituent parts. Such constructions have grammatical relations of the normal kind, but these grammatical relations do not correspond with semantic roles in the normal way. For example, the sentence *Mary is pulling John's leg* means that Mary is trying to trick or deceive John. The word *leg* bears the OBJ relation, but no semantic role; it is the possessor (in this case, *John*) which bears the semantic role of patient. Similarly, in the sentence *John's goose is cooked* neither *goose* nor *cook* can be interpreted literally. *Goose* is the SUBJ, but not the patient. There is no act of cooking, thus no "cook-ee" in the patient role. The crucial point, then, is that fixed elements of the idiomatic phrase cannot bear any independent semantic role.

Since idioms do have normal grammatical relations, the SUBJ of an idiom is eligible to be a controllee just like any other SUBJ. If a "chunk" of an idiomatic expression (e.g., *John's goose* in [45a], repeated below) appears as the subject of a Raising predicate, the idiomatic meaning of the expression as a whole is not destroyed. Raising predicates assign no semantic role to their subjects; the only semantic role assigned to the controller in a Raising construction would be the one it inherits from the controllee, which in this case is the idiom's SUBJ. Thus the control relation has no effect on the semantic content of the idiom.

(45) a   John's goose seems to be cooked.
     b   #John's goose tries to be cooked.

With Equi predicates, however, the situation is quite different. An Equi predicate assigns a semantic role to its subject. But in order to receive this semantic role, any idiom chunk which appears in the subject position must be interpreted literally. This not only destroys the idiomatic meaning but often leads to violations of selectional restrictions as well, as illustrated above in (44b)–(47b).

5.5.3   Lexical entries for *try* and *seem*

Having explored some of the differences between Raising and Equi predicates, let us attempt to make our analysis more precise and explicit by formulating lexical entries for each of these types. In the case of Equi predicates, which assign semantic roles in the normal way to all their grammatical arguments, we can simply modify the lexical entries proposed in (18) for *promise* and *persuade*.

The Equi predicates discussed in this section, e.g., *try*, take only two semantic arguments as indicated in (53). The control equation states that the SUBJ of the XCOMP is controlled by the SUBJ of *try*.

(53)   *try* < agent, Action >
                      | |
                 SUBJ XCOMP
            [SUBJ = XCOMP SUBJ]

A Raising predicate, in contrast, assigns a grammatical relation to its subject but no semantic role. This fact suggests that the subject of a Raising predicate is not a semantic argument at all. This intuition is supported by the fact that many of the Raising constructions we have discussed in this section can be paraphrased using the EXTRAPOSITION construction, as in (54b):

(54) a   All the girls seem to like John.
     b   It seems [that all the girls like John].

Extraposition involves a dummy subject before the main verb and a sentential complement (S-COMP) after it. Since the dummy subject is clearly not a semantic argument, the only semantic argument in (54b) is the proposition expressed by the S-COMP. Since the two sentences in (54) are highly synonymous, it seems natural that they should have the same basic argument structure.

So the lexical entry for the Raising predicate *seem* (as it is used in 54a) must include two grammatical relations (SUBJ and XCOMP), but only one semantic argument. The SUBJ relation is not associated with any semantic role. We could represent this situation in the following way:

(55)   *seem* < Proposition >   Ø
                      | |
                  XCOMP   SUBJ
            [SUBJ = XCOMP SUBJ]

This entry says that the verb *seem* takes only a single semantic argument, a Proposition, expressed as an XCOMP. The subject in a sentence like (54a) gets no semantic role from *seem*; but it controls the subject of the XCOMP.

The extraposition structure in (54b) involves the same basic argument structure. But in this form, the propositional argument is linked to a finite sentential complement (a *that* clause), rather than an XCOMP; and there is no control relation. Once again, the SUBJ is not associated to a semantic role. This construction corresponds to the lexical entry in (56).

(56)   *seem* < Proposition >   Ø
                       | |
                  S-COMP   SUBJ (*it*)

The systematic relationship between pairs of lexical entries like (55) and (56) could be expressed in terms of a lexical rule.

5.6   Functional vs. anaphoric control

We have defined control as a relationship in which the "missing" subject of a subordinate clause is interpreted as being coreferential with some argument of the matrix clause. The control constructions we have considered thus far involve a single NP functioning as an argument of both the matrix and the subordinate clause at the same time. The shared argument is assigned a grammatical relation by both verbs, and so these two relations are said to be FUNCTIONALLY IDENTIFIED.

As we mentioned in section 5.3, Bresnan (1982b) refers to this pattern as FUNCTIONAL CONTROL. She points out that some languages also allow a different type of control relation, which she refers to as ANAPHORIC CONTROL. In this second pattern, the relationship between the controller and controllee is not functional identification (two grammatical relations assigned to a single argument) but rather anaphora, similar to the relationship between a pronoun and its antecedent. In fact, the controllee in this pattern is best described as being an invisible (or NULL) pronoun.

Following Mohanan (1983b), we will illustrate the difference between these two types of control using the contrast between English participles (functional control) vs. gerunds (anaphoric control). First, the null pronoun controllee in an anaphoric control construction can often be replaced by an overt pronoun (57); but this is typically not possible in a functional control construction (58).

position of the controllee in each example is indicated by "__." Many of
the examples contain a reflexive pronoun which must take the controllee as its
antecedent; the form of the reflexive helps us to identify the controller.)

(57) a   __ Praising himself got John into trouble.
    b   His praising himself got John into trouble.

(58) a   __ Hearing the warning, John dodged the falling brick.
    b   *Him/he hearing the warning, John dodged the falling brick.

Second, an anaphoric control construction can sometimes have no controller
at all, in which case the controllee is interpreted with arbitrary reference (59a–b).
This pattern is sometimes referred to as ARBITRARY CONTROL. In a functional
control relation, however, the arbitrary control interpretation is not available; the
controller is obligatory (59c).

(59) a   __ Praising oneself is frowned upon.
    b   __ Mimicking oneself offends the critics.
    c   *While __ praising oneself/himself, the situation may become ludicrous.

Third, since the controllee in anaphoric control is actually a pronoun, it can
take a controller (or antecedent) which is not an element of the immediate matrix
clause. The controller may be found in some higher clause (60a) or even a separate
sentence (60b). In a functional control relation, however, the controller must be
an argument of the immediate matrix clause (61).

(60) a   John asked his wife to explain to their clients why __ surrendering
           himself/herself/themselves to the police was necessary.
    b   Lord Peter glanced at his watch. __ Presenting himself too soon would
           certainly arouse suspicion.

(61) a   John asked his brother to inform their clients that, while __ surrendering
           herself/*himself/*themselves to the police, Susan had promised to
           cooperate with the investigation.
    b   Lord Peter glanced at his watch. *__ Presenting himself to the duchess, she
           became suspicious.

Fourth, since functional control involves two grammatical relations assigned to
a single argument, the controller is normally identified with a specific grammatical
relation in the matrix clause. The examples in (62) show that the controller of a
bare participial clause must be the subject of the matrix clause. But the controller
in an anaphoric control construction may bear a variety of grammatical relations:
SUBJ (63a), OBJ (63b), or even possessor (63c).

(62) a   __ Addressing himself/*herself to the senate, Nero blamed his mother
           for the fire.
    b   __ Locking herself/*himself in the bedroom, John's wife called the police.

(63) a   John denied __ voting for himself
    b   __ Presenting himself to the duchess got Peter into trouble.
    c   __ Locking his cousins in the basement is Henry's idea of a good joke.

Bresnan also mentions that, in some languages, the controllee in an anaphoric control construction need not be the SUBJ of its clause, although it is normally a term (direct argument). In functional control, however, the controllee is always a grammatical subject.

A final difference relates to the structure of the subordinate clause. In a functional control construction, the subordinate clause has no independent SUBJ; it assigns its SUBJ relation to some argument of the matrix clause. We use the labels XCOMP and XADJ for these "open" complement and adjunct clauses. In an anaphoric control construction, however, the subordinate clause has an independent SUBJ, which happens to be a null pronoun. In this case the subordinate clause is not "open" but fully sentential (S-COMP or S-ADJ), even though the subject may not be visible. But since the construction allows (or requires) an S-COMP or S-ADJ, it may also allow the subordinate clause to contain an overt subject NP as in (64). Thus the null pronoun in anaphoric control may alternate with an overt subject NP, but this is not normally the case with the controllee in a functional control construction (65).

(64) a   John's praising himself always makes me sick.
     b   Microsoft sharing their source code would satisfy the court's demands.

(65) a   While __ defending himself, Arthur committed perjury.
     b   *While Arthur defending himself, Susan committed perjury.

Tagalog is a language which allows both functional control and anaphoric control into complement clauses. Most Equi predicates in Tagalog allow the anaphoric control pattern, in which the controllee must be the agent of the complement clause but need not be the subject. Tagalog has a very rich voice system, similar in many ways to the systems discussed in chapter 11, section 11.5. "Passive" type constructions like that in (66b), in which the agent is not the grammatical subject, are quite common. Crucially, as discussed at length in chapter 11, the genitive agent in these constructions is not demoted to oblique status, but remains a term and so is eligible to be a controllee.

(66) a   H-um-iram   siya   ng=pera   sa=bangko.
           AV.PERF-borrow 3sg.NOM GEN=money DAT=bank
           'He borrowed money from the bank.'

     b   H-in-iram-Ø   niya   ang=pera   sa=bangko.
           PERF-borrow-OV 3sg.GEN NOM=money DAT=bank
           'He borrowed the money from the bank.'
           (lit.: 'The money was borrowed from the bank by him.')

Examples (67–68) illustrate anaphoric control into a complement clause, using "PRO" to represent the null pronoun controllee. The controllee in (67a) is both the agent and the subject of the complement clause, because the complement verb is marked for active voice (AV). The controllee in (67b) is the agent but not the subject, because the complement verb is marked for a non-active voice. The same is true in (68a). In (68b), however, the controllee is the subject but not the agent, and the resulting sentence is ungrammatical.

(67)   (Schachter, 1977:293–294)

   a   Nag-atubili   siya=ng[9]   [h-um-iram PRO$_{\text{NOM}}$ ng=pera   sa=bangko].
       PERF.AV-hesitate 3sg.NOM=COMP AV-borrow   GEN=money DAT=bank
       'He hesitated to borrow money from the bank.'

   b   Nag-atubili   siya=ng   [hiram-in   PRO$_{\text{GEN}}$ ang=pera   sa=bangko].
       PERF.AV-hesitate 3sg.NOM=COMP borrow-OV   NOM=money DAT=bank
       'He hesitated to borrow the money from the bank.'

(68) a   Nag-atubili   si=Maria=ng   [bigy-an PRO$_{\text{GEN}}$ ng=pera   si=Ben].
       PERF.AV-hesitate NOM=Maria=COMP give-DV   GEN=money NOM=Ben
       'Maria hesitated to give money to Ben.'

   b   *Nag-atubili   si=Maria=ng   [bigy-an PRO$_{\text{NOM}}$ ng=pera   ni=Ben].
       PERF.AV-hesitate NOM=Maria=COMP give-DV   GEN=money GEN=Ben
       (intended: 'Maria hesitated to be given money by Ben.')

Examples (67–68) show that the grammatical relation of the controllee is variable, as long as the controllee is the complement's agent. Similarly, example (69) illustrates how the case marking and grammatical relation of the controller (in this case, *Maria*) may vary, depending on the voice marking of the matrix verb. The identity of the controller is determined by the semantics of the specific Equi predicate, so again the semantic role is what is crucial rather than the grammatical relation.

(69) a   B-in-awal-an   ko   si=Maria=ng   [kain-in PRO$_{\text{GEN}}$ ang=litson].
       PERF-forbid-DV 1sg.GEN NOM=Maria=COMP eat-OV   NOM=roast.pig
       'I forbade Maria to eat the *lechon*.'

   b   Nag-bawal   ako   kay=Maria=ng   [kain-in PRO$_{\text{GEN}}$ ang=litson].
       PERF.AV-forbid 1sg.NOM DAT=Maria=COMP eat-OV   NOM=roast.pig
       'I forbade Maria to eat the *lechon*.'

The null pronoun in the complement clause can often be replaced by an overt resumptive pronoun, as in (70). Some speakers find this less natural when the resumptive pronoun is a grammatical subject, as in (70a).

(70) a   Binalak   ni=Miguel   na   [bumili (?siya)   ng=kotse].
       PERF-plan-OV GEN=Miguel COMP AV-buy 3sg.NOM GEN=car
       'Miguel planned to buy a car.'

   b   Binalak   ni=Miguel   na   [bilhin (niya)   ang=bago=ng   kotse].
       PERF-plan-OV GEN=Miguel COMP buy-OV 3sg.GEN NOM=new=LNK car
       'Miguel planned to buy the new car.'

When the complement verb is marked for non-volitive modality, the lexically specified control relation does not apply. This may be due to a clash between the semantic requirements of the Equi predicate and the semantic properties of the non-volitive form. With some Equi predicates this situation creates an "arbitrary control" interpretation: the agent of the complement clause is understood to be some arbitrary person not named in the sentence, as in (71).

(71)　　Nag-atubili　　si=Maria=ng　　　[ma-bigy-an　　PRO_{GEN}
　　　　PERF.AV-hesitate NOM=Maria=COMP INVOL-give-DV
　　　　ng=pera　　si=Ben].
　　　　GEN=money NOM=Ben
　　　　'Maria hesitated for Ben to be given money (by someone).'

　　In addition to the anaphoric control pattern described above, a few Equi predicates also allow a functional control relation. In this pattern, both the controller and the controllee must be the SUBJ of their respective clauses, regardless of the semantic roles involved. Example (72a) cannot be an example of anaphoric control, because the controllee is not the agent of its clause. Notice that both the controller and the controllee bear the SUBJ relation. In (72b), the controller (*Maria*) is a non-subject; for this reason, functional control is impossible and the sentence is ungrammatical. The same contrast is observed in (73).[10]

(72)　　(adapted from Ramos, 1971:132)
　a　Nagpilit　　　　si=Maria=ng　　　[bigy-an __NOM ng=pera　　ni=Ben].
　　　PERF.AV-insist.on NOM=Maria=COMP give-DV　　　GEN=money GEN=Ben
　　　'Maria insisted on being given money by Ben.'

　b　*Pinilit　　　　ni=Maria=ng　　　[bigy-an __NOM ng=pera　　ni=Ben].
　　　PERF-insist.on-OV GEN=Maria=COMP give-DV　　　GEN=money GEN=Ben
　　　(for: 'Maria insisted on being given money by Ben.')

(73) a　H-in-imok　　ng=Tatay　　si=Josie=ng　　　[halik-an __NOM ng=Lola　　　niya].
　　　persuade-OV GEN=father NOM=Josie=LNK kiss-DV　　　GEN=gr.mother her
　　　'Father persuaded Josie to be kissed by her grandmother.'

　b　*Tatay ang　h-um-imok　kay=Josie=ng　　[halik-an __NOM ng=Lola　　　niya].
　　　father NOM persuade-AV DAT=Josie=LNK kiss-DV　　　GEN=gr.mother her
　　　(for: 'It was Father who persuaded Josie to be kissed by her grandmother.')

　　Raising is another construction in Tagalog that involves functional control, and the same constraints apply: both controller and controllee must bear the SUBJ relation. This is illustrated in (74). There is no control relation in (74a); the verb *inasahan* in this example takes a sentential complement (S-COMP). In (74b), the SUBJ of the complement clause is raised into the matrix clause, where it also bears the SUBJ relation. Example (74c) shows that a non-subject agent cannot be raised; that is, the controllee must be a SUBJ. Example (74d) is also ungrammatical, no matter what case marker (represented by "??") is added to the raised argument. The Active Voice marking on the matrix verb *umaasa* requires that the experiencer (*ako*) be the SUBJ of the matrix clause. This means that Raising is impossible, because the raised argument (i.e., the controller) would also have to be the matrix SUBJ, creating a structure which would violate the uniqueness principle.

(74) a   Inasahan   ko   na   [awit-in ni=Linda   ang=pambansang.awit].
           expect-DV I(GEN) COMP   sing-OV GEN=Linda   NOM=national.anthem
           'I expected (for) Linda to sing the national anthem.'

     b   Inasahan   ko   ang=pambansang.awit na   [awit-in ni=Linda   ___NOM].
           expect-DV I(GEN)   NOM=national.anthem   COMP   sing-OV GEN=Linda
           'I expected the national anthem to be sung by Linda.'

     c   *?Inasahan   ko   si=Linda   na   [awit-in ang=pambansang.awit   ___GEN].[11]
           expect-DV I(GEN) NOM=Linda   COMP   sing-OV NOM=national.anthem

     d   *Umaasa   ako   ??=pambansang.awit na   [awit-in ni=Linda   ___NOM].
           AV-expect I(NOM)   ??=national.anthem   COMP   sing-OV GEN=Linda

A critical difference, then, between the two types of control in Tagalog is the way they are determined. Anaphoric control relations are specified on the basis of semantic roles: for most Equi predicates, the controllee must be the agent, while the role of the controller depends on the semantics of the matrix verb. Functional control relations, on the other hand, are specified on the basis of grammatical relations: both controller and controllee must be the SUBJ of their respective clauses.

Exercise 5-A: Transitive Equi and Raising predicates

All of the examples we considered in section 5.5 involved intransitive Equi and Raising predicates. However, transitive predicates of each type exist as well. The following examples illustrate the difference between Equi verbs such as *persuade, order, force, forbid, urge*, etc. and Raising verbs such as *believe, consider, expect, imagine*, etc.

(A1) a   John believed it to be raining.
     b   #John persuaded it to be raining.

(A2) a   John expected there to be a high tide that night.
     b   #John forced there to be a high tide that night.

(A3) a   John expected his guitar to fit into his backpack.
     b   #John persuaded his guitar to fit into his backpack.

(A4) a   Mary expected Dr. Benson to examine John.
     b   Mary expected John to be examined by Dr. Benson.
           (no difference in meaning)

(A5) a   Mary urged/persuaded/ordered Dr. Benson to examine John.
     b   Mary urged/persuaded/ordered John to be examined by Dr. Benson.
           (clear difference in meaning)

(A6) a   Mary considered/believed John's goose to be cooked.
     b   #Mary persuaded/urged/ordered John's goose to be cooked.

(A7) a   Mary persuaded herself to enter the dance contest.

    b   Mary expected herself to win the dance contest.

(A8) a   Doctor Chong was persuaded to examine Mary's son.

    b   Doctor Chong was expected to examine Mary's son.

Task 1: Briefly comment on the significance of each of these examples: what does the data tell us and why?

Task 2: We have already proposed a lexical entry for *persuade* (see 18a). Try to formulate a lexical entry for the transitive Raising verb *believe*. (Note: in [11] above we proposed a lexical entry for the non-Raising usage of this verb.)

Notes

1. The facts illustrated in (5b,c,d) are most naturally interpreted as objecthood properties, and for verbs like *persuade* this conclusion is not controversial. Within the Government-Binding framework a different analysis, based on a special mechanism called "Exceptional Case Marking" (ECM), has been proposed for similar facts in the case of Raising predicates like *expect* and *believe* (see section 5.5). In this book we will assume that the same basic structure is required for both classes of predicates.

2. With some verbs in this class, the complementizer *for* can optionally be deleted; see McCawley (1988) for discussion. For some speakers *hope* and *wish* can also be used in this pattern:

   Mary was hoping for Mrs. Thatcher to resign.
   Many people wish for the war to end.

   Other speakers find such examples unnatural.

3. The infinitival complement selected by verbs like *persuade* and *promise* is a type of predicate complement. The abbreviation XCOMP is motivated by the fact that other verbs (e.g. copular *be*) select predicate complements belonging to other syntactic categories: adjectival, nominal, or prepositional. For some adjectival examples, see section 10.1.6. Some writers have argued that it is necessary to distinguish four types of predicate complement, namely NCOMP, ACOMP, PCOMP, and VCOMP. In this book we follow standard LFG practice in assuming that only one, underspecified label is needed, XCOMP.

4. Gibson (1978).

5. Vamarasi (1999:154, ex. 8.86) cites a possible counter-example to this generalization.

6. We are ignoring here such possible figurative, somewhat humorous, expressions as "It is trying to rain," "It refused to rain," "It pretended to rain," etc.

7. Again, we are ignoring figurative, semi-humorous, expressions such as "Your radio is just asking to be confiscated."

8. The words "falling leaves" here are not to be interpreted as an NP.

9. The clitic =*ng* is the normal form of this complementizer after vowels. After consonants, the allomorph *na* is used.

10. In (73b) a Cleft construction is used in order to make the active voice form of the matrix verb more natural. The sentence becomes grammatical, under anaphoric control, if the complement verb is marked for non-volitive modality: *mahalikan*.

11. Example (74c) becomes grammatical if the gap in the complement clause is replaced with an overt resumptive pronoun. This construction, which is sometimes referred to as "Copy Raising," has different grammatical properties from the type of Raising under discussion here. Some Tagalog speakers do accept examples like (74c), apparently assuming the presence of a null pronoun in the gapped position.

6   Pragmatic functions: topic and focus

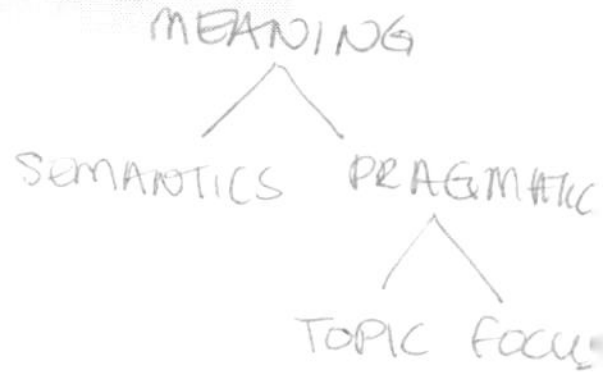

[handwritten marginal note:]
MEANING
SEMANTICS   PRAGMATICS
TOPIC FOCUS

The basic information content of a single sentence is largely determined by the meanings of each individual word, together with the rules for how these word meanings combine into larger units of meaning. But, as each sentence is produced, the speaker also provides various signals about what *kind* of information the various elements in the sentence represent. A given piece of information could be new to the hearer in one context (e.g., at the beginning of a story) but familiar (or known) to the hearer in another context (e.g., at the end of the story). It could be vitally important in one context, but only of marginal or incidental interest in another. These signals help the hearer integrate the various pieces of information into a coherent message.

Variations in word order are often used to make one part of the sentence more prominent than another. Even in a language like English, which has fairly rigid word order, the elements of a sentence can be rearranged in various ways to produce different shades of meaning. Compare the effect of the "basic" word order in sentence (1a) with the "marked" orders in sentences (1b–c):

(1) a   I leave my stamp collection to my youngest brother.
    b   My stamp collection I leave to my youngest brother.
    c   To my youngest brother I leave my stamp collection.

Each of these three sentences contains the same basic information: the same participants play the same roles in the situation, etc. But the information is packaged differently in these three versions. Each version would be appropriate in slightly different contexts, and raises different expectations about what will follow. All three sentences seem to be taken from someone's "last will and testament." The choice among the three versions might depend on how the text as a whole is organized. Sentence (1b) would be appropriate if the will is organized as a list of possessions and their disposal; the next clause could be something like *My bass fiddle I leave to my dear cat Felix*. Sentence (1c), on the other hand, would be more appropriate if the will is organized as a list of heirs and their inheritance; the next clause might be something like *To my sister's children I leave my entire portfolio of stocks and bonds*. Sentence (1a) is relatively neutral, and would probably be acceptable in either context.

In this chapter, we will introduce two basic concepts relating to the packaging of information within sentences, namely TOPIC and FOCUS, and describe some constructions in various languages which are used to mark a topic or focus element for special prominence.

6.1   Pragmatic functions

There are two distinct branches of linguistics which deal with meaning. SEMANTICS (narrowly defined) is the study of word meanings and how they combine in phrases and sentences. PRAGMATICS is the study of how meaning is affected by context.

like fa!

As noted above, every language has ways of indicating whether a particular piece of information is "old" (known to the hearer) or "new" (unknown to the hearer) in a given context. Every language has ways of highlighting certain pieces of information within a sentence as being more significant (or more prominent) than others. Obviously these distinctions are highly dependent on context, and so are a part of the pragmatic rather than semantic content of the sentence. For example, we would probably say that all of the sentences in (1) have the same semantic content, but they are clearly different from one another in terms of their pragmatic structure.

Linguists often refer to two PRAGMATIC FUNCTIONS which elements of a sentence may bear, namely FOCUS and TOPIC. FOCUS can be defined as "the essential piece of new information that is carried by a sentence" (Comrie, 1981). Focus is marked in all languages by intonational prominence (FOCAL STRESS), but in many languages it is also indicated by word order and/or special particles or clitics.

The TOPIC is often defined intuitively as the thing which the sentence is "about." Now, in order to say something about a particular entity, the speaker must assume that the hearer can identify that entity. Thus the topic is normally something that the hearer has some knowledge about. It may be "old information," i.e., something already mentioned in the preceding discourse. It may relate to some kind of shared knowledge, i.e., something in the world which both speaker and hearer already know about (e.g., *the moon* or *the Prime Minister*) or something in the immediate speech context (e.g., *you* or *I*). It may be predictably associated with a known individual, e.g., a body part, close relative, article of clothing, etc. Whatever the mechanism, this is a crucial difference between topic and focus: the focused element is new or unpredictable information at the point in which it appears, while a topic is normally known, predictable, or inferable.

The topic of a sentence, when it is the same as the topic of the preceding sentence, needs no special marking. It can often be referred to with an unstressed pronoun, an agreement marker (as in the "pro-drop" languages), or even by being omitted entirely ("zero anaphora"). But in certain contexts the topic may require more elaborate marking. This may happen when there is a change in topic, a contrast between one topic and another, or a choice among several available topics.

In this chapter we will concentrate on the syntactic effects of topic and focus, rather than their role in discourse. In particular, we will consider certain sentence types in which a particular element is marked for special prominence, and is also associated with a particular pragmatic function. We will refer to these sentences as "marked" topic or focus constructions.

6.2   Marked topic and focus constructions in English

In English, the marked topic or focus element is normally fronted. If the fronted element is a topic, we will refer to the remainder of the sentence as the COMMENT. If the fronted element bears the focus function, we will refer to the remainder of the sentence as the PRESUPPOSITION. Thus the sentence as a whole can be described as having either a topic-comment or focus-presupposition structure.

MARKED USUALLY FRONTED IN ENGLISH

6.2.1   Topic–comment constructions

Some examples of topic–comment sentences are given in (2) through (4). In all three constructions, the marked topic phrase (underlined) is followed by a comment which presents new information about that topic.

(2)   **Contrastive Topic:**
a   This ice cream I like(, but the stuff we had yesterday was awful).
b   (Your mother is all right, but) your sister I can't stand.
c   John we managed to rescue; his dog we never found.
d   To Mary he gave a golden locket, but to the rest of the children he gave only ribbons and paper dolls.
e   Out of his pocket John pulled a crumpled $100 bill.

selects one topic from a list of topics

(3)   **Left-Dislocation:**
a   My friend John, a snake bit him on the hand and he lost three fingers.
b   This man that I know, his wife won $1 million in the lottery.

begins a new story in discourse or introduces new topic for discussion

(4)   **External Topic:**
a   As for John, a python swallowed his dog.
b   As for Clinton, most of the voters still don't trust him.
c   As for Manila, the traffic is unbelievable.

signals return to previous topic or inferred topic

These three constructions are similar, in that they all follow the general topic–comment pattern, but there are important structural differences among them. Perhaps the most striking of these is the fact that the CONTRASTIVE TOPIC construction in (2) contains a "gap" (i.e., a missing element; see chapter 7) in the body of the clause (the comment). The topic phrase is interpreted as bearing the grammatical relation which corresponds to this gap. For example, *John* in (2c) is interpreted as the OBJ of *rescue*, and *to Mary* in (2d) is interpreted as the oblique recipient of *gave*. (Linguists often speak of the topic phrase in such a construction as having been "extracted" from its normal position.) But in the LEFT-DISLOCATION and EXTERNAL TOPIC constructions, shown in (3) and (4) respectively, there is no gap in the comment clause, and the topic phrase is not assigned a grammatical relation. In these constructions, the comment clause frequently contains a pronoun which takes the topic phrase as its antecedent. This pronoun is called a RESUMPTIVE PRONOUN. However, there is no resumptive pronoun in (4c). In this example, the relationship between topic and comment is purely semantic, with no overt grammatical marking.

In addition to their structural differences, the three constructions also have somewhat different functions. All three of them are used to signal a change in discourse topic. (A discourse topic which does not change, i.e., which is continuing from the preceding clause, would typically be expressed in English with an unstressed pronoun.) However, they are not interchangeable; each would be appropriate in certain contexts, but not in others.

The Contrastive Topic construction, which is often referred to simply as "topicalization," frequently has the effect of selecting one topic from among a set of possible topics. The sentences in (1b) and (1c) are both examples of the Contrastive Topic construction, but they differ in terms of the topic set from which the new topic is chosen. In (1b), the topic set is the set of things to be inherited, while in (1c), the topic set is the set of heirs. Left-Dislocation has a number of different uses. In informal or conversational speech it is frequently used to begin a new story or section of discourse, and to introduce the proposed topic for discussion.[1] The External Topic construction might be used to signal a return to a previously mentioned or inferred topic.

6.2.2 Focus–presupposition constructions

Some examples of marked focus constructions are shown in (5) and (6). In a CLEFT SENTENCE (or "*it*-cleft"), shown in (5), the focused element is preceded by a dummy subject (*it*) plus the copular verb *be* and followed by a complement clause. The focused constituent contains information which is new or unpredictable in a particular context, while the clause which follows it contains old or presupposed information. Thus the structure of the sentence as a whole is focus-presupposition. In the PSEUDO-CLEFT (or "Wh-cleft") construction shown in (6), the focused constituent appears at the end of the sentence, with the presupposition stated in an initial interrogative clause.[2]

(5)   **Clefting:**
a   It was <u>Mary</u> that John gave the flowers to(, not Susan).
b   It is <u>the Permanent Secretary</u> who will visit us(, not the Minister).
c   It was <u>on this very spot</u> that Gen. Lee surrendered to Gen. Grant in 1865.

(6)   **Pseudo-Clefts:**
a   What John gave to Mary was <u>a bunch of flowers</u>(, not a diamond ring).
b   What I like for breakfast is <u>cold pizza</u>.

Another construction which involves a focused element is the content question. Content questions involve a request for a specific piece of new information. The question word bears pragmatic focus, since it specifies the crucial piece of new information which is required; the rest of the question is part of the presupposition. (Since question words in English are normally fronted, content questions involve a focus–presupposition pattern.) Similarly in the answer to a question, the word or phrase which corresponds to the question word will bear the focus function; other participants, being part of the presupposition, will normally be pronominalized.

(7) a   <u>What</u> did John give his mother for her birthday?
    b   He gave her <u>a jade necklace</u>.

The beginning of a sentence is a highly prominent position, and is used for both marked topics and focused elements in many languages. However, this is by no means a universal pattern. A number of languages have distinct positions for topic and focus. In Hungarian, for example, a focused element must immediately precede the finite verb, while a sentence topic, if there is one, will occur in sentence initial position, preceding the focus. Everything else in the sentence follows the verb. Comrie (1981:57) shows that in Hungarian, both a question word and its answer must appear in the focus position, as we would expect, immediately preceding the verb.

6.3   Structural representation

In sentences (2a–c), we noted that the fronted element has two functions in the sentence: it is simultaneously a topic and a direct object. Topic and focus are sometimes referred to as "overlay functions," because they are typically assigned <u>in addition to</u> some other clause-level function in this way. That is, the topic or focus element bears its pragmatic function in the sentence <u>in addition to</u> a clause-level grammatical relation.

A simple phrase structure analysis for example (2a) is given in (8a). The functional structure of this topic–comment sentence might be represented as in (8b). This diagram indicates that the fronted constituent bears both the topic function, by virtue of its structural position, and the OBJ relation, which is required by the subcategorization of the verb *like*.

(8) a   *This ice cream I like.*

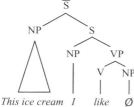

b
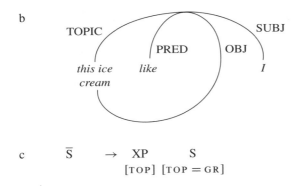

c $\overline{\text{S}}$ →   XP   S
                  [TOP] [TOP = GR]

The Contrastive Topic construction in (8a–b) could be licensed by a phrase structure rule similar to that shown in (8c). The annotation of this rule means that a topic phrase of any category ("XP") is identified with some grammatical relation ("GR") in the clause that follows. As it stands, this annotation is both too restrictive and too general;[3] however, it provides a basic idea of the kind of rule that is needed. As we will see in the next chapter, different languages impose different constraints on this kind of construction, which can be captured by replacing the "GR" with something more specific.

The structure of a content question like (7a), the simplest of the focus-presupposition constructions we have discussed thus far, is shown in (9). The "inversion" of the subject NP with the first auxiliary element in English questions (and certain other constructions) is a very interesting phenomenon, but we will not be able to discuss it in any detail here.[4] For present purposes, we will simply assume that English has a special "inverted" clause type in which a single auxiliary precedes the subject, as suggested in (9a).

The functional structure in (9b) is very similar to that proposed in (8b). The fronted question word *what* bears the focus function. In this case it is a secondary object (OBJ_2) which is missing from the body of the clause, so this is the grammatical relation which is assigned to the focus phrase. Again, a somewhat simplified PS rule is given in (9c).

(9) a   *What did John give his mother?*

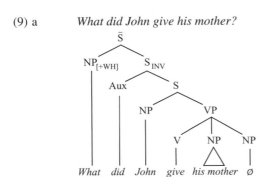

b

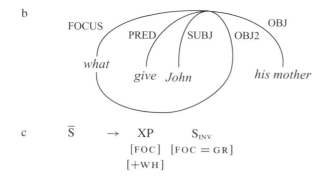

c $\bar{\text{S}}$ →   XP S_{INV}
                 [FOC]   [FOC = GR]
                 [+WH]

6.4   Basic word order

We have said that "marked" (or special) word order is often used to indicate pragmatic topic or focus. More generally, variations in word order are usually motivated by discourse or pragmatic factors. But we cannot recognize marked word orders unless we know the "unmarked," or basic, word order.

In a language like English it is not too difficult to determine the basic order, at least with regard to the major constituents of the clause (SVO, followed by oblique arguments and complement clauses). But other languages allow much more freedom of word order than English. How then can we decide which of the possible orders for a particular sentence type is the most "basic"? The following criteria can help us make this decision; see also chapter 11 for further discussion of MARKEDNESS.

a   **frequency**: the basic order is usually the most frequently used in discourse.

b   **mood, polarity, and voice**: basic sentences are normally indicative (statements, not questions or commands) and positive (not negated). In most theories of grammar, active sentences are also assumed to be more basic than passive.

c   **distribution**: marked sentence types tend to be appropriate only in certain specific contexts. Neutral word order is generally the order that has the widest distribution, i.e., which can occur in the greatest number of different contexts.

d   **avoid pronouns**: pronouns often have special word order properties, so basic word order should be based on the order of full NP and PP arguments.

e   **subordinate clauses take priority**: in many languages, main clauses allow more variation in word order than subordinate clauses. Thus if we observe special restrictions on word order within subordinate clauses, these restrictions may reflect the most basic word-order pattern for that language.

interesting

6.5   Topic and focus in other languages

6.5.1   Topicalization in Mandarin Chinese

Mandarin Chinese is often described as a "topic-prominent" language.[5] Chinese has almost no inflectional morphology, and so the word order is fairly rigid. The most basic word order is SVO, and any element which occurs before the subject is normally referred to as a "topic." A topic phrase may optionally be separated from the rest of the sentence by a pause, or by one of the topic-marking particles: *a, me, ne,* or *ba.* However, Li and Thompson (1981) state that these particles are rarely used in spoken Mandarin. Some examples of the topic–comment sentence pattern, with topic phrases underlined, are presented in (10).[6]

(10) a   zhèi-ge   zì   wǒ bù rènshì.
         this-CLASS character I not recognize
         'This character (i.e., word) I don't recognize.'

  b   nèi-kē   shù yèzi hěn dà.
      that-CLASS tree leaf very big
      'That tree, (its) leaves are very big.'

  c   zuótiān   tā 12 diǎnzhōng shuìjiào.
      yesterday he 12 o'clock   sleep
      'Last night, he went to bed at 12 o'clock.' (Xu and Langendoen, 1985:19)

  d   wǔ-ge   píngguǒ liǎng-ge   huài le.
      five-CLASS apples   two-CLASS spoil PERF
      '(Of) the five apples, two are spoiled.'

The element which occupies this sentence-initial topic position has several properties which are characteristic of pragmatic topics. First, the topic element may be definite or generic, as in (11a–b), but not indefinite (11c). This follows from the fact that a topic is generally something which the speaker assumes that the hearer knows about.

(11) a   gǒu wǒ yǐjing   kàn-guo le.
         dog I   already see-PAST PERF
           (i) 'The dog I have already seen.'
           (ii) 'Dogs (generic) I have already seen.'
           (iii) but not: *'A dog I have already seen.'

  b   nèi-zhī   gǒu wǒ yǐjing   kàn-guo le.
      that-CLASS dog I   already see-PAST PERF
      'That dog I have already seen.'

  c   *yi-zhī   gǒu wǒ yǐjing   kàn-guo le.
      one-CLASS dog I   already see-PAST PERF
      *'A dog I have already seen.'

Second, a question word may not appear in topic position, as illustrated in (12). This follows from the fact that a question word must bear pragmatic focus, which is incompatible with the topic function.

(12)   *shénme tā chī le?   (Tan, 1991:179)
           what   he eat PTCLE
          *'What he ate (it)?'

Third, the topic phrase establishes what the rest of the sentence is "about."[7] The following examples (from Guo, 1995:136) involve coordinate sentences expressing a comparison between two things. In each case, the topic phrase at the beginning of the sentence establishes the discourse topic for both of the conjoined clauses that follow. If the topic is a particular speaker, we can compare his levels of fluency in two languages (13a). If the topic is a particular language, we can compare the fluency of two speakers (13b). But sentence (13c) is incoherent, because the second clause has nothing to do with the sentence topic.

(13) a   <u>LǐSì</u> Zhōngwén hěn hǎo, Yīngwén yě   kěyǐ.
          LiSi Chinese   very good English also can
          'As for Li Si, his Chinese is very good. His English is also OK.'

     b   <u>Zhōngwén</u> LǐSì hěn hǎo, Zhāngsān bù tài hǎo.
          Chinese   LiSi very good ZhangSan not too good
          'As for Chinese, Li Si is very good but Zhang San is not very good.'

     c   ??<u>Zhōngwén</u> LǐSì hěn hǎo, Yīngwén yě   kěyǐ.
          Chinese   LiSi very good English also can
          'As for Chinese, Li Si is very good. His English is also OK.'

An interesting feature of Chinese is that a single clause may have more than one topic phrase, as illustrated in (14). This is frequently less acceptable in some other languages, as the awkwardness of the English translations for these examples suggests.

(14) a   <u>Lǐ xiānsheng</u> zuótiān   wǒ kànjiàn le.
          Li Mr.   yesterday I see   PERF
          'Mr. Li, yesterday I saw (him).' (Xu and Langendoen, 1985:17)

     b   <u>zhè-jiàn   shì</u>   <u>Lǐ</u> xiānsheng wǒ gàosu guo.
          this-CLASS matter Li Mr.   I inform PAST
          'This matter, Mr. Li, I have told (him) about.' (Xu and Langendoen, 1985:17)

6.5.1.1   Topicalization of objects

As the examples in (10) suggest, a variety of different elements may appear in the topic position. The structure of the topic–comment sentence depends in part on the grammatical relation of the topic phrase. One common pattern, illustrated in (10a), is the topicalization of a direct object. Two more examples of this type are presented in (15).

(15) a   Zhèi-běn xiǎoshuō Zhāngsān kàn wán le.
          this   novel   Zhangsan read finish PERF
          'This novel Zhangsan has finished reading.'

     b   Júzi   wǒ bu chī le.
          orange I   not eat PERF
          'Oranges I don't eat.' or: 'The orange I will not eat.'

These sentences seem quite similar to the Contrastive Topic construction in English, which was illustrated in (2a–c). In these examples, the comment clause by itself looks incomplete because the verb seems to lack a direct object; but in fact the topicalized NP bears the direct object relation. The structure of these sentences could be represented as in (16).

(16)   (= example 15a)

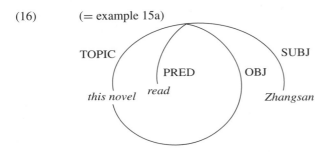

6.5.1.2   Topicalization of possessors, OBJ$_2$, OBL, etc.

Example (10b) involves the topicalization of a possessor. This pattern is extremely common in Chinese; some additional examples are presented in (17a–c). In each of these sentences, the topic phrase is interpreted as the possessor of the subject NP. Tan (1991) shows that this construction is actually ambiguous: in addition to the topic–comment structure which we are interested in, the possessor NP plus the following noun could also be interpreted as a single NP, because the possessive particle *de* is optional; this possibility is shown in (17d). In order unambiguously to specify the topic–comment sentence pattern, the topic phrase can be separated from the rest of the sentence by a pause, or by one of the topic-marking particles as in (17e). Of course, when the possessor of an element of a subordinate clause is topicalized, as in (17f), the result is unambiguously a topic–comment sentence.

(17) a   zhèi-ge   nǚhái yǎnjing hěn dà.
          this-CLASS girl   eye   very big
          'This girl, her eyes are very big.'

     b   Zhāngsān nǚ-péngyǒu duō.
          Zhangsan girlfriend   many
          'As for Zhangsan, his girlfriends are many.'

c   <u>xiàng</u>   bízi   cháng.
        elephant nose long
        'As for elephants, their noses are long.'

d   [[zhèi-ge   nǚhái]$_{NP}$ (de) yǎnjing]$_{NP}$ hěn dà.
        this-CLASS girl   POSS eye   very big
        'This girl's eyes are very big.'

e   <u>zhèi-ge</u>   <u>nǚhái</u> ne, yǎnjing hěn dà.
        this-CLASS girl   TOP eye   very big
        'This girl, her eyes are very big.'

f   <u>zhèi-ge</u>   <u>rén</u>   wǒ juéde jìxing tèbié   hǎo.
        this-CLASS person I   feel   memory exceptionally good
        'As for this man, I feel that (his) memory is extremely good.'
        (Xu and Langendoen, 1985:19)

Xu and Langendoen (1985:25) point out that possessors of non-subjects can also be topicalized, but a different strategy is required. The examples in (18) all contain the same possessed NP: 'these people's children.' This phrase occurs as a subject in (18a), but as an object in (18b–c). Example (19a) shows that the possessor of the subject can be topicalized using the same construction illustrated in (17) and (10b). However, the possessors of non-subjects can only be topicalized if a resumptive pronoun is left within the NP (19b–c). If these pronouns were not present, the examples would be ungrammatical.[8]

(18) a   zhé-xiē   rén   de   zǐnǚ   zài Harvard shàng xúe.
         this-CLASS person POSS children at Harvard attend school
         'These people's children go to school at Harvard.'

    b   Harvard lùqǔ   le   zhé-xiē   rén   de   zǐnǚ.
         Harvard accept PERF this-CLASS person POSS children
         'Harvard accepted these people's children.'

    c   Wáng lǎoshī jiāo zhé-xiē   rén   de   zǐnǚ   zhōngwén.
         Wang prof. teach this-CLASS person POSS children Chinese
         'Prof. Wang teaches these people's children Chinese.'

(19) a   zhé-xiē   rén,   Ø zǐnǚ   zài Harvard shàng xúe.
         this-CLASS person Ø children at Harvard attend school
         'These people, (their) children go to school at Harvard.'

    b   zhé-xiē   rén,   Harvard lùqǔ le   <u>tāmen</u> de   zǐnǚ.
         this-CLASS person Harvard accept PERF 3pl   POSS children
         'These people, Harvard accepted their children.'

    c   zhé-xiē   rén,   Wáng lǎoshī jiāo <u>tāmen</u> de   zǐnǚ   zhōngwén.
         this-CLASS person Wang prof. teach 3pl   POSS children Chinese
         'These people, Prof. Wang teaches their children Chinese.'

Another example of a topicalized possessor is given in (20a). Resumptive pronouns can also be used to topicalize secondary objects, objects of prepositions or serial verbs, etc. Some examples are presented in (20b–e). However, there appears to be a significant degree of dialect variation with respect to the conditions under which resumptive pronouns are permitted or required. Some speakers find examples like (20d–e) more natural in a contrastive context, e.g., where there is implied contrast with other members of the group under discussion.

(20)   (Xu and Langendoen, 1985; Koshimizu, 1985)

a   Cáo Yú wǒ xǐhuan tā de jùbèn, bù xǐhuan tā de shīgē.
     Cao Yu I like his LNK play NEG like his LNK poem
     'Cao Yu, I like his plays but not his poems.'

b   Wú xiānsheng wǒ gěi le tā liǎng běn shū.
     Wu Mr.   I give PERF him two CLASS book
     'Mr. Wu, I gave him two books.'

c   Lǐ xiānsheng wǒ chúle tā méi rén rènshi.
     Li Mr.   I except him NEG person know
     'Mr. Li, except for him I don't know anyone.'

d   Zhè bǎ   dāo, wǒ yòng tā qiē ròu.
     this CLASS knife I use it cut meat
     'As for this knife, I use it to cut meat.'

e   Nǐ shuó de nèi.ge tóng-xué, tā zài nǎr?
     you say REL that class-mate he at where
     'That classmate you mentioned, where is he?'

In sentences like those in (17), the topic phrase is identified with the possessor of the subject NP. The structure of this construction is shown in (21).

(21)   (= example 17a)

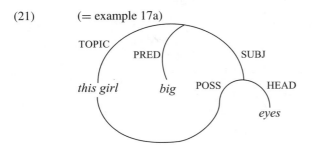

In a sentences like (19b–c), however, the topic phrase is not assigned a grammatical relation within the clause. Rather, the topic functions as the antecedent of the resumptive pronoun, which is contained in some non-subject NP in the body of the clause. This anaphoric relationship is represented in (22) by CO-INDEXING the possessive pronoun with the topic.

(22)   (= example 20a)

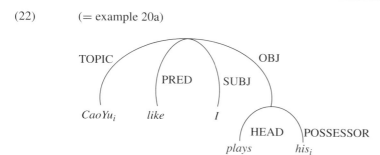

6.5.1.3   Adjunct topics vs. "dangling topics"

Examples (10c–d) seem in many ways very similar. They do not contain resumptive pronouns, yet there is no obvious gap in the comment clause. In (10c) the topic is an adjunct, specifically an adverbial time expression. It is not surprising that the comment clause in this sentence does not seem incomplete, since adjuncts can be freely added or omitted. Some further examples of adjunct topics are given in (23).

(23) a   <u>nèi</u> <u>kuài</u> <u>tián</u>, dàozi zhǎngde hěn dà.
             that piece land rice   grow   very big
             '(On) that piece of land, the rice grows very big.'

    b   <u>shàng-ge</u>   <u>yuè</u>   tiānqi   fēichang   mèn.
             last-CLASS month weather extremely humid
             'Last month the weather was extremely humid.'

    c   <u>zài</u> <u>Táiběi</u> kéyi chī de   hěn hǎo.
             at Taipei can eat ADVBL very good
             'In Taipei one can eat very well.'

The relationship of the topic phrase in (10d) to the clause which follows it is somewhat harder to characterize. In this sentence the topic names a set or domain ('five apples') of which the subject ('two [apples]') is a subset. Some similar examples of "domain topics" are presented in (24a–b). In other cases, the topic phrase may name a point of comparison between two things, as in (24c), or an activity about which the following clause makes some comment, as in (24d). So a wide variety of things may appear in topic position, provided that it is "relevant" in some way to the clause which follows. A topic that has no apparent connection to the rest of the sentence, such as (24e), is ungrammatical. Xu and Langendoen (1985), Tan (1991), and Shi (2000), among others, have tried to define this "relevance" constraint in a more precise way, but this is a complex issue which we will not address here.

(24) a   <u>shuǐguǒ</u> tā zuì   xǐhuan píngguǒ. (Xu and Langendoen, 1985:19)
             fruit   he most like   apple
             'As for fruit, he likes apples best.'

    b   <u>miàn</u> wǒ zuì   xǐhuān chī là   de.
           noodle I   most like   eat   spicy NMLZR
           'Noodles, I like to eat spicy (ones) best.'

    c   <u>wùjià</u> Dōngjīng bǐ   Běijīng guì.
           price Tokyo   than Beijing expensive
           'As for prices, Tokyo is more expensive than Beijing.'
           (Chen, 1996, ex. 21a)

    d   <u>zhù</u>, Táiběi zuì   fāngbiàn;   <u>chī</u>, háishi Xiānggǎng hǎo.
           live Taipei most convenient eat still   Hong Kong good
           'Housing, Taipei is most convenient; eating, Hong Kong is still better.'

    e   *<u>zhè-jiàn</u>   <u>shì</u>,   wǒ dǎ le   tā.
           this-CLASS matter I   hit PERF him
           *'This matter, I hit him.'

The topic phrases in (24a–d) do not bear any grammatical relation to the clause that follows; rather, the link between the topic and its comment seems to be purely semantic or conceptual. This kind of topic is sometimes called a "dangling topic," because it is not grammatically linked to the rest of the sentence. We will argue that the structure of the examples in (24) is different from that of adjunct topics like those in (23). One piece of evidence for this is that the topic phrases in (10d) and (24a–d) could not occur as the head of a relative clause, whereas this is possible for most other topics. (Relative clauses will be discussed in more detail in chapter 7.)

Chen (1996) and Shi (2000) point out that most but not all topics can be relativized; this pattern is illustrated in (25). In sentence (25a) (repeated from 10a) the topic phrase is the direct object. The corresponding relative clause is shown in (25b). Note in particular that the grammatical relation assigned to the head noun in (25b) is identical to that of the topic NP in (25a). Both possessor topics (26) and adjunct topics (27–29) can be relativized in the same way.

(25) a   <u>zhèi-ge</u>   <u>zì</u>   wǒ bù rènshì.
        this-CLASS character I   not recognize
        'This character (i.e., word) I don't recognize.'

    b   [wǒ bù rènshì   de] zì
        I   not recognize REL character
        'the character that I don't recognize'

(26) a   <u>nèi-kē</u>   <u>shù</u> yèzi hěn dà.
        that-CLASS tree leaf very big
        'That tree, (its) leaves are very big.'

    b   [yèzi hěn dà de] shù
        leaf very big REL tree
        'a/the tree whose leaves are very big'

(27) a   <u>shàng-ge</u>   <u>yuè</u> tiānqi fēicháng mèn.
        last-CLASS month weather extremely humid
        'Last month the weather was extremely humid.'

b   [tiānqi fēichang mèn de] yuè
     weather extremely humid REL month
     'the month when the weather was extremely humid'

(28) a   zài Táiběi kéyi chī de   hěn hǎo.
          at Taipei can eat ADVBL very good
          'In Taipei one can eat very well.'

     b   [kéyi chī de   hěn hǎo de] dìfāng
          can   eat ADVBL very good REL place
          'the place where one can eat very well'

(29) a   nèi kuài tián, dàozi zhǎngde hěn dà.
          that piece land rice   grow   very big
          '(On) that piece of land, the rice grows very big.'

     b   [dàozi zhǎngde hěn dà de] tián
          rice   grow   very big REL land
          'land on which the rice grows very big'

However, "dangling topics" cannot be relativized in this way. Example (30), adapted from Tan (1991:34), illustrates this. The topic phrase in (30a) names a domain, specifically a set of people, while the subject NP names a subset of the domain. In (30b) this topic is expressed as the head of a relative clause, but the result is ungrammatical. Similar results are demonstrated for other "dangling topics" in (31–32).

(30) a   zhé-xiē   rén,   sān-ge   shì wǒ-de péngyou.
          this-CLASS person three-CLASS be my   friend
          '(Among) these people, three are my friends.' (Tan, 1991:34)

     b   *[sān-ge   shì wǒ-de péngyou de] rén
          three-CLASS be my   friend   REL person
          (for: 'people among whom three are my friends')

(31) a   shǔiguǒ wǒ zuì   xǐhuan xiāngjiāo.
          fruit   I   most like   banana
          '(Among all) fruits, I like bananas best.' (Shi, 2000, ex. 55)

     b   *[wǒ zuì   xǐhuan xiāngjiāo de] shǔiguǒ
          I   most like   banana REL fruit
          *'the fruit that I like bananas best'

(32) a   wùjià Dōngjīng bǐ   Běijīng guì.
          price Tokyo   than Beijing expensive
          'As for prices, Tokyo is more expensive than Beijing.'
          (Chen, 1996, ex. 21)

     c   *[Dōngjīng bǐ   Běijīng guì   de] wùjià
          Tokyo   than Beijing expensive REL price
          *'the prices that Tokyo is more expensive than Beijing'

So we see that, in spite of superficial similarities between examples like (10c) and (10d), "dangling topics" have different structural properties from adjunct topics. We suggested above that the crucial difference lies in the fact that adjuncts are grammatically related to the comment clause, whereas "dangling topics" are not. This structural difference can be represented as in (33). The diagram in (33a) shows a topic phrase which is also a locative adjunct, as in (23a). The diagram in (33b) shows a domain topic which has no other grammatical function within the sentence, as in (24a).

(33) a　　　(= example 23a)

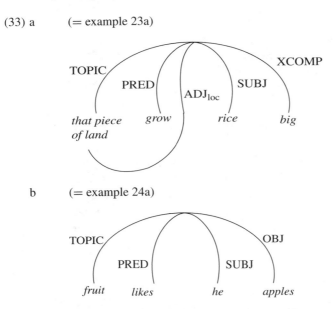

b　　　(= example 24a)

We have proposed a distinction between two different types of topics in Chinese, which we might refer to as normal topics and "dangling topics." We have seen that normal topics employ two different topicalization strategies, which differ in terms of how the topic phrase is related to the body of the clause. In the extraction strategy, the linkage is functional: the topic phrase bears a clause-level grammatical relation in addition to its pragmatic function. In the resumptive pronoun strategy, the linkage is anaphoric: the topic phrase functions as the antecedent of a pronoun within the comment clause. "Dangling topics" employ a third strategy. In this construction the linkage is primarily semantic: the topic phrase defines what the sentence is "about," but does not seem to have any grammatical function within the comment clause.

6.5.2　Topic marker in Japanese

Sentence topics in Chinese are identified primarily on the basis of word order, i.e., by their sentence-initial position. In Japanese, however, topics are marked by a special particle, *wa*.

Japanese is an SOV language with four case-marking particles: *ga* 'NOM,' *o* 'ACC,' *ni* 'DAT/LOC,' *no* 'GEN.' The topic marker *wa* appears most often on the subject of a clause, but can occur on other arguments as well, as in (34b–d). The constituent which is marked as topic frequently occurs in initial position, although this is not a requirement. In this and other respects, Japanese word order is much freer than Chinese. When the topic is an argument which would otherwise take NOM or ACC case marking, the topic marker *wa* replaces the normal case marker, as seen in (34a–b).[9]

(34) a   Taroo=wa   sono hon=o   yondeiru.
          Taroo=TOP that   book=ACC reading
          'Taroo is reading that book.'

     b   Sono hon=wa   Taroo=ga   yondeiru.
          that   book=TOP Taroo=NOM reading
          'That book, Taroo is reading.'

     c   Hongoo=ni=wa   Toodai=ga   arimasu.
          Hongoo=LOC=TOP U.of.Tokyo=NOM exist
          'In Hongoo is the University of Tokyo.'

     d   Nihon kara=wa   Tanaka sensei=ga   mieta.
          Japan from=TOP Tanaka Prof.=NOM came
          'From Japan came Prof. Tanaka.'

Let us review some of the linguistic evidence for identifying *wa* as a topic marker. First, as we have seen, topics must be something which the hearer can identify. Thus in Japanese, as in Chinese, the topic element may be generic as in (35a), or definite as in (35b); but not indefinite (35c–d).

(35) a   Kuzira=wa   honyuu-doobutu desu. (GENERIC)
          whale=TOP mammal   is
          'A whale is a mammal.'

     b   Zyon=wa   watakusi=no tomodati desu. (DEFINITE)
          John=TOP 1sg=GEN   friend   is
          'John is my friend.'

     c   Dareka={ga/*wa}   kimasita. (NON-GENERIC and
          someone=NOM/*TOP came   INDEFINITE)
          'Someone has come.'

     d   *Oozei=no   hito=wa   paatii=ni   kimasita. (NON-GENERIC and
          many=GEN people=TOP party=DAT came   INDEFINITE)
          (for: 'Many people came to the party.')

Second, we have noted that the question word in content questions takes pragmatic focus. It represents the crucial new piece of information. Since topic and focus are mutually exclusive, a question word should not be able to occur in a topic position. As we would predict, there is a well-known constraint in Japanese

which states that a question word can never be marked with *wa*; this is illustrated
in (36a) and (37a). The same holds for the part of the answer which corresponds
to the question word, as illustrated in (36b) and (37b).[10]

(36) a Dare={ga/*wa}   kimasita ka?
        who=NOM/*TOP   came   Q
        'Who came?'

     b Taroo={ga/*wa}   kimasita.
        Taroo=NOM/*TOP came
        'Taroo came.'

(37) a Dare={o/*wa}   Taroo=ga[11] mimasita ka?
        who=ACC/*TOP   Taroo   saw   Q
        'Who did Taroo see?'

     b Hanako={o/*wa}   mimasita.
        Hanako=ACC/*TOP saw
        '(He) saw Hanako.'

In main clauses, the subject is normally marked by *wa* unless some other
constituent is marked as a topic. Therefore when the subject takes the nominative
case marker *ga* rather than *wa*, in the absence of some other topic phrase, it
normally indicates that the subject NP is not an eligible topic for some reason.
Kuno (1973) identifies two basic uses of *ga* in this context: either it marks the
subject in a "neutral" clause, i.e., one which contains entirely new information, or
it marks a subject which gets contrastive focus. Kuno refers to this second usage
as the "exhaustive listing" sense, meaning that the subject NP names the only
individual(s) among a certain class for which the predicate is true.

(38) a Zyon=ga mainiti   gakkoo=ni   iku. (EXHAUSTIVE LISTING)
        John   every.day school=DAT goes
        'It is John who goes to school every day.'
        (Among those under discussion, only John goes to school every day.)

     b Taihen da!   Zyon=ga/*wa zisatusita. (NEW INFO.)
        good.heavens John   killed-self
        'Oh, my goodness! John has committed suicide!'

     c Oya, ame=ga/*wa hutte   iru. (NEW INFO.)
        oh   rain   falling is
        'Oh, it is raining.'

Kuno states that when there is only one person under discussion (i.e., a unique,
known topic), *ga* would be ungrammatical; *wa* must be used instead. For example,
in a connected discourse which begins with sentence (39a), the speaker would
never continue with (39b), using *ga*, but would use (39c) instead:

(39) a Zyon=ga   tazunete kimasita.
        John=NOM visiting came

b   *{Zyon/kare}=ga omiyage=ni   kudamono=o kuremasita.
      John/he =NOM   present=DAT fruits=ACC   gave-me

*[handwritten: no need for ga
because info is not here]*

c   {Zyon/kare}=wa omiyage=ni   kudamono=o kuremasita.
      John/he =TOP   present=DAT fruits=ACC   gave-me
      'John called on me. John/he gave me fruits as a present.'

However, when there are several people under discussion (i.e., several available topics), *ga* can be used to select one from among this set of available topics, as in the following short discourse. Sentence (40b) implies that, out of the three visitors, it was only John who brought a gift of fruit.

(40) a   Zyon to   Marii to   Biru=ga   tazunete kimasita.
            John and Mary and Bill=NOM visiting came

     b   Zyon=ga   omiyage=ni   kudamono=o kuremasita.
            John=NOM present=DAT fruits=ACC   gave-me
            'John, Mary, and Bill called on me. John gave me fruits as a present.'

Kuno also points out that subject "deletion" (or zero anaphora) is only possible for subjects which would otherwise be marked with *wa*, and not for those that would be marked with *ga*. This is consistent with our earlier observation that zero-anaphora is frequently used for continuing topics in discourse. In the second clause of (41a), for example, the subject pronoun is marked by *wa*, and so could be omitted as in (41b). In the context of the question in (42a), it would be more natural for the subject of (42b) to be marked with *ga* instead of *wa*. Thus (42c) is not a possible answer to the same question, because a pronoun marked with *ga* cannot be omitted.

(41) a   Boku=ga ikite iru uti wa, boku={wa/*ga} kare=ni   sonna koto=o   sasenai.
            I=NOM   alive am while I   him=DAT such thing=ACC let-do-not
            'As long as I am alive, I will not let him do such a thing.'

     b   Boku=ga ikite iru uti wa, Ø kare=ni   sonna koto=o   sasenai.
            I=NOM   alive am while   him=DAT such thing=ACC let-do-not
            'As long as I am alive, I will not let him do such a thing.'

(42) a   Dare=ga   bosu=ni   naru=no?
            who=NOM boss=DAT become=INTERROG
            'Who will become the boss?'

     b   Boku=ga ikite iru uti wa, boku={?wa/ga} kono kaisya=no   bosu da.
            I=NOM   alive am while I   this company=GEN boss am
            'As long as I am alive, I am the boss of this company.'

     c   *Boku=ga ikite iru uti wa, Ø kono kaisya=no   bosu da.
            I=NOM   alive am while   this company=GEN boss am

In addition to the usage illustrated in the above examples, which involve what Kuno calls the thematic topic, Kuno states that there is another use of *wa* which we might refer to as the "Contrastive Topic" use. These two uses are distinguished partly on the basis of intonation: NPs which take the contrastive *wa*, like the subject NPs in (43b), are pronounced with "prominent intonation," i.e., contrastive emphasis (shown below with capital letters), whereas normal ("thematic") topics like the subject in (43a) are not.

(43) a   Zyon=wa sono hon=o   yonda.
          John=TOP that book=ACC read
          'Speaking of John, he read that book.'

    b   ZYON=wa sono hon=o   yonda ga, MARII=wa yomanakatta.
          John=TOP that book=ACC read but Mary=TOP did.not.read
          'John read that book, but Mary didn't.'

But there are some grammatical differences as well. For example, certain indefinite NPs which could not occur as normal topics do occur in the Contrastive Topic construction. This is illustrated in (44).

(44) a   *Oozei=no   hito=wa   paatii=ni   kimasita.
          many=GEN people=TOP party=DAT came
          (for: 'Many people came to the party.')

    b   Oozei=no   hito=wa   paatii=ni   kimasita ga,
          many=GEN people=TOP party=DAT came   but
          omosiroi hito=wa   hitori mo imasen.desita.
          interesting people=TOP one   even was.not
          'Many people came to the party, but there was not one who was interesting.'

It is possible for both uses of *wa* to occur in the same sentence, as illustrated in (45).[12] Kuno (1973:48–49) states that any given sentence can have only one thematic topic. If a sentence contains more than one constituent marked with *wa*, the first one must be the thematic topic, and all the others must be Contrastive Topics.

(45)   Boku=wa SAKE=wa nomu ga BIIRU=wa nomanai.
          1sg=TOP sake=TOP drink but beer=TOP do.not.drink
          'As for me, *sake* I drink but beer I do not drink.'

In summary, we have seen that *wa* marks continuing discourse topics. It is incompatible with pragmatic focus (e.g., in content questions and answers) and indefiniteness. Zero anaphora is limited to constituents which would otherwise be marked with *wa*. All of these facts are consistent with the hypothesis that constituents marked with *wa* bear the topic function.

6.5.3   Focus marking in Indonesian and Russian

We have considered topic-marking strategies in Chinese and Japanese in some detail. Now we will look more briefly at certain types of marked focus constructions, i.e., constructions which give special prominence to a particular piece of new information. We will draw examples from two languages, namely Indonesian and Russian.

6.5.3.1   Declarative focus in Indonesian

In addition to using intonation and word order to mark focused elements, Indonesian also makes use of two clitic particles. The particle =*lah* is used in declarative and imperative sentences (statements and commands, respectively), while =*kah* appears in interrogative sentences (questions).

Mashudi (1981:21–22) states that the constituent marked by =*lah* contains the most novel (i.e., new or unpredictable) information in the sentence; in other words, =*lah* marks the focus of the sentence. In Indonesian the focused element normally occurs at the beginning of the sentence. This is less strictly true in other varieties of Malay, in particular Bahasa Malaysia (standard Malaysian), where non-initial focus seems to be more acceptable. And even in Indonesian the focus particle may attach to a negative element in non-initial position, as well as to certain other kinds of modifiers within non-initial phrases. However, in this chapter we will restrict our attention to the marked focus construction in which the focused element appears at the beginning of its clause. Some typical examples are given in (46).[13]

(46) a   Di.sana=lah kami   menghadapi imperialisme. . . .
       there=FOC 1pl.EXCL AV-face   imperialism
       'It was there that we faced imperialism . . .'

    b   [Sejak tahun itu]=lah   Indonesia secara.resmi menjadi jajahan Belanda
       since year that=FOC Indonesia officially   become colony Dutch
       'It was from that year that Indonesia officially became a Dutch colony.'

In both of the sentences in (46) the focused constituent is an adjunct. It is also quite common for a verb or auxiliary to be focused. In narrative discourse especially, the verb often appears in clause-initial position, before the subject; and in this position it may carry the focus particle, as illustrated in (47). Hopper (1979, 1983) points out that this verb-initial order is used to mark the crucial, "main-line" events in the narrative. But this pattern is only possible with intransitive or passive verbs, for reasons which will be discussed below.

(47) a   Di.sini hati saya hancur. <u>Menangis=lah</u> saya dengan sangat sedih.
       here   liver 1sg break   weep=FOC   1sg with   very   sad
       'Here my heart broke. I cried very sadly.'

    b   Sesudah mengucapkan kata-kata itu,
       after   speak   words   that
       <u>bangkit=lah</u> dia dari kursi dan terus   pergi . . .
       arise=FOC   3sg from chair and straight go
       'After uttering those words, he got up from his chair and immediately went away . . .'

    c   Pada hari itu <u>ter-cipta=lah</u>   suatu negara Indonesia merdeka.
       on   day that PASS-create=FOC one   country Indonesia independent
       'On that day was created a free country of Indonesia.'

A subject NP in its normal position may not be focused. Mashudi (1981) notes that the subject of a basic Malay sentence normally contains given or presupposed information. Alsagoff (1991) shows that both active and passive subjects in Malay have a number of topic-like properties. For example, the crucial new information in the answer to a question cannot appear in subject position. This is illustrated in (48–49), taken from Alsagoff (1991:95–96). In each example, the first answer (A1) is inappropriate because the crucial new information appears in subject position.

(48) Q: Siapa yang men-cubit doktor itu?
          who REL AV-pinch doctor that
          'Who pinched the doctor?'

   A1: #Mariam men-cubit doktor itu.
        Mariam AV-pinch doctor that
        #'Mariam pinched the doctor.'

   A2: Doktor itu di-cubit   oleh Mariam.
        doctor that PASS-pinch by Mariam
        'The doctor was pinched by Mariam.'

(49) Q: Siapa yang di-cubit   oleh Mariam?
          who REL PASS-pinch by Mariam
          'Who was pinched by Mariam?'

   A1: #Doktor itu di-cubit   oleh Mariam.
        doctor that PASS-pinch by Mariam
        #'The doctor was pinched by Mariam.'

   A2: Mariam men-cubit doktor itu.
        Mariam AV-pinch doctor that
        'Mariam pinched the doctor.'

Since the subject position has these topic-like properties, and topics cannot take pragmatic focus, it is not surprising that =lah cannot mark the subject NP in a basic sentence. This is illustrated in (50b). But there is a way to assign focus to the subject NP, namely by using a Cleft sentence as in (50c). Cleft sentences in Indonesian (as in many other languages) have the form of an equative clause, in which the focused element is equated to a headless relative clause.

(50) a   Orang itu mencuri dompet saya.
          person that steal   wallet my
          'That person stole my wallet.'

     b   *Orang itu=lah   mencuri dompet saya.
          person that=FOC steal   wallet my
          (for: 'That person stole my wallet.')

     c   Orang itu=lah   yang mencuri dompet saya.
          person that=FOC REL steal   wallet my
          'It was that person who stole my wallet.'

We noted above that transitive verbs may not be focused in the same way as intransitive or passive verbs. The reason for this is that the verb and its object may not be separated from each other. This is illustrated in (51). In example (47) we saw several examples of intransitive verbs occurring in the initial focused position. These examples contrast with the ungrammatical sentence (51a), in which the transitive verb *makan* 'eat' is fronted leaving the object NP "stranded." However, when the same verb is used intransitively, as in (51b), it can be focused. Moreover, it is possible to focus the verb plus object as a unit, i.e., the entire VP, as shown in (51c).

(51) a   *<u>Makan</u> =lah   dia   nasi.
             eat   =FOC   3sg   cooked.rice
             (for: 'He is <u>eating</u> rice.')

     b   <u>Makan</u> =lah   dia.
             eat   =FOC   3sg
             'He is <u>eating</u>.'

     c   [<u>Makan   nasi</u>]   =lah   dia.
             eat   cooked.rice   =FOC   3sg
             'He is <u>eating rice</u>.'

Another consequence of the prohibition against separating a verb from its object is that direct objects cannot be independently focused. In order to focus the patient of a clause without focusing the VP as a whole, it is necessary to use a Cleft construction as in (52c). Notice that the headless relative clause in this example must contain a passive verb form; that is, in order to be clefted the patient must be expressed as a passive subject. The reason for this will be discussed in chapter 7.

(52) a   Kami   paling meng-gemari wayang.kulit.
             1pl.EXCL   most   AV-admire   shadow.puppet
             'We most admire/enjoy the shadow puppets.'

     b   *<u>Wayang.kulit=lah</u>   kami   paling meng-gemari.
             shadow.puppet=FOC   1pl.EXCL   most   AV-admire
             (for: 'We most admire/enjoy <u>the shadow puppets</u>.')

     c   <u>Wayang.kulit=lah</u>   yang paling kami   Ø-gemari.
             shadow.puppet=FOC   REL   most   1pl.EXCL   PASS-admire
             'It is the shadow puppets that we most admire/enjoy.'

6.5.3.2   Interrogative focus in Indonesian

The distribution of the interrogative focus particle =*kah* is quite similar to that of =*lah*. Sneddon (1996:320) states that in standard Indonesian =*kah* is used primarily in writing or formal speech. However, in standard Malaysian this particle is quite commonly used in all registers.

Basic yes–no questions can be signaled purely by intonation, or by an overt interrogative marker: sentence-initial *apakah* in Indonesian; sentence-final *=kah* in Malaysian. Alternatively, a particular element within the question may be marked for special prominence. In this construction the focused element is shifted to the beginning of the sentence and marked with *=kah*.

If the verb or VP is focused in this way, as in (53), the pragmatic focus interpretation applies to the sentence as a whole. But if any other element of the sentence is focused, this element would be interpreted as the main point of the question; the rest of the question would be presupposed. The examples in (54) show that the focused element may be an auxiliary, adverb, or adjunct PP. (Note that auxiliaries like *akan* and *sudah* normally occur immediately before the verb.)

(53) a   Jatuh=kah dia?
          fall=FOC   3sg
          'Did she fall?'

     b   Mahu=kah kamu   ikut?
          want=FOC you(familiar) follow
          'Do you want to come along?'

     c   Terlalu gemuk=kah anda?
          too   fat=FOC   you(formal)
          'Are you too fat?'

     d   Sudah   pergi=kah ia?
          already go=FOC   3sg
          'Has she already gone?'

(54) a   Sudah=kah   hal   ini kau=pikirkan?
          already=FOC matter this 2sg=think.about
          'Have you already thought about this matter?'

     b   Akan=kah pertemuan=nya dengan Presiden Soeharto batal?
          FUT=FOC meeting=3sg   with   President Soeharto cancel
          'Will his meeting with President Soeharto be cancelled?'

     c   Sering=kah dia pergi ke sana?
          often=FOC 3sg go   to there
          'Does she go there often?'

     d   Di sekolah=kah Ahmad menulis surat itu?
          at school=FOC Ahmad write   letter that
          'Did Ahmad write that letter at school?'   (Ramli, 1989:118)

As demonstrated in the preceding section with respect to *=lah*, subjects cannot generally be focused *in situ*. Thus Sneddon (1996:317) notes that, while some Indonesian speakers accept sentences like (55a), for most speakers the Cleft sentence in (55b) would be strongly preferred. And, once again, because direct objects cannot be separated from their verb (56b), the patient of a transitive verb can only be focused by passivization plus clefting (56c).

(55) a 　?*Wawan=kah　menulis surat itu?
　　　　　Wawan=FOC write　　letter that
　　　　　(for: 'Did <u>Wawan</u> write that letter?')

　　b 　Wawan=kah　yang menulis surat itu?
　　　　　Wawan=FOC REL write　　letter that
　　　　　'Was it Wawan who wrote that letter?'

(56) a 　Saya telah　mem-beli sepeda itu.
　　　　　1sg　PERF AV-buy　bicycle that
　　　　　'I bought that bicycle.'

　　b 　*Sepeda itu=kah　saya telah　mem-beli?
　　　　　bicycle that=FOC 1sg　PERF AV-buy
　　　　　(for: 'Did I buy <u>that bicycle</u>?')

　　c 　Sepeda itu=kah　yang telah　saya Ø-beli?
　　　　　bicycle that=FOC REL PERF 1sg　PASS-buy
　　　　　'Was it that bicycle that I bought?'

In addition to its usage in yes–no questions, the clitic =*kah* can also be used in content questions, where it optionally attaches to the question word. But this is only possible when the question word appears in initial position. Question words may remain *in situ*; in this case they cannot take the focus particle, as illustrated in (57a) and (58a). But when they are fronted (57b) or clefted (58b), =*kah* may be added.

(57) a 　Bapak tinggal di.mana(*=kah)?
　　　　　father dwell　where(*=FOC)
　　　　　'Where do you live, sir?'

　　b 　Di.mana(=kah) Bapak tinggal?
　　　　　where(=FOC)　father dwell
　　　　　'Where do you live, sir?'

(58) a 　Anda　　menemui siapa(*=kah)?
　　　　　you(formal) AV-meet　who(*=FOC)
　　　　　'Who did you meet?'

　　b 　Siapa(=kah) yang anda　　Ø-temui?
　　　　　who=FOC　REL you(formal) PASS-meet
　　　　　'Who did you meet?'

We have seen that the focus particles in Indonesian are used to mark the crucial new information in a sentence. It is interesting to contrast the distribution of these particles with Japanese *wa*. Indonesian =*kah* frequently attaches to a question word, whereas *wa* can never be used in this way. Conversely, in most Japanese sentences *wa* marks the subject, whereas the Indonesian focus particles can mark subjects only if they are clefted. This reflects the fact that subjects are the preferred or default topic in most languages.

6.5.3.3   Interrogative focus in Russian

Russian has a question-marking particle which is in many ways similar to the =*kah*
of Indonesian; but there are some interesting differences as well.

Yes–no questions in Russian may be formed either by the use of question
intonation alone, as in (59b), or by the use of a clitic particle -*li*, as in (59c).
The element which hosts the clitic appears in sentence-initial position. As (60)
shows, the clitic may attach either to the verb or to some other element within
the sentence. If the clitic attaches to the verb, as in (60b), the entire proposition is
being questioned. If the clitic attaches to another element, as in (60c), that element
becomes the focus of the question.

(59)   **Russian** (King, 1995)
    a   On živet zdes'.
             he   live   here
             'He lives here.'

    b   On živet zdes'?
             he   live   here
             'He lives here?'

    c   živet=li   on zdes'?
             live=QUES he here
             'Does he live here?'

(60) a   Anna pročitala knigu.
             Anna read   book
             'Anna read a book.'

    b   Pročitala=li Anna knigu?
             read=QUES Anna book
             'Did Anna read a book?'

    c   Knigu=li   Anna pročitala?
             book=QUES Anna read
             'Was it a book that Anna read?'

As we saw in the preceding sections, focus clitics in Indonesian normally
follow the syntactic constituent which they mark. However, the position of the
focus clitic in Russian is more complex. King (1995) states that the interrogative
particle attaches as an enclitic to the first PHONOLOGICAL WORD of the focused
constituent. So the position of the clitic depends on phonological constituent
boundaries as well as syntactic structure.

Verbs always constitute a single phonological word, but a given phrasal constituent (such as an NP) may contain more than one phonological word. When a
phrasal constituent which contains more than one phonological word is focused,
the clitic will occur inside the boundaries of the constituent which it marks, as
in (61a–b). In (61b), the preposition *na* is not a phonological word; so the clitic

attaches to the string *na etom* 'at this,' which is a single phonological word even though it is not a syntactic constituent.

(61) a   [Interesnuju=li   knigu Ivana]   on čitaet?
          interesting-ACC=QUES book Ivan-GEN he reads
          'Is it an interesting book of Ivan's that he is reading?'

     b   [Na etom=li   zavode] on rabotaet?
          at   this =QUES factory he work
          'Is it at this factory that he works?'

     c   *[Na etom zavode]=li   on rabotaet?
          at   this   factory =QUES he work

Notice that in Russian content questions, the question word always occurs in initial position. Unlike Indonesian, the interrogative clitic -*li* may not co-occur with a question word (62d).

(62) a   Kto priexal k vam?
          who came   to you
          'Who visited you?'

     b   čto ty   kupila?
          what you buy
          'What did you buy?'

     c   Komu   ženščina xotela napisat'?
          who-DAT woman   want   write-INF
          'Who did the woman want to write to?'

     d   *čto=li   ona delaet?
          what=QUES she do

6.6   Identifying topic and focus

We have defined FOCUS as new or unpredictable information and TOPIC as known or given information. But it is not always easy to tell which of these functions is associated with a particular construction. For example, the topic–comment constructions illustrated in examples (2–4) may not seem to fit comfortably into either definition. Because they serve to signal a *change* in discourse topic, they give prominence to information that is in some way unpredictable at that point in the discourse. Why then do we identify the fronted constituent in these constructions as bearing the topic function? More generally, if we are investigating a marked sentence type in a particular language, how can we determine its pragmatic structure?

In order to identify the pragmatic function of a particular construction, we need to examine the contexts in which it is appropriate to use that construction. Our basic assumption is that a single element cannot function as both topic and focus at the same time, since the same piece of information cannot be simultaneously old and new in a single context. Thus, if a particular sentence type assigns the topic function to one of its constituents, it will not be appropriate to use the construction in contexts where that constituent should receive pragmatic focus.

One of the clearest contexts of this kind is the Content (or Wh-) question. As we have said, the answer to a Wh- question places natural focus on the element which corresponds to the question word. Thus question–answer pairs can provide very useful tests for identifying the pragmatic function of marked elements.

Example (63) contains a content question followed by three possible answers. Each of these answers involves one of the pragmatically marked English sentence types discussed in section 6.2: Wh-Cleft, Contrastive Topic, and External Topic, respectively. And in each case, the NP which is given structural prominence (*a paperweight*) provides the crucial new information which corresponds to the question word; in other words, that is the element which must bear pragmatic focus in this context.

(63)   Q: What did you give John for his birthday?
         A1.   I almost bought him a pet boa, but what I actually gave him was a
               paperweight.
         A2.   #A pet boa sounded attractive, but a paperweight I actually gave him.
         A3.   #As for paperweights, I actually gave him one.

As these data indicate, the Wh-Cleft construction (answer 1) is a perfectly appropriate way to give marked prominence to the focused element. But the Contrastive Topic and External Topic constructions in answers 2 and 3 would not be appropriate in this context.

We can explain this contrast based on the pragmatic functions we proposed for these three sentence types in section 6.2. If the Wh-Cleft construction assigns focus to the clefted NP, there is no problem using this construction in contexts where this NP must bear pragmatic focus. On the other hand, if the Contrastive Topic and External Topic constructions assign the topic function to the fronted NP, they would be inappropriate in contexts where this NP must bear pragmatic focus. This is because focus and topic are mutually incompatible; a single element cannot bear both functions at the same time.

Another context which involves pragmatic focus is illustrated in example (64). The first speaker makes a statement (S) which contains a false presupposition. The second speaker's reply is an attempt to correct this false presupposition. In the reply, the crucial new information (*Mary*) bears pragmatic focus and stands in contrast to the false information (*John*). This type of focus is often referred to as CONTRASTIVE FOCUS.

Four different versions of this reply are given in (64). The first version (R1) is expressed using normal, basic word order; the focused element is marked only by intonational prominence, i.e., FOCAL STRESS (marked here with italics). In the second version (R2), a Cleft sentence is used to give prominence to the crucial new information; the result is perfectly natural, perhaps even better than (R1).

However, the Contrastive Topic and External Topic constructions, as in versions R3 and R4, would be inappropriate in this context.

(64)   S: I take it you finally caught up with John.
       R1.   I was looking for *Mary*, not John.
       R2.   It's *Mary* I was looking for, not John.
       R3.   #Mary I was looking for, not John.
       R4.   #As for Mary, I was looking for her, not John.

Once again we see that clefting is compatible with pragmatic focus, whereas the Contrastive Topic and External Topic constructions are not. These facts support our earlier claim that clefted NPs bear the focus function, while the fronted element in the Contrastive Topic and External Topic constructions bear the topic function.

We can also examine the behavior of these sentence types in contexts which establish a specific discourse topic. For example, when someone asks a question about *John*, as in (65), *John* is established for the moment as the topic of conversation. Any reference to *John* in the answer would normally use an unstressed pronoun, as in both of the possible answers provided.

(65)   Q: What ever became of John?
       A1.   He's got a job selling used cars out in Santa Fe.
       A2.   The police finally caught up with him, but I think he's out of jail now.

If the questioner establishes a set of two possible topics, as in (66), then a marked topic construction is perfectly appropriate as a way of choosing one of them; Contrastive Topic is used in answer A1, External Topic in answer A2. But a marked focus construction such as clefting is inappropriate in this context, as indicated by the "#" before answer A3. The phrase *Mary* cannot naturally be clefted in this case, because it has already been established as a possible topic. In other words, clefting is incompatible with topichood, which supports our claim that a clefted element bears the focus function.

(66)   Q: How are John and Mary doing?
       A1.   John I never hear from at all, but Mary's doing fine; she's got a job selling used cars.
       A2.   Mary's doing fine; she's got a job selling used cars. As for John, I never hear from him anymore. Maybe the police finally caught up with him.
       A3.   #It is Mary that is doing fine, not John.

The basic strategy, then, is to find a discourse context where a particular element must bear a known pragmatic function, either topic or focus. We then test to see whether this element can occur in the prominent position of a marked sentence type in this context. If a particular sentence type seems clearly inappropriate in that context, this fact may provide evidence that the pragmatic function of the marked construction itself clashes with the function established by the discourse context.

Notes

1. For a discussion of other possible functions of the Left-Dislocation construction, see Prince (1997); Geluykens (1992); K.-H. Kim (1995); and references cited by these authors.

2. Other examples of Clefts and Pseudo-Clefts were given in chapter 2, section 2.2.1.

3. The rule in (8c) is too restrictive because (interpreted strictly) it accounts only for monoclausal examples; see chapter 7 for a discussion of long-distance extraction. It is too general because it would allow subjects to be topicalized in this construction. See Falk (2001) and Dalrymple (2001) for a discussion of the formal notation ("functional uncertainty") needed to state language-specific constraints on extraction.

4. Falk (2001) and Dalrymple (2001) also present a formal analysis of Subj-Aux inversion.

5. See, for example, Li and Thompson (1976).

6. The examples in this section are from Li and Thompson (1976, 1981), unless another citation is given.

7. Tan (1991) shows that a sentence topic is not always the same as the discourse topic. Where there is a mismatch, it is the discourse topic which controls phenomena such as zero anaphora.

8. The examples in (18) and (19) are adapted from Tan (1991:32–33).

9. Most of the examples in this section come from Kuno (1972, 1973) and Makino (1982).

10. Thanks to Yo Matsumoto (p.c.) for providing some of these data, and for helpful discussion of these issues.

11. In most contexts, it is more natural for the subject of a Wh- question (when the subject itself is not the question word) to be marked with *wa*, rather than *ga*. But (37a) shows that even when the subject takes *ga*, the question word cannot take *wa*.

12. Example (45) is from Tsutsui (1981), cited in Makino (1982).

13. Unless otherwise indicated, the examples in this section are taken from Sneddon (1996) and MacDonald (1976).

7 Filler–gap dependencies and relativization

A RELATIVE CLAUSE CONSTRUCTION is a noun phrase which contains a clausal modifier. For example, the subject NP in sentence (1) consists of a determiner (*the*), the head noun (*woman*), and a modifying clause (*I love*). The modifying clause is introduced by a RELATIVIZER (*that*).

(1)   [The woman [that I love]$_{S'}$]$_{NP}$ is moving to Argentina.

Note that the modifying clause in this example seems incomplete: it lacks a direct object, even though its verb (*love*) requires one. Nevertheless, this sentence is perfectly grammatical. We can give an intuitive explanation for this fact by suggesting that the head noun *woman* is "understood" to be the object of *love*. Another way of expressing this intuition is to say that the modifying clause contains a "gap," while the head noun is interpreted as the thing which fills this gap, making the sentence complete.

In English, this kind of "filler–gap" structure is also found in content (or Wh-) questions and several other constructions, such as clefting and topicalization (i.e., the Contrastive Topic construction). Constructions of this type have some unique and interesting properties, which have stimulated a great deal of syntactic research. One characteristic property of these constructions is that the "filler" may be very far from the "gap." In English Wh- questions, for example, the question word may occur an arbitrarily long distance away from the verb which assigns its semantic role and grammatical relation.

In the first section of this chapter we will present a brief overview of the filler–gap relation, using data primarily from English. In the following sections we will look in more detail at relative clauses in various languages, reviewing some of the basic typological patterns in section 7.2 and proposing structural analyses for various types of relative clauses in section 7.3.

7.1   The filler–gap relation

7.1.1   Filler–gap constructions in English

The sentences in (2) illustrate that the verb *fall* is intransitive, and cannot take a direct object; while the verb *annoy* is transitive and requires a direct object. This explains why the intransitive sentence in (2a) is grammatical, while the one in (2b) is not. But when we use the very same strings as clausal modifiers, the pattern of grammaticality is reversed: (3b) is grammatical, while (3a) is not.

(2) a   John fell.
    b   *John annoyed.
    c   *John fell his sister.
    d   John annoyed his sister.

(3) a   *This is the sister that [John fell].
    b   This is the sister that [John annoyed].

These examples illustrate the most obvious way in which the head noun in a relative clause is understood to fill a gap in the modifying clause: the head noun must be assigned a grammatical function within the modifying clause. In other words, the head noun must be included when the modifying clause is evaluated for Completeness and Coherence (see chapter 1, section 1.2.5). If there is no gap in the modifying clause, as in (3a), the relative clause is ill-formed. The same principle is illustrated in (4).

(4) a   There is the man that [__ gave me his watch].
    b   There is the woman that [John gave his watch to __].
    c   This is the watch that [John gave me __].
    d   *There is the man that [John gave me his watch].
    e   *This is the watch that [John gave me his watch].

The head noun behaves like an integral part of the modifying clause in other ways as well. Example (5) illustrates the selectional restrictions which the verbs *iron* and *annoy* impose on their objects: the OBJ of *annoy* must be animate, while the OBJ of *iron* must be a flat, soft object, normally made of cloth. As (6) demonstrates, when the modifying clause lacks an object, these same selectional restrictions are imposed on the head noun. We noted in chapter 1 that selectional restrictions of this type are associated with particular semantic roles. Thus the examples in (6) suggest that the head noun bears the semantic role of the gap, as well as its grammatical relation.

(5) a   John ironed his shirt.
    b   John annoyed his sister.
    c   #John ironed his sister.
    d   #John annoyed his shirt.

(6) a   This is the shirt that [John ironed __].
    b   This is the sister that [John annoyed __].
    c   #This is the sister that [John ironed __].
    d   #This is the shirt that [John annoyed __].

As noted above, an interesting feature of filler–gap relations is that the filler (in this case the head noun) can be quite far removed from the gap (the position of the missing element in the modifying clause). This fact is illustrated in (7). As these examples suggest, there is no definite limit as to how far the filler may

be from its gap. For this reason, filler–gap relations are sometimes referred to as
LONG DISTANCE DEPENDENCIES.

(7) a   There is a man that [___ admires himself too much].
    b   There is the man that [Mary thinks
            [___ admires himself/*herself too much]].
    c   There is the man that [Alice said [Mary thinks [___ admires himself/*herself
            too much]].
    d   There is the man that [Susan told me that [Alice said [Mary thinks
            [___ admires himself/*herself too much]]]].

Of course, the term "long distance" does not refer to the sheer length of an
utterance as measured in number of words or syllables. The ungrammaticality of
herself in (7b–d) indicates that the gap is separated from all potential feminine
antecedents (*Mary, Alice*, or *Susan*) by one or more clause boundaries. Such examples indicate that the filler may be separated from the gap by an arbitrary number of
nested clause boundaries, and this is what syntacticians mean by "long distance."
    But notice that, even though the head noun in (7b–d) is also separated from
the gap by one or more clause boundaries, it is still eligible to function as the
antecedent of the reflexive *himself*. If this were not true the examples would be
ungrammatical, because reflexives in English require an antecedent within their
minimal clause. So once again the head noun behaves as if it were an element of
the modifying clause.
    As noted in the introduction to this chapter, there are several other construc-
tions in English which have properties similar to those we have been discussing,
including Wh- questions, topicalization, and Cleft sentences. Some examples of
Wh- questions, parallel to the relative clause examples in (2–7), are given in (8).
Examples of topicalization and Cleft sentences were presented in chapter 6.

(8)   **Wh– questions:**
    a   Who did John annoy?
    b   *Who did John fall?
    c   Which shirt / #sister did John iron?
    d   Which #shirt / sister did John annoy?
    e   Who did you say Mary thinks (that) John loves?
    f   Who did you say Bill told you (that) Mary thinks (that) John loves?
    g   Which man does Mary think admires himself/*herself too much?
    h   Which man did you say (that) Alice told you (that) Mary thinks admires
            himself/*herself too much?

7.1.2   "Islands" and resumptive pronouns

We have seen that the filler in a long-distance dependency may be separated from the gap by an arbitrary number of nested clause boundaries. However,
this does not mean that there are no limits at all on the relative positions of the gap
and its filler. Ross (1967, 1986) identified several types of constructions in English
which cannot contain gaps if they do not also contain the corresponding filler.

He referred to these constructions as "islands." They include coordinate structures (9), indirect questions (10), and "complex NPs" (i.e., NPs which contain an embedded clause) as in (11).

(9)   a   The police captured [Butch Cassidy and Al Capone] on the same day.

    b   *There is the man whom the police captured [Butch Cassidy and __] on the same day.

    c   *Who did the police capture [Butch Cassidy and __] on the same day?

(10) a   I don't know [how much money Al Capone offered (to) Eliot Ness].

    b   *Eliot Ness is the guy that I don't know [how much money Al Capone offered (to) __].

    c   I don't know [why Butch was arrested].

    d   *Butch is the guy that I don't know [why __ was arrested].

    e   *Who don't you know [why __ was arrested]?

(11) a   The police are denying [reports that someone helped Butch (to) escape].

    b   *I just saw the guy that the police are denying [reports that someone helped __ (to) escape].

    c   *Who are the police denying [reports that someone helped __ (to) escape]?

Because these constituents may not contain gaps, it is generally not possible to question, relativize, topicalize, or cleft an element within such a structure. However, speakers of some non-standard dialects of English do in fact relativize etc. out of at least some of these constructions, by making use of resumptive pronouns:

(12) a   %Eliot Ness is the guy that [I don't know how much money Al Capone offered him].

    b   %Butch is the guy that [I don't know why he was arrested].

    c   %I just saw the guy that the police are denying [reports that someone helped him (to) escape].

In fact, as a number of authors have pointed out,[1] even speakers of "standard" English dialects sometimes use resumptive pronouns in these contexts, in spite of the fact that resumptive pronouns are generally considered ungrammatical in standard English. Some examples from natural speech are listed in (13):

(13) a   There are always guests who [I am curious about what they are going to say.] (Dick Cavett, cited in Prince, 1990)

    b   Apparently there are . . . bees in the area which [if you're stung by them, you die]. (cited in Prince, 1990)

    c   That idiot X, who [I loathe and despise [the ground he walks on]], . . . (adapted from Prince, 1990)

    d   He jumped over the fence (of the cattle yard) and into something that [if he had known what it was, he would have jumped further left]. (Garrison Keillor on A Prairie Home Companion; cited in Bickford, 1998:339)

Similar patterns are reported in other languages. For example, Borer (1984) shows that in Hebrew, as in English, coordinate structures (15a) and complex NPs (15b) may not contain a gap. An element within one of these constructions can only be relativized by using resumptive pronouns:

(15)   **Israeli Hebrew** (Borer, 1984:221, 226)

   a   ha-yeled she=[Rina ?ohevet [*Ø / oto   ve=?et   ha-xavera shelo]]
         the-boy REL=Rina loves   Ø / him(ACC) and=ACC the-friend of-his
         'the boy that Rina loves him and his girlfriend'

   b   ha-yeled she=[Dalya makira [?et ha-?isha   she=?ohevet *Ø / oto]]
         the-boy REL=Dalya knows ACC the-woman REL=loves   Ø / him(ACC)
         'the boy that Dalya knows the woman who loves him'

However, there is an important difference between Hebrew and English: resumptive pronouns in Hebrew are not considered to be speech errors or markers of a non-standard dialect. Rather, they are fully grammatical, and are used in many contexts where English allows gaps. For example, complement clauses of indirect speech in English may contain gaps, as illustrated in (7). But this is not allowed in Hebrew.

Givón (1973) shows that there is a contrast between simple clauses and complement clauses in Hebrew with respect to relativization. He states that resumptive pronouns are strongly disfavored when the subject of a simple clause with basic SVO word order is relativized, as in (16a). Resumptive pronouns are optional when the object of a similar clause is relativized (16b).[2] However, when either the subject or the object of a complement clause is relativized, gaps are not allowed; a resumptive pronoun is obligatory (17a–b).[3]

(16)   **Hebrew main clause relativization** (Givón, 1973)

   a   ha-ish   she=[Ø / *hu   hika et   ha-kelev]
         the-man REL=Ø / he(NOM) hit   ACC the-dog
         'the man that (*he) hit the dog'

   b   ha-ish   she=[Yoav raa Ø / oto   etmol]
         the-man REL=Yoav saw Ø / him(ACC) yesterday
         'the man that Yoav saw (him) yesterday'

(17)   **Hebrew complement clause relativization** (Givón, 1973)

   a   ha-ish   she=yadati   she=[*Ø / hu   avad   etmol]
         the-man REL=1sg.knew COMP= Ø / he(NOM) worked yesterday
         'the man that I knew that he worked yesterday'

   b   ha-ish   she=yadati   she=[ha-kelev nashax *Ø / oto   etmol]
         the-man REL=1sg.knew COMP=the-dog bit   Ø / him(ACC) yesterday
         'the man that I knew that the dog bit him yesterday'

The general pattern in most languages is that gaps are less likely to occur in deeply embedded positions, and resumptive pronouns are more likely to occur in these positions. We will return to this issue in section 7.2.3.

7.1.3   Representing the filler–gap relation

The examples presented in section 7.1.1 pose the following paradox: the grammatical and semantic properties of a filler (including grammatical relations, semantic roles, selectional restrictions, and reflexive binding) are those associated with the position of the gap; but the filler actually occupies a very different position. We might even say that the filler seems to occupy two positions at once.

There are several different ways in which this paradox can be resolved. In transformational approaches to syntax (based on Chomsky 1965, 1981, and a huge volume of related work), the relationship between a gap and its filler is expressed in terms of a transformational rule called WH- MOVEMENT. This rule moves an element from its initial, or basic, position (the gap) into its final, visible position (the filler). (This process is sometimes referred to as EXTRACTION, a term that is often used to refer to filler–gap dependencies even in non-transformational frameworks.)

The movement analysis is an intuitively appealing way of describing elements which seem to occupy two positions at once. However, the use of such transformational rules introduces a much higher level of potential complexity into the grammar. For this reason, among others,[4] we will adopt a different approach. The essentials of this approach were introduced in chapter 6.

Constructions which involve a filler–gap relation are typically used to encode a special pragmatic function, i.e., topic or focus. As we saw in chapter 6, Wh-questions involve a request for a particular piece of new information, so the question word will bear the focus function. To use a specific example, the functional structure of the question in (8a) could be represented as in (18):

(18)   *Who did John annoy?*

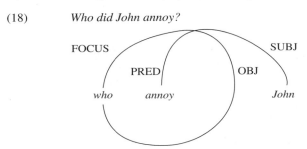

This diagram represents the dual status of the filler (*who*) in terms of dual function assignment. On the one hand, it bears the focus function associated with a question word. On the other hand, it bears the grammatical relation (OBJ) associated with the gap. This grammatical relation carries with it a particular semantic role, binding properties, etc.

The phrase structure we proposed for questions in chapter 6 is shown in (19). Notice that this tree contains an empty NP position (i.e., one with no phonetic content) corresponding to the gap. Since the filler-gap relationship is already

represented in functional structure, this empty NP does no work in the analysis.
A number of linguists have taken the position that there is actually no position in
phrase structure corresponding to the gap; in this example, that would mean that
the VP simply lacks an object NP. However, Bresnan (2001) argues that this is in
fact an empirical question: some languages (including English) provide evidence
for an empty position in phrase structure, while others do not.[5] We adopt her
analysis of English here, without implying that all languages must have empty
positions in phrase structure.

(19)
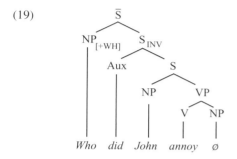

The relational network diagram in (18) is independent of language-specific
details such as word order. Since the pragmatic function of content questions is
much the same in all languages, the functional structure of content questions in
various languages is likely to be quite similar even when the phrase structure
configuration is very different. For example, the form of a content question in
Japanese is quite different from that of a content question in English, as illustrated
by the examples in (20):

(20)   **Japanese** (adapted from Merrifield *et al.*, 1987, prob. 271)
  a   Josei=ga   kodomo=ni okashi=o   ageta.
       woman=NOM child=DAT cake=ACC gave
       'The woman gave the cake to the child.'

  b   Dare=ga   kodomo=ni okashi=o   ageta ka?
       who=NOM   child=DAT cake=ACC gave Q
       'Who gave the cake to the child?'

  c   Josei=wa   dare=ni   okashi=o   ageta ka?
       woman=TOP who=DAT cake=ACC gave Q
       'To whom did the woman give the cake?'

  d   Josei=wa   kodomo=ni nani=o   ageta ka?
       woman=TOP child=DAT what=ACC gave Q
       'What did the woman give to the child?'

The most obvious difference is that in English, the question word appears at the
beginning of the sentence, while in Japanese it appears *in situ*, that is, in its normal

position based on its grammatical relation. However, the pragmatic function of the question word (focus) is presumably the same in both languages. Therefore it seems reasonable to assume that questions in the two languages have essentially the same functional structure: in both languages, the question word bears both a pragmatic function (focus) and a grammatical relation within the sentence. The difference is primarily a matter of word order, which will be represented in the phrase structure.

As we have seen, the filler may be separated from its gap by a clause boundary, and there seems to be no fixed limit as to how deeply embedded the gap may be. This long-distance effect is illustrated in the phrase structure and functional structure diagrams for example (8e), which are shown in (21):

(21) a   Phrase structure

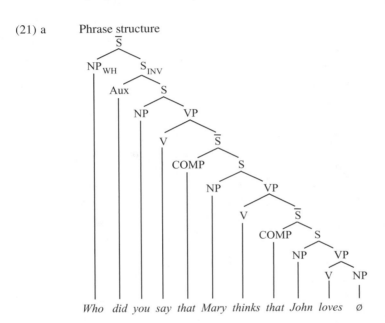

Who   did   you   say   that   Mary   thinks   that   John   loves   ∅

b   Functional structure

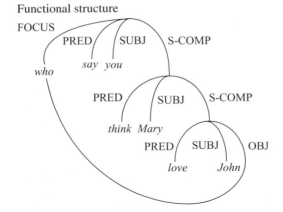

7.1.4   Differences between control and the filler–gap relation

A filler–gap relation, such as the relation between the fronted element in a Wh- question and the "missing argument" which it corresponds to, looks superficially very similar to the relation between controller and controllee which was discussed in chapter 5. However, there are a number of differences between the filler–gap relation and control. The most obvious of these is illustrated in figure (21b) above, which shows that a filler–gap relation may cross multiple clause boundaries; that is, it may extend down through an arbitrary number of multiply embedded clauses. Control relations, in contrast, are generally LOCAL (or CLAUSE-BOUNDED). This means that the controller must be an element of the clause that immediately dominates the clause that contains the controllee. Note the contrast between the long-distance (filler–gap) dependencies in (22) vs. the control relations in (23) and (24).

(22) a   Who did you say Mary thinks (that) John loves __?
     b   Who did you say (that) Bill told you (that) Mary thinks (that) John loves __?

(23) a   Babe Ruth tried to hit a home run.
     b   Alice longed for Babe Ruth to hit a home run.
     c   *Babe Ruth tried (for) Alice to long for __ to hit a home run.
     d   *Babe Ruth tried (that) Alice longs for __ to hit a home run.
     e   *Babe Ruth tried (for) Alice to bet that __ would hit a home run.

(24) a   Joe seems to like trigonometry.
     b   Dad is eager for Joe to like trigonometry.
     c   *Joe seems (for) Dad to be eager for __ to like trigonometry.
     d   *Joe seems (that) Dad is eager for __ to like trigonometry.
     e   *Joe seems (for) Dad to believe that __ likes trigonometry.

Example (23) involves an Equi predicate, while (24) involves a Raising predicate. The locality constraint on these constructions is so strong that it is somewhat difficult even to invent examples which might illustrate long-distance control; but (23c–e) and (24c–e) provide some idea of what would be involved. No matter what combination of finite and infinitival clauses is used, the result is totally unacceptable. These examples illustrate that the controller and controllee must belong to adjacent clauses.

In a control construction, the controller can be separated from the controllee only if each of the intervening clauses contains a control predicate of the appropriate type. In other words, apparent cases of long-distance control are actually composed of a series of local (clause-bounded) control relations, as illustrated in (25). The functional structure of (25a) is shown in (26).

(25) a   John planned to promise Mary to try to behave himself.
     b   Bill seems to be expected to pretend to love Alice.

(26)   *John planned to promise Mary to try to behave himself.*

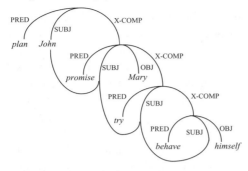

A second difference between control and the "filler–gap" relation is that control relations are often LEXICALLY GOVERNED, i.e., only possible with certain matrix verbs such as Equi or Raising predicates. We discussed several examples of such predicates in chapter 5. Filler–gap relations are not lexically governed; virtually any declarative sentence can be turned into a Wh- question, relative clause, etc.

A third difference is that in English (and many other languages), control relations are possible only when the controllee is an element of a non-finite clause (infinitival or participial). Filler–gap relations, on the other hand, may exist equally in finite and non-finite clauses. Examples (2–8) and (22) above illustrate filler–gap relations into finite clauses. The following sentences illustrate filler–gap relations into infinitival (27a) and participial (27b) clauses.

(27) a   Who did John plan to invite __ to his party?
     b   What secrets was Bill accused of selling __ to the Russians?

A fourth difference is that in a control relation, the controller bears two clause-level grammatical relations (e.g., SUBJ or OBJ): one assigned by the matrix predicate; the other assigned by the subordinate clause. In a filler–gap construction, however, the filler bears only one grammatical relation, namely the one associated with the position of the gap. But in addition, the filler bears a pragmatic function (topic or focus).

7.2   Typology of relative clauses

The filler–gap relation is a feature of relative clauses in many languages, including some (such as Japanese and Chinese) which do not use this strategy for Wh- questions. But the structure of a relative clause is in some ways more complex than that of a question or topicalized sentence, because in a relative clause the filler–gap construction is embedded within an NP.

In discussing example (1), repeated below, we noted that a relative clause construction has three basic parts: a head noun (*woman*), a modifying clause (*I love*), and, in some languages, a RELATIVIZER (*that*). An interesting property of relative clause constructions is that the head noun bears two grammatical relations at the same time. In example (1), *woman* is the subject of the matrix predicate *is moving*, but it is also interpreted as being the object of *love* in the modifying clause. We will refer to the grammatical relation which the head noun gets from the modifying clause as the RELATIVIZED FUNCTION. Thus the relativized function in (1) is the OBJ.

(1)   [The woman [that I love]_{S'}]_{NP} is moving to Argentina.

In general, there are few restrictions on the function of a relative clause within the matrix sentence; relative clauses can appear wherever normal NPs are allowed. However, many languages place restrictions on the relativized function. Moreover, languages employ a variety of strategies for identifying the relativized function, i.e., for indicating the relation of the head noun to the modifying clause. In English, as we have seen, the relativized function is normally marked by a gap; but other languages may use resumptive pronouns or other strategies in particular contexts.

When we compare the ways in which relative clauses are formed in large numbers of languages around the world, two very interesting patterns emerge. First, certain functions are easier to relativize (i.e., more "accessible") than others. Second, the choice of relativization strategy often correlates with "accessibility" in this sense.

In this section we provide a brief review of some of the basic structural and typological features of relative clauses, including some of the cross-linguistic findings on accessibility. In section 7.3 we will develop a slightly more formal analysis of the structure of various types of relative clauses.

7.2.1   Restrictive vs. non-restrictive relatives

The sentences in (28) illustrate a contrast between two kinds of relative clause found in English. The object NP in (28a) contains a RESTRICTIVE relative clause, while that in (28b) is NON-RESTRICTIVE.

(28) a   The police are looking for [the man who escaped from prison yesterday].
     b   The police are looking for [Al Capone, who escaped from prison yesterday].

In a restrictive relative clause like (28a), the head noun is generally a common noun which could refer to a large number of different individuals. The specific reference of the NP as a whole is determined by the clausal modifier. A non-restrictive relative clause like (28b) is one in which the referent of the head noun is already known, or can be identified independently; the clausal modifier simply presents additional information about that participant. Thus proper names frequently occur as the head noun of a non-restrictive relative clause, but never as the head noun of a restrictive relative clause.

There are a number of other grammatical differences between restrictive and non-restrictive relative clauses in English; see McCawley (1988:417–432) for a detailed discussion. In other languages, such as Japanese (Kuno, 1973), there are no grammatical differences. In this chapter we will focus primarily on restrictive relative clauses.

7.2.2   Relativization strategies

Keenan (1985b:141–170) discusses three basic strategies which are used to mark the relativized function in various languages. In comparing these strategies and their distribution, it is very important to remember that the term "relativized function" refers to the function of the head noun in relation to the modifying clause, not the matrix clause. Thus the relativized function in (1) is (as we have already noted) the OBJ, while the relativized function in (28a) is the SUBJ.

For convenience we will use the abbreviation "S_{REL}" to refer to the modifying clause.[6] The three strategies which account for the vast majority of relative clauses in most of the world's languages are: (a) the GAP (or "extraction") strategy; (b) the RESUMPTIVE PRONOUN (or PRONOUN RETENTION) strategy; and (c) the RELATIVE PRONOUN strategy. The first two of these strategies are very similar to topicalization strategies which we discussed in chapter 6.

The GAP strategy, as the name implies, involves a filler–gap relation. The nominalized element is simply omitted from S_{REL}, and the head noun is interpreted as filling this gap. Most of the English examples which we have considered, aside from the "non-standard" examples in (12) and (13), make use of this strategy.

In this construction the relativized function must be identified on the basis of negative evidence, i.e., by observing what is missing. This will involve comparing the subcategorization of the embedded verb with the NPs which actually occur inside S_{REL}. This strategy works most efficiently in a language with rigid verb-medial word order, like English, or a language with a rich system of morphological case marking, like Korean. In other languages the use of gaps may result in ambiguity, as illustrated in (29).

(29)   **Isthmus Zapotec** (Mexico; Payne, 1997)

   a   najii Juan junaa
            loves Juan woman
            'Juan loves a woman.'

   b   najii junaa   Juan
            loves woman Juan
            'A woman loves Juan.'

   c   junaa   ni   [najii Juan __]
            woman REL loves Juan
            'a woman that Juan loves'

   d   junaa   ni   [najii __ Juan]
            woman REL loves   Juan
            'a woman that loves Juan'

Isthmus Zapotec has basic VSO word order, and there is no case or agreement morphology to distinguish subjects from objects. Since gaps are invisible (i.e., not pronounced), examples (29c) and (29d) would sound exactly the same; a hearer would have to determine which structure was intended based on the context in which it was used.

In the PRONOUN RETENTION strategy, the relativized function is assigned to a pronominal copy of the head noun, i.e., a resumptive pronoun. These resumptive pronouns are regular personal pronouns which agree with the head noun in gender and number. As example (31) illustrates, if pronouns in a given language are normally marked for case, the case marking of a resumptive pronoun will reflect the grammatical relation of the relativized function. (The resumptive pronouns are underlined in the following examples.)

(30)   **Persian** (Keenan, 1985b)
          Man [zan-i   râ   ke   [John be u   sibe zamini dâd]] mishenasam.
          I   woman-the ACC REL John to her potato   gave know
          'I know the woman that John gave the potato to (her).'

(31)   **Israeli Hebrew** (Givón, 1973)
   a   ha-ish   she=[etmol   raiti   oto]
          the-man REL=yesterday 1sg-saw him(ACC)
          'the man that I saw (him) yesterday'

   b   ha-ish   she=[etmol   natati   lo   et   ha-sefer]
          the-man REL=yesterday 1sg-gave him(DAT) ACC the-book
          'the man that I gave the book to (him) yesterday'

The third common strategy involves the use of a RELATIVE PRONOUN. Relative pronouns can be described as anaphoric elements which introduce the modifying clause and take the head noun as their antecedent. Unlike resumptive pronouns, which occur *in situ*, relative pronouns normally occur just to the left of the modifying clause, i.e., between S$_{REL}$ and the head noun. The words which function as relative pronouns are different from the normal personal pronouns of the language. They are often derived from demonstratives or, as in English, from interrogative elements. The use of the relative pronouns *who, which, whose*, and *whom* is illustrated in (32) and (33).

(32) a   the spy who loves me
     b   the spy who(m) I love
     c   the spy from whom I bought these documents
     d   the spy who I bought these documents from
     e   the spy whose sister I love

(33) a   the professor who/*which my brother studied under
     b   the monkey which/??who(m) my brother trained
     c   the book which/*who(m) my brother edited

Now *that* and *who(m)* are often interchangeable in English relative clauses; the relativizer *that* could take the place of the relative pronoun in all of these examples except (32c and e). But, if that is true, why do we call one form a relative pronoun and the other a relativizer? More generally, how do we distinguish relative pronouns from relativizers in any language?

The crucial difference is that a relative pronoun is a special type of pronoun, i.e., an anaphoric NP, while a relativizer is not. The clearest evidence for the anaphoric nature of the relative pronoun is agreement, i.e., a change in the form of the relative pronoun depending on some features of the head noun (gender, number, animacy, etc.). Moreover, a relative pronoun is typically inflected for case, which is a property of NPs. A relativizer, in contrast, is normally an invariant particle (one that doesn't change shape), much like a complementizer. If there are changes in the shape of the relativizer, they are usually morphophonemic in nature and do not reflect agreement or case features.

In English, neither case nor agreement are strongly reflected in the morphology. Vestigial case marking can be observed in the choice between *who* (nominative), *whom* (dative/accusative), and *whose* (genitive). (The form *whom* is now rarely used in informal conversation. It is optional when the relativized position is a direct object [32b], and obligatory only when it follows a preposition, as in [32c].) A kind of animacy agreement determines the choice between *who* (for humans) and *which* (for non-humans), as illustrated in (33). In contrast, the relativizer *that* never changes form; it is not marked for case or agreement, occurring equally with subject or object, animate or inanimate.

The case and agreement features of the relative pronoun are much more obvious in other languages. German provides a very clear example. The relative pronoun in German is identical in form with the definite article. It agrees with the head noun for gender and number, and its case marking indicates the grammatical relation which the head noun is understood to bear within the modifying clause. In other words, it bears the case marking which would be assigned to the gap. Example (34) illustrates this change in case marking.

(34)   **German** (Stern and Bleiler, 1961)

    a   der Reiseführer, [der   uns die Stadt zeigt]
        the guide   who(SG.MASC.NOM) us the city shows
        'the guide who shows us the city'

    b   der Reiseführer, [dessen   Adresse wir haben wollen]
        the guide   who(SG.MASC.GEN) address we have want
        'the guide whose address we want to have'

    c   der Reiseführer, [dem   ich ein gutes Trinkgeld gegeben habe]
        the guide   who(SG.MASC.DAT) I a   good tip   given   have
        'the guide to whom I gave a good tip'

    d   der Reiseführer, [den   ich Ihnen empfehlen kann]
        the guide   who(SG.MASC.ACC) I   you   recommend can
        'the guide whom I can recommend to you'

If a relative pronoun is marked for case, its case marking will generally be the one which corresponds to the relativized function as in German. But in a few languages (e.g., Latin and Greek), the case marking of the relative pronoun may correspond to the grammatical function of the head noun in the larger (matrix) sentence.

A fourth strategy which may be used is that the relativized argument may be expressed by a full NP. This strategy is not common, but occurs in at least two different constructions. A few languages have INTERNALLY HEADED relative clauses, in which the head noun appears inside the modifying clause. The Bambara language from West Africa is a well-known case.[7]

(35)   **Bambara** (West Africa; Keenan, 1985b)
  a   Ne ye   so   ye.
          I   PAST horse see
          'I saw a horse.'

  b   Tye ye   [ne ye   <u>so</u>   min ye] san.
          man PAST I   PAST horse REL see   buy
          'The man bought the horse which I saw.'

Another type of relative construction in which the relativized argument is expressed by a full NP is the CORRELATIVE. In this construction the head noun occurs both inside and outside the modifying clause. An example is provided in (36).[8]

(36)   **Hindi** (Keenan, 1985b)
          <u>Jis</u>   <u>aadmi</u>=ka kutta bemaar hai, <u>us</u> <u>aadmi</u>=ko mai=ne dekha.
          which man=GEN dog   sick   is   that man=OBJ I=ERG   saw
          'I saw the man whose dog is sick.'
          (lit.: 'Which man's dog is sick, that man I saw.')

Internally headed relative clauses and correlative constructions are relatively rare, and we will not discuss them further in this book. We will focus instead on the more familiar, externally headed relative clauses.

7.2.3   Word order

In describing the structure of an externally headed relative clause, one of the first questions to be asked is whether the clausal modifier (S_{REL}) precedes or follows the head N. It turns out that there is a correlation between the position of S_{REL} and other basic word-order patterns in the language. Verb-initial languages (VSO or VOS) almost always have postnominal relatives, i.e., S_{REL} follows the head N. Verb-final (SOV) languages usually have prenominal relatives, with S_{REL} preceding the head N. Examining the data in greater detail, we find two basic tendencies at work:

a   Clausal modifiers tend to occupy the same position as other NP modifiers, e.g., adjectives. Thus languages with A-N order (notably the V-final languages) will tend to have Rel-N (prenominal relative clauses). Languages with N-A order (notably the V-initial languages) will tend to have N-Rel (postnominal relative clauses). This pattern is part of the principle of typological "harmony."

b   Clausal modifiers tend to occur in final position within the NP. This is part of a general tendency for "heavy" constituents to occur near the end of the phrase or sentence which contains them.

These two tendencies reinforce each other in the case of V-initial languages, with the result that these languages almost never have prenominal relative clauses.[9] The two tendencies compete with each other in the case of V-final languages. Thus in some SOV languages (e.g., Yaqui), the postnominal pattern is preferred; but in many others (Japanese, Korean, Tibetan, Turkish, etc.) prenominal relative clauses are the normal pattern. A Turkish example is given in (11). Notice that, in this example, the verb of the modifying clause ('give') is nominalized, and its subject ('John') takes genitive case marking. This is a very common pattern in languages with prenominal relative clauses.

(37)   **Turkish** (Keenan, 1985b)
        [John='un Mary=ye   ver-dig-i]   patates-i   yedim.
        John=GEN Mary=DAT give-NMLZR-his potato=ACC 1sg.ate
        'I ate the potato that John gave to Mary.'
        (lit.: 'I ate the potato of John's giving to Mary.')

SVO languages like English, which tend to be typologically mixed, show a strong preference for postnominal relative clauses. This preference seems like a natural outcome of the tendency to place heavy constituents last, given the absence of any strong harmonic effect in many of these languages.

In addition to the word-order correlations noted above, we also find some correlations between word order and relativization strategies. Prenominal relative clauses almost always make use of the gap strategy. Relative pronouns are found only in postnominal relative clauses (Keenan, 1985b:149), and (as noted above) almost always occur at the beginning of S_{REL}. Resumptive pronouns are normally found only in postnominal relative clauses; Chinese is the only known counterexample to this generalization (Keenan, 1985b:149).

7.2.4   The Accessibility Hierarchy

Two generalizations emerged from our discussion of "islands" (i.e., constraints on extraction from certain positions) in section 7.1.2. First, some positions are harder to relativize (less accessible) than others; for example, elements of a subordinate clause are generally less accessible than elements of a main clause. Second, there is a correlation between relativization strategy and accessibility.

We have seen that the gap strategy tends to be avoided in the more inaccessible positions, such as coordinate structures and embedded clauses, while resumptive pronouns tend to be preferred in these positions.

Even within a simple clause, certain functions tend to be more accessible than others. For example, in many languages prepositional objects (i.e., obliques and adjuncts) are harder to relativize (less accessible) than subjects and direct objects. Keenan and Comrie (1977) described this general pattern in terms of an ACCESSIBILITY HIERARCHY, a ranking of positions or functions within the clause based on accessibility to relativization. This hierarchy is very similar to the Relational Hierarchy that we presented in chapter 4, in discussing the relative prominence constraint on reflexive binding. A simplified version of the Accessibility Hierarchy (adapted from Comrie, 1981) is shown in (38):

(38)   ACCESSIBILITY HIERARCHY:
            SUBJ > OBJ > OBL > Possessor

The basic intuition is that positions at the left end of the scale are easier to relativize than positions on the right. This basic intuition can be elaborated in several specific ways. For example, the following generalization holds for a large majority of the world's languages:

(39)   **Generalization 1:**
            "If a language can form relative clauses on a given position on the
            hierarchy, then it can also form relative clauses on all positions higher
            (to the left) on the hierarchy."   (Comrie, 1981: § 7.3.1)

In other words, any language which can relativize objects can also relativize subjects; any language which can relativize obliques can also relativize objects (as well as subjects); any language which can relativize possessors can also relativize obliques and all higher positions.

This generalization predicts that if a language has relative clauses at all, it must be able to relativize subjects; and if there is only one type of argument which can be relativized in a language, that argument will be the subject. If a language allows relativization on only two functions, those functions must be the subject and the object.

Malagasy, Tagalog, and most Philippine-type languages are examples of languages which can relativize only on subjects. The following Tagalog examples are taken from Schachter (1976). Sentences (40a–b) illustrate the structure of simple active and passive clauses, together with the basic verb forms used in each case. These clauses form the basis for the relative clauses shown in (41) and (42). In (41a), the head noun corresponds to the active subject of S_{REL}, while in (41b) the head noun corresponds to the passive subject. Both examples in (42) are ungrammatical, because in both cases the relativized function is a non-subject argument: the passive agent in (42a), the active direct object in (42b).[10]

(40) a   Bumasa ang=lalaki ng=diyario.
            AV-read NOM=man GEN=newspaper
            'The man read a newspaper.'

   b   Binasa ng=lalaki ang=diyario.
            OV-read GEN=man NOM=newspaper
            'The newspaper was read by a/the man.'

(41) a   Matalino ang=lalaki=ng bumasa ng=diyario.
            intelligent NOM=man=REL AV-read GEN=newspaper
            'The man who read a newspaper is intelligent.'

   b   Interesante ang=diyario=ng   binasa ng=lalaki.
            interesting NOM=newspaper=REL OV-read GEN=man
            'The newspaper which the man read is interesting.'

(42) a   *Matalino ang=lalaki=ng binasa ang=diyario.
            intelligent NOM=man=REL OV-read NOM=newspaper

   b   *Interesante ang=diyario=ng   bumasa ang=lalaki.
            interesting NOM=newspaper=REL AV-read NOM=man

Many Bantu languages allow relativization only of subjects and objects. In order to relativize an oblique argument, it must be promoted to object using the applicative construction (see chapter 3). The following examples are from Luganda. Sentence (43a) illustrates a basic transitive clause with the instrument expressed as a PP. This oblique instrumental phrase cannot be relativized, as demonstrated in (43b). However, when the verb is marked with the instrumental applicative suffix, as in (43c), the instrument becomes the primary object, and so becomes eligible for relativization (43d).

(43)   **Luganda** (Bantu; Keenan, 1985b:158–159)
   a   John yatta enkonko n'=ekiso.
            John killed chicken with=knife
            'John killed the chicken with a knife.'

   b   *ekiso John (na) kye-yatta enkonko (na)
            knife John with REL-killed chicken with
            (for: 'the knife with which John killed the chicken')

   c   John yatt-is-a   ekiso enkonko.
            John kill-APPL-ASP knife chicken
            'John killed with a knife the chicken.'

   d   ekiso John kye-yatt-is-a   enkonko
            knife John REL-kill-APPL-ASP chicken
            'the knife with which John killed the chicken'

Generalization 1 expresses a strong cross-linguistic tendency; but it does not hold as an absolute universal. For example, Keenan and Comrie (1979) and Comrie (1981) point out that Malay and a number of other western Indonesian languages are exceptions to this generalization. Malay allows relativization only of subjects and possessors, but not of objects or obliques.[11] But it is important to note that different strategies are employed in the two types of relative clause: subjects are relativized using the gap strategy (44a), whereas possessors are relativized using the resumptive pronoun strategy (44b).

(44)   (based on Comrie, 1981)

a   **Gap strategy**

Gadis [yang __ duduk di.atas bangku] itu   kakak   Ali.
girl   REL   sit   on   bench   that older.sister Ali
'The girl who is sitting on the bench is Ali's big sister.'

b   **Resumptive pronoun**

Gadis [yang abang=nya   memukul saya] itu   sedang datang.
girl   REL older.brother=her hit   me   that PROG arrive
'The girl whose elder brother hit me is coming now.'

Notice also that Malay allows relativization of possessors of subjects (45a), but not of other possessors (45b). We will return to this point below.

(45)   **Malay** (based on Comrie, 1981)

a   Di.mana orang yang abang=nya   memukul saya itu?
where   person REL older.brother=his hit   me   that
'Where is the person whose big brother hit me?'

b   *Di.mana orang yang saya memukul abang=nya   itu?
where   person REL I   hit   older.brother=his that
(for: 'Where is the person whose big brother I hit?')

Keenan and Comrie (1977) emphasize the need to interpret the Accessibility Hierarchy as applying to specific strategies. They propose the following generalizations:

(46)   **Hierarchy Constraints:**

a   every language which has relative clauses can relativize on subjects;
b   any relative clause strategy within a particular language must apply to a continuous segment of the accessibility hierarchy.

This formulation accounts for Malay (and most of the other Indonesian exceptions to Generalization 1), because relativization of subjects uses the gap strategy, whereas relativization of possessors uses the resumptive pronoun strategy. In fact, very few counter-examples to these Hierarchy Constraints have been found. Most of the proposed counter-examples involve syntactically ergative languages like Dyirbal, in which transitive patients can be relativized but transitive agents cannot. However, under the analysis which will be developed in chapter 11, Dyirbal too conforms to these constraints (in particular [46a]).[12]

We have already noted that positions near the left end of the accessibility hierarchy are more likely to be relativized by the gap strategy, while positions near the right end of the scale are more likely to be relativized by the resumptive pronoun strategy (Keenan, 1985b:148). The situation described by Givón (1973) for Hebrew is fairly typical. As noted above, when S_{REL} preserves the basic SVO word order, resumptive pronouns are strongly disfavored when the subjects are relativized (47a), optional when objects are relativized (47b), and obligatory when secondary objects (47c) or oblique arguments are relativized.

(47)   **Hebrew main clause relativization** (Givón, 1973)

a   ha-ish   she=[Ø / *hu   hika et   ha-kelev]
          the-man REL=Ø / he(NOM) hit   ACC the-dog
          'the man that (*he) hit the dog'

b   ha-ish   she=[Yoav raa Ø / oto   etmol]
          the-man REL=Yoav saw Ø / him(ACC) yesterday
          'the man that Yoav saw (him) yesterday'

c   ha-ish   she=[Yoav natan *Ø / lo   et   ha-sefer][13]
          the-man REL=Yoav gave   Ø / him(DAT) ACC the-book
          'the man that Yoav gave (him) the book'

Aside from the "mixed-ergative" languages discussed in note 11, genuine counter-examples to this generalization (i.e., languages which require resumptive pronouns at a higher position but allow gaps in a lower position) appear to be quite rare. A possible counter-example is Vata, a Kru language of West Africa. Koopman (1983, 1984) states that in Vata, resumptive pronouns are obligatory when the subject is relativized (48a) and impossible in all other positions.

(48)   **Vata** (W. Africa; Koopman, 1983)

a   kɔ   mɔmɔ [*Ø / ɔ le-ɓɔ   saka]
          man whoREL Ø / he eat-REL rice
          'the man who (he) is eating rice'

b   saka mama   [kɔ le-ɓɔ   Ø / *ma]
          rice whichREL man eat-REL Ø / it
          'the rice which the man is eating (*it)'

Nevertheless, the general tendency for resumptive pronouns to occur in less-accessible positions is quite strong. It has been suggested that this tendency is motivated by processing factors such as the need to preserve information concerning the relativized function, but we will not pursue this idea here.

7.3   Relative clause structures

7.3.1   Relativization and topicalization

Now let us consider how we might represent the structure of relative clauses. We have already noted that two of the relativization strategies discussed in section 7.2 are very similar to topic–comment patterns which were discussed in chapter 6. This is clearly not accidental; the structural similarities between relative clauses and topic–comment sentences in a number of languages suggest that the two constructions are in fact closely related.

Kuno (1973) presents a variety of evidence suggesting that there are strong parallels between relative clauses and topic–comment constructions in Japanese. For example, in most cases an NP can be relativized if and only if it can be topicalized with the particle *wa*. In example (49), the prepositional object *John* cannot be topicalized (49b),[14] nor can it be relativized (49c). (In Japanese there is no structural difference between non-restrictive relative clauses, like (49c), and restrictive relative clauses.) However, when the adverbial element *issyo-ni* 'together' is added, *John* can be both topicalized (50b) and relativized (50c).

(49)   **Japanese** (Kuno, 1973)
   a   Marii=ga   Zyon=to   benkyoo-sita.
        Mary=NOM John=with studied
        'Mary studied with John.'

   b   *Zyon=wa   Marii=ga   benkyoo-sita.
        John=TOP Mary=NOM studied

   c   *[Marii=ga   benkyoo-sita] Zyon
        Mary=NOM studied   John
        (for: 'John, with whom Mary studied')

(50) a   Marii=ga   Zyon=to   issyo-ni benkyoo-sita.
        Mary=NOM John=with together studied
        'Mary studied with John.'

   b   Zyon=wa   Marii=ga   issyo-ni benkyoo-sita.
        John=TOP Mary=NOM together studied
        'John Mary studied with.'

   c   [Marii=ga   issyo-ni benkyoo-sita] Zyon
        Mary=NOM together studied   John
        (for: 'John, with whom Mary studied')

Kuno presents a large number of similar examples, as well as a few exceptions to his generalization.[15] While the correlation between topicalization and relativization is not perfect, the parallels are quite striking. Similar parallels are found in other languages as well. For example, Bresnan and Mchombo (1987) show that the distribution of incorporated vs. independent object pronouns in Chichewa relative clauses is the same as in topicalization. A topicalized OBJ NP may be coreferential with an incorporated pronoun (51a) but not with a free pronoun (51b). In the same way, the head N of a relative clause may be coreferential with an incorporated pronoun (52a) but not with a free pronoun (52b).

(51)   **Chichewa** (Bresnan and Mchombo, 1987:769; tone not marked)[16]

   a   Mkango uwu fisi   a-na-u-dy-a.
        lion(3)   this hyena(1) SUBJ(1)-PAST-PRO(3)-eat-INDIC
        'This lion, the hyena ate it.'

   b   *?Mkango uwu fisi   a-na-dy-a   iwo
        lion(3)   this hyena(1) SUBJ(1)-PAST-eat-INDIC PRO(3)

(52) a   mkango u-mene fisi   a-na-u-dy-a.
        lion(3) 3-REL hyena(1) SUBJ(1)-PAST-PRO(3)-eat-INDIC
        'the lion which the hyena ate (it)'

   b   *?mkango u-mene fisi   a-na-dy-a   iwo
        lion(3) 3-REL hyena(1) SUBJ(1)-PAST-eat-INDIC PRO(3)

The incorporated object pronouns are inherently topic-oriented. They cannot be used when the object is questioned, as seen in (53b), because the question word must bear pragmatic focus. Bresnan and Mchombo use this contrast between questions and relative clauses to support their claim that the head of a relative clause bears the topic function.

(53)   **Chichewa** (Bresnan and Mchombo, 1987:759–760; tone not marked)

   a   (Kodi) mu-ku-fun-a   chiyani?
        QUES you.SUBJ-PRES-want-INDIC what(7)
        'What do you want?'

   b   ??(Kodi) mu-ku-chi-fun-a   chiyani?
        QUES you.SUBJ-PRES-PRO(7)-want-INDIC what(7)
        (lit: 'What do you want it?')

In section 7.2.4 we noted that Malay allows possessors of subjects to be relativized (using the resumptive pronoun strategy), but not other possessors (see example [45]). This is also true for Indonesian. Sneddon (1996) reports that the same constraint applies to the topicalization of possessors. In this construction, the topicalized NP must be the possessor of the subject of the clause. The possessor of a passive subject can be topicalized in this way (54b), but not the possessor of a direct object in an active clause (54c).

(54) a   Sopir itu, nama=nya Pak Ali.
        driver that name=his Mr. Ali
        'About that driver, his name is Mr. Ali.'

   b   Mahasiswa itu, rambut=nya tidak pernah di-sisir.
        student   that hair=his   not ever PASS-comb
        'That student, his hair is never combed.'

   c   *Mahasiswa itu, polisi telah memotong rambut=nya.
        student   that police PAST cut   hair=his
        (for: 'That student, the police have cut his hair.')

Thus we find a striking parallelism between topicalization of possessors and relativization of possessors in Indonesian: both constructions employ the resumptive pronoun strategy, and both apply only to the possessor of the subject NP. These facts suggest that the two constructions are structurally similar.

More generally, the strong similarities between topicalization and relativization in a number of languages provide evidence that these constructions have many structural features in common. In describing relative clauses which involve the gap and resumptive pronoun strategies, it seems natural to adopt the same basic analysis which we proposed in chapter 6 for topic–comment patterns involving those strategies. This analysis will be outlined in section 7.3.2. An analysis of the relative pronoun strategy, which does not seem to have a close parallel in any topic–comment structure, will be outlined in section 7.3.3.

7.3.2   Gaps and resumptive pronouns in relative clauses

As we have seen, Malay employs both the gap and the resumptive pronoun strategies: the former in subject-relatives (55a); the latter in possessor-relatives (55b).

(55) a   [Budak yang memukul saya itu] kurang ajar   betul.
          child   REL hit   me   that less   teach truly
          'The child who hit me is very impolite.'

     b   [Budak yang abang=<u>nya</u>   memukul saya itu] tidak bersekolah.
          child   REL older.brother=his hit   me   that not   go.to.school
          'The child whose elder brother hit me does not go to school.'

The S_{REL} functions as a modifier of the head noun in both cases, but the relationship between the head noun (*budak*) and its modifying clause is different in these two examples. In (55a), which involves the gap strategy, the head noun is assigned the SUBJ relation by the embedded predicate *memukul*, as represented in (56a). But in (55b), the head noun has no direct grammatical relation to the embedded predicate. Rather, it is anaphorically related as the antecedent of the possessive pronoun =*nya*. This pattern is represented in (56b).

(56) a   **Gap strategy**

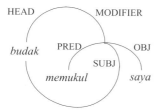

b   **Resumptive pronoun**

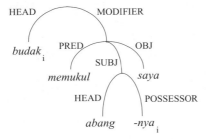

7.3.3   Relative pronouns

In the following German example, taken from Keenan (1985b), the relative pronoun *den* agrees with the head noun *Mann* for number and gender, indicating that an anaphoric relationship exists. That is, the head noun is the antecedent of the relative pronoun. At the same time, the relative pronoun is inflected for case (in this example accusative) to reflect its grammatical relation (direct object) within the modifying clause.

In these respects, a relative pronoun is very similar to a resumptive pronoun. But the relative pronoun differs from the resumptive pronoun in one important respect: it always precedes the modifying clause, rather than occurring in the normal, clause-internal position associated with its grammatical relation. Crucially, example (57a) contains a gap in S$_{REL}$ corresponding to the relativized function, whereas resumptive pronoun examples like (55b) contain no gap. We can account for both the case-marking and the position of the relative pronoun by assuming that it is the filler for the gap in S$_{REL}$, and functions as the topic of the modifying clause. The structure of the relative clause as a whole can be represented as in (57b):

(57) a   der   Mann, <u>den</u>   Marie liebt
           the(NOM.MASC.SG) man   PRO(ACC.MASC.SG) Marie loves
           'the man whom Marie loves'

b
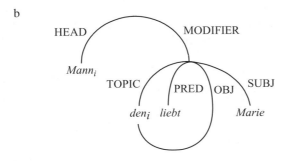

The relative pronoun bears a dual function here: it is anaphorically related to the head noun, but functionally identified with the gap in the modifying clause. This analysis is supported by cases where the head noun itself cannot be interpreted as the filler of the gap, e.g., possessor relatives in English like (58a). This example can only mean that it was the dog, and not the man, who got killed. In this case the topic of S_{REL} and the filler of the gap (i.e., the understood object of *killed*) is the phrase *whose dog*. The head noun *man* is not the filler; it functions as the antecedent of the possessor of the object phrase, i.e., of the relative pronoun *whose*.

(58) a   the man$_i$ [whose$_i$ dog [John killed __]]

   b

Here the dual relationships of a relative pronoun are clearly distinguished: the filler–gap relationship involves the whole phrase headed by *dog*, whereas the anaphoric relationship involves only *whose*.

7.4   Conclusion

As we have seen, filler–gap constructions have a number of distinctive properties. Most strikingly, the "filler" can bear a grammatical relation and semantic role within a clause which it is not structurally a part of (i.e., the position of the filler is outside the clause boundaries). In addition to its clause-level grammatical relation, the filler typically bears a special pragmatic function such as topic or focus. In many languages, there is no fixed limit on the number of clause boundaries that can intervene between filler and gap; in this case, the dependency between the two is said to be unbounded. However, the more deeply embedded the gap is in relation to the filler, the more likely it is that the "gap" will be occupied by a resumptive pronoun.

Relative clauses are an especially interesting type of filler–gap construction. The head noun functions as the filler, and is assigned a grammatical relation and semantic role within its modifying clause. But the entire NP containing the relative clause is itself an element of a larger clause. So in addition to the normal constraints on filler–gap constructions in the language, the structure of a relative clause is also determined by the rules for NPs in general, and by the syntax of the larger clause within which it occurs. Perhaps because of this added degree of complexity, relative clauses in some languages employ a special strategy for signaling the relationship between filler and gap, namely the relative pronoun.

Notes

1. See, for example, Kroch (1981), Prince (1990), Bickford (1998); and Cann, Kaplan, and Kempson (in press).
2. Givón states that resumptive pronouns become obligatory whenever a non-subject element is fronted to initial position within S_{REL}.
3. Givón points out that the resumptive pronouns could be omitted in (17) if these sentences are interpreted as double relative constructions, e.g., 'the man whom I knew, and whom the dog bit yesterday.' But this interpretation is irrelevant to the issue under discussion here.
4. See Kaplan and Bresnan (1982); Bresnan (2001); and references cited there for a discussion of this issue.
5. One piece of evidence which is often cited as supporting the existence of an empty NP position comes from the possibility of using contracted forms like *wanna* for *want to* in American English. However, Sag and Fodor (1994) and Pullum (1997) have presented strong arguments for analyses of these facts which do not posit the existence of a gap in phrase structure.
6. This abbreviation was used by Keenan and Comrie (1977) and has been adopted in much subsequent work.
7. Example (35b) has been very widely cited for the past thirty-five years. However, while this book was being typeset Youssouf Dembele (p.c.) informed me that most Bambara speakers would actually consider the sentence ungrammatical. This fact is also noted by Creissels (2000). For more reliable examples of internally headed relative clauses from West Africa, see Culy (1990).
8. As Keenan (1985b:164) points out, such examples are technically not relative clauses because the restrictive clause is not a modifier within a noun phrase. But they serve the same function as relative clauses in other languages.
9. Tagalog allows both N-Rel and Rel-N orders, perhaps because it also allows both orders for adjectives (N-A and A-N). But N-Rel seems to be preferred.
10. The voice marking affixes in these examples are glossed AV for "Active Voice" and OV for "Objective Voice", which is similar to a passive construction. See chapter 11 for a discussion of voice in some related languages.
11. This generalization applies only to Bahasa Malaysia. Sneddon (1996) points out that in Bahasa Indonesia, objects and obliques can be relativized using the resumptive pronoun strategy. Even in Indonesian, however, some speakers find examples involving relativized objects quite odd.
12. Keenan and Comrie (1977) note that Tongan appears to be a counter-example. In Tongan, resumptive pronouns are allowed and sometimes required when a transitive subject is relativized, and are obligatory for obliques and possessors; but resumptive pronouns are not allowed when a transitive object is relativized. Thus the resumptive pronoun strategy applies to a discontinuous segment of the hierarchy. Comrie (1981) notes that Tongan syntax displays a significant degree of ergativity, although whether Tongan can be described as a syntactically ergative language has been a topic of debate

(Dukes, 1998). Similarly, some Mayan languages seem to be syntactically ergative, while others present mixed properties which, like Tongan, pose a challenge to the Hierarchy Constraints in (46).

13. Givón states that the resumptive pronoun in such examples can be omitted if the head noun itself is marked for dative case.

14. Example (49b) would be grammatical if the post-position = *to* 'with' were retained before the topic particle, as in: *Zyon=to=wa Marii=ga benkyoosita*. Yo Matsumoto (p.c.) informs me that both (49b) and (49c) could be grammatical under the less plausible reading that John is the object of Mary's study, e.g., 'John, whom Mary studied.'

15. See Yoshiko Matsumoto (1997) for a discussion of various challenges to Kuno's analysis.

16. The numbers in the glosses of these examples refer to Bantu noun classes.

8   Causative constructions

Consider the following three sentences:

(1) a   My cat died.
   b   The Mayor caused my cat to die.
   c   The Mayor killed my cat.

Sentence (1a) is a simple clause which describes an event involving one argument, namely *my cat*. Sentence (1b) is a biclausal construction involving two participants, and describing two distinct events. The complement clause in (1b) describes the same event that was expressed in (1a), while the matrix clause refers to a different event in which the Mayor performed some unspecified action. Clearly there is a logical connection between the two events: one is the result of the other. In other words, the first event (the Mayor's action) is seen as the cause of the second (my cat dying).

Sentences (1b) and (1c) are similar in meaning, but not perfectly synonymous. Sentence (1c) seems to imply that the Mayor personally killed my cat, while (1b) would be more appropriate if the cat's death was an indirect result of some action on the Mayor's part (e.g., ordering that all the dogs in the dog pound should be released). Nevertheless, there is a substantial overlap in meaning between the two sentences. Both imply a cause-and-effect relationship between two events; the causing event in both cases is something the Mayor did; and the effect (or result) in both cases is the event described in (1a).

Both (1b) and (1c) are examples of CAUSATIVE constructions. Causatives describe semantically complex situations in which one event causes another. The Actor of the first event is called the CAUSER. The event that results from his action is called the CAUSED EVENT. The most prominent argument of the caused event, i.e., the argument which would be expressed as the subject of a simple clause describing that event, is called the CAUSEE. So for both (1b) and (1c), *the Mayor* is the causer, *my cat* is the causee, and (1a) describes the caused event.

8.1   Three ways of expressing causation

Even though (1b) and (1c) are very similar in meaning, they are very different in terms of grammatical structure. Sentence (1b) contains two verbs and two distinct clauses, as noted above. Sentence (1c), on the other hand, is (like

[1a]) a simple sentence containing a single verb and just one clause. The complex nature of the causative situation is directly reflected in the structure of (1b), with each event being expressed in a separate clause. In (1c), however, the complexity is entirely due to the semantics of the verb *kill*; both the cause and the result are inherent parts of the meaning of this verb.

Causative constructions are traditionally classified into three major types, based on these kinds of differences in grammatical structure. Sentence (1b) is an example of a PERIPHRASTIC (or ANALYTIC) CAUSATIVE. This label indicates that the causative expression "cause to X" is expressed by two separate verbs. The biclausal periphrastic causative found in English, and in many other languages, is a lexically determined control construction similar to those discussed in chapter 5. We will not have much more to say about these constructions in this chapter. In the next chapter, however, we will discuss another kind of periphrastic causative which involves two verbs occurring within a single clause.

Sentence (1c) is an example of a LEXICAL CAUSATIVE. This label is used for verbs that include the sense of causation as a part of their basic semantic content. The word *kill* means (roughly) 'cause to die,' but there is no morphological relationship between the words *kill* and *die*. Other similar verbs in English include *feed* 'cause to *eat*' and *inform* 'cause to *know*.' Sometimes there is a phonological similarity between the causative verb and the corresponding basic verb, e.g., *seat* 'cause to *sit*'; *fell (a tree)* 'cause to *fall*'; *lay* 'cause to *lie*'; *walk* (e.g., a dog) 'cause to *walk*.' But the phonological correspondences between these pairs of verbs are irregular. There is no productive morphological process which relates the causative verb to the corresponding basic predicate, so these cases are also examples of lexical causatives.

The third basic type of causative construction is the MORPHOLOGICAL CAUSATIVE. This term indicates that the causative form meaning "cause to X" is derived from a basic predicate meaning "X" through a regular morphological process, e.g., affixation. One such example is the causative prefix *po-* in Kimaragang Dusun, which can be added to a verb root like *suwang* 'enter' to derive *po-suwang* 'cause to enter.' English has derivational suffixes which create causative forms, as in *short* + *-en* → *shorten*; *normal* + *-ize* → *normalize*. However, these affixes also involve a change of category, since they derive verbs from adjectives (or sometimes nouns). There is no productive morphological process in English for deriving causative verbs from verbal roots.

Most comparative studies of causatives have focused on the morphological type. The derivation of a causative verb will involve changes to the argument structure of the base verb, since a new participant (the causer) is introduced. Thus causative formation is a VALENCE-INCREASING process; the semantic valence of the causative verb will always be one greater than the valence of the base verb.

This change in valence will of course affect the assignment of grammatical relations. The causer is almost always encoded as the subject of the causative construction, while the causee receives different grammatical relations in different languages. However, when we examine morphological causatives in many different languages, we find that two basic patterns are available for expressing the causee. These will be discussed in the next section.

8.2   The status of the causee

The grammatical relation of the causee depends first of all on the valence of the basic predicate from which the causative is derived. (We are restricting our discussion primarily to languages which have a morphological causative.) In causatives formed from intransitive roots, the causee is normally encoded as direct (or primary) object in all languages. In Turkish, the primary object takes accusative case (2b). In Swahili, the primary object is indicated by an optional object-agreement marker on the verb (3b).[1]

(2)   **Turkish** (Aissen, 1974)
    a   Hasan   öl-dü.
        Hasan   die-PAST
        'Hasan died.'

    b   Mehmet Hasan-ï   öl-dür-dü.[2]
        Mehmet Hasan-ACC die-CAUS-PAST
        'Mehmet caused Hasan to die, killed Hasan.'

(3)   **Swahili** (Bantu; Comrie, 1976)
    a   Mtungi u-me-ja-a.
        pot   S.agr-PERF-fill-INDIC
        'The pot has filled.'

    b   Ni-me-(u-)ja-z-a   mtungi.
        1sg.S-PERF-O.agr-fill-CAUS-INDIC pot
        'I have filled the pot.'

A more interesting picture emerges when we examine causatives derived from transitive roots. Baker (1988) has pointed out that the grammatical relation of the causee in a transitive causative is largely predictable from the marking of the recipient in basic (underived) ditransitive constructions in the same language. For the sake of concreteness, let us assume that a language has ditransitive verbs with argument structures similar to the one shown in (4):

(4)   *give* < agent, recipient, theme >

Dryer (1986) states that languages have two main options for expressing such predicates. First, the recipient may be realized as primary object (OBJ) and the theme as a secondary object (OBJ$_2$). In this pattern both objects are typically expressed as NPs with the same case marking, which is either accusative or zero. Swahili is an example of a language that chooses this pattern, as illustrated in (5).

(5)   **Swahili** (Vitale, 1981:130)
          Halima a-li-m-p-a   Fatuma zawadi.
          Halima S.agr-PAST-O.agr-give-ASP Fatuma gift
          'Halima gave Fatuma a gift.'

The other option is for the theme to be realized as the primary object (OBJ), with the recipient appearing either as an oblique argument (OBL), or as a secondary object (OBJ$_2$) with distinctive case marking (e.g., dative). Turkish employs the latter pattern, as illustrated in (6).

(6)   **Turkish** (Comrie, 1981)
          Müdür Hasan-a   mektub-u göster-di.
          director Hasan-DAT letter-ACC show-PAST
          'The director showed the letter to Hasan.'

Baker's generalization is this: if the recipient is expressed as a primary object, as in (5), then there is a strong tendency for a transitive causee also to be marked as a primary object. If the recipient is expressed as a secondary object (as in [6]) or oblique argument, then there is a strong tendency for a transitive causee also to be marked as a secondary object or oblique argument.[3] (The term "transitive causee" is used here for convenience to refer to the causee of a causative verb derived from a transitive root.) We will discuss these two options in the following two sections.

8.2.1   Causee as primary object

Examples (7) and (8) show how causative verbs are formed from transitive roots in Swahili. Based on the data in (5), which show that the recipient of a basic ditransitive is realized as the primary object, Baker's theory of causative formation predicts that transitive causees should also be expressed as primary objects; and that is exactly what we find in these examples.

(7)   **Swahili** (Comrie, 1976)
   a   Msichana a-li-(u-)fungu-a   mlango.
          girl   S.agr-PAST-O.agr-open-INDIC door
          'The girl opened the door.'

   b   Mwalimu a-li-m-fungu-zish-a   msichana mlango.
          teacher S.agr-PAST-O.agr-open-CAUS-INDIC girl   door
          'The teacher made the girl open the door.'

(8)   **Swahili** (Vitale, 1981:32, 164)
   a   Halima a-na-pik-a   ugali.
          Halima S.agr-PRES-cook-INDIC porridge
          'Halima is cooking porridge.'

   b   Sudi a-li-m-pik-ish-a   mke wake uji.
          Sudi S.agr-PAST-O.agr-cook-CAUS-INDIC wife his   gruel
          'Sudi made his wife cook some gruel.'

What is the evidence for identifying the causees in these examples as primary objects? First, word order: the preferred order is for the primary object to occur immediately after the verb.[4] Second, as mentioned above, the object agreement marker must agree with the noun class of the primary object. As we see in (7b) and (8b), the object agreement marker on the causative verb agrees with the causee. The patient of the basic predicate (e.g., 'door' in [7b]) occurs as a secondary object, and cannot trigger object agreement. This is demonstrated in (9), which is identical to (7b) except that the object agreement marker agrees with 'door' instead of 'girl'; the result is ungrammatical.

(9)   *Mwalimu a-li-u-fungu-zish-a   msichana mlango.
        teacher   S.agr-PAST-O.agr-open-CAUS-INDIC   girl   door
        (Obj-agr agrees with *mlango* 'door')

A third important piece of evidence is that only primary objects can be passivized (i.e., promoted to subject by the passive rule). In a basic ditransitive clause like (5), only the recipient can be passivized (10a), because it is the primary object. If the theme (the secondary object) is passivized, as in (10b), the result is ungrammatical.

(10)   **Swahili** (Vitale, 1981:131)
     a Fatuma a-li-p-ew-a   zawadi na Halima.
        Fatuma S.agr-PAST-give-PASS-INDIC gift   by Halima
        'Fatuma was given a gift by Halima.'

     b *zawadi i-li-p-ew-a   Fatuma na Halima.
        gift   S.agr-PAST-give-PASS-INDIC Fatuma by Halima
        (for: 'The gift was given to Fatuma by Halima.')

In the same way, a transitive causee can be passivized, as in (11a), because it is the primary object. The patient of the basic predicate cannot be passivized (11b), because it is the secondary object.

(11)   **Swahili** (Vitale, 1981:165)
     a mke wake a-li-pik-ish-w-a   uji   na Sudi.
        wife his   S.agr-PAST-cook-CAUS-PASS-INDIC gruel by Sudi
        'His wife was made to cook gruel by Sudi.'

     b *uji   u-li-pik-ish-w-a   mke wake na Sudi.
        gruel S.agr-PAST-cook-CAUS-PASS-INDIC wife his   by Sudi
        (for: 'The gruel was caused to be cooked by his wife by Sudi.')

Other languages which follow this "double object" pattern of causative formation include Chimwiini (Kisseberth and Abasheikh, 1977; Marantz, 1984), Malagasy (Andrianierenana, 1996), and Chamorro (Gibson, 1980; Gibson and Rapposo, 1986). The Chamorro facts are especially interesting, because there is an overt case marker which distinguishes secondary objects from primary objects. In a basic ditransitive clause like (12a), the secondary object (i.e., the theme, *babui*) takes the case-marking preposition *nu* ~ *ni*. (The same marker is also used for instruments and passive agents.) When a causative is formed from a basic transitive root (12c), the patient takes this same prepositional marker; the causee, like the primary object in (12a), is unmarked.

(12)   **Chamorro** (Austronesian; Gibson and Rapposo, 1986)

a   In=nä'i   si   tata-n-mami   nu   i   bäbui.
       1pl.EX=give PERS   father-LNK-our   OBJ₂   the   pig
       'We gave our father the pig.'

b   In=taitai   esti.na lebblu.
       1pl.EX=read   this   book
       'We read this book.'

c   Ha=na'-taitai   häm   i   ma'estru ni⁵   esti.na lebblu.
       3sg=CAUS-read   1pl.EX.ABS   the   teacher   OBJ₂   this   book
       'The teacher made us read this book.'

Now let us consider the other major option for marking transitive causees.

8.2.2   Causee as OBJ₂ or OBL

As we saw in example (6), recipients in Turkish are expressed as secondary objects with dative case. The theme of a basic ditransitive predicate is realized as the primary object. Baker's theory predicts that when causative verbs are formed from transitive roots, the root's patient should appear as primary object, with the causee expressed as either OBJ₂ or OBL. As the following examples show, this prediction is correct. The patient takes ACC case, while the causee takes DAT case.

(13)   **Turkish** (Aissen, 1974; Comrie, 1981)

a   Müdür   mektub-u   imzala-dï.
       director   letter-ACC   sign-PAST
       'The director signed the letter.'

b   Dişçi   mektub-u   müdür-e   imzala-t-tï.
       dentist letter-ACC   director-DAT   sign-CAUS-PAST
       'The dentist got the director to sign the letter.'

(14)   **Turkish** (Aissen, 1974)

a   Kasap   et-i   kes-ti.
       butcher meat-ACC   cut-PAST
       'The butcher cut the meat.'

b   Hasan kasab-a   et-i   kes-tir-di.
       Hasan butcher-DAT   meat-ACC   cut-CAUS-PAST
       'Hasan had the butcher cut the meat.'⁶

In addition to the difference in case marking, passivization again provides important evidence about the grammatical relations assigned to each argument. In a basic ditransitive clause, only the theme (i.e., the OBJ) can be passivized, as in (15b). The recipient (OBJ₂) cannot passivize, as seen in (15c).

(15)   **Turkish** (Gibson and Özkaragöz, 1981)

    a   çocuǧ-a   pasta-yï   ver-di.
           child-DAT cake-ACC give-PAST
           'He/she gave the cake to the child.'

    b   pasta   çocuǧ-a   ver-il-di.
           cake-NOM child-DAT give-PASS-PAST
           'The cake was given to the child.'

    c   *çocuk   pasta-yï   ver-il-di.
           child-NOM cake-ACC give-PASS-PAST
           (for: 'The child was given the cake.')

Similarly, in transitive causative constructions only the patient (OBJ) can passivize, as in (16c). The causee (OBJ₂) cannot passivize, as seen in (16d).

(16)   **Turkish** (Aissen, 1974)

    a   Hasan bavul-u   açtï.
           Hasan suitcase-ACC open-PAST
           'Hasan opened the suitcase.'

    b   Mehmet Hasan-a   bavul-u   aç-tïr-dï.
           Mehmet Hasan-DAT suitcase-ACC open-CAUS-PAST
           'Mehmet had Hasan open the suitcase.'

    c   Bavul   Mehmet tarafïndan Hasan-a   aç-tïr-ïl-dï.
           suitcase Mehmet by   Hasan-DAT open-CAUS-PASS-PAST
           'The suitcase was caused by Mehmet to be opened by Hasan.'

    d   *Hasan Mehmet tarafïndan bavul-u   aç-tïr-ïl-dï.
           Hasan Mehmet by   suitcase-ACC open-CAUS-PASS-PAST
           (for: 'Hasan was caused by Mehmet to open the suitcase.')

Malayalam, a Dravidian language of southern India, is similar to Turkish both in its case marking and in its pattern of causative formation. In a basic ditransitive clause, the theme is realized as the primary object, taking ACC case if animate and NOM case if inanimate. The recipient is a secondary object taking DAT case. As the examples in (17) demonstrate, only the theme (OBJ) can passivize; the recipient (OBJ₂) cannot passivize. These facts are parallel to the Turkish pattern illustrated in (15).

(17)   **Malayalam** (Mohanan 1982:509, and p.c.)

    a   kuṭṭi   amma-kkə aana-ye   koṭuṭṭu.
           child(NOM) mother-DAT elephant-ACC gave
           'The child gave the elephant to the mother.'

    b   kuṭṭiyaal   amma-kkə aana   koṭukkappeṭṭu.
           child-INSTR mother-DAT elephant(NOM) give-PASS-PAST
           'The elephant was given to the mother by the child.'

c   *kuṭṭiyaal   amma   aana-ye   koṭukkappeṭṭu.
       child-INSTR mother(NOM) elephant-ACC give-PASS-PAST
       (for: 'The mother was given an elephant by the child.')

When a causative verb is derived from an intransitive predicate, the causee is expressed as a primary object, as in all of the other languages we have considered thus far. The intransitive causee can passivize just like any other OBJ, as demonstrated in (18c).

(18) a   kuṭṭi   kaḷiccu.
           child(NOM)   played
           'The child played.' (1982:586)

     b   acchan   kuṭṭi-ye   kaḷippiccu.
           father(NOM)   child-ACC   play-CAUS-PAST
           'The father made the child play.'

     c   acchan-aal   kuṭṭi   kaḷippikkappeṭṭu.
           father-INSTR child(NOM)   play-CAUS-PASS-PAST
           'The child was made to play by father.'

When a causative verb is derived from a transitive predicate, it is the patient of the base predicate (not the causee) which is expressed as primary object, as predicted by Baker's generalization. The most obvious difference between Malayalam and Turkish concerns the marking of the transitive causee. Whereas the transitive causee in Turkish is a secondary object taking DAT case, in Malayalam it is an oblique argument (OBL) taking the post-position *koṇṭə* 'with.'

(19) a   kuṭṭi   aana-ye   ṇuḷḷi.
           child(NOM)   elephant-ACC pinched
           'The child pinched the elephant.' (1983a:59)

     b   amma   kuṭṭi-ye=kkoṇṭə aana-ye   ṇuḷḷiccu.
           mother(NOM)   child-ACC=with   elephant-ACC pinch-CAUS-PAST
           'Mother made the child pinch the elephant.'

Oblique causees are found, at least as a possible option, in a large number of languages; further examples will be given below. In most of these languages, the preposition which is used to mark oblique causees is either the same one used for passive agents, as in Turkish and French, or the one used for oblique recipients, as in Chichewa. Malayalam is unusual in this respect: oblique causees take a postposition which is used for instruments, but not for passive agents.[7]

Since the transitive causee is an oblique argument it cannot passivize, as demonstrated in (20b). Only the patient of the base predicate can be passivized, as seen in (20a). Notice that the causee is not expressed in this example. The potential for expressing causees in Malayalam depends on the transitivity of the root. In active causative clauses, intransitive causees are obligatory but transitive causees are optional. When an intransitive causative verb is passivized the causee is expressed as the subject, as in (18c); but when a transitive causative verb is passivized, the causee cannot be expressed at all, as seen in (20c).

(20) a   amma-yaal   aana   ṇuḷḷikkappeṭṭu.
          mother-INSTR elephant(NOM) pinch-CAUS-PASS-PAST
          'The elephant was caused by Mother to be pinched.' (1983a:63–64)

    b   *amma-yaal   kuṭṭi   aana-ye   ṇuḷḷikkappeṭṭu.
          mother-INSTR child(NOM) elephant-ACC pinch-CAUS-PASS-PAST
          (for: 'The child was caused by Mother to pinch the elephant.')

    c   *amma-yaal   kuṭṭi-ye=kkoṇṭə aana   ṇuḷḷikkappeṭṭu.
          mother-INSTR child-ACC=with elephant(NOM) pinch-CAUS-PASS-PAST
          (for: 'The elephant was caused by Mother to be pinched by the child.')

8.2.3   Causatives derived from ditransitive roots

Let us summarize the marking of causees we have observed thus far. In languages like Swahili, which mark recipients as primary objects, the causee is always a primary object. In languages like Turkish, which mark themes as primary objects and recipients as OBJ$_2$, the marking of the causee depends on the valence of the base predicate. If the base verb is intransitive, subcategorizing for only a SUBJ, the causee will be an OBJ. If the base verb is transitive, subcategorizing for SUBJ and OBJ, the causee will be an OBJ$_2$. What grammatical relation would you predict the causee to bear when the base verb is ditransitive?

There are a number of languages which have morphological causatives but which do not allow morphological causatives to be derived from basic ditransitive verbs. This is not altogether surprising, as the result of such a derivation would be a verb with four core arguments. Different languages set different limits as to the number of arguments which a single verb may take. However, Turkish does allow such constructions, as seen in (21). As this example illustrates, the ditransitive causee is an OBL argument marked with the postposition *tarafından*, the same postposition used to mark passive agents.

(21)   **Turkish** (Comrie, 1976, 1981)
    a   Müdür Hasan-a   mektub-u göster-di.
        director Hasan-DAT letter-ACC show-PAST
        'The director showed the letter to Hasan.'

    b   Dişçi Hasan-a   mektub-u müdür tarafından göster-t-ti.
        dentist Hasan-DAT letter-ACC director by   show-CAUS-PAST
        'The dentist got the director to show the letter to Hasan.'

Malayalam also allows ditransitive causatives. The causee in this construction takes the same instrumental postposition used with transitive causatives.

(22)   **Malayalam** (Mohanan, 1982:575)

a   amma kuṭṭi-kkə puṣṭakam koṭuttu.
mother child-DAT book   gave
'The mother gave a book to the child.'

b   accʰan amma-ye=kkonṭə kuṭṭi-kkə puṣṭakam koṭuppiccu.
father mother-ACC=with child-DAT book   give-CAUS-PAST
'Father caused mother to give a book to the child.'

[handwritten: mother is marked with ACC and takes the instrumental 'with']

Comrie (1976) reports that such constructions are also possible in Swahili, although they do not seem to be entirely natural. The result of the derivation is a clause with three objects (one primary and two secondary), as shown in (23b). The object agreement marker in this example agrees with the causee, *Johni*. This is consistent with the general pattern of Swahili causatives: the causee is always the primary object.

(23)   **Swahili** (Comrie, 1976)

a   Johni a-li-wa-lip-a   watoto pesa.
John S.agr-PAST-O.agr-pay-INDIC children money
'John paid the money to the children.'

b   ?Maria a-li-m-lip-ishiz-a   Johni watoto pesa.
Mary S.agr-PAST-O.agr-pay-CAUS-INDIC John children money
'Mary made John pay the money to the children.'

8.2.4   Causee as "next available GR"

Comrie (1981) has pointed out that the GR of the causee in languages like Turkish can be predicted from the Relational Hierarchy: the causee will always get the highest relation on the hierarchy which is not part of the subcategorization of the base verb. In other words, the causee is assigned the "next available" GR. This pattern, which we have seen demonstrated in the examples above, is summarized in (24):

(24)
SUBCAT. OF BASE VERB	GR OF CAUSEE
{SUBJ}	OBJ
{SUBJ, OBJ}	OBJ$_2$
{SUBJ, OBJ, OBJ$_2$}	OBL

Based on this generalization, what do you predict would happen to the causee when the base verb takes a SUBJ and either an OBJ$_2$ or an OBL argument, but no primary object? The "next available" GR in this case would be OBJ. The verb meaning 'start' in Turkish is one such predicate; its second argument is marked for dative case, as seen in (25a), suggesting that it is not a primary object. Example (25b) illustrates what happens when a causative verb is formed from this root. As predicted by Comrie's hierarchy, the causee (*Hasan*) is expressed as an OBJ, taking accusative case.

(25)   **Turkish** (data from Zimmer, 1976)

    a   Hasan   okul-a   başla-dï.
        Hasan(NOM) school-DAT start-PAST
        'Hasan started school.'

    b   Baba-sï Hasan-ï   okul-a   başla-t-tï.
        father-his Hasan-ACC school-DAT start-CAUS-PAST
        'His father made Hasan start school.'

Similarly, the Malayalam verb meaning 'climb' takes an agent and an oblique locative argument. When this verb is causativized the causee becomes the OBJ, as indicated by its case marking (26b) and the fact that it can passivize (26c).

(26)   **Malayalam** (T. Mohanan, unpublished MS)

    a   kuṭṭi   bass-il   kayarum.
        child(NOM) bus-LOC climb-FUT
        'The child will get on the bus.'

    b   acchan   kuṭṭi-ye bass-il   kayattum.
        father(NOM) child-ACC bus-LOC climb-CAUS-FUT
        'The father will put the child on the bus.'

    c   kuṭṭi   acchan-aal bass-il   kayattappeṭum.
        child(NOM) father-INSTR bus-LOC climb-CAUS-PASS-FUT
        'The child will be put on the bus by the father.'

In Japanese (as in Turkish), intransitive causees normally take accusative case while transitive causees take dative case. This normal pattern is illustrated in (27). Once again there are a few roots which take two arguments, neither of which is a primary object. When a causative is derived from such a root, as in (28b), the causee (*John*) takes the next available GR, namely OBJ, and so gets accusative case.

(27)   **Japanese** (Ishikawa, 1985)

    a   Reiko=ga   Taroo=o   hasir-ase-ta.
        Reiko=NOM Taroo=ACC run-CAUS-PAST
        'Reiko made Taroo run.'

    b   Reiko=ga   Tony=ni   nattoo=o   tabe-sase-ta.
        Reiko=NOM Tony=DAT fermented.soybeans=ACC eat-CAUS-PAST
        'Reiko made Tony eat fermented soybeans.'

(28)   **Japanese** (Sells, 1990)

    a   John=ga   Mary=ni   soodan-sita.
        John=NOM Mary=DAT consult-do-PAST
        'John consulted Mary.'

    b   Bill=ga   John=o   Mary=ni   soodan-saseta.
        Bill=NOM John=ACC Mary=DAT consult-do-CAUS-PAST
        'Bill made John consult Mary.'

8.2.5   Summary

For languages which have a morphological causative, we might think of the causative affix as representing an abstract predicate (CAUSE) that takes two arguments: the causer and the caused event. The caused event is named by the base predicate, which takes its own arguments. The causee would be the SUBJ of the base predicate if it occurred alone, but in a causative construction the causer bears the SUBJ relation. As illustrated in (29), this situation creates a potential violation of the uniqueness condition, which says that a single clause cannot contain more than one SUBJ (see chapter 1).

(29)

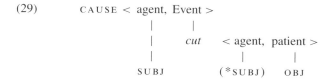

In order for the resulting clause to be grammatical, the causee must take some other grammatical relation. As we have seen, when the base predicate is intransitive (i.e., does not take an OBJ) the causee gets the OBJ relation. When the base predicate is transitive, there are two main options. In some languages, e.g., Swahili, the causee gets the OBJ relation and the patient of the base predicate gets "bumped" down to OBJ$_2$. This pattern is illustrated in (30), based on example (8b).

(30) a   Sudi a-li-m-pik-ish-a   mke wake uji.   (=8b)
        Sudi S.agr-PAST-O.agr-cook-CAUS-INDIC wife his   gruel
        'Sudi made his wife cook some gruel.'

    b

In other languages, e.g., Turkish, the patient of the base predicate retains the OBJ relation and the causee gets some other relation, either OBL or OBJ$_2$. This pattern is illustrated in (31), based on example (14b).

(31) a   Hasan kasab-a   et-i   kes-tir-di.   (=14b)
        Hasan butcher-DAT meat-ACC cut-CAUS-PAST
        'Hasan had the butcher cut the meat.'

    b

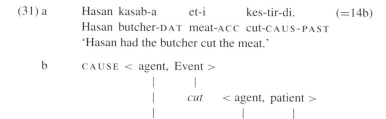

Up to this point, we have talked as if there were only one possible way of marking the causee in each of the constructions we have discussed. In fact, a number of languages allow a certain amount of variation in this regard. These alternations frequently correlate with semantic contrasts involving factors such as affectedness, degree of control on the part of the causee, or direct vs. indirect action by the causer. We will illustrate some of these contrasts in the next section.

8.3   The semantics of causative constructions

Let us now briefly consider some of the semantic distinctions which may be indicated by variation in the grammatical form of a causative construction. We will see that the general term "causation" actually includes a variety of different concepts. Let us begin by illustrating some of the relevant issues using English examples.[8]

(32) a   The captain caused his boat to sink (by drilling holes in the bottom).
     b   The captain caused his boat to sink (by allowing too many passengers to come aboard).

(33) a   John made his daughter watch the rugby match on TV.
     b   John allowed his daughter to watch the rugby match on TV.

(34) a   John put his (sleeping) daughter into her car seat.
     b   John made his (*sleeping) daughter get into her car seat.

The contrast in (32) relates to the nature of the linkage between the causer's action and the caused event. The term DIRECT CAUSATION is used when the causer does or says something directly to the causee, usually with the intention of bringing about the caused event, as in (32a). The term INDIRECT (or MEDIATED) CAUSATION implies that there is no such direct action; the caused event may be an unintended consequence of the causer's actions, as in (32b).

The examples in (33) illustrate the difference between COERCION (33a), in which the causer (*John*) actively works to bring about the caused event; vs. PERMISSION (33b), in which he simply allows the event to happen (i.e., refrains from preventing it). Obviously this contrast relates to the degree of volitionality which is retained by the causee: how much choice does the causee have?

The examples in (34) illustrate the difference between physical MANIPULA-TION (34a) vs. verbal DIRECTION (34b). In the first sentence, the causer (*John*) takes some direct, physical action to bring about the caused event; while the second example suggests that he says something to his daughter to achieve the desired event.

8.3.1   Direct vs. mediated causation

In discussing example (1) above, we noted that the lexical causative *kill* used in (1c) always implies direct causation, whereas the periphrastic expression *cause to die* used in (1b) allows an interpretation which involves indirect causation.

A similar pattern is found in many other languages as well. For example, Malayalam has two different types of causative affixation. Mohanan (1983a) identifies the form illustrated in (35b), which is less productive in modern Malayalam, as a lexical causative. The more productive causative form, which is illustrated in (35c), is clearly a morphological causative. Mohanan states that lexical causatives in Malayalam always express direct causation, as in (35b). Where the same verb root can take either form, as in this case, the morphological causative (35c) expresses indirect causation. (Recall that the OBJ in Malayalam takes ACC case if it is animate, NOM otherwise.)

(35) a   boottə   muŋŋi.
           boat(NOM) sink(intr.)-PAST
           'The boat sank.'

    b   kuṭṭi   boottə   mukki.   (LEXICAL CAUSATIVE)
           child(NOM) boat(NOM) sink(tr.)-PAST
           'The child sank the boat.'

    c   kuṭṭi   boottə   muŋŋiccu.   (MORPH. CAUSATIVE)
           child(NOM) boat(NOM) sink(intr.)-CAUS-PAST
           'The child caused the boat to sink.' (1983a:58)

8.3.2   Manipulation vs. direction

As noted above, direct causation may involve either physical or verbal action on the part of the causer. Lexical causatives, like the verb *put* in (34a) above, often carry a sense of physical manipulation, while the corresponding periphrastic causative in (34b) allows a purely verbal interpretation. We find a similar contrast between the lexical causative *feed (someone)*, which implies that the causer physically puts the food in the causee's mouth, vs. the periphrastic *make/have (someone) eat*, which is more likely to involve an invitation, command, threat, urging, or some other verbal action.

In Japanese, certain lexical causatives necessarily involve physical manipulation, and can only be used with inanimate causees. In (36b), the use of the morphological causative is ungrammatical with the inanimate causee *book*, because it would imply that the causation was achieved verbally. With an animate causee, however, the lexical causative is not permitted (36c); but the morphological causative is grammatical, and can be used in either the manipulative or directive sense (36d).

(36)   **Japanese** (data from Shibatani, 1976b)
    a   Boku=wa sono hon=o   tate-ta.   (LEXICAL CAUSATIVE)
           I=TOP   that book=ACC stand(tr.)-PAST
           'I stood that book up.'

    b   *Boku=wa sono hon=o   tat-ase-ta.   (MORPH. CAUSATIVE)
        I=TOP   that book=ACC stand-CAUS-PAST
        (for: 'I made that book stand up.')

    c   *Boku=wa kodomo=o tate-ta.   (LEXICAL CAUSATIVE)
        I=TOP   child=ACC stand(tr.)-PAST
        (for: 'I stood the child up.')

    d   Boku=wa kodomo=o tat-ase-ta.   (MORPH. CAUSATIVE)
        I=TOP   child=ACC stand-CAUS-PAST
        'I made the child stand up.' or: 'I stood the child up.'

This contrast between physical manipulation and verbal direction is brought out by the example in (37). The first clause contains the lexical causative *kise-*, meaning 'to dress (someone),' which indicates that the causer performs the action himself; the causee could be totally passive or even asleep. The second clause contains the morphological causative *ki-sase-*, meaning 'to have (someone) get dressed.' When this form is used, it is the causee who actually performs the action; the causer merely directs him to do so. If the lexical and morphological causatives had the same meaning, the sentence would be self-contradictory; but in fact, it is perfectly natural and meaningful.

(37)   **Japanese** (Shibatani, 1976b)
        Sono kodomo=ni huku=o   kise-ta   no   de wa   naku,
        that child=DAT shirt=ACC dress(tr.)-PAST COMP is EMPH not
        ki-sase-ta   no   da.
        dress(intr.)-CAUS-PAST COMP is
        'I didn't dress the child, but I had him get dressed.'

In other languages, alternations in the case marking of the causee may be used to mark similar contrasts. Note the contrast in the following examples from Telugu (Dravidian, southern India). When the causee takes dative case (38b), the sentence implies direct physical involvement on the part of the causer. When the causee is expressed as an instrumental OBL (38c), there is no such implication.

(38)   **Telugu** (Rao and Bashir, 1985:229)
    a   siita   tammudu   annam   tinn-aa-du.
        Siita(NOM) younger.brother(NOM) food(NOM) eat-PAST-3sg
        'Siita's younger brother ate his food.'

    b   siita   tammudi-ki   annam   tini-pinc-indi.
        Siita(NOM) younger.brother-DAT food(NOM) eat-CAUS-PAST.3sg
        'Siita fed her younger brother.' (e.g., by hand)

    c   siita   tammudi-ceeta   annam   tini-pinc-indi.
        Siita(NOM) younger.brother-INST food(NOM) eat-CAUS-PAST.3sg
        'Siita fed her younger brother.' (told him to eat or supervised his eating)

A similar pattern is found in the Malayalam examples in (39). The intransitive verb *roll* in Malayalam has two uses: an agentive sense, as when a child or dog rolls on the ground for fun; and a patient-like sense, which could be used for a ball or stone rolling down a hill. When the causative suffix is added to this root, the interpretation depends on the case marking of the causee. Example (39a), with the causee marked for ACC case, requires the non-agentive sense of the verb; the mother is interpeted as physically helping the child to roll. But (39b), where the causee is expressed as an oblique argument, requires the agentive sense of the verb; the mother causes the rolling to take place simply by instructing or ordering the child to do so.

(39)   **Malayalam** (T. Mohanan, unpublished MS.)
   a   amma   kuṭṭiye   ṇilaṭṭə   uṟuḷik'k'um.
         mother(NOM) child-ACC floor-LOC roll-CAUS-FUT
         'Mother will roll the child on the floor.'

   b   amma   kuṭṭiye-kkoṇṭə ṇilaṭṭə   uṟuḷik'k'um.
         mother(NOM) child(ACC)-with floor-LOC roll-CAUS-FUT
         'Mother will make the child roll on the floor.'

8.3.3   Coercion vs. permission

In (33) above, we contrasted a coercive causative (33a) with the corresponding permissive form (33b). These two forms, repeated below, differ in terms of the degree of initiative and control exercised by the causer, and in terms of the degree of control or choice retained by the causee. In the coercive example, all the initiative rests with the causer; the causee has no choice at all. In the permissive example, the initiative seems to rest with the causee; the causer does not need to do anything, but only to refrain from preventing a particular action by the causee.

These two types of causation seem to represent extreme ends on a scale. A third type, illustrated in (33c), lies somewhere between the two. In this sentence, the initiative may come from the causer, but the causee may well retain a fair degree of control, e.g., the right to refuse. We will refer to this third type as NEUTRAL or BALANCED CAUSATION. Of course, in the real world we may find many different degrees and combinations of relative control by each party, but for our purposes these three types will be sufficient.

(33) a   John made his daughter watch the rugby match on TV.
     b   John allowed his daughter to watch the rugby match on TV.
     c   John had his daughter watch the rugby match on TV.

In languages like English which depend primarily on periphrastic causatives, we often find different matrix verbs used to express each of these types as in (33). But morphological causatives are frequently ambiguous, and may allow any of these three interpretations. The following Tagalog sentence, for example, can be used in any of these three ways:

(40)   **Tagalog**
         Nagpabili   kay=Maria ng=bigas ang=Nanay.
         PERF.AV-CAUS-buy DAT=Maria GEN=rice NOM=mother
         'Mother let/made/had Maria buy some rice.'

Once again, alternations in the case marking of the causee may be used to indicate the degree of control retained by the causee. Consider the examples in (41). Both sentences involve a morphological causative derived from the intransitive root *laugh*. Normally, of course, the causee of an intransitive causative will be marked as an OBJ, taking accusative case; but in Japanese it is often possible to use dative case instead, with a slightly different interpretation. Sentence (41a), with the causee *Hanako* marked for dative case, implies that she is laughing volitionally. For example, *Taroo* may be a movie director who instructs the actress *Hanako* to laugh. Sentence (41b) on the other hand, with the causee taking accusative case, allows an involuntary interpretation: *Taroo* may be telling a joke or doing something funny which causes *Hanako* to laugh whether she wants to or not.

(41)   **Japanese** (Shibatani, 1976b)

  a   Taroo=wa   Hanako=ni   waraw-ase-ta.
      Taroo=TOP Hanako=DAT laugh-CAUS-PAST
      'Taroo had Hanako laugh.'

  b   Taroo=wa   Hanako=o   waraw-ase-ta.
      Taroo=TOP Hanako=ACC laugh-CAUS-PAST
      'Taroo made Hanako laugh.'

The semantic effect of this case marking alternation is highlighted in (42). In these examples, each of the two possible case markers (ACC and DAT) is shown in combination with one of two adverbial phrases: 'forcibly,' which indicates that the causee has little choice or control over his actions, vs. 'by gently persuading,' which indicates that the causee retains essentially full control over his actions. As these examples show, ACC is fully natural with 'forcibly' (42d), but unnatural with 'by gently persuading' (42c); whereas the pattern for DAT case is exactly the opposite (42a–b). These data confirm that, where both case-marking options are possible, ACC case on the causee tends to indicate coercion, while DAT case indicates permission or "balanced" causation.

(42)   **Japanese** (Shibatani, 1976b)

  a   Boku=wa yasasiku.iikikasete Zyon=ni   ik-ase-ta.
      I=TOP   gently.persuading John=DAT go-CAUS-PAST
      'I caused John to go by gently persuading him.'

  b   ?Boku=wa tikarazuku.de Zyon=ni   ik-ase-ta.
      I=TOP   forcibly   John=DAT go-CAUS-PAST
      'I forcibly caused John to go.'

  c   ?Boku=wa yasasiku.iikikasete Zyon=o   ik-ase-ta.
      I=TOP   gently.persuading John=ACC go-CAUS-PAST
      'I caused John to go by gently persuading him.'

  d   Boku=wa tikarazuku.de Zyon=o   ik-ase-ta.
      I=TOP   forcibly   John=ACC go-CAUS-PAST
      'I forcibly caused John to go.'

8.3.4   Ingestives and affectedness

In a number of languages, including many South Asian languages in particular, morphological causatives derived from certain transitive roots follow the pattern of case marking otherwise associated with intransitive causatives. This class of roots typically includes verbs of ingestion and perception (e.g., 'eat,' 'drink,' 'smell,' 'hear,' 'see,' 'learn,' 'understand,' etc.). The verbs which trigger this pattern are often referred to as INGESTIVE verbs (Masica, 1976; Saksena, 1980).

Consider the following examples from Marathi, an Indo-Iranian language of northern India. In Marathi, as in Malayalam, a transitive causee is normally realized as an oblique argument marked with the postposition *kaḍun* 'by.' This transitive pattern is illustrated in (43a). With ingestive roots, however, the causee takes ACC case (43b), the same marking used for intransitive causees. Essentially the same pattern is found in Hindi (Saksena, 1980).

(43)   **Marathi** (Alsina and Joshi, 1991)
  a   sumaa-ni   shaam-laa raam-kaḍun maarawle.
      Suma-ERG Sham-ACC Ram-by   beat-CAUS
      'Suma made Ram beat Sham.'

  b   sumaa-ni   raam-laa   paaṇi paaḍzle.
      Suma-ERG Ram-ACC water drink-CAUS
      'Suma made Ram drink water.'

In Kimaragang Dusun, the difference between transitive and intransitive causatives only emerges when the causee is passivized. In this construction, the normal causative prefix *po-* is replaced in transitive causatives by a different prefix *poN-* (glossed "TRANS" in the following examples), as seen in (44b). The normal causative prefix is retained in intransitive causatives, as seen in (44a). Transitive roots of the ingestive type (including 'eat,' 'drink,' 'smoke,' 'chew betel,' 'know,' 'hear,' 'look at,' etc.) follow the intransitive pattern, taking the normal causative prefix *po-* as seen in (44c–d). (A literal passive translation is given only for [44a], but in all of these examples the causee is the grammatical subject.)

(44)   **Kimaragang Dusun** (Kroeger, in press)
  a Po-odop-on   kuh   poh itih   tanak.
     CAUS-sleep-OV 1sg.GEN yet this(NOM) child
     'I will put the baby to sleep.'
     (lit.: 'This baby will be caused to sleep by me.')

  b Pangalapako'(poN-lapak-o') yalo   dinoh   niyuw.
     TRANS-split-OV.IMPER   3sg.NOM that(ACC) coconut
     'Get him to split those coconuts.'

  c Penumon(po-inum-on) (nuh)   ih   tanak nuh ditih   tubat.
     CAUS-drink-OV   2sg.GEN NOM child your this(ACC) medicine
     '(You) have your child drink this medicine.'

d   Pa-akan-on   kuh   poh ih   Jaiwan tu'   witilon.
        CAUS-eat-OV Isg.GEN yet NOM Jaiwan because hungry
        'I'll have Jaiwan eat something (i.e., give him something to eat), because
        he is hungry.'

Saksena (1980) suggests that ingestive verbs in Hindi are different from normal transitive verbs because they describe actions in which the agent, as well as the patient, is affected. The person who eats, drinks, or smokes is clearly affected by the action.

Another way of looking at affectedness is to ask, who or what is the causer (as Actor) acting upon? In a basic transitive situation an Actor does something to another participant (sometimes called the UNDERGOER);[9] thus the Undergoer is the participant which is acted upon. In a basic transitive verb the patient corresponds to the Undergoer.

In many transitive causative constructions, e.g., *Mary made John kill the snake*, the causer seems to be primarily interested in the effect of the action on the patient, rather than the causee; thus the patient would be the Undergoer. With ingestives, however, the causer's action seems to be directed primarily toward the causee. These examples would often be translated by non-causative constructions in English, e.g., *Give her something to eat; give him a drink; give me a smoke.* In causatives of this type it seems to be the causee, rather than the patient, who is seen as being acted upon. One indication of this is that, in Kimaragang, the patient is frequently omitted entirely, as in (44d).

Consider the following data from Malayalam. As noted above, in causatives based on normal transitive roots the causee must be expressed as an oblique argument (45). However, in causatives based on "ingestive" transitive roots, the causee may be expressed either as an OBJ (46a) or as an oblique argument (46b). In this example the case-marking alternation also correlates with a contrast between two different causative verb forms: lexical (46a) vs. morphological (46b).

(45)   **Malayalam** (T. Mohanan, unpublished MS.)
    a   amma   kuṭṭiye-kkoṇṭə   wirakə   .   weṭṭik'k'um.
          mother(NOM) child(ACC)-with firewood(NOM) cut-CAUS-FUT
          'Mother will make the child cut firewood.'

    b   *amma   kuṭṭiye   wirakə   weṭṭik'k'um.
          mother(NOM) child-ACC firewood(NOM) cut-CAUS-FUT

(46) a   amma   kuṭṭiye   maaṇṇa   ṭiittum.
          mother(NOM) child-ACC mango(NOM) eat-CAUS-FUT
          'Mother will feed the child a mango.'

    b   amma   kuṭṭiye-kkoṇṭə   maaṇṇa   ṭinnik'k'um.
          mother(NOM) child(ACC)-with mango(NOM) eat-CAUS-FUT
          'Mother will have the mango eaten by the child.'

Sentence (46a), in which the causee is expressed as an object, suggests that the mother's purpose is to nourish the child. In (46b), on the other hand, the mother's main purpose is to get the mango eaten. Thus only (46a) would be an appropriate response to the question, *What did Mother do to the child?*; while only (46b) would be an appropriate response to the question, *What did Mother do to the mango?*

In some languages, a similar contrast is possible even with non-ingestive predicates. Alsina (1992) reports that in the Bantu language Chichewa a transitive causee may appear either as a primary object (47b) or as an oblique argument (47a). The difference between the two sentences in (47) is related to the intentions of the causer. In (47a), the porcupine's main goal is to get the pumpkins cooked; the owl plays almost an instrumental role. In (47b), however, the porcupine's action is directed toward the owl, with the aim of getting him to do the cooking. Thus only (47a) would be an appropriate response to the question, *What did the porcupine do to the pumpkins?*; while only (47b) would be an appropriate response to the question, *What did the porcupine do to the owl?*.

(47)   **Chichewa** (Bantu; Alsina, 1992:523)
    a   Nungu   i-na-phik-its-a   maungu   kwa kadzidzi.
          porcupine(9) 9.SUBJ-PAST-cook-CAUS-ASP pumpkins(6) to   owl(1a)
          'The porcupine had the pumpkins cooked by the owl.'

    b   Nungu   i-na-phik-its-a   kadzidzi maungu.
          porcupine(9) 9.SUBJ-PAST-cook-CAUS-ASP owl(1a) pumpkins(6)
          'The porcupine made the owl cook the pumpkins.'

8.4   The structure of causative clauses

In section 8.1 we noted that English lexical causatives behave like simple transitive predicates, while periphrastic (or phrasal) causatives are similar to other control constructions. Thus example (1c) consists of one simple clause, whereas (1b) contains two clauses, one (the complement clause) embedded within the other (the matrix clause).

The structure of morphological causatives, in languages that have them, is a very interesting issue about which a great deal has been written. We will be concerned here primarily with functional structure rather than phrase structure, since in most cases the phrase structure configuration required by a morphological causative is also required by some simple, non-causative verb in the language. That is, morphological causatives do not usually differ from simple clauses in terms of phrase structure.

A basic question that must be addressed is whether the functional structure associated with a morphological causative consists of one clausal unit or two. For most languages with morphological causatives, the answer seems to be one. We will examine some of the evidence for this claim in section 8.4.1. In a few languages, however, certain morphological causatives seem to require a different analysis; we will mention two such cases in section 8.4.2.

8.4.1   Evidence for a monoclausal analysis

Reflexive pronouns in Turkish must find an antecedent within their minimal clause, as demonstrated in (48c–d), and regular pronouns cannot take an antecedent within their minimal clause, as demonstrated in (48a–b). Note in particular that in a Raising construction like (48d), the matrix subject cannot be the antecedent for a reflexive OBJ within the complement clause.

(48)   **Turkish** (Aissen, 1974:330, 334)

a   Kendim-i/*ben-i   yïkadïm.
         myself-ACC/*me-ACC I.washed
         'I washed myself.'

b   Kendiniz-i/*siz-i   vurdunuz.
         yourself-ACC/*you-ACC you.hit
         'You hit yourself.'

c   (Ben) [Hasan-ïn   ben-i/*kendim-i   yïka-masïna]   sevindim.
         (I)   Hasan-GEN me-ACC/*myself-ACC wash-PRTCPL I.was.pleased
         'I was pleased that Hasan washed me.'

d   (Ben) Hasan-ï   [ben-i/*kendim-i   yïkadï] sanïyorum.
         (I)   Hasan-ACC me-ACC/*myself-ACC washed I.believe
         'I believe Hasan to have washed me.'

Under a biclausal analysis of causatives, a morphological causative would have essentially the same functional structure as the English control construction in (1b). The causer would be the matrix subject. However, as example (49) shows, the causer in Turkish can be the antecedent of any reflexive argument of the causative verb, but not of a regular pronoun in the same positions. This shows that the causative examples in (49) consist of a single functional-structure clause, in contrast to the biclausal examples (48c–d).

(49)   **Turkish** (Aissen, 1974:330)

a   Hasan-a   kendim-i/*ben-i   yïka-t-tïm.
         Hasan-DAT myself-ACC/*me-ACC wash-CAUS-PAST.Isg
         'I made Hasan wash me.'

b   Kitab-ï   kendim-e/*bana   verdittim.
         book-ACC myself-DAT/*me-DAT give-CAUS-PAST.Isg
         'I made (someone) give me the book.'

Under a biclausal analysis of morphological causatives, the causee would function as the subject of a subordinate clause (or, more precisely, as the controller of a subordinate SUBJ). Thus, in order to determine the clause structure of a causative sentence, it is important to ask whether the causee retains any of the properties associated with grammatical subjects.

One useful test for subjecthood in Korean is subject honorification. The honorific suffix -*si* may be added to a verb to show that the subject of that verb is a person to whom the speaker defers or shows respect. Example (50a) involves a biclausal Equi construction. In this sentence the honorific suffix has been added to the complement verb. This marker indicates that the speaker feels respect for the complement SUBJ, namely the controllee, which is functionally identified with the controller *professor*.

Korean has two causative constructions, one periphrastic and the other involving a causative affix.[10] In the periphrastic causative (50b), the honorific suffix can be added to the complement verb to show the speaker's respect for the causee. This indicates that the causee in (50b) is in fact a SUBJ; and since the sentence also contains another SUBJ, namely *students*, this sentence must be biclausal. In the morphological causative (50c), however, the honorific suffix cannot be used to show respect for the causee. The sentence could only be interpreted as showing respect for the causer, which in this example is quite unnatural. (Example [50d] is identical except that it lacks the honorific suffix.) This is a clear indication that the causee in (50c) is not a SUBJ, and that the sentence is monoclausal.

(50) **Korean** (adapted from Shibatani, 1976a)[11]

a Haksayng-tul=un kyoswu=eykey kanguy-ha-si-ki-lul
   student-PL=TOP professor=DAT lecture-do-HON-NMLZR-ACC
   yocheng-ha-ess-ta.
   request-do-PAST-INDIC
   'The students requested the (honored) professor to lecture.'

b Haksayng=un kyoswu=eykey wus(u)-si-key   ha-ess-ta.
   student=TOP professor=DAT smile-HON-COMP cause-PAST-INDIC
   'The student made the (honored) professor smile.'

c #Haksayng=un kyoswu=lul   wus(u)-ki-si-ess-ta.
   student=TOP professor=ACC smile-CAUS-HON-PAST-INDIC
   (honorific could only refer to student)

d Haksayng=un kyoswu=lul   wus(u)-ki-ess-ta.
   student=TOP professor=ACC smile-CAUS-PAST-INDIC
   'The student made the professor smile.'

As we saw in chapter 4, reflexive pronouns in Malayalam must take a grammatical subject as their antecedent, but they are not clause-bounded; their antecedent may be the SUBJ of their immediate clause or any higher clause within the same sentence. Example (51a) shows that in a simple clause only the SUBJ may be the antecedent, while (51b) shows that in a subordinating construction the SUBJ of a higher clause may also be the antecedent. Example (51c) contains a morphological causative. If the causee were the SUBJ of a subordinate clause, as predicted under a biclausal analysis, it should be an eligible antecedent of the reflexive. But, as this example shows, the reflexive can only refer to the causer. This is very good evidence that the causee is not a SUBJ, and thus example (51c) is monoclausal.

(51)   **Malayalam** (Mohanan 1982, 1983a)

a   jooni   meeriye   swantam wiiṭṭil   wecca umma weccu.
  Johnny-NOM Mary-ACC self's   house-LOC at   kiss   put
  'Johnny kissed Mary at self's (=Johnny's/*Mary's) house.'

b   [[swantam makan   buḍḍhimaan aana enna] ṛaajaawina
  self's   son-NOM intelligent   is   that king-DAT
  ṭoonni enna] raani   manṭriye   wiŝwasippiccu.
  thought that   queen-NOM minister-ACC made.believe
  'The queen convinced the minister that the king thought that self's
  (= the king's / queen's / *minister's) son was intelligent.'

c   accʰan   kuṭṭi-ye   swantam wiiṭṭil   wecca kaḷippiccu.
  father(NOM) child-ACC self's   house-LOC at   play-CAUS-PAST
  'The father made the child play at self's (= father's/*child's) house.' (1983a:61)

Further evidence for the claim that morphological causatives are monoclausal comes from the pattern of causee realization discussed in section 8.2. Much of this data can be explained in terms of the Uniqueness condition: a single clause may not contain more than one subject or one primary object. Since the causer is always expressed as SUBJ, the argument which would be the SUBJ of the base predicate (i.e., the causee) must be demoted to some other grammatical relation. If the base predicate takes an OBJ, either this OBJ must be demoted to make way for the causee, as in Swahili and Chamorro, or the causee must take a lower GR, as in Turkish and Malayalam. In either case, the resulting clause will have only one SUBJ and one OBJ. This contrasts with a typical biclausal Equi construction like *John made his dog bite the robber*, in which both the matrix clause and the complement clause may contain a primary object.

Baker's generalization points out that there is at least a very strong tendency for the arguments of a morphological causative to be linked to grammatical relations in much the same way as those of an underived predicate which has the same number of arguments. Thus the subcategorization of an intransitive causative is usually the same as that of a basic transitive verb; the subcategorization of a transitive causative is usually the same as (or very similar to) that of a basic ditransitive verb; etc. Moreover, if the language imposes a limit on the maximum number of arguments which may be expressed in a single clause, the same limit typically applies to causative verbs as to underived predicates.

We noted above that in a number of languages, it is impossible to form a morphological causative from a ditransitive root; Song (1991) mentions Abkhaz,[12] Basque, Afar (Eastern Chadic), and Babungo (Cameroon) as examples. These languages seem to allow at most three core arguments per clause. Other languages impose an even stricter limit of two core arguments, deriving morphological causatives only from intransitive roots and not from transitive roots. Song lists the following languages as examples of this type: Lamang (Nigeria), Moroccan Berber, Urubu-Kaapor (Brazil), Turkana (Eastern Nilotic), and Uradhi and

Kayardild (Australia). Another strategy which many languages adopt for coping with the "over-crowding" problem is to leave one or more arguments unexpressed in a transitive or ditransitive causative construction.

However, all of these restrictions make sense only in a monoclausal structure. We would expect that a biclausal structure could potentially have twice as many arguments as a simple clause, but this is clearly not what we find with respect to morphological causatives. So there are good reasons to assume that the functional structure of a morphological causative in most languages consists of a single clausal unit.

The argument structure of the morphological causative is a much more complex issue, and a wide variety of proposals have been advanced. For the sake of concreteness, we will simply assume that lexical causatives have the same basic argument structure as underived predicates,[13] while morphological causatives have a more complex argument structure in which one predicate is an argument of another. Thus we might represent the Malayalam examples in (35b,c) with argument structures like those shown in (52–53).

(52) a   kuṭṭi   booṭṭə   mukki.   (LEXICAL CAUSATIVE)
          child(NOM) boat(NOM) sink(tr.)-PAST
          'The child sank the boat.'

     b   *sink(tr.)* < agent, patient >
                          | |
                        SUBJ   OBJ

(53) a   kuṭṭi   booṭṭə   muṇṇiccu.   (MORPH. CAUSATIVE)
          child(NOM) boat(NOM) sink(intr.)-CAUS-PAST
          'The child caused the boat to sink.'

     b   CAUSE < agent, Event >
                     | |
                     | *sink* < patient >
                     | |
                   SUBJ   OBJ

The details of the argument structure are not of crucial importance here. We are primarily interested in the fact that the functional structures and grammatical relations of the two sentences are the same: both involve a single clause containing a SUBJ and an OBJ.

The examples in (46) illustrate a similar contrast for lexical vs. morphological causatives derived from a basic transitive predicate. Argument structure and functional structure diagrams corresponding to these examples are suggested in (54–55). T. Mohanan (1988) demonstrates that in the ingestive construction, the causee is the primary object. Notice that in this case, unlike (52–53), there is a difference in the grammatical relations assigned; but both sentences are still monoclausal in their functional structure.

(54) a   amma kuṭṭiye   maaṇṇa ṭiittum.   (LEXICAL CAUSATIVE)
           mother child-ACC mango eat-CAUS-FUT
           'Mother will feed the child a mango.'

   b   *feed* < agent, recip/ben theme >

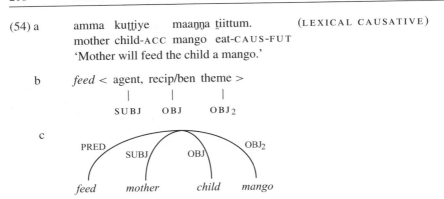

(55) a   amma kuṭṭiye-kkoṇṭə   maaṇṇa ṭinnik'k'um.   (MORPH. CAUSATIVE)
           mother child(ACC)-with mango eat-CAUS-FUT
           'Mother will have the mango eaten by the child.'

   b   CAUSE < agent, Event >

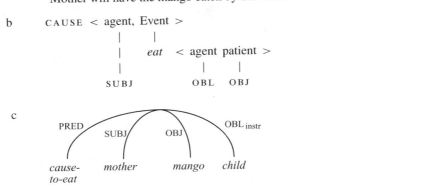

8.4.2   Biclausal morphological causatives

As we mentioned above, there a few languages for which the monoclausal analysis discussed in section 8.4.1 does not seem to work. Morphological
causatives in such languages have at least some properties that suggest the existence of an internal clause boundary. For example, Marantz (1984) states that
the reflexive pronoun *ru:hu* in Chimwiini must be an OBJ, and must take the
SUBJ of its immediate clause as its antecedent. As (56a) demonstrates, a reflexive causee can take the causer as antecedent, indicating that causee and causer
are "clause-mates" (elements of the same minimal clause). Similarly, a reflexive
which occurs as the patient of the base predicate can take the causee as antecedent
(56b). But a reflexive patient cannot take the causer as antecedent (56c). The ungrammaticality of (56c) indicates that the causer and patient are not elements
of the same minimal clause. Moreover, in light of the constraints on reflexives
mentioned above, example (56a) shows that the causer is a SUBJ and the causee
is an OBJ; while example (56b) shows that the causee is a SUBJ and the patient is
an OBJ. So these sentences each contain two SUBJ and two OBJ, and thus must
be biclausal. A functional-structure diagram for (56b) is shown in (57).

(56)   **Chimwiini** (Bantu; Abasheikh, 1979; cited in Marantz, 1984)

a   Mi m-pik-ish-ize   ru:hu-ya cha:kuja.
      1sg S.agr-cook-CAUS-ASP self-1sg food
      'I made myself cook food.'

b   Mi ni-m-big-ish-ize   mwa:na ru:hu-ye.
      1sg S.agr-O.agr-hit-CAUS-ASP child   self-3sg
      'I made the child hit himself.'

c   *Mi ni-m-big-ish-ize   Ali ru:hu-ya.
      1sg S.agr-O.agr-hit-CAUS-ASP Ali self-1sg
      (for: 'I made Ali hit myself.')

(57)

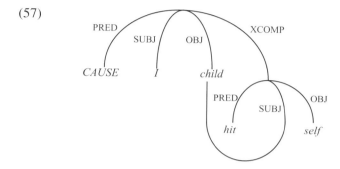

Matsumoto (1996, 1998) shows that morphological causatives in Japanese may be either monoclausal or biclausal. Moreover, this structural ambiguity correlates with a semantic contrast. He presents a variety of evidence which demonstrates that permissive causatives are functionally biclausal, whereas coercive causatives are functionally monoclausal. The central issue here is the status of the causee. In biclausal structures the causee will function as a grammatical subject, while in monoclausal structures it will not. Thus the crucial data come from tests for grammatical subjecthood.

One such test involves control of preposed *while* clauses: the subject of the adverbial clause must be controlled by the subject of the main clause. Sentence (58a) is an example of a coercive causative. In this sentence, only the causer (*teacher*) and not the causee (*John*) can be interpreted as the controller. But sentence (58b), involving the permissive interpretation of the same causative verb form, is ambiguous: either the causer or the causee could be interpreted as the controller. Thus in the permissive causative, both causer and causee seem to function as grammatical subjects; but this is possible only if the sentence contains two clauses.

(58)   **Japanese** (Matsumoto, 1996 and p.c.)

a   [terebi=o mi-nagara] sensee=wa   muriyari Jon=ni
      TV=ACC watch-while teacher=TOP forcefully John=DAT
      hon=o   yom-ase-ta.
      book=ACC read-CAUS-PAST
      'Teacher forced John to read the book while watching TV.'
      (coercive; unambiguous: only the teacher could be watching TV)

b   [terebi=o mi-nagara]   sensee=wa   Jon=ni   sonomama
      TV=ACC watch-while teacher=TOP John=DAT as.it.is
      hon=o   yom-ase-ta.
      book=ACC read-CAUS-PAST
      'Teacher allowed John to (continue to) read the book while watching TV.'
      (permissive; ambiguous: either John or the teacher could be watching TV)

A second test for grammatical subjecthood involves the interpretation of certain adverbs. When these adverbs are not immediately adjacent to the verb, they can only be interpreted as describing the grammatical subject of their clause. One such adverb is *omoikiri-yoku* 'without hesitation.' In sentence (59a), a coercive causative, the adverb must be interpreted as describing the causer (*John*) and not the causee (*Bill*). In the permissive sentence (59b), the adverb could potentially be interpreted as describing either the causer or the causee, although in this example it is more natural to assume that it refers to the causee (*horse*). So, once again, we see the causee functioning as a grammatical subject in the permissive causative, but not in the coercive causative.

(59)   **Japanese** (Matsumoto, 1996 and p.c.)
  a   Jon=wa   omoikiri-yoku   muriyari Biru=o   hashir-ase-ta.
      John=TOP without.hesitation forcefully Bill=ACC run-CAUS-PAST
      'John without hesitation forcibly made Bill run.'

  b   Jon=wa   omoikiri-yoku   sono uma=ni   hashir-ase-ta.
      John=TOP without.hesitation the   horse=DAT run-CAUS-PAST
      'John let the horse run as fast as it wanted.'

A third subjecthood test is honorification. There are several different kinds of honorific marker in Japanese. In the pattern we will be concerned with here, a prefix *o-* is added to the verb, which is then followed by the copula *=ni* plus an auxiliary *naru*. This marking indicates that the speaker is showing respect for the grammatical subject of the marked verb. When this marking is added to a causative verb, the causative suffix *-(s)ase* may either appear following the auxiliary *naru*, or it may attach to the verb root, preceding the copula.

Example (60) illustrates the first of these possibilities. In (60a), a permissive causative, the subject honorification marker is understood to refer to the causee *prince*. This shows that the causee is functioning as a grammatical subject, and hence that the sentence is biclausal. In the coercive example (60b), the subject honorific cannot refer to the causee because the causee is not a grammatical subject, so the sentence is highly unnatural.

(60)   **Japanese** (Matsumoto, 1998 and p.c.)
  a   Daijin=wa   ooji=ni   sonomama sono kutsushita=o
      minister=TOP prince=DAT as.it.is   the socks=ACC
      o-haki=ni   nar-ase-rare-mashi-ta.
      HON-wear=COP HON-CAUS-HON-POL-PAST
      'The minister let the prince (continue to) wear/put the socks on his feet.'
      (honorific refers to causee 'prince')

b   ??Karera=wa muriyari   ooji=ni   sono kutsushita=o
     they=TOP   forcefully prince=DAT the   socks=ACC
     o-haki=ni   nar-ase-rare-mashi-ta.
     HON-wear=COP HON-CAUS-HON-POL-PAST
     'They forced the prince put the socks on his feet.'
     (honorific cannot refer to prince)

(It may be helpful to explain a bit more about the verb form used in these sentences. In addition to the subject honorification marker described above, a second honorific marker *-rare* is used to show respect for the causer. This is because it would be pragmatically odd for a non-respected person to force a prince to do anything. In addition, the politeness marker *-mashi* is used, because honorifics are used primarily in polite speech.)

When the causative suffix *-(s)ase* appears inside the honorific marking, together with the verb root, the pattern of grammaticality is reversed. In that case only the causer can be selected by subject honorification, and the coercive reading is much more natural than the permissive reading.

Matsumoto's conclusion, based on these and other types of evidence, is that a coercive causative construction contains only one clause with the causer functioning as grammatical subject. In a permissive causative, however, both the causer and the causee are grammatical subjects, and so two functional clauses are involved. In this permissive usage the causative affix itself functions as a control predicate,[14] with the base verb functioning as the XCOMP. The causer is the matrix SUBJ and the causee is the controllee. This permissive structure is illustrated in (61), using sentence (59b) as an example:

(61) a

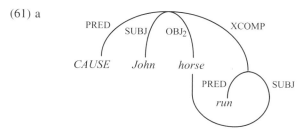

b   Jon=wa   omoikiri-yoku   sono uma=ni   hashir-ase-ta.
     John=TOP without.hesitation the   horse=DAT run-CAUS-PAST
     'John let the horse run as fast as it wanted.'

8.5   Conclusion

Causative constructions are fascinating for a number of reasons. Causatives reveal in a very clear way how intricate the relationships between morphology, syntax, and semantics can be. They also demonstrate the potential independence of phrase structure, functional structure, and argument structure, in that an expression which constitutes a single clause in one of these structures may turn out to be biclausal in one or both of the others. Causatives have also proven to be a fruitful topic for cross-linguistic comparison, with interesting patterns of similarity, both syntactic and semantic, emerging across a wide variety of languages.

We have seen that the marking of the causee is of special interest in several respects. Syntactically, the causee needs to be assigned a grammatical relation in such a way as to preserve the Uniqueness of SUBJ and OBJ within the clause. This poses a special challenge when a causative is derived from a transitive or ditransitive root. Moreover, whenever there is more than one option for marking the causee, the choices often have semantic implications. In general, causees are more likely to be marked as objects where they retain less control over the situation, less freedom of choice, or where they are more directly acted upon or affected by the action. Causees are more likely to be marked as oblique arguments where they retain greater control and freedom of choice, or where the causation is more indirect.

Notes

1. Object agreement is obligatory if the primary object is animate, or when the object is deleted or topicalized; it is optional otherwise (Vitale, 1981:20, 24).
2. The symbol [ï] is used here for the high back unrounded vowel, normally written in Turkish as [ı].
3. In fact, Baker predicts that this correlation should be universal. Hebrew (Cole, 1976) may be a counter-example to this claim: with agentive transitive roots, the causee is expressed as the primary object of a double object construction, but the double object pattern is not permitted with basic ditransitive verbs. However, the productivity of the morphological causative in Hebrew is fairly limited. Gilyak and Amharic may also be counter-examples (Comrie, 1976).
4. This order appears to be obligatory if there is no object agreement marker on the verb. When object agreement is marked, as it normally is in double object constructions, the primary and secondary object may occur in either order; however, the preferred order still places the primary object adjacent to the verb (Vitale, 1981:44, 130).
5. The descriptions by Topping (1973) and Cooreman (1988) seem to indicate the *nu* form should be used here, rather than *ni*.
6. The relative order of the primary and secondary objects is different in (14b) from (13b). Underhill (1976:70) states that the ordering of definite NP arguments is flexible and largely determined by discourse/pragmatic factors.
7. Instruments in Malayalam may be marked either by a semantic case suffix -*aal*, or by the postposition *koɳʈə*. The postposition is more commonly used in informal speech. Passive agents are always marked with the instrumental case suffix, and never with the postposition; whereas transitive causees normally take the postposition and never take the case suffix.
8. Much of the terminology in sections 8.3.1–8.3.3 is based on Shibatani (1976a,b).
9. Foley and Van Valin (1984).
10. Some uses of the causative affix in Korean appear to be lexicalized, but we take the examples in (50c–d) to be morphological causatives.

11. Thanks to Shin-Ja Hwang for helping to clarify these examples. She states that the causative and honorific suffixes in (50c) can only occur in the order shown.
12. Hewitt (1979:171) notes that Abkhaz is different in this respect from the closely related Abaza language; in Abaza, causatives can be derived from ditransitive roots.
13. Matsumoto (1998) discusses several tests in Japanese which indicate that the causee of a lexical causative does not function as a logical subject. This implies that lexical causatives in Japanese have a simple, or "monoclausal," argument structure. In contrast, causees of morphological causatives (both coercive and permissive) do behave like logical subjects, indicating that these causatives have complex, or "biclausal," argument structures.
14. Matsumoto (1996) analyzes explicit permissives as Equi constructions and implicit permissives as Raising constructions.

9   Serial verbs and related issues

A SERIAL VERB construction (or SVC) is one in which a single clause contains two or more verbs, neither of which is an auxiliary. The term "serial verb" has been used by different authors in slightly different ways, and linguists sometimes disagree about whether a particular construction in a given language is "really" a serial verb or not. We will not attempt here to formulate a precise definition that will clear up all these gray areas. Rather, we will focus on describing the most important features of the "prototypical" SVC, i.e., characteristics of those serial verb constructions which everyone agrees belong to this category. As a way of introducing this discussion, let us consider a type of causative construction which is similar in many ways to those discussed in chapter 8, but also different in ways which make it relevant to the current chapter.

9.1   Causative constructions in French

Causative constructions in Romance languages are periphrastic, in the sense that they contain a verb meaning 'cause' which is morphologically independent of the base verb. However, they can also have many of the properties associated with morphological causatives. In particular, some of these constructions can be shown to be monoclausal, even though they contain two verbs. In this sense they are similar to serial verb constructions.

French, like English, lacks a morphological causative; but it has two different types of periphrastic causative. The first type, illustrated in (1), is a normal, biclausal Equi construction. The second type involves the verb *faire* 'make'; this pattern is illustrated in (2a).[1]

(1)   Jean a   laissé Marie partir.
         Jean has let   Marie leave
         'John let Marie leave.'

(2) a   J'ai   fait   partir Maurice.
         I-have made leave Maurice
         'I made Maurice leave.'

     b   *J'ai fait   Maurice partir.
         I-have made Maurice leave
         'I made Maurice leave.'

Notice the position of the causee in these examples. In (1), the causee appears immediately after the matrix verb, the normal position for the matrix OBJ. But with *faire* the causee follows both verbs, as in (2a). The usual word order is impossible in this case, as shown in (2b).

More generally, in the *faire* construction the two verbs can never be separated from each other; no other element may appear between them. The verbs appear to be more tightly bound to each other than in a normal Equi construction like (1). In fact, a variety of evidence suggests that example (2a) consists of just a single clause, even though it contains two verbs.

A very important piece of evidence for the monoclausal status of the *faire* causative comes from clitic placement. In French, as in other Romance languages, clitic OBJ and OBJ$_2$ pronouns attach to the verb which heads their immediate clause; normally, this is the verb which assigns their grammatical relation. In a biclausal Equi construction, clitic arguments of the downstairs verb must remain with that verb, as illustrated in (3):

(3) a   Marie a   laissé Paul lire ces   romans.
            Marie has let   Paul read these novels
            'Marie has let Paul read these novels.'

     b   Marie a   laissé Paul les   lire.
            Marie has let   Paul 3pl.ACC read
            'Marie has let Paul read them.'

     c   *Marie les   a   laissé Paul lire.
            Marie 3pl.ACC has let   Paul read

But in the *faire* construction, this is impossible; all clitic pronouns must attach to the initial verb, as illustrated in (4). This fact indicates that both verbs belong to the same minimal clause.

(4) a   Pierre fera   acheter ces livres à   Jean.
            Peter will-make buy   these books DAT John
            'Pierre will make Jean buy these books.'

     b   Pierre les   fera   acheter à   Jean.
            Pierre 3pl.ACC will-make buy   DAT Jean
            'Pierre will make Jean buy them.'

     c   *Pierre fera   les   acheter à   Jean.
            Pierre will-make 3pl.ACC buy   DAT Jean

The monoclausal causative construction with *faire* has many of the same properties as the morphological causatives that we discussed in the previous chapter. For example, when the complement verb is transitive, the causee is marked for dative case like a secondary object (5b). Compare this pattern with the normal Equi construction in (5a), in which the causee appears as the matrix OBJ.

(5) a   J'ai   laissé l'enfant   manger un gâteau.
         I-have let   the-child eat   a   cake
         'I let the child eat a cake.'

   b   J'ai   fait   manger un gâteau à   l'enfant.
         I-have made   eat   a   cake DAT the-child
         'I made the child eat a cake.'

When the causee in the *faire* construction is a pronoun, the dative form is used:

(6) a   J'ai   fait   préparer la mayonnaise à   Maurice.
         I-have made   prepare the mayonnaise DAT Maurice
         'I made Maurice prepare the mayonnaise.'

   b   Je lui   ai   fait   préparer la mayonnaise.
         I 3sg.DAT have   made   prepare the mayonnaise
         'I made him/her prepare the mayonnaise.'

When the complement verb is ditransitive, with OBJ and OBJ_2 already part of its basic subcategorization, the causee in the *faire* construction takes the "next available" GR according to Comrie's generalization, namely OBL. It is marked with the same preposition used for passive agents, namely *par*:

(7)   Je ferai   écrire une lettre à Jean par Daniel.
         I will.make write a   letter to Jean by Daniel
         'I will have Daniel write a letter to Jean.'

If the complement verb subcategorizes for an OBJ_2 or OBL argument but no direct object, then the causee is marked as OBJ:

(8) a   Cela fera   téléphoner Pierre à   ses parents.
         that will-make telephone Pierre to his parents
         'That will make Pierre telephone his parents.'

   b   Cela le   fera   téléphoner à   ses parents.
         that 3sg.m.ACC will-make telephone to his parents
         'That will make him telephone his parents.'

   c   Je les   ai   fait écrire au   Père   Noël.
         I 3pl.ACC   have made write to-the Father Christmas
         'I had/made them write to Father Christmas.'

   d   Cela le   fera   voter pour vous.
         that 3sg.m.ACC will-make vote for   you
         'That will make him vote for you.'

Recall that this "next available GR" pattern is motivated by the Uniqueness constraint: any single clause may contain no more than one SUBJ or OBJ. Thus the data in (5)–(8) only make sense if the *faire* construction is in fact a single clause, with the two verbs together assigning a single set of GRs. This conclusion is further supported by evidence from passivization.

In the previous chapter we discussed passivization patterns for morphological causatives. In languages like Turkish, we saw that the causee becomes the passive SUBJ if the base verb is intransitive; but when the base verb is transitive, it is the basic patient that is promoted to SUBJ, rather than the causee. The *faire* causative in French cannot be passivized, but the cognate construction in Italian does allow passivization. Consider the following examples:

(9) a   Maria fa   lavorare Giovanni.
             Maria makes work   Giovanni
             'Maria makes Giovanni work.'

    b   Giovanni e stato fatto lavorare (molto).
             Giovanni was   made work   (a lot)
             'Giovanni was made to work.'

(10) a   Maria ha   fatto riparare la   macchina a   Giovanni.
             Maria has made fix   the car   DAT Giovanni
             'Maria made Giovanni fix the car.'

    b   La macchina fu   fatte riparare a   Giovanni.
             the car   was made fix   DAT Giovanni
             'The car was made to be fixed by Giovanni.'

    c   *Giovanni e stato fatto riparare la   macchina.
             Giovanni was   made fix   the car

When the complement verb is intransitive, as in (9a), the causee is expressed as an OBJ, and becomes the SUBJ of the corresponding passive form (9b). But when the complement verb is transitive, as in (10a), the patient is expressed as an OBJ while the causee takes the next available GR, namely secondary object. When this sentence is passivized, it is the patient that is promoted to SUBJ (10b), and never the causee (10c).

The pattern of grammaticality observed in these data is exactly what we would predict given the following assumptions: (i) passive promotes OBJ to SUBJ; (ii) each clause contains at most one OBJ; (iii) the *faire* causative construction consists of a single clause.

Another similarity between the *faire* construction and the morphological causatives discussed in the previous chapter relates to variation in the marking of the causee. In the examples we have considered thus far, transitive causees have always been marked as secondary objects, taking dative case. However, in many cases it is also possible to use the preposition *par* instead, as illustrated in the following examples.

(11)   J'ai   fait   manger les pommes à/par   Paul.
             I-have made eat   the apples DAT/by Paul
             'I made Paul eat the apples.'

(12) a   J'ai   fait   préparer la mayonnaise à   Maurice.
             I-have made prepare the mayonnaise DAT Maurice
             'I made Maurice prepare the mayonnaise.'

b   J'ai   fait   préparer la   mayonnaise par Maurice.
     I-have made prepare   the mayonnaise by Maurice
     'I have had the mayonnaise prepared by Maurice.'

This contrast in the marking of the causee often correlates with semantic contrasts of the kind discussed in the previous chapter. Compare the following two examples, from Hyman and Zimmer (1976):

(13) a   J'ai   fait   nettoyer les toilettes au   général.
          I-have made clean   the toilets   to-the general
          'I made the general clean the toilets.'

     b   J'ai   fait   nettoyer les toilettes par le général.
          I-have made clean   the toilets   by the general
          'I had the toilets cleaned by the general.'

The authors describe the contrast as follows:

> As can be seen in the two glosses, there is an important difference between these sentences. In (13a) it is the case that I did something to the general, e.g., because I did not like him, I made him do an undesirable task. In (13b) the general is more incidental to the task. I wanted to get the toilets cleaned and it happened to be the general that I got to clean them. In (13a) it is important to get the general to do the toilet-cleaning, whereas in (13b) it is important that the toilet be cleaned (by someone). While the difference does not always come out as clearly as in these examples, it is apparently always possible to assign such interpretations to *à NP* and *par NP*. (p. 199)

We have argued that the *faire* causative in French is a construction which contains two verbs in the same minimal clause. For this reason, we could describe it as a special type of serial verb. In the next section, we will discuss more typical examples of serial verb constructions, which everyone would agree belong to this category. In sections 9.3 and 9.4 we will examine other constructions which may be confused with SVCs.

9.2   Serial verbs

As stated above, a serial verb construction (or SVC) is one in which a single clause contains two or more verbs, neither of which is an auxiliary. Serial verbs seem to be characteristic of certain linguistic areas and families, including the languages of Western Africa, mainland Southeast Asia (Chinese, Thai, Khmer, etc.), and many pidgin and creole languages; but constructions which are identified as "serial verbs" have been reported in all corners of the world. However, as we have noted, there is some disagreement as to what types of construction should be included under this label.

We will begin our discussion by illustrating some of the most common functions or uses of SVCs, that is, the semantic patterns which these constructions are commonly used to express. Then we will examine some of the structural features of these constructions.

9.2.1   Functions of the SVC

The two (or more) verbs in a serial verb construction normally function together to express a single event; but because both verbs contribute to the meaning of the clause, the resulting expression is semantically more complex than the meaning of either verb on its own. This complexity may take several different forms. One very common use of the serial verb pattern is to add an additional argument, such as an instrument (14) or beneficiary (15).

(14) a   **Nupe** (Hyman, 1975; tone not indicated)
Musa la   ebi   ba nakā.
Musa take knife cut meat
'Musa cut the meat with a knife.'

b   **Sranan** (Suriname; Sebba, 1987)
Mi teki a.nefi   koti a.brede.
1sg take the.knife cut the.bread
'I cut the bread with a knife.'

(15) a   **Sranan** (Suriname; Sebba, 1987)
Mi e   prani a.karu gi   yu.
1sg ASP plant the.corn give you
'I am planting the corn for you.'

b   **Anyi** (Ivory Coast; Van Leynseele, 1975, cited by Foley and Van Valin, 1984:199; tone not marked)
ajo tɔ̄   alɪɛ mā Kasi.
Ajo cook-HABIT food give Kasi
'Ajo cooked food for Kasi.'

Another very common function of the SVC is to express the goal or direction of motion, as in (16). Serialization may also be used to express the result or extent of an action, as in (17).

(16) a   **Khmer** (Schiller, 1990a; tone not marked)
kŏat yɔɔk mhoup mɔɔk phtĕah.
he   take food   come house
'He brought the food home.'

b   **Yoruba** (W. Africa; Stahlke, 1970; tone not shown)
mo mu iwe   wa   fun ɛ.
I   took book came gave you
'I brought you a book.'

c   **Saramaccan** (Suriname; Byrne, 1987)
a bi   tsá   di.meliki go na   di.konde.
3sg PAST carry the.milk go LOC the.village
'He had taken the milk to the village.'

(17) a   **Sranan** (Suriname; Sebba, 1987)

Kofi naki Amba kiri.

Kofi hit   Amba kill

'Kofi struck Amba dead.'

b   **Tok Pisin** (PNG)

Ol   i-sutim pik i-dai.

they shoot   pig die

'They shot the pig dead.'

c   **Yoruba** (W. Africa; Bamgboṣe, 1974; tone not shown)

olu ti   ɔmɔ naa šubu.

Olu push child the fall

'Olu pushed the child down.'

d   **White Hmong** (SE Asia; Jarkey, 1991; cited by Durie, 1997)

kuv nrhiav   tau kuv nti   nplhaib.

I   search.for get my CLASS ring

'I found my ring.'

In a pattern related to this resultative use, serial verbs are often used to express completive aspect, as in (18). Other aspectual uses are also possible; these often involve verbs which denote bodily movements or postures, as in (19a).

(18)   **Saramaccan** (Suriname; Byrne, cited in Seuren, 1990)

Kofi nyan di   ganya   kabá.

Kofi eat   the chicken finish

'Kofi has already eaten the chicken.'

(19)   **Yatyɛ** (W. Africa; Stahlke, 1970; tone not indicated)

a   *Continuous:*

odide ahyɛ ibi   itywi.

man   squat come home

'The man is coming home.'

b   *Habitual:*

odide aga   ibi   itywi.

man   wander come home

'The man usually comes home.'

c   *Repetitive:*

odide ibu   ibi   itywi.

man   return come home

'The man came home again.'

Other uses include purpose (20a), manner (20b), causation, etc. Finally, specific combinations of serial verbs often take on an idiomatic meaning, as illustrated in (21).

(20) a   **Chrau** (Vietnam; Thomas, 1971, cited in Durie, 1997:305)

něh hao   chhɔ pĭq pai-vunh.

3sg climb tree pick gourd

'He climbed the tree to pick gourds.'

b   **Yoruba** (W. Africa; Stahlke, 1970; tone not marked)
     mo fi   ɔgbɔn   ge igi.
     I   took cleverness cut tree
     'I cut the tree cleverly.'

(21) a   **Akan** (Schachter, 1974)
          Kofi gyee   Amma dii.
          Kofi receive-PAST Amma eat-PAST
          'Kofi believed Amma.'

b   **Yoruba** (Baker, 1989, from Laniran and Sonaiya, 1987; tone not marked)
     olu rɛ bɔla jɛ.
     Olu cut Bola eat
     'Olu cheated Bola.'

c   **Vagala** (W. Africa; Pike, 1966)
     ù lé   û há.
     he get-PAST him throw
     'He saved him.'

9.2.2   Characteristic and diagnostic features of SVCs

Beyond the basic formulation given above (one clause, two or more verbs), it is very difficult to find a definition of serial verbs which all linguists would accept. In fact, different linguists sometimes disagree as to whether a particular construction in some language is really a serial verb construction or not. The examples presented in section 9.2.1 were "classic" or prototypical serial verbs, i.e., cases which everyone would accept as true SVCs. But in other cases there is less agreement as to whether constructions which some authors have called "serial verbs" really belong to this category.

Rather than try to formulate an explicit definition of SVCs, we will describe the prototypical cases by listing some of their characteristic features. A proposed list of properties is given in (22); some of these properties will be discussed immediately below, others in subsequent sections. Then we will mention a few diagnostic tests which have been proposed for determining whether or not a particular construction is in fact a "true" SVC.

(22)   **Characteristic properties of SVCs**
   a   A prototypical SVC contains two or more morphologically independent verbs within the same clause, neither of which is an AUX.
   b   There are no conjunctions or other overt markers of subordination or coordination separating the two verbs.
   c   The serial verbs belong to a single intonation contour, with no pause separating them.
   d   The entire SVC refers to a single (possibly complex) event.
   e   A true SVC may contain only one specification for tense, aspect, modality, negation, etc., though these features are sometimes redundantly marked on both verbs.
   f   The two verbs in the SVC share at least one semantic argument.

g   Obligatory non-coreference: a true SVC will not contain two overt NPs which refer to the same argument.

h   A prototypical SVC contains only one grammatical subject.

First, and most importantly, an SVC comprises a single clause. There will be no intonational or grammatical indication of a clause boundary between the two verbs; no markers of subordination (e.g., complementizers); and (in general) no overt markers of coordination (i.e., conjunctions). Note the following contrast between a true SVC (23a) and a coordinate sentence (23b) in Nupe, a language of West Africa:

(23)   **Nupe** (Hyman, 1975; tone not indicated)

a   Musa la   ebi   ba nakã.
        Musa take knife cut meat
        'Musa cut the meat with a knife.'

b   Musa la   ebi   <u>tʃi</u> ba nakã.
        Musa take knife <u>and</u> cut meat
        'Musa took the knife and (then) cut the meat.'

These examples also illustrate a second property of prototypical SVCs, namely that the two verbs together express a single event, as in (23a). Compare this with the coordinate structure in (23b) which expresses a sequence of two distinct events.

Related to this single-event interpretation, it is generally not possible for the two (or more) verbs in an SVC to have independent marking for tense and aspect. If both verbs are marked, they must agree in tense and aspect. In example (24a), both verbs are marked for past tense. In (24b), the first verb is past but the second verb is perfect, which makes the SVC ungrammatical. In a coordinate structure like (24c), however, the two verbs can have different tense marking.

(24)   **Akan** (Akuapem dialect; Schachter, 1974)

a   me-kɔɔ-e me-baa-e.
        I-go-PAST I-come-PAST
        'I went and came back.'

b   *me-kɔɔ-e maba.
        I-go-PAST I-come-PERF

c   me-kɔɔ-e <u>na</u> maba.
        I-go-PAST <u>and</u> I-come-PERF
        'I went and I have come back.'

One clear indication that the two serialized verbs express a single event is that we cannot negate one verb while asserting the truth of the other. Compare the SVC in (25a), where the result of the action cannot be negated, with the corresponding biclausal construction (25b) where this negation is perfectly acceptable:

(25)   **Sranan** (Suriname; Sebba, 1987)

a   Mi   teki   a.nefi   koti   a.brede   (#ma   no   koti   en).
       1sg   take   the.knife   cut   the.bread   but   not   cut   it
       'I cut the bread with a knife (#but didn't cut it).'

b   Mi   teki   a.nefi   fu   koti   a.brede   (ma   no   koti   en).
       1sg   take   the.knife   for   cut   the.bread   but   not   cut   it
       'I took a knife in order to cut the bread (but didn't cut it).'

In Ewe, as in a number of other languages, negation is marked by a circumfix.
The Ewe circumfix has the form *me-*. . . . *o*: the prefix *me-* attaches to the verb of
the clause which is being negated, while the particle *o* appears at the end of that
clause. In an SVC both verbs must be included within a single instance of the
circumfix (26b). It is not possible to negate one verb without the other (26c). But
in a biclausal structure like (26d),[2] either clause can be negated independently as
illustrated in (26e).

(26)   **Ewe** (W. Africa; Agbedor, 1993; Felix Ameka, unpublished MS.)

a   Me-šle   agbale   ná   Áma.
       1sg-buy   book   give   Ama
       'I bought a book for Ama.'

b   Nye   me-šle   agbale   ná   Áma   o.
       1sg   NEG-buy   book   give   Ama   NEG
       'I did not buy a book for Ama.'

c   *Me-šle   agbale   me-ná   Áma   o.
       1sg-buy   book   NEG-give   Ama   NEG

d   Me-yɔ!-e   wò-tɔ.
       1sg-call-3sg   3sg-respond
       'I called him (and) he responded.'

e   Me-yɔ!-e   mé-tɔ   o.
       1sg-call-3sg   NEG-respond   NEG
       'I called him (but) he did not respond.'

In a typical SVC, each argument will be expressed by only one overt NP. Thus
a non-reflexive pronoun within the SVC must be NON-COREFERENTIAL with
all of the other arguments; that is, the pronoun cannot take some other argument
within the SVC as its antecedent. This constraint is illustrated in (27), specifically
by the fact that the pronoun *en* in (27b) cannot refer to 'the match' if the sentence
is interpreted as a serial verb construction.

(27)   **Sranan** (Suriname; Sebba, 1987)

a   Kofi   teki   a   swarfu   bron.
       Kofi   take   the   match   burn
       'Kofi burned the match.'

b   Kofi   teki   a   swarfu   bron   en.
       Kofi   take   the   match   burn   it
       'Kofi burned it with the match.' (*it* cannot refer to *match*)

Sebba (1987) states in that Sranan, when a coreferential pronoun does occur as in (28b), the sentence is not a serial verb construction but rather a special type of coordinate structure which does not contain any overt conjunction. This coordinate structure must be interpreted as describing two separate events, and the two verbs may be separated by a pause. Thus (28b) has the same structure as (28c), which clearly describes two distinct events. (This coordinate interpretation is also possible for [27b], with the meaning 'Kofi took the match and then burned it' and an optional pause between the two clauses.) When no pronoun is present, as in (28a), we have a true SVC which must be interpreted as a single event, and which cannot contain a pause. A similar pattern is found in Papiamentu, a Portuguese-based creole (29). A tree diagram for the unmarked coordinate structure in (28c) is given in (30).

(28) a   Kofi naki Amba (*,) kiri.
          Kofi hit Amba   kill
          'Kofi struck Amba dead.'

     b   Kofi naki Amba (,) kiri en.
          Kofi hit   Amba   kill 3sg
          'Kofi struck Amba and killed her.'

     c   Kofi sutu   Amba (,) kiri Kwaku.
          Kofi shoot Amba   kill Kwaku
          'Kofi shot Amba and killed Kwaku.'

(29)   **Papiamentu** (W. Africa; Bendix, 1972; cited in Sebba, 1987)
     a   korta e   barika habri
          cut   the belly open
          'cut the belly open'

     b   korta e   barika habri-e
          cut   the belly open-it
          'cut the belly and then open it' (two actions)

(30)
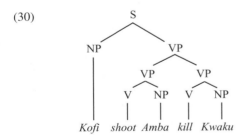

Baker (1989) points out that a number of authors have failed to distinguish between these unmarked coordinate constructions and true SVCs, which has led to considerable confusion in the literature about serial verbs. For this reason it is important to identify criteria which will allow us to distinguish true SVCs from other similar constructions. We have already mentioned a number of these criteria:

scope of negation, uniqueness of tense and aspect marking, the non-coreference constraint, etc.

Another helpful test comes from filler–gap constructions such as Wh- questions or relative clauses. Recall from chapter 7 that coordinate structures in many languages are extraction "islands," meaning that they cannot contain a gap. In languages where this constraint applies, neither object can be extracted from coordinate structures like (28c), repeated below as (31a). In contrast, both objects can be questioned or relativized from a true SVC like (32a).

(31)   **Sranan (unmarked coordination)** (Sebba, 1987)
   a   Kofi sutu   Amba kiri Kwaku.
      Kofi shoot Amba kill Kwaku
      'Kofi shot Amba and killed Kwaku.'

   b   *Suma Kofi sutu   Amba kiri —?
      Who Kofi shoot Amba kill
      (*'Who did Kofi shoot Amba and kill?')

   c   *Suma Kofi sutu   — kiri Kwaku?
      Who Kofi shoot   kill Kwaku
      (*'Who did Kofi shoot and kill Kwaku?')

(32)   **Sranan (true SVC)** (Sebba, 1987)
   a   Kofi teki a.nefi   koti a.brede.
      Kofi take the.knife cut the.bread
      'Kofi cut the bread with the knife.'

   b   San   Kofi teki a.nefi   koti —?
      what Kofi take the.knife cut
      'What did Kofi cut with the knife?'

   c   San   Kofi teki — koti a.brede?
      what Kofi take   cut the.bread
      'What did Kofi cut the bread with?'

9.2.3   "Single event" interpretation

There is a great deal more to be said about the syntactic properties of SVCs. However, let us now turn to some of the semantic issues which these constructions raise. In particular, let us consider the question of what it means to say that a true SVC must refer to a "single event."

As noted in the preceding section (see point [22d] above), the event named by an SVC may be semantically complex. For example, the serialized verbs may refer to a sequence of closely related actions which together are viewed as making up a single event, as in (24). Some further examples of this type are shown in (33).

(33) a   **Yoruba** (W. Africa; Lord, 1974; tone not shown)
      Dada ra   burɛdi jɛ.
      Dada buy bread eat
      'Dada bought bread to eat and ate it.'

b   **Kalam** (PNG; Lane, 1991, cited in Durie, 1997)
      byn   pataj ogok am yg pak dad   ap-elgp-al . . .
      woman young these go dig hit carrying come-PAST-HABIT-3pl
      'The young women dig and fetch (these animals) . . .'
      (i.e., 'The young women go hunting')

Durie (1997) points out that in order for SVCs of this type to be grammatical,
it must be possible for speakers of the language to interpret the various actions
as comprising a single coherent event. It appears that different languages impose
different restrictions as to which specific combinations of verbs are permissible,
and that these restrictions are sometimes due to cultural factors. In the following
Yoruba examples, there seems to be no grammatical explanation for the difference
in grammaticality between (34a) and (34b), or between (35a) and (35b).

(34)   **Yoruba** (W. Africa; Bamgboṣe, 1974)
    a   ó   ra   išu   wá.
          she bought yams came
          'She bought yams and came.'

    b   *ó ta   išu   wá.
          she sold   yams came

(35) a   ó   jɛun sùn.
          he ate slept
          'He ate and then slept.'

    b   *ó jɛun padà.
          he ate returned

Similarly, serial verbs are sometimes used to express simultaneous actions,
but only when these are viewed by the speakers as comprising a single event.
Durie notes that in Hmong culture, dancing and playing the bamboo pipes always
go together; they are viewed as one event, and so may be combined in a serial
construction (36a). Listening to music, on the other hand, is viewed as a separate
event from dancing, so these two verbs may not serialize (36b); rather, a coordinate
construction must be used (36c).

(36)   **White Hmong** (SE Asia; Jarkey, 1991; cited in Durie, 1997)
    a   nws dhia   tshov qeej.
          he dance blow bamboo.pipes
          'He dances playing the pipes.'

    b   *nws dhia   mloog nkauj.
          he   dance listen song

    c   nws dhia   thiab mloog nkauj.
          he dance and   listen song
          'He dances (while) listening to music.'

The Alamblak language of Papua New Guinea has a very productive process of V+V compounding, which exhibits a number of features associated with

prototypical SVCs in other languages. One such point of similarity is that, in order to form a permissible compound, two verb roots must name actions which can be conceived of as a single event (Bruce, 1988:28). This constraint involves both cultural and pragmatic factors. For example, all speakers accept the compound form in (37a), since climbing a tree to look for insects is a common activity in that culture. All speakers reject (37b), since climbing a tree and looking at the stars have no connection in people's minds. But, given a context in which it is important to see the stars for some reason, speakers will accept the very similar form in (37c).

(37)   **Alamblak** (PNG; Bruce, 1988)

a   miyt   ritm   muh-hambray-an-m.
          tree   insects   climb-search.for-1sg-3pl
          'I climbed the tree and looked for insects/ looking for insects.'

b   *miyt guñm muh-hëti-an-m.
          tree   stars   climb-see-1sg-3pl
          (for: 'I climbed the tree and saw the stars.')

c   ?miyt guñm muh-hëti-marña-an-m.
          tree   stars   climb-see-well-1sg-3pl
          'I climbed the tree and saw the stars clearly.' (acceptable in specific context)

9.2.4   Morphological features in SVCs

As we have noted, it is generally not possible for the two (or more) verbs in an SVC to have independent marking for tense and aspect. Usually tense and aspect will be marked only once for the entire clause, typically on the first verb as in (38a–b). A number of languages allow tense "doubling" or "spreading," with both verbs taking identical marking for tense and aspect as in (38c–d); see also (16b, 20b, 21a). In some languages, e.g., Akan, this tense spreading may even be obligatory, at least for certain types of SVC. Byrne (1990) reports that in Saramaccan and a few other Atlantic creole languages, tense may be marked on either or both verbs (38e); but this pattern seems to be quite rare. Of course, if both verbs are marked the indicated values of tense and aspect must be identical.

(38) a   **Sranan** (Suriname; Jansen *et al.*, 1978, cited by Byrne, 1990)
          Roy e   tyari a   pikin go na   oso.
          Roy PAST carry the child go LOC house
          'Roy took the child home.'

b   **Bamileke** (W. Africa; Hyman, 1971)
          á   ká   láh càk usá? ha   a.
          he PAST take pot come give me
          'He brought the pot for/to me.'

c   **Akan** (W. Africa; Schachter, 1974)
          Kofi yɛ-ɛ   adwuma ma-a   Amma.
          Kofi do-PAST work   give-PAST Amma
          'Kofi worked for Amma.'

d   **Ewe** (W. Africa; Collins, 1997)
Kofi <u>a</u>   tsɔ ati-ε   <u>a</u> fo Yao.
Kofi FUT take stick-DEF FUT hit Yao
'Kofi will hit Yao with the stick.'

e   **Saramaccan** (Suriname; Byrne, 1990)
a <u>(bi)</u> tsa di.meliki <u>(bi)</u> go na   di.konde.
3sg PERF carry the.milk PERF go LOC the.village
'He had taken the milk to the village.'

Similarly, in languages where negation is marked by a verbal affix, it must be marked on both verbs in some languages:

(39) a   **Akan** (W. Africa; Schachter, 1974)
Kofi n-yε   adwuma m-ma   Amma.
Kofi NEG-do work   NEG-give Amma
'Kofi does not work for Amma.'

b   **Anyi** (Ivory Coast; Van Leynseele, 1975, cited by Foley and Olson, 1985; tone not marked)
cʊa n-jɪ   akɔ   n-ˈni.
dog NEG-catch-HABIT chicken NEG-eat-HABIT
'The dog never eats a chicken.'

Since there is normally only one grammatical subject, if both verbs are marked for subject agreement they must show identical agreement features, as in (40). It is very interesting to note that in some languages, even when the subject is not a semantic argument of the second verb, that verb may still be marked for agreement with the grammatical subject, as illustrated in (41).

(40) a   **Akan** (Africa; Schachter, 1974)
me-yε-ε   adwuma me-ma-a   Amma.
I-do-PAST work   I-give-PAST Amma
'I worked for Amma.'

b   **Tariana** (Brazil; Aikhenvald, 1999)
nha-ritu na-inu=pidana   ñaña.
3pl-catch 3pl-kill=REM.PAST madi.fish
'They caught some madi fish.'

c   **Kisar** (Maluku, Indonesia; Blood, 1992)
Idedinamene Dedi n-amkuru n-amaka.
just.now   Dedi 3sg-sleep 3sg-awaken
'Dedi just woke up from his sleep.'

d   **Kisar** (Maluku, Indonesia; Blood, 1992)
A=m   la=m   pahar.[3]
ai   m-la   m-pahar
1pl.EXCL 1pl.EXCL-go 1pl.EXCL-wash (clothes)
'We (excl.) are going to wash clothes.'

(41) a   **Akan** (Africa; Schachter, 1974)[4]
me-de aburow mi-gu nsu-m.
I-take corn   I-flow water-in
'I pour corn into the water.'

    b   **Tariana** (Brazil; Aikhenvald, 1999)
ka: ru=ka nuha nu-a=mahka   nu-hyā=niki
fearing   1sg 1sg-give=REC.PAST 1sg-eat=completely
piri=nuku   iniri=nuku.
your.son=ACC traira.fish=ACC[5]
'Being afraid, I let the traira-fish eat your son.'

    c   **Obolo** (Durie, 1997; tone not shown)
e-gwen emi e-nu.
PL-call 1sg PL-come
'Let them call me to come.'

Examples like those in (41) provide strong evidence that the grammatical relation between a verb and its subject may be independent of any semantic roles assigned by that verb. It is the grammatical relation which is crucial for identifying SVCs. In a typical SVC, both verbs must assign the SUBJ relation to the same NP, even if that NP does not get any semantic role from the second verb.

9.2.5   Word order

Thus far we have discussed primarily those features which can be used to identify true SVCs in any language. In this section we will consider a structural feature which provides a notable point of difference among serial verb languages, namely the position of object NPs.

Serial verbs occur most frequently in SVO languages, but they are also found in SOV languages. They almost never occur in verb-initial languages, although Schiller (1990b) cites the Mon-Khmer language Ravüa as one such case. Obviously the position of the object NPs in a serial verb construction will depend in part on the position of the object within a simple, one-verb clause. But, aside from this contrast between VO and OV word order, there is another parameter of variation in serial verb constructions. In most serial verb languages, each object NP will occur adjacent to the verb which selects it. But in some languages, all the verbs may "cluster" together, with the NPs grouped either before or after the verbs.

Let us begin with the situation in which the SVC contains two transitive verbs, each of which has an overt object NP. As we have just noted, the most common pattern is for each object to be adjacent to the verb that selects it. In SVO languages, each object will follow its verb as in (42), while in SOV languages the object precedes its verb as in (43).

(42)   **Sranan** (Suriname; Sebba, 1987)
   a   Mi teki a.nefi   koti a.brede.
       1sg take the.knife cut the.bread
       'I cut the bread with a knife.'

   b   Mi e   prani a.karu gi   yu.
       1sg ASP plant the.corn give you
       'I am planting the corn for you.'

(43)   **Ịjọ** (West Africa; Williamson, 1965; tone not marked)
   a   eri ogidi   akı-nı   indi pεı-mı.
       he machete take-Ø[6] fish cut.up-PAST
       'He cut up a fish with a machete.'

   b   araʊ zu.ye akı buru teri-mı.
       she basket take yam cover-PAST
       'She used a basket to cover a yam.'

A great many proposals have been made concerning the structure of these examples. Without going into all the details, let us simply assume that each verb together with its object forms a constituent which we will label V'. The patterns in (42–43) could then be represented by the tree diagrams shown in (44):

(44) a   (SVO languages; cf. [42a])

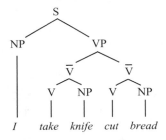

   b   (SOV languages; cf. [43a])

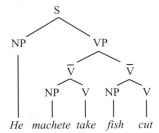

Next, consider the situation in which there is only one object NP which is shared between two transitive verbs. Assuming that the NP position is optional within each V', the structures proposed in (44) would allow a shared object NP to occur within either the first or the second V'. Most languages seem to prefer to express the object in the first V', as in (45a). But Sebba notes that the order in (45b) was used in nineteenth-century Sranan, and is still accepted by some speakers.

(45)   **Sranan** (Suriname; Sebba, 1987)
  a   Kofi naki Amba kiri.
       Kofi hit   Amba kill
       'Kofi struck Amba dead.'

  b   Kofi naki kiri Amba. (*archaic?*)
       Kofi hit   kill Amba
       'Kofi struck Amba dead.'

Some languages, such as Hmong, seem to prefer to express shared objects as far to the right as possible (46c–d).[7]

(46)   **White Hmong** (SE Asia; Jarkey, 1991; in Durie, 1997)
  a   nws xuab riam txiav nqiaj qaib.
       3sg grasp knife cut   meat chicken
       'She cut some chicken with a knife.'

  b   nws xa   ib   qho   khoom pub kuv.
       3sg send one CLASS goods give 1sg
       'She sent some things to me (as a present).'

  c   kuv nrhiav   tau kuv nti   nplhaib.
       1sg search.for get my CLASS ring
       'I found my ring.'

  d   nws tua   raug   liab.
       3sg shoot.at hit.the.mark monkey
       'He shot a monkey.'

The SVCs we have considered so far can be analyzed as a sequence of V′s, and as we have noted this is the most common pattern. However, there are some languages in which all the verbs cluster together, with all the object NPs either following (for SVO languages, as in [47]) or preceding (for SOV languages, as in [48]) the verbs. Languages of this type clearly involve a different kind of structure. One possible analysis is presented in (49).

(47)   **Jeh** (Vietnam; Gradin, 1976; Cohen, 1976)
  a   Au rŭp dĕk   kanei.
       1sg catch strangle rat
       'I caught and strangled a rat.'

  b   ĕn chŏk bùh cha ka.
       3sg take roast eat fish
       'He roasted and ate a fish.'

  c   Baă tənoh dòh băl.ĕn tədrong i . . .
       father explain give them matter this
       'Father explained this matter to them . . .'

d   mi ruat dòh au phei.
      you buy give me rice
      'You buy rice for me.'

e   ĕn loh chièu reng   rŭp   bùh cha chŏl 'wăn.
      3sg exit go   search catch roast eat pig   their
      'He went out, got somebody's pig, roasted and ate it.'

(48)   **Barai** (PNG; Foley and Olson, 1985:43–44)

a   fu burede ije sime abe ufu.
      he bread   the knife take cut
      'He cut the bread with the knife.'

b   fu na ire   ifej-ie   i.
      he me food help-1sg.OBJ eat
      'He helped me eat food.'

c   a na ine tua   kore-j-ie.
      you me stick break.off throw-TRANS-1sg.OBJ
      'You broke off and threw at me a stick.'

(49) a   (SVO languages; cf. [47d])

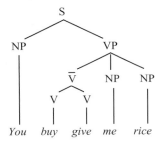

b   (SOV languages; cf. [48b])

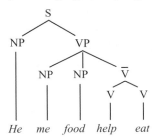

9.2.6   Non-canonical serialization

    As we noted in section 9.2.2, the two verbs in a prototypical SVC are
morphologically independent, i.e., two distinct words. But there are languages
such as Alamblak in which a highly productive V+V compounding process seems
very similar to serialization. In these languages compound verbs, in which two
or more roots join to form a single complex stem, are used to express many of

the same functions we saw in section 9.2.1. Some further examples are given in (50); see also (37a) above.

(50) a   **Alamblak** (PNG; Bruce, 1988)
        na   yawyt yimam wikna-hay-më-an-m.
        1sg dog   people buy-give-REM.PAST-1sg-3pl
        'I bought a dog for the people.' or: 'I bought a dog and gave it to the people.'

     b   **Yimas** (PNG; Foley and Olson, 1985)
        mabargat   ya-na-park-bi-kapik-bi-warki-k.[8]
        coconut.branches 3pl.OBJ-3sg.SUBJ-split-*-break.up-*-tie-REM.PAST
        'He split, broke into small pieces, and tied together the coconut branches.'

This type of "compounding serialization" is most common in SOV languages. However, it is also found in Igbo, an SVO language of West Africa. Interestingly, Déchaine (1993) reports that Igbo uses a "normal" serial verb construction to express instrument, manner, comitative, etc., as illustrated in (51a–b). But there are no benefactive, recipient, or resultative serial verb constructions in the language; these functions can only be expressed by using a V+V compound, as in (51c–d).

(51)   **Igbo** (W. Africa; Déchaine, 1993; Lord, 1975)
     a   ó   wè-re   úkwʊ gà-á   ahyá.
        he take-ASP leg   go-ASP market
        'He went to the market on foot.'

     b   ó ji-ri   ɔhʊhʊ ri-e   ihé.
        he use-ASP hurry eat-ASP thing
        'He ate hurriedly.'

     c   ó tⁱi-gbù-rù   nwóké áhʊ.
        he hit-kill-ASP man   that
        'He beat that man to death.'

     d   ó bì-nye-re   Adhá akwà.
        he borrow-give-ASP Adha cloth
        'He lent some cloth to Adha.'

Another construction which has been described as serialization but does not exhibit all of the diagnostic properties listed in section 9.2.2 is illustrated in (53). Several Austronesian languages spoken in Vanuatu and northern Papua New Guinea have constructions that look like normal SVCs with subject agreement marked on each verb, as in (52a). In some of these languages it is also possible for the second verb to appear in the default third person singular form, as in (52b). (Notice that the object NP in that example is plural, so the second verb does not agree with either the subject or the object.) This pattern is sometimes referred to as "ambient" serialization.

(52)   **Numbami** (PNG; Bradshaw, 1993)
     a   ma-pa-andalowa ma-woti   ma-ma   ma-solonga teteu.
        1pl.ex-make-way 1pl.ex-descend 1pl.ex-come 1pl.ex-enter village
        'We walked down here into the village.'

b   "Ambient" serialization (default 3sg marking)

ma-pisa   ai i-iye taun.

1pl.ex-find 3pl 3sg-lie town

'We found them in town.'

A very few examples have been published in which both verbs agree, but not with the same argument. In other words, the two verbs have different grammatical subjects, and each verb agrees with its own subject. This pattern, illustrated in (53), is sometimes called "switch-subject" serialization.

(53) a   **Loniu** (Manus Island, PNG; Hamel, 1993)

utó   ko'oluweni   wow ala   tan.

1pl.ex IRR-NONSG-move.with.rope 2sg IRR-2sg-go down

'We will lower you down (into the water).'

b   **Paamese** (Vanuatu; Crowley, 1987:48)

kaik komuasinau   nauvā   netan.

2sg 2sg-REAL-hit-1sg 1sg-REAL-go down

'You hit me down.'

These examples are extremely interesting, because we expect normal SVCs to contain just one grammatical subject. One hypothesis which we might want to test is that the sentences in (53) could be analyzed as examples of CLAUSE CHAINING. Of course, before we can consider that question, we need to understand what "clause chaining" means. This is the topic of the next section.

9.3   Clause chaining and switch-reference

CLAUSE CHAINING is a complex sentence pattern which is sometimes mistakenly identified as a serial verb construction (SVC). In languages which allow this pattern, a single sentence may consist of many clauses strung together in a "chain," with none of them necessarily being subordinate to any of the others. The similarity to serial verbs lies in this fact. Both serial verbs and clause chaining have been described by some authors as examples of "co-subordination,"[9] meaning a sequence of similar units which are neither in a subordinate nor a true coordinate relationship to each other. The crucial difference between serial verbs and clause chaining is the size of the unit involved. Serial verbs, we have argued, may involve sequences of verbs or V's, whereas clause chaining involves sequences of clauses. In particular, each clause in the chain may potentially contain its own subject NP.

True clause chaining is found primarily in verb-final (SOV) languages.[10] It is especially common in the Papuan languages of New Guinea, but is also found in Central and South America and various other parts of the world. As noted above, a sentence in these languages may consist of many clauses strung together in a "chain." Only the last verb in the chain carries complete inflectional marking for tense, aspect, and mood (TAM); so verbs which are fully inflected for TAM are called FINAL VERBS. Verbs which occur in the non-final clauses (MEDIAL VERBS) take a reduced set of tense markers, as discussed below. The basic pattern of the sentence looks something like this:

(54)   S$_{medial}$ S$_{medial}$ S$_{medial}$ . . . S$_{final}$

Longacre (1985, 1996) compares this sentence pattern to a train, with the final verb being like a locomotive which pulls a long string of medial verbs behind it.

A very common system of tense marking on the medial verbs is a simple two-way contrast between SEQUENTIAL VS. SIMULTANEOUS action. A medial verb carries the "simultaneous" marker when the event it refers to occurs at the same time as the event named in the following clause, while the "sequential" marker indicates that one event follows the other. This contrast is illustrated in (55a–b). Comparing (55a) with (55c), we can see how the tense marking of the final verb determines the time reference for the medial verbs as well.

(55)   **Amele** (PNG; Roberts, 1988:53)
   a   Ho busale-ce-b   dana age qo-ig-a.
            pig run.out-DS(SEQ)-3sg man PL hit-3pl-REC.PAST
            'The pig ran out and (then) the men killed (it).'

   b   Ho bu-busale-n   dana age qo-ig-a.
            pig SIMUL-run.out-3sg.DS man PL hit-3pl-REC.PAST
            'As the pig ran out the men killed (it).'

   c   Ho busale-ce-b   dana age qo-qag-an.
            pig run.out-DS(SEQ)-3sg man PL hit-3pl-FUT
            'The pig will run out and the men will kill (it).'

The gloss "DS" in these examples stands for "different subject," and illustrates another typical feature of clause-chaining languages. In a clause-chaining construction, each medial verb can be marked to indicate whether its subject is the same as, or different from, the subject of the following clause. This type of marking (Same Subject vs. Different Subject) is referred to as a SWITCH-REFERENCE system.

In the simplest case, then, we have a two-way tense distinction which combines with the two switch-reference categories to produce a total of four possible medial verb forms. This four-way contrast is illustrated in (56). In these Kâte examples, the first suffix on each medial verb is a portmanteau, indicating a specific combination of tense and switch-reference category. Notice that the DS (Different Subject) medial verbs in (56c–d) carry a subject agreement suffix (in this case, third plural), whereas the SS (Same Subject) verbs in (56a–b) have no agreement marker. This is a very common pattern, since any subject-agreement marking on the medial verb would be redundant when it is marked for SS.

(56)   **Kâte** (PNG; Longacre, 1983:187; 1985:267)

  a   Fisi-huk   na-wek.
      arrived-SS(SIMUL) eat-3sg.PAST
      'As he$_i$ arrived, he$_i$ was eating.'

  b   Fisi-rã   na-wek.
      arrived-SS(SEQ)   eat-3sg.PAST
      'He$_i$ arrived, then he$_i$ ate.'

  c   Mu-ha-pie   kio-wek.
      speak-DS(SIMUL)-3pl weep-3sg.PAST
      'As they spoke, he wept.'

  d   Mu-Ø-pie   kio-wek.
      speak-DS(SEQ)-3pl weep-3sg.PAST
      'After they spoke, he wept.'

Many languages have more complex systems of tense marking on medial verbs, but it is still the case that the time reference of the medial verbs is at least partially dependent on the tense of the following verb. For this reason, medial verbs are sometimes referred to as DEPENDENT forms, and final verbs as INDEPENDENT forms.

Our examples so far have involved very simple chains consisting of just two clauses; but in natural speech, chains are typically much longer and may contain dozens of medial clauses before a final clause is reached. Each of the following Usan examples consists of a single chain, with the end of the chain marked by the occurrence of an independent (fully inflected) verb form. Note that in Usan, medial verbs are normally unmarked for tense. The sequence of these unmarked medial verbs is "iconic," meaning that they must appear in the same order as the events they refer to in the story.[11] As in the Kâte examples in (56), only DS verbs are marked for subject agreement.

(57)   **Usan** (PNG; Reesink, 1987:346)

  a   irai   eng ba-ub   di-ab   wuri-s-a   n-unor.
      shrimp the take-SS come.up-SS them-give-2sg.DS eat-3pl.FUT(uncertain)
      'Take these shrimps, come up and give them to them and they may eat.'

  b   wo namanimun gumat   big-a   gâb   qâmâr-ari ig-uminei.
      he letter   write.SS put-3sg.DS see-SS say-3pl.DS hear-1pl.REM.PAST
      'He wrote a letter, put (it), they saw (it), told, and we heard.' (i.e., 'We have heard it said that he sent a letter.')

  c   igâm-a   wai   yar   saragaim-a   ig-ub   mâgib   ar-a
      be-3sg.DS animal come rustle-3sg.DS hear-SS whistle-SS call-3sg.DS
      inaun weib   di   wai   sir   wo-t   âriram-a   wâr-a
      moon appear.ss come.up animal very him-at throw-3sg.DS shoot-3sg.DS
      inaun nob qâm-ar: "..."
      moon with say-3sg.REM.PAST

"He was there, and an animal came rustling, and he heard it and whistled and called, and the moon appeared and threw (its light) right on the animal, and he shot (the animal) and the moon said to (him): ('Father, give me the animal's blood to drink.')"

9.3.1   Medial vs. subordinate clauses

Although the morphological differences between medial and final verbs are sometimes described as a contrast between "dependent" vs. "independent" forms, the medial clauses in examples (55) to (57) are not subordinate to (i.e., embedded within) their final clause. One clear indication of this is the difference in word order between medial clauses and true subordinate clauses.

Complement clauses in verb-final languages normally precede their matrix verb. In the Amele example in (58a), the complement clause occurs in the middle of the matrix clause, between the subject and verb. This kind of embedding is impossible for medial clauses (58b); rather, each medial and final clause in the chain must form a continuous constituent. (All Amele examples are taken from Roberts, 1988.)

(58) a   **Complement clause**

Ija [dana age ija   na   ho qo-ig-a]   d-ugi-na.
1sg man PL 1sg POSS pig hit-3pl-REC.PAST know-1sg-PRES
'I know that the men killed my pig.'

   b   **Embedded medial clause** (cf. 55a)
*dana age [ho busale-ce-b]   qo-ig-a.
man PL pig run.out-DS(SEQ)-3sg hit-3pl-REC.PAST

Subordinate adverbial clauses in Amele exhibit variable word order. In the case of adverbial purpose clauses, the preferred ordering is for the subordinate clause to appear inside the matrix clause, as in (59a); but it may also be preposed to initial position, as in (59b). Conditional clauses may occur either before or after the main clause, as illustrated in (60).

(59)   **Purpose adverbial clause**

   a   Dana age [ho qo-qag-an   nu]   ho-ig-a.
man PL pig hit-3pl-FUT PURPOSE come-3pl-REC.PAST
'The men have come to kill the pig.'

   b   [Ho qo-qag-an   nu]   dana age ho-ig-a.
pig hit-3pl-FUT PURPOSE man PL come-3pl-REC.PAST
'In order to kill the pig the men have come.'

(60)   **Conditional adverbial clause**

   a   [Ija ja hud-ig-en   fi] uqa sab man-igi-an.
1sg fire open-1sg-FUT if 3sg food roast-3sg-FUT
'If I light the fire she will cook the food.'

b   Uqa sab man-igi-an   [ija ja hud-ig-en   fi].
3sg food roast-3sg-FUT 1sg fire open-1sg-FUT if
'She will cook the food if I light the fire.'

The ordering relationship between a medial clause and the final clause in a clause chain is totally different. We have already seen that the medial clause can never be embedded inside the final clause (58b). Example (61) illustrates the fact that the order of clauses cannot be reversed: the medial clause must precede the final clause.

(61)   **Medial clause post-posing**

a   [Ho busale-ce-b]   dana age qo-ig-a.
pig run.out-DS(SEQ)-3sg man PL hit-3pl-REC.PAST
'The pig ran out and the men killed (it).'

b   *dana age qo-ig-a   [ho busale-ce-b].
man PL hit-3pl-REC.PAST pig run.out-DS(SEQ)-3sg

9.3.2   Medial clauses vs. coordinate clauses

Medial clauses in Amele exhibit some striking similarities to coordinate clauses, but also some important differences. The most obvious difference relates to the potential marking for tense and mood.

Amele has a fairly rich system of tenses, distinguishing the following categories: present, future, three degrees of past tense (earlier today, yesterday, and remote past), habitual past, negative past, negative future, and "relative future." As we saw above, only the final verb in a chain can be inflected for the full range of tense categories. The time reference of medial verbs depends on the tense marking of the final verb, as illustrated in (55a,c) (repeated below as [62a–b]). However, in both subordinate and coordinate clauses verbs take full independent tense inflections, as illustrated in (62c–d); see also (58a), (59), and (60).

(62)   **Amele** (PNG; Roberts, 1988:52)

a   Ho busale-ce-b   dana age qo-ig-a.
pig run.out-DS(SEQ)-3sg man PL hit-3pl-REC.PAST
'The pig ran out and the men killed (it) (today).'

b   Ho busale-ce-b   dana age qo-qag-an.
pig run.out-DS(SEQ)-3sg man PL hit-3pl-FUT
'The pig will run out and the men will kill (it).'

c   **Subordinate clause**
Dana age [ho qo-qag-an   nu]   ho-ig-a.
man PL pig hit-3pl-FUT PURPOSE come-3pl-REC.PAST
'The men have come to kill the pig.'

d   **Coordinate clauses**
Fred cum   ho-i-an   qa Bill   uqadec h-ugi-an.
Fred yesterday come-3sg-YESTER.PAST but Bill tomorrow come-3sg-FUT
'Fred came yesterday, but Bill will come tomorrow.'

When a yes–no question is formed from a coordinate clause, either or both conjuncts may be marked for interrogative mood by adding a question particle after the verb. This same is true for subordinate clauses: the subordinate clause can be marked for interrogative mood independently from the matrix clause, for example to form an indirect question. But medial verbs in a clause chain cannot take this marking; whenever the yes–no question particle appears on the final verb, it is understood to apply equally to the medial verbs.

Similarly, negation of medial verbs is only possible when the final verb is also negated, but in subordinate and coordinate structures either clause may be independently negated. See Roberts (1988) for examples and discussion.

Nevertheless, there are some important similarities between medial clauses and coordinate clauses in Amele, properties which distinguish these two clause types from subordinate clauses. For example, a pronoun in a preposed subordinate clause may take an NP in the following matrix clause as its antecedent, as in (63a). The subject pronoun is optional, because the identity of the subject is also specified by the agreement marking on the verb; so even with no overt pronoun in the first clause, the interpretation of the sentence is the same. In a coordinate structure, however, a pronoun (whether overt or not) in the first clause cannot take an antecedent in the following clause; this fact is illustrated in (63b). In the same way, a pronoun in a medial clause of a clause chain cannot take an NP in the final clause as its antecedent (63c).

(63) a **Subordinate clause**
(Uqa_i) sab j-igi-an   nu   Fred_i ho-i-a.
3sg   food eat-3sg-FUT PURPOSE Fred come-3sg-REC.PAST
'In order for him_i to eat food Fred_i came.'
(i.e., 'Fred came in order to eat food.')

b **Coordinate clauses**
*Ø_i/*Uqa_i ho-i-a   qa Fred_i sab   qee je-l-Ø.
3sg   come-3sg-REC.PAST but Fred food not eat-NEG.PAST-3sg
*'He_i came but Fred_i did not eat.'

c **Clause chain**
*Ø_i/*Uqa_i bi-bil-i   Fred_i je-i-a.
3sg   SIMUL-sit-3sg-SS Fred eat-3sg-REC.PAST
*'While he_i sat Fred_i ate.'

The same patterns hold when the potential antecedent is a Wh- (content question) word:

(64) a **Subordinate clause**
(Uqa_i) sab j-igi-an   nu   in_i ho-i-a?
3sg   food eat-3sg-FUT PURPOSE who come-3sg-REC.PAST
'Who came in order to eat food?'

b **Coordinate clauses**
*Ø_i/*Uqa_i ho-i-a   qa in_i sab qee je-l-Ø?
3sg   come-3sg-REC.PAST but who food not eat-NEG.PAST-3sg
(for: 'Who came but did not eat?')

    c   **Clause chain**

       *Ø$_i$/*Uqa$_i$ bi-bil-i   in$_i$ je-i-a?

       3sg   SIMUL-sit-3sg-SS who eat-3sg-REC.PAST

       (for: 'Who sat and ate?')

The contrast observed here between subordinate and coordinate clauses suggests that the rules for pronominal reference in Amele may include the following constraint. (This constraint has also been proposed for a number of other languages.)

(65)   In order for a pronoun (whether overt or not) to take as its antecedent an NP within the same sentence, that NP must either precede or command the pronoun.

An NP is said to "command" a pronoun when every phrase structure node which dominates the NP also dominates the pronoun.[12] So, for example, in (66a) the subject NP (*Fred*) of the matrix clause S$_1$ will command any pronoun within the subordinate clause S$_2$. This is true because the only node which commands the matrix subject NP is S$_1$, and this node also dominates everything in S$_2$. But no NP within a coordinate clause will command any element within a sister clause. For example, the NP *Fred* in (66b) is dominated by S$_3$, but S$_3$ does not dominate the pronoun *he* within S$_2$. Thus *Fred* neither precedes nor commands *he*, and so cannot function as its antecedent.

(66) a   (subordinate clause; cf. [63a])

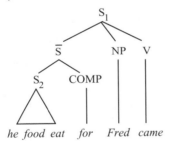

    b   (coordinate clause; cf. [63b])

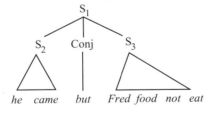

If the statement in (65) correctly describes the Amele rules of pronominal coreference, then we would expect that the coordinate sentence in (67) should be perfectly acceptable, because the antecedent precedes the pronoun. In fact, this is the case (Roberts, p.c.).

(67)   Fred$_i$ ho-i-a   qa (uqa$_i$) sab   qee je-l-Ø.
            Fred come-3sg-REC.PAST but 3sg   food not eat-NEG.PAST-3sg
            'Fred$_i$ came but he$_i$ did not eat.'

Based on these results, the pattern of pronominal reference in a clause-chaining construction, which is similar to the pattern observed in a coordinate sentence, tells us something about the phrase structure of the clause chain. Specifically, the fact that (63c) and (64c) are ungrammatical shows that medial clauses are not subordinate to (i.e., embedded within) the final clause. Rather, medial and final clauses must be sisters, in a configuration similar to the coordinate structure in (66b). On the other hand, we have seen that medial clauses are different from normal coordinate clauses in a number of ways. A coordinate clause takes independent tense and agreement marking, can be independently marked for interrogative mood or negation, etc., whereas medial clauses have none of these properties. Moreover, the order of coordinate clauses can often be reversed, whereas this is impossible in a clause chain.

We will not attempt to provide here a detailed formal analysis of the clause-chaining construction, but it will be helpful to suggest a possible approach which such an analysis might take. One way of characterizing the basic difference between clause chaining and coordinate sentences might be to assign them the same configuration but assume a difference in category. In a standard coordinate structure the two conjuncts are identical in category, and are immediately dominated by another node of that same category. Thus in (66b) we see two sister nodes of category S dominated by another node of category S.

But clause chaining does not behave like normal coordination, which suggests that the category of the mother node is different from that of the daughters. For simplicity we will assume here that both medial and final clauses have category S, although different morphological constraints will need to be stated for the two clause types. Let us introduce a new category, "S-double bar" (S″), to function as the root node of the clause chain.[13] The structure of a simple clause chain would then look something like (68).

(68)   clause chaining; cf. (55a)

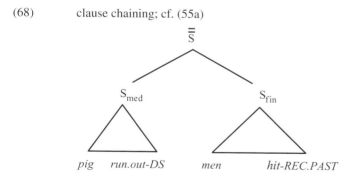

Some reasons to think that the clause chain as a whole is not simply a constituent of category S include the fact that it is very often much longer than a "normal" sentence; its function within a discourse seems closer to that of a paragraph in

English. Furthermore, the clause chain can only occur at the "root" level of the tree; that is, it cannot occur embedded within another S.

9.3.3   Clause chaining vs. SVCs

At this stage we may summarize the following differences which we have mentioned between a typical clause chain and a canonical serial verb construction:

a   Each clause in the clause chain may contain its own distinct subject, whereas a typical SVC has only one grammatical subject.

b   Each clause in the clause chain may refer to a distinct event, whereas a typical SVC describes a single complex event.

c   The final verb in a clause chain is morphologically distinguished from medial verbs; only the final verb is fully specified for tense, aspect, modality, etc. In SVCs, both verbs may take identical marking for tense, agreement, etc. If only one verb is marked it is most likely to be the first verb.

d   There is no obligatory argument sharing within the clause chain; each verb may take a totally distinct set of arguments.

e   Pronouns cannot refer to another NP within the same SVC; but pronouns can take an antecedent within the same clause chain. (Zero anaphora seems to be preferred in many chaining languages when there is no reason to emphasize the pronoun, but the use of overt pronominals is quite common.)

At the end of section 9.2 we noted a few examples of reported SVCs in which the affixation on the two verbs suggests that they have different subjects. Hale (1991) reports similar examples in Miskitu and some closely related languages. These languages also have typical clause-chaining constructions with switch-reference marking. Hale states that there is no morphological or structural difference between clause chaining and serial verbs in these languages. The difference is primarily semantic: does the sentence describe one event or two? Most examples are ambiguous between these two interpretations, as illustrated in (69).

(69)   **Miskitu** (Nicaragua; Hale, 1991)
        witin ai   pruk-an   kauhw-ri.
        3sg   1sg strike-DS.3   fall-PAST.1
        'He hit me and I fell down.' [clause chain]
        or: 'He knocked me down.' [SVC]

The two interpretations can be distinguished by syntactic tests such as negation, Wh- questions, etc. But Hale's conclusion is that serialization in Miskitu is "just a special case of chaining," i.e., a clause chain which allows a single-event interpretation. If a similar analysis can be supported for languages like Loniu and Paamese, the sentences in (53) might be better treated as examples of clause chaining rather than SVCs with two subjects. However, this hypothesis remains to be investigated.

9.4   Serial verbs vs. auxiliary verbs

We have characterized a serial verb construction as "a single clause that contains two or more verbs, neither of which is an auxiliary." This formulation implies that, in order to identify SVCs, we need to be able to distinguish auxiliary verbs from main verbs. In this section we will briefly mention some of the criteria which can help us to make this distinction.

Steele (1978) defines an AUXILIARY as an element of the clause which

(i)   is separate from the verb (i.e., it is a clitic or independent word, rather than an affix);

(ii)   expresses the categories of tense, aspect and/or mood;[14] and

(iii)   does not subordinate the main verb (i.e., the auxiliary and main verb occur within the same minimal clause).

She distinguishes between auxiliary verbs, which share at least some of the properties of prototypical verbs (e.g., subject agreement), vs. non-verbal auxiliaries. Auxiliary verbs tend to express primarily aspectual categories, while non-verbal auxiliaries primarily express modality.

Perhaps the key insight here is that auxiliary verbs do not function as independent semantic predicates; they do not take their own arguments as normal verbs do. The semantic content of auxiliary verbs is usually grammatical rather than lexical; they are used to express elements of meaning that would be expressed by inflectional affixes in other languages: tense, aspect, mood, voice, and polarity (or negation).

Because auxiliary verbs do not assign semantic roles or determine the number of arguments in a clause, they typically cannot appear as the only verb in an independent clause. An auxiliary must normally co-occur with a regular (non-auxiliary) verb, and it is this main verb which determines the transitivity, subcategorization, and selectional restrictions within the clause. Of course, sentences like those in (70) are acceptable in certain very restricted environments, such as in answer to a question. Such sentences are understood to be ELLIPTICAL, meaning that the main verb (together with its complements) has been left out and must be recovered from the immediate discourse context.

(70) a   John will/can/should/must.
     b   John has.
     c   John is.

In the prototypical SVC, however, each verb may carry lexical semantic content, may assign semantic roles to its own arguments, and has the potential to function on its own as the only verb in a simple clause.[15] A related observation is that the set of auxiliary verbs in a particular language always forms a small, closed class, whereas this is not necessarily true of any verb in an SVC.[16]

Auxiliary verbs are often morphologically defective in some way, lacking regular inflected forms for tense, agreement, etc. For example, the English MODAL auxiliaries, including *can*, *may*, *must*, *will*, *shall*, and *should*, are invariant forms. They are not inflected for tense or agreement. However, the other auxiliary verbs in English, *have* and *be*, are inflected when they occur as the first verbal element in a sentence. Notice, too, that in English only the first verbal element in a clause may be inflected in this way. The kind of "double marking" or "spreading" of inflectional features which is sometimes found in SVCs does not normally occur in Aux + main verb constructions.

Auxiliary verbs often have unique word-order properties which are different from those of regular verbs. For example, in Luiseño (Uto-Aztecan, California) the auxiliary elements (modality, agreement, and tense) always occur in second position: that is, they must immediately follow the first word or phrase of their clause. If the auxiliary elements occur in any other position, the sentence is ungrammatical (71c–d). The order of other words in the sentence is quite free, as illustrated in (71a–b).

(71)   **Luiseño** (Akmajian, Steele, and Wasow, 1979:8)

a   noo <u>xu=n=po</u>   pati   hunwuti.
        1sg MOD=1sg=FUT shoot bear.ACC
        'I should shoot a bear.'

b   hunwuti   <u>xu=n=po</u>   (noo) pati.
        bear.ACC MOD=1sg=FUT 1sg   shoot
        'I should shoot a bear.'

c   *noo hunwuti   <u>xu=n=po</u>   pati.
        1sg bear.ACC MOD=1sg=FUT shoot

d   *<u>xu=n=po</u>   (noo) hunwuti   pati.
        MOD=1sg=FUT 1sg   bear.ACC shoot

A similar situation is found in the Australian language Warlpiri. Hale (1981) states that the words in a Warlpiri clause may occur in virtually any order, provided that the auxiliary verb occurs in second position. A few examples are given in (72), but many other permutations are grammatically possible.

(72)   **Warlpiri** (Hale, 1981)

a   kurdu-jarra-rlu   <u>ka-pala</u>   maliki-Ø wajilipi-nyi   wita-jarra-rlu.
        child-DUAL-ERG   PRES-DUAL dog-ABS chase-NONPAST small-DUAL-ERG
        'The two small children are chasing the dog.'

b   maliki-Ø <u>ka-pala</u>   kurdu-jarra-rlu   wajilipi-nyi   wita-jarra-rlu.
        dog-ABS PRES-DUAL child-DUAL-ERG   chase-NONPAST small-DUAL-ERG
        'The two small children are chasing the dog.'

c   wita-jarra-rlu   <u>ka-pala</u>   maliki-Ø wajilipi-nyi   kurdu-jarra-rlu.
        small-DUAL-ERG   PRES-DUAL dog-ABS chase-NONPAST child-DUAL-ERG
        'The two small children are chasing the dog.'

d   wajilipi-nyi   <u>ka-pala</u>   kurdu-jarra-rlu   maliki-Ø wita-jarra-rlu.
chase-NONPAST PRES-DUAL child-DUAL-ERG dog-ABS small-DUAL-ERG
'The two small children are chasing the dog.'

English auxiliaries also have special word-order properties. The most obvious of these is that all auxiliary verbs must precede the main verb in their clause. In addition, there are several constructions in English that contain a specific position which only an auxiliary verb may fill. These include yes–no questions, in which the first auxiliary must precede the subject (73b); negated finite clauses, in which the first auxiliary must precede the negative, *not* or *-n't* (73c); and what Huddleston (1984) calls "Polarity Emphasized" clauses (73d–e). When one of these constructions is formed from a basic clause which contains no auxiliary element, the "dummy" verb *do* is inserted in the obligatory auxiliary position, as illustrated in (74).

(73) a   Marie Antoinette could have been bribing the Bishop.
    b   Could Marie Antoinette have been bribing the Bishop?
    c   Marie Antoinette could not have been bribing the Bishop.
    d   Yes Marie Antoinette COULD have been bribing the Bishop.
    e   She COULD TOO (have been bribing the Bishop).

(74) a   Marie Antoinette kissed the Bishop.
    b   *Kissed Marie Antoinette the Bishop?
         Did Marie Antoinette kiss the Bishop?
    c   *Marie Antoinette kissed not the Bishop.
         Marie Antoinette did not kiss the Bishop.
    d   *Yes Marie Antoinette KISSED the Bishop.
         Yes Marie Antoinette DID kiss the Bishop.
    e   *She KISSED TOO (the Bishop).
         She DID TOO (kiss the Bishop).

These constructions give us a way to test whether or not a particular element is functioning as an auxiliary. For example, in British (but not American) English, *ought, need*, and *dare* can be used as modals, and so may occur in these restricted auxiliary positions. The verbs *have* and *be* are special. *Be* can occur in auxiliary positions even when it is used as a main verb (or copula). In British English, both the main verb *have* and the auxiliary *have* may occur in auxiliary positions, but in American English sentences like (75b) are ungrammatical.

(75) a   **Aux**: Have you eaten banana fritters?
    b   **Main verb**: (* in US) Have you any banana fritters?

Finally, in a number of languages auxiliaries place restrictions on the form of the main verbs with which they co-occur, e.g., requiring that the main verb appear in the infinitive or a participial form. In an SVC, however, the specific form of each verb (typically either a bare stem or a fully inflected finite form) is generally determined by the construction itself, and not by one of its co-verbs.

A single English clause may contain between zero and four auxiliary verbs, with each auxiliary determining the inflectional form of the immediately following verb. The auxiliaries in a clause must occur in a fixed order, as shown in the following chart. As noted above, the MODAL auxiliaries include *can, may, must, will, shall*, and *should*; only one of these may occur in any single clause.[17]

(76)   **Aux. element:**   Modal   perfect *have*   progressive *be*   passive *be*
            following V-form: bare infinitive past participle present participle past participle

All of these elements are optional, and they may occur in any combination provided that (a) they occur in the order shown; (b) only one instance of each element occurs in any given clause; and (c) tense and agreement are marked only on the first verbal element of the clause, i.e., on the first auxiliary if there is one, otherwise on the main verb. The sentences in (77) illustrate these points.

(77) a   John ate.
     b   John will/can/should/must eat.
     c   John has eaten.
     d   John is eating.
     e   John was eaten.
     f   John will be eating when we arrive.
     g   John will have been eating for two hours by the time we arrive.
     h   John must have been being eaten when the police arrived.

One familiar way of analyzing auxiliary verbs is to treat them as a special type of Raising predicate (see chapter 5). This analysis captures the fact that auxiliary verbs do not take their own semantic arguments or assign semantic roles. Falk (1984) presents an analysis of the English auxiliary system in this vein.

More recent work has adopted the hypothesis that auxiliary verbs and main verbs function as "co-heads" of their clauses. The main verb provides the lexical semantic content, semantic roles, and subcategorization, while the auxiliary verb provides inflectional information. See Bresnan (2001) and Falk (2001) for a discussion of this approach.

9.5   Conclusion

Serial verbs are difficult to analyze within most syntactic frameworks. Both verbs in the serial construction play a role in determining the semantic content and syntactic structure of the clause. In other words, both verbs seem to function as predicates and heads of the same clause. This pattern is especially challenging because in most other constructions we have good reasons to assume that predicates must be unique within their clauses.

In order to appreciate the nature of the challenge more fully, let us contrast the serial verb constructions described in section 9.2 with a partially similar construction, the COMPLEX PREDICATE. Complex predicates typically consist of a "light" verb plus at least one other word, which may be an abstract noun, adjective, participle, etc. Some examples are presented in (78–79).

(78)   **Hindi** (Mohanan, 1994)

a   raam-ne   mohan-par   b^harosaa   kiyaa.
 Ram-ERG Mohan-LOC reliance(NOM) do-PERF
 'Ram relied on Mohan.'

b   ilaa-ne   mohan-ko   pasand   kiyaa.
 Ila-ERG Mohan-DAT liking(NOM) do-PERF
 'Ila liked/approved of Ram.'

c   mohan-ko   hasii   aaii.
 mohan-DAT laughter(NOM) come-PERF
 'Mohan had the urge to laugh.'

(79)   **Japanese** (Matsumoto, 1996)

a   Jon=wa   Tookyoo=ni ryokoo=o shita.
 John=TOP Tokyo=LOC trip=ACC do-PAST
 'John made a trip to Tokyo.'

b   seehu=wa   sono chihoo=e   busshi=no   yusoo=o   shita.
 gov't=TOP the region=LOC goods=GEN transportation=ACC do-PAST
 'The government transported the goods to the region.'

Mohanan (1994), Matsumoto (1996), and Butt (1995) have demonstrated quite clearly that the two words in these complex predicates, even though they are morphologically distinct, combine to function as a single predicate within the clause. They share a single argument structure and a single subcategorization. Moreover, the assignment of semantic roles and grammatical relations is determined by the specific combination of elements (N + V in these examples) which is present, and not by either of them individually. (In this respect the light verb is quite different from an auxiliary verb, which does not contribute to the argument structure or subcategorization of the clause.) In a serial verb construction, however, both verbs seem to retain the ability to assign their own distinct semantic roles and grammatical relations, though they normally share at least one argument in common.

But even though both verbs in the SVC can assign grammatical relations, we have argued that a serial verb construction (at least in the prototypical case) may not contain more than one grammatical SUBJ. This is one of the critical features that distinguishes SVCs from clause chaining. In addition, we have seen that the verbs in an SVC must share the same features for tense, aspect, polarity, etc. Thus an important goal of our analysis of the SVC must be to achieve the correct balance between independence and sharing of information. This challenge remains a very active focus of current research.

Notes

1. Examples in this section are taken from Gibson and Rapposo (1986); Hyman and Zimmer (1976); and Rouveret and Vergnaud (1980).
2. Felix Ameka, unpublished MS., states that the unmarked coordinate clause in (26d) is distinguished from an SVC like (26a) by various features including obligatory subject agreement on both verbs, the potential for distinct grammatical subjects, and the possibility of different tense marking on the two verbs.
3. The agreement prefixes in Kisar cliticize to the preceding word when the verb stem begins with a consonant, as in (40d). The first line of this example shows how the sentence is pronounced, the second line shows the underlying morphemic form.
4. Thanks to Lars Hellan and Florence Dolphyne for clarifying this example.
5. Aikhenvald glosses the case marker -*nuku* as meaning "topical non-subject." I use the term "accusative" here for simplicity.
6. The linker -*nɪ* is inserted for purely phonological reasons.
7. We do not have enough data available to determine whether this is the only grammatical order, or merely a preference.
8. Foley and Olson describe the -*bi* in this form as a generalized derivational suffix. No gloss is given in this example.
9. Olson (1981); Foley and Van Valin (1984); Foley and Olson (1985).
10. Switch-reference systems are found in languages of all word-order types. However, the presence of a switch-reference system does not necessarily mean that a language has clause chaining, because switch-reference is frequently marked in subordinate and/or coordinate clauses. As we will see below, clause chaining is distinguished from subordination and coordination by important structural properties.
11. Unmarked medial verbs may also refer to simultaneous or partly overlapping events.
12. Syntacticians often refer to the structural "command" relation defined here as C-COMMAND.
13. Aissen (1992) uses the category E (for Expression) in a somewhat similar way, following a proposal by Banfield (1973).
14. Schachter (1985) adds to this list the categories of voice and polarity (or negation).
15. It is not uncommon for one verb in an SVC to lose some of its lexical semantic content over time. For this reason, serial verbs are a common historical source for grammatical functors such as prepositions and auxiliary verbs.
16. In some languages, one verb in at least some kinds of SVC must come from a restricted set, e.g., verbs of motion, etc.
17. This may not be true in all dialects, e.g., southern US colloquial: "I might could be persuaded."

10 "Quirky case" and subjecthood

In this chapter we will examine some examples of "irregular" or atypical case marking. Case is a morphological feature used to indicate the function of an NP within its clause. But, as we will see, case marking is not always a reliable guide for determining the grammatical relation of a particular NP: an NP may be a grammatical subject or object even though its case marking suggests something quite different.

In fact, it is not uncommon to find this kind of "mismatch" (or irregular correlation) between morphological features and syntactic functions. For this reason, it is important that grammatical relations be identified on the basis of syntactic evidence, and not on purely morphological grounds. In this chapter we will be primarily interested in the mismatch between case marking and grammatical relations. Examples of this kind will help us to clarify the kinds of syntactic evidence which can be used to identify grammatical relations (subjects in particular) when there is reason for uncertainty.

We begin by looking at examples from German and Icelandic which show how the regular case-marking rules for subjects and objects can be overridden by the lexical requirements of a particular verb. As a way of introducing this issue, we will first consider the marking of prepositional objects in German. In the second section of this chapter we will consider the "dative subject" construction, taking examples primarily from South Asian languages.

10.1   Lexically specified case marking in Germanic

Four morphological cases are distinguished in German: nominative, accusative, dative, and genitive. Case is marked primarily on determiners (e.g., articles and demonstratives), but adjectives and nouns may also register case distinctions. In general, all the elements in a noun phrase must agree in number, gender, and case, though adjectives take reduced endings when preceded by a fully inflected determiner. The forms of the definite article are shown below:

(1)

	Masculine	Feminine	Neuter	Plural
nominative	der	die	das	die
genitive	des	der	des	der
dative	dem	der	dem	den
accusative	den	die	das	die

10.1.1   Objects of prepositions

In English, the case form of pronouns that follow a preposition is entirely predictable: it is always the same form that would appear as the direct object of a verb.

(2) a to me/him/her/us/them
  b *to I/he/she/we/they
  c from me/him/her/us/them
  d *from I/he/she/we/they
  e behind me/him/her/us/them
  f *behind I/he/she/we/they

But in German, the case marking of a prepositional object is not predictable at all, unless we know which specific preposition is involved. Certain prepositions require that the NP which appears as their object be marked for accusative case. These prepositions include: *bis* 'until,' *durch* 'through,' *für* 'for,' *gegen* 'against,' *ohne* 'without,' *um* 'around,' *wider* 'against.' Some examples are given in (3).

(3) durch den Wald 'through the forest'
   gegen den Wind 'against the wind'
   um die Erde   'around the world'

Other prepositions require that their objects appear in the dative case: *aus* 'out of, from,' *ausser* 'except,' *bei* 'at,' *mit* 'with,' *nach* 'after,' *seit* 'since,' *von* 'from,' *zu* 'to.'

(4) aus der Stadt 'from the city'
   bei der Kirche 'near the church'
   mit dem Zug 'with the train (by train)'

Another class of prepositions may take either dative or accusative objects, depending on the meaning of the preposition phrase as it is used in a particular context. Dative case is used to designate a static location or position, while accusative case signals motion to the designated position.[1] Prepositions of this type include: *an* 'at,' *auf* 'on,' *hinter* 'behind,' *in* 'in,' *neben* 'beside,' *über* 'above,' *unter* 'below,' *vor* 'in front of,' *zwischen* 'between.' Some examples are given in (5).

(5)

DATIVE		ACCUSATIVE	
an der See	'at the seaside'	an die See	'to the seaside'
auf dem Tisch	'on the table'	auf den Tisch	'onto the table'
im (in dem) Hause	'in the house'	ins (in das) Haus	'into the house'

A few prepositions take genitive objects, although some of these are reported to be archaic or rarely used in common speech. Some examples of such prepositions include: *anstatt* 'instead of,' *laut* 'according to,' *trotz* 'in spite of,' *während* 'during,' *wegen* 'because of,' *zwecks* 'for the purpose of.'

The general pattern, then, is that an NP which appears as the object of a preposition in German may be marked for accusative, dative, or genitive case, depending on the particular preposition involved. The case marking associated with each preposition must be learned on a word-by-word basis. Adult students of German are often required to memorize lists of the prepositions which belong to each class, like those given above, because there is no way to predict the appropriate case marking in advance. In other words, the choice of case is lexically determined: this information must simply be included as part of the lexical entry of each preposition.

10.1.2 "Quirky case" objects

As noted above, direct objects normally take accusative case. However, with certain verbs this rule does not apply. Some transitive verbs consistently assign dative case to their objects. These include: *antworten* 'to answer,' *begegnen* 'to meet,' *danken* 'to thank,' *fluchen* 'to curse,' *folgen* 'to follow,' *gefallen* 'to please,' *helfen* 'to help,' *trauen* 'to trust.'[2] Some examples are given in (6):

(6) a   Ich   helfe   dem   Mann.
        I(NOM) help-1sg.PRES the(MASC.DAT) man
        'I help the man.'

    b   Ich   danke   dir.
        I(NOM) thank-1sg.PRES 2sg.DAT
        'I thank you.'

While these verbs seem to share certain semantic properties, e.g., non-affectedness of the patient, the irregular case marking of these objects cannot be predicted on purely semantic grounds. It must be specified as part of the lexical entry of these verbs. One way in which this might be done is illustrated in (7). However, in section 10.1.5 we will see evidence which suggests that, at least for Icelandic, the case feature should be associated with the appropriate semantic role (e.g., beneficiary, in this example) rather than the grammatical relation (OBJ).

(7)   *help* < agent, beneficiary >
                 | |
             SUBJ   OBJ
       [OBJ CASE dative]

A very few German verbs take genitive objects, e.g., *gedenken* 'to remember, commemorate.' These could be treated in essentially the same way.

(8)   Ich   gedenke   des   Mannes.
        I(NOM) remember-1sg the(MASC.GEN) man(GEN.SG)
        'I remember the man.'

These irregular, lexically determined patterns of case assignment are often referred to as "quirky case," because the choice of case marking depends on the idiosyncratic lexical requirements of the verb rather than on a general rule of the grammar.

10.1.3   "Quirky case" in Icelandic

Icelandic, another Germanic language, has essentially the same four-case system as German. However, in addition to the irregular (non-accusative) case marking of certain direct objects, Icelandic also has "quirky" case marking on subjects.

A relatively large number of verbs assign cases other than the nominative to their subjects. Verbs which take accusative subjects include those which mean 'long to,' 'dream about,' 'melt,' 'drift,' 'lack,' and 'freeze.' Verbs which take dative subjects include those which mean 'speak' (intr.), 'capsize,' 'slope,' 'seem,' 'resemble', 'recover from,' and 'be cold.' A very few verbs take genitive subjects, e.g., 'be noticeable.' Some examples of accusative and dative subjects, taken from Andrews (1982), are given in (9).[3] In each of these sentences, the initial NP is considered to be the subject.

(9) a   Mig   langar að fara til Íslands.
             me(ACC) longs to go to Iceland
             'I long to go to Iceland.'

    b   Drengina   vantar mat.
             the.boys(ACC) lacks food(ACC)
             'The boys lack food.'

    c   Honum mæltist vel í kirkjunni.
             he(DAT) spoke well in the-church
             'He spoke well in the church.'

    d   Barninu   batnaði   veikin.
             the.child(DAT) recovered.from the.disease(NOM)
             'The child recovered from the disease.'

    e   Henni   hefur alltaf þótt   Ólafur   leðinlegur.
             she(DAT) has   always thought Olaf(NOM) boring(NOM)
             'She has always considered Olaf boring.'

Quirky-case objects may appear in either the dative or the genitive, as in German. Verbs that take dative objects include 'rescue' and 'finish.' Verbs that take genitive objects include 'await' and 'visit.'

Now let us stop and think about these "non-nominative subjects" and "non-accusative objects." What do we mean by this? If an NP is marked for accusative or dative case, why would we want to call it a subject? For intransitive examples, like (9a) and (9c), this may not seem like a major problem since there is only one NP candidate for subject. (Of course, for these examples one might suggest that the sentence simply lacks a subject.) But where there are two NPs, neither of which takes nominative case (as in [9b]), how do we know which is the subject? And, worst of all, why should we consider the dative NP in examples like (9d–e) to be the subject rather than the nominative NP?

10.1.4   Subjecthood tests in Icelandic

As stated above, grammatical relations must be identified on the basis of syntactic evidence, and not just on the basis of morphological features like case and agreement. In this section we will look at some of the evidence which can be used to identify the grammatical subject in Icelandic. The examples cited below are taken from Zaenen, Maling, and Thráinsson (1985) and Andrews (1982).

10.1.4.1   Reflexive binding

First, only a reflexive pronoun can be used to refer to a grammatical subject within the same clause, and (at least for many speakers) only the subject can serve as the antecedent of a reflexive.[4] This is illustrated in (10a–b) for a normal transitive verb ('hit') which takes a nominative subject and accusative object: when the antecedent is the subject, as in (10a), only the reflexive is possible; but when the antecedent is the object, as in (10b), the opposite pattern holds. In (10c), we see that the dative experiencer of 'think' can be the antecedent of a reflexive pronoun within its minimal clause, and that a non-reflexive pronoun is impossible in the same position. This shows that the dative experiencer NP is in fact the grammatical subject of the clause.

(10) a   Sigga$_i$ barði mig   með dúkkunni   sinni$_i$/*hennar$_i$.
        Sigga$_i$(NOM) hit   me(ACC) with doll(DAT) self's$_i$/*her$_i$
        'Sigga$_i$ hit me with her$_i$ doll.'

     b   Ég   barði Siggu$_i$ með dúkkunni   *sinni$_i$/hennar$_i$.
        I(NOM) hit   Sigga$_i$(ACC) with doll(DAT) *self's$_i$/her$_i$
        'I hit Sigga$_i$ with her$_i$ doll.'

     c   Henni$_i$ þykir bróðir   sinni$_i$/*hennar$_i$ leðinlegur.
        she$_i$(DAT) thinks brother(NOM) self's$_i$/*her$_i$ boring(NOM)
        'She$_i$ considers her$_i$ brother boring.'

10.1.4.2   Subject ellipsis

A second piece of evidence comes from a pattern of NP ellipsis. In a coordinate sentence consisting of two conjoined clauses, the subject NP may be omitted from the second conjunct when it is coreferential with the subject of the first conjunct. For example, both clauses in the coordinate sentence (11a) have the same subject; therefore, the subject of the second clause can be omitted, as in (11b). Example (11c) shows that the object NP cannot be omitted, even when it is coreferential with the object of the first clause. Even if the first clause is passivized, as in (11d), so that the object of the second clause is coreferential with the subject of the first, the object NP still cannot be omitted.[5]

(11) a   þeir   fluttu   líkið   og þeir grófu það.
        they(NOM) moved the.corpse and they buried it
        'They moved the corpse and they buried it.'

b   þeir   fluttu líkið   og __ grófu það.
     they(NOM) moved the.corpse and (they) buried it
     'They moved the corpse and buried it.'

c   *þeir   fluttu líkið   og þeir grófu __.
     they(NOM) moved the.corpse and they buried (it)
     *'They moved the corpse and they buried.'

d   *Líkið   var flutt   og þeir grófu __.
     the.corpse was moved   and they buried (it)
     *'The corpse was moved and they buried.'

Now consider the coordinate sentences in (12). The second clause in each example contains the verb 'find,' which assigns dative case to its experiencer. This dative experiencer can be omitted when it is coreferential with the subject of the first clause, as in (12b). In light of the facts illustrated in (11), this pattern shows that the dative experiencer of 'find' is in fact the grammatical subject of its clause. Contrast this example with the pattern in (12c), in which the stimulus NP (which would be assigned nominative case) cannot be omitted even though it is coreferential with the subject of the first clause. This contrast shows that the acceptability of ellipsis in coordinate sentences is based on the grammatical relations of the two subject NPs, rather than simple identity of case marking.

(12) a   Hann   segist vera duglegur, en honum finnst verkefnið   of þungt.
          he(NOM) claims to.be diligent   but he(DAT) finds the.homework too hard
          'He claims to be diligent, but he finds the homework too hard.'

     b   Hann   segist vera duglegur, en __   finnst verkefnið   of þungt.
          he(NOM) claims to.be diligent   but (he.DAT) finds the.homework too hard
          'He claims to be diligent, but finds the homework too hard.'

     c   *Hann   segist vera duglegur, en mer   finnst __   latur.
          he(NOM) claims to.be diligent   but I(DAT) finds (him.NOM) lazy
          *'He claims to be diligent, but I find (him) lazy.'

10.1.4.3   Subject–verb inversion

Icelandic word order is much less rigid than that of English. However, in both yes–no questions and content questions, the subject NP must appear immediately after the tensed verbal element. This pattern is illustrated in the following examples. The yes–no question (13b) is identical to the corresponding declarative form (13a) except that the tensed auxiliary verb is shifted to initial position. The subject NP *Sigga* immediately follows the auxiliary; if any other element intervenes, as in (13c), the result is ungrammatical. The same observations hold for the content question in (13d–e).

(13) a   Sigga   havði aldrei hjálpað Haraldi.
          Sigga(NOM) had   never helped Harald(DAT)
          'Sigga had never helped Harald.'

b   **Yes-No question:**
Havði Sigga   aldrei hjálpað Haraldi?
had   Sigga(NOM) never helped Harald(DAT)
'Had Sigga never helped Harald?'

c   *Havði Haraldi   Sigga   aldrei hjálpað?
had   Harald(DAT) Sigga(NOM) never helped

d   **Wh- question:**
Hvenær havði Sigga   hjálpað Haraldi?
when   had Sigga(NOM) helped Harald(DAT)
'When had Sigga helped Harald?'

e   *Hvenær havði Haraldi   Sigga   hjálpað?
when   had Harald(DAT) Sigga(NOM) helped

Now consider the example which is repeated in (14a). When this sentence
is changed into a yes–no question (14b), the dative experiencer NP must occur
immediately after the tensed auxiliary. If anything else intervenes, even the NP
which bears nominative case as in (14c), the result is ungrammatical. This contrast
supports the claim that the subject of (14a) is the dative NP, and not the nominative
NP.

(14) a   Henni   hefur alltaf þótt   Ólafur   leðinlegur.
she(DAT) has   always thought Olaf(NOM) boring(NOM)
'She has always considered Olaf boring.'

b   Hefur henni   alltaf þótt   Ólafur   leðinlegur?
has   she(DAT) always thought Olaf(NOM) boring(NOM)
'Has she always considered Olaf boring?'

c   *Hefur Ólafur   henni   alltaf þótt   leðinlegur?
has   Olaf(NOM) she(DAT) always thought boring(NOM)

10.1.4.4   Raising

Icelandic has both "Raising to subject" predicates (like English *seem*) and "Raising to object" predicates (like English *believe* or *expect*). As in English and most
other languages which have a Raising construction, only the grammatical subject
of the complement clause can be raised (i.e., can be functionally controlled). Examples (15b–c) show that the accusative experiencer (or possessor) of 'lack' can
be raised with both types of predicates; and examples (16b–c) show the same for
the dative argument of 'recover.' This evidence indicates that the NPs in question
are the grammatical subjects of the basic clauses (15a) and (16a), even though
they do not take nominative case.

(15) a   Hana   vantar peninga.
she(ACC) lacks   money(ACC)
'She lacks money.'

b   Hana   virðist vanta peninga.
    she(ACC) seems to.lack money(ACC)
    'She seems to lack money.'

c   Hann   telur   mig   (í barnaskap sínum) vanta peninga.[6]
    he(NOM) believes me(ACC) (in foolishness his) to.lack money(ACC)
    'He (in his foolishness) believes me to lack money.'

(16) a   Barninu   batnaði   veikin.
    the.child(DAT) recovered.from the.disease(NOM)
    'The child recovered from the disease.'

b   Barninu   virðist hafa batnað   veikin.
    the.child(DAT) seems to.have recovered.from the.disease(NOM)
    'The child seems to have recovered from the disease.'

c   Hann   telur   barninu   (í barnaskap sínum) hafa
    he(NOM) believes the.child(DAT) (in foolishness his) to.have
    batnað   veikin.
    recovered.from the.disease(NOM)
    'He (in his foolishness) believes the child to have recovered from the disease.'

10.1.5   Case preservation

We have discussed four tests for subjecthood in Icelandic, all of which independently lead to the same conclusion: certain verbs assign some case other than the nominative to their subjects. Zaenen, Maling, and Thráinsson (1985) present a number of other tests which provide additional evidence confirming the identity of the subject in examples like (9). Before concluding our discussion of Icelandic, we will briefly discuss an interesting property of lexically specified case marking in this language.

Compare the Raising examples in (15) and (16) with example (17), in which the complement verb 'love' follows the default case assignment pattern (nominative SUBJ, accusative OBJ). In (17), the controller 'Harold' appears in nominative case when it is raised to subject position (17b), and accusative case when it is raised to object position (17c). This is, of course, just what we would expect.

(17) a   Haraldur   elski Maríu.
    Harold(NOM) loves Maria(ACC)
    'Harold loves Maria.'

b   Haraldur   virðist elska Maríu.
    Harold(NOM) seems to.love Maria(ACC)
    'Harold seems to love Maria.'

c   þeir   telja   Harald   elska Maríu.
    they(NOM) believe Harold(ACC) to.love Maria(ACC)
    'They believe Harold to love Maria.'

But with the "quirky" case verbs in (15) and (16), we find the same case marking on the raised argument in the (b–c) examples as we find on the corresponding argument of a simple clause in the (a) examples. That is, the controller in the Raising examples bears the case marking which would be assigned (within the complement clause) to the controllee. Another way of stating this is to say that lexically specified case is "preserved" under Raising.

A similar pattern of case preservation can be observed in passive sentences. Our discussion thus far has been focused on quirky-case subjects, but we also noted the fact that certain transitive verbs assign quirky case to their objects. Two such verbs are presented in (18): 'help,' which takes a dative object; and 'miss,' which takes a genitive object.

(18) a   Ég   hjálpaði þeim.
          I(NOM) helped   them(DAT)
          'I helped them.'

     b   Ég   mun sakna hennar.
          I(NOM) will miss her(GEN)
          'I will miss her.'

One of the strongest pieces of evidence for claiming that the post-verbal NPs in (18) are in fact direct objects is that they can passivize, as demonstrated in (19). All of the subjecthood tests discussed in the preceding sections confirm that the initial NPs in (19) are true subjects;[7] see Zaenen, Maling, and Thráinsson (1985) for the relevant examples. But notice that the case marking of the passive subjects in (19) is identical to that of the corresponding active objects in (18): dative for 'help' and genitive for 'miss.' In other words, lexically specified case seems to be preserved under passivization as well.

(19) a   þeim   var hjálpað.
          them(DAT) was helped
          'They were helped.'

     b   Hennar   var saknað.
          her(GEN) was missed
          'She was missed.'

Zaenen *et al.* argue that these case preservation effects provide an important clue about how quirky case is assigned. Specifically, the fact that case marking remains constant even when the grammatical relation changes is an indication that lexically specified case is associated with a particular semantic role, rather than a particular grammatical relation. Any irregular case feature assigned by a particular verb to one of its arguments must be represented in the lexical entry of the verb, in something like the following way:

(20) a   *help* < agent, beneficiary >
                              |
                        [CASE dat]

b   *lack* < possessor, theme >
                    |
              [CASE acc]

c   *recover from* < experiencer,   stimulus >
                        | |
                  [CASE dat] [CASE nom]

The regular case-marking rules of the language assign nominative case to subjects, accusative case to objects, etc., but lexically specified case takes priority. If a case feature is lexically specified for a particular argument, the regular rules are blocked and cannot apply. This is an instance of a very widespread pattern in the application of morphological rules: a more specific pattern blocks (or preempts) the application of a more general rule.[8]

10.1.6   Case marking and control

Finally, let us consider the patterns of case preservation in various types of control construction. We have already seen that quirky case is preserved under Raising, which (as discussed in chapter 5) involves a functional control relation. Another type of construction which typically involves functional control is the predicate complement (XCOMP). (All examples in this section come from Andrews [1982, 1990].)

An adjective which functions as a predicate complement in Icelandic agrees with the noun it describes (i.e., is predicated of) for number, gender, and case. This agreement pattern is illustrated in (21). In each of the three sentences, the adjective 'popular' appears as a predicate complement describing 'she/her.' As the grammatical relation of the pronoun changes, undergoing first Raising to object (21b) and then passivization of the matrix verb (21c), its case changes from NOM to ACC and back to NOM; and these same changes are mirrored in the case of the agreeing pronoun.

(21) a   Hún   er vinsæl.
            she(NOM) is popular(NOM)
            'She is popular.'

      b   þeir   telja   hana   vera vinsæla.
            they(NOM) believe her(ACC) to.be popular(ACC)
            'They believe her to be popular.'

      c   Hún   er talin   vera vinsæl.
            she(NOM) is believed to.be popular(NOM)
            'She is believed to be popular.'

This is exactly what we would expect under the model of functional control outlined in chapter 5. The implicit subject (or controllee) of the XCOMP is functionally identified with the controller ('she/her'); any changes to the case or other functional features of the controller will automatically be shared by the controllee. The form of the adjective reflects agreement with its implicit SUBJ, i.e., the controllee.

Example (22) involves a verb ('describe') which assigns lexical dative case to its object, and allows an adjective to appear as predicate complement. The lexically specified case of the object in (22a) is mirrored in the case marking of the adjectival complement 'dangerous.' When the verb is passivized (22b), the lexical dative case is retained on the passive subject. Since this subject is the controller of the adjectival XCOMP, and the adjective must agree with its implicit SUBJ (the controllee), the adjective too is marked for dative case.

(22) a   Lögreglan   lýsti   glæpamönnunum   sem stórhættulegum.
         the.police(NOM) described   the.criminals(DAT.PL) as   very.dangerous(DAT.PL)
         'The police described the criminals as extremely dangerous.'

     b   Glæpamönnunum   var lýst   sem stórhættulegum.
         the.criminals(DAT.PL) was described   as   very.dangerous(DAT.PL)
         'The criminals were described as extremely dangerous.'

These examples illustrate how the case features of controller and controllee are automatically shared, no matter whether the case marking of a particular argument is lexically specified or assigned by regular rule (e.g., on the basis of its grammatical relation). Again, these results follow as an automatic consequence of our conception of functional control: since controller and controllee correspond to the same unit in functional structure, they must share all of the same functional information, regardless of where that information comes from.

Now let us compare these constructions with an example of anaphoric control. As discussed in chapter 5, the controller and controllee in an anaphoric-control relation are not functionally identified; that is, they are not associated with the same unit in functional structure. Rather, the controllee is a kind of null (invisible) pronoun, which must take the controller as its antecedent. Each has its own independent functional structure, and so the two may have different syntactic features.

Andrews (1982) argues, based on a variety of evidence, that a certain class of Equi constructions in Icelandic involves anaphoric rather than functional control. The Equi predicates we are interested in here, which include 'hope,' 'decide,' 'promise,' 'request,' 'order,' etc., take infinitival complements marked with the complementizer að.

Based on the picture of anaphoric control outlined above, there is no reason to expect that the controller and controllee should necessarily share the same case features; and in fact they do not, as illustrated in (23–24). In both (23b) and (24b), we see a passive subject marked with lexically specified case. In the corresponding (c) examples, these passive sentences are embedded as complements to the Equi predicate 'hope.' But the controller (i.e., the matrix subject) in these

examples must take nominative case, rather than the case assigned to the controllee by the complement verb.[9] So controller and controllee must have distinct case features; but this is perfectly grammatical in an anaphoric-control
relation.

(23) a   Stúlkan   beið   mín.
          the.girl(NOM) awaited me(GEN)
          'The girl waited for me.'

     b   Mín   var beðið.
          me(GEN) was awaited
          'I was awaited.'

     c   Ég/*mín   vonast til að   verða beðið.
          I(NOM/*GEN) hope   to COMP be   awaited
          'I hope to be awaited.'

(24) a   þeir   björguðu honum.
          they(NOM) rescued   him(DAT)
          'They rescued him.'

     b   Honum   var bjargað.
          he(DAT) was rescued
          'He was rescued.'

     c   Hann/*honum   vonast til að   verða bjargað.
          he(NOM/*DAT) hopes to COMP be   rescued
          'He hopes to be rescued.'

The fact that controller and controllee have distinct case features in examples
like (23c) and (24c) can be made even more clear by adding a predicate adjunct
(XADJ). In (25), the adjective 'alone' appears as a predicate adjunct modifying
the implicit subject of the complement clause, i.e., the controllee. Since it must
agree with the complement subject, the case marking on the adjective reflects
the case (GEN or ACC) which would be assigned by the complement verb to its
subject. But once again the case marking on the matrix subject, the controller, is
nominative. This difference clearly shows that the case features of the controller
and controllee in this construction are distinct.

(25) a   Ég   vonast til að   verða vitjað   eins.
          I(NOM) hope   to COMP be   visited alone(GEN)
          'I hope to be visited alone.'

     b   Ég   vonast til að   vanta ekki einan   í tímanum.
          I(NOM) hope   to COMP lack not alone(ACC) in class
          'I hope not to be the only one missing from class.'

So the behavior of quirky case in Icelandic reflects in a very direct way the
structural difference between anaphoric and functional control.

10.2   Dative subject constructions in South Asian languages

Icelandic provides a particularly striking example of how the default case-marking rules of a language can be overridden by the lexical requirements of a particular verb. A number of other languages also reveal various types of "non-canonical" case marking, i.e., constructions which appear to violate the normal case-marking patterns of the language. A very common example of this is the DATIVE SUBJECT construction, which is found in a wide variety of languages but seems to be especially characteristic of South Asian languages.

The label "dative subject construction" suggests that an NP which bears dative case functions as the grammatical subject of its clause; but of course this is a hypothesis that needs to be tested. We will begin by giving some examples from various South Asian languages to illustrate the surface form and semantic functions of the construction. Then we will apply some of the tests for subjecthood in two particular languages, namely Malayalam and Hindi, in order to decide which argument, if any, is actually the grammatical subject.

First let us summarize some relevant facts about case marking and agreement. In many South Asian languages, direct objects take accusative case only if they are animate. Inanimate objects remain unmarked (i.e., appear in the nominative form). This is illustrated in the Malayalam and Hindi examples in (26–27).[10]

(26)   **Malayalam** (Mohanan, 1982:539)
  a   puucca   eli-ye   tiṇṇu.
      cat(NOM) rat-ACC ate
      'The cat ate the rat.'

  b   puucca   roṭṭi   tiṇṇu.
      cat(NOM) bread(NOM) ate
      'The cat ate the bread.'

(27)   **Hindi** (Mohanan, 1994:59, 80)
  a   niinaa   bacce-ko ut^{h}aayegii.
      Nina(NOM) child-ACC lift-FUT.FEM.SG
      'Nina will pick the child up.'

  b   niinaa   haar   ut^{h}aayegii.
      Nina(NOM) necklace(NOM) lift-FUT.FEM.SG
      'Nina will pick up the necklace.'

It is also very common for the verb to agree only with nominative NPs. If the subject bears nominative case, as in (28a), the verb agrees with the subject (*Raam* is a man's name, therefore grammatically masculine). Otherwise, it will agree with the most prominent nominative NP.[11] In Hindi, subjects of perfective verbs take ergative case marking. For this reason, the verb in (28b) cannot agree with the subject, but agrees with the nominative object instead (the word for 'book' is grammatically feminine). If the clause does not contain any nominative NP, then the verb takes default agreement marking. In Hindi, this would be third person singular masculine, as illustrated in (28c) (note that *Niina* is a woman's name, therefore grammatically feminine); in some other languages, the default category is third person singular neuter.

(28)   **Hindi** (Mohanan, 1994)

a   raam   kitaabā   kʰariidegaa.
Ram(NOM) books(NOM) buy-FUT.MASC.SG
'Ram will buy books.'

b   raam-ne   kitaabā   kʰariidñ̄.
Ram-ERG books(NOM) buy-PERF.FEM.PL
'Ram bought books.'

c   niinaa-ne   baalikaa-ko utʰaayaa.
Nina-ERG girl-ACC   lift-PERF.MASC.SG
'Nina lifted up the girl.'

10.2.1   Functions of dative subjects

One very common type of dative subject construction involves EXPERIENCER VERBS (or "psych verbs"); that is, predicates which express some mental, emotional, or perceptual state. The first argument of the verb typically bears the experiencer semantic role, and is assigned dative case. The second argument of the verb, if any, is typically a stimulus or non-affected patient. In the languages we will look at here, this argument is assigned accusative case if it is animate and nominative case if it is inanimate, the normal pattern for direct objects. Some examples from various languages are given below.

(29)   **Tamil** (N. Asher, 1985:105–106)

a   enakku   oru glassu ṭii   veeṇum.
1sg.DAT one glass tea(NOM) want
'I want a glass of tea.'

b   avanukku   anta paaṭam   puriyale.
3sg.M.DAT that lesson(NOM) understand-NEG
'He didn't understand that lesson.'

c   avare   enakku   teriyaatu.
3sg.M.ACC 1sg.DAT know-FUT-NEG
'I don't know him.'

d   avaḷukku   tampiye   piṭikkaatu.
3sg.F.DAT younger.brother(ACC) like-FUT-NEG
'She doesn't like little brother.'

e   enakku   pacikkutu.
1sg.DAT hunger-PRES-3sg.NEUT[12]
'I am hungry.'

(30)   **Malayalam** (Mohanan, 1982:540, 554)
  a   awaḷkkə   wišaṇṇu.
         she-DAT   hungered
         'She was hungry.'

  b   enikkə   weeḍaniccu.
         I-DAT   felt.pain
         'I felt pain.'

  c   kuṭṭikkə   saṇkaṭam   aaṇə.
         child-DAT   sorrow-NOM   is
         'The child is unhappy.'

  d   kuṭṭikkə   aanaye   weruppə   aaṇə.
         child-DAT   elephant-ACC   hatred-NOM   is
         'The child hates the elephant.'

(31)   **Hindi** (Mohanan, 1994:141)
  a   tuṣaar-ko   caand   dikʰaa.
         Tushar-DAT   moon(NOM)   see-PERF
         'Tushar saw the moon.'

  b   tuṣaar-ko   kʰušii   huii.
         Tushar-DAT   happiness(NOM) happen-PERF
         'Tushar became happy.'

  c   tuṣaar-ko   cuhee-se   ḍar   lagtaa   hai.
         Tushar-DAT   mouse-INSTR   fear(NOM)   struck-IMPERF be-PROG
         'Tushar is afraid of mice.'

Another common use of the "dative subject" construction is to express possession. Notice that in Tamil, the patient or theme in this construction takes NOM case even when it is animate, unlike the "psych verb" construction in (29).

(32)   **Tamil** (N. Kome and J. Hoshino, field notes)
  a   enakku   oru makal   irukkiral.
         1sg.DAT   one daughter(NOM) be-3sg.F
         'I have one daughter.'

  b   enakku   aintu pillee-kal   irukkirarkal.
         1sg.DAT   five child(NOM)-PL   be-3pl
         'I have five children.'

(33)   **Kannada** (Sridhar, 1979:101)
         avaḷige   ibbaru makkaḷu iddāre.
         she-DAT   two   children are
         'She has two children.'

(34)   **Malayalam** (Mohanan and Mohanan, 1990:45)
         kuṭṭikkə   dʰaaṛaaḷam panam   uṇṭə.
         child-DAT   plenty   money(NOM) has
         'The child has plenty of money.'

(35)   **Hindi** (Mohanan, 1994:141)
    tuṣaar-ko   kitaab   milii.
    Tushar-DAT book(NOM) get-PERF
    'Tushar found/received a book.'

In some languages, the choice between dative and nominative case on the subject corresponds with a contrast between volitional vs. non-volitional events or states:

(36)   **Malayalam** (Mohanan and Mohanan, 1990:53–54)
    a   baalanə   ii   paaṭʰam   manass-il-aa-yi.
          boy-DAT this lesson(NOM) mind-LOC-become-PAST
          'The child understood this lesson.' (non-volitional)

    b   baalan   ii   paaṭʰam   manass-il-aa-kk-i.
          boy(NOM) this lesson(NOM) mind-LOC-become-CAUS-PAST
          'The child caused himself to understand this lesson.' (volitional)

    c   kuṭṭikkə   kaṇṇil   weḷḷam   niraññu.
          child-DAT eyes-LOC water(NOM) fill(intr.)-PAST
          'The child's eyes filled with tears.'

    d   kuṭṭi   kaṇṇil   weḷḷam   niraccu.
          child(NOM) eyes-LOC water(NOM) fill-CAUS-PAST
          'The child filled his eyes with tears (i.e., pretended to cry).'

(37)   **Kannada** (Sridhar, 1979:102)
    a   avanu   ī   suddi tiḷidukoṇḍanu.
          he-NOM this news learned
          'He learned this news.' (actively, intentionally)

    b   avani-ge ī   suddi tiḷiyitu.
          he-DAT this news became.known
          'He came to know this news.' (unintentionally)

    c   avanu   jvara barisikoṇḍa.
          he-NOM fever CAUS-come-PAST
          'He got a fever (intentionally).'

    d   avanige jvara bantu.
          he-DAT fever came
          'He caught a fever (unintentionally).'

(38)   **Hindi** (Mohanan, 1994:141–142)
    a   tuṣaar-ko   caand   dikʰaa.
          Tushar-DAT moon(NOM) see-PERF
          'Tushar saw the moon.'

    b   tuṣaar-ne   caand   dekʰaa.
          Tushar-ERG moon(NOM) look.at-PERF
          'Tushar looked at the moon.'

In Malayalam, modal suffixes expressing permission and desire require that the subject take dative case:

(39)   **Malayalam** (Mohanan, 1982:541–542)
  a   awaḷkkə uraṇṇ-aam.
      she-DAT sleep-may
      'She may (is permitted to) sleep.'

  b   kuṭṭikkə aanaye   ṇuḷḷ-aṇam.
      child-DAT elephant-ACC pinch-wants
      'The child wants to pinch the elephant.'

Hindi has periphrastic constructions which express similar meanings, and also take dative subjects:

(40)   **Hindi** (Mohanan, 1994:142)
  a   tuṣaar-ko miṭʰaaii   kʰaanii   hai.
      Tushar-DAT sweets(NOM) eat-NON.FIN be-PROG
      'Tushar wants to eat sweets.'

  b   tuṣaar-ko davaaii   piinii   paḍii.
      Tushar-DAT medicine(NOM) drink-NON.FIN fall-PERF
      'Tushar had to drink the medicine.'

Having illustrated some of the uses of the "dative subject" construction, let us return to the question posed above: are the dative arguments in these examples really the grammatical subjects of their clauses? We will consider evidence from two languages, Malayalam and Hindi.

10.2.2   Subjecthood tests in Malayalam

Mohanan (1982:566–569) discusses two tests for subjecthood in Malayalam. First, the antecedent of the possessive reflexive pronoun *swaṇtam* 'self's' must always be a grammatical subject. In (41a) the antecedent of *swaṇtam* is 'the king,' which is the subject of the clause, so the sentence is fully grammatical. Example (41b) is ungrammatical, because in this sentence the antecedent of *swaṇtam* (again 'the king') is the object of the clause. More relevant to our immediate purposes, (41c) shows that a dative secondary object cannot function as the antecedent of a reflexive.

(41) a   ṟaajaawə   swaṇtam bhaaṟyaye ṇuḷḷi.
         king$_i$-NOM self's$_i$ wife-ACC pinched
         'The king pinched his own wife.'

    b   *ṟaajaawine swaṇtam bhaaṟya   ṇuḷḷi.
         king$_i$-ACC self's$_i$ wife-NOM pinched
         (for: 'His own wife pinched the king.')

    c   *ṟaajaawə makaḷkkə   swaṇtam bhartaawine koṭuttu.
         king-NOM daughter$_i$-DAT self's$_i$ husband-ACC gave
         (for: 'The king gave (his) daughter her own husband.')

We can use this test to examine the structure of the examples discussed in section 10.2.1. As sentence (42) illustrates, the dative arguments of these examples can be the antecedent of a reflexive, in contrast to the dative secondary object of (41c). This evidence supports the claim that a dative experiencer is indeed the subject of its clause.

(42)   raajaawinə swaṇṭam bhaaṟyaye iṣṭamaaṇə.
          king_i-DAT self's_i   wife-ACC liking-is
          'The king likes his own wife.'

A second test for subjecthood in Malayalam relates to possible control relations in a particular type of adverbial clause. The examples in (43) illustrate a temporal clause expressing simultaneous actions, formed with the postposition *koṇṭə* 'while, with.' When the subject of a 'while'-clause is omitted, it must be interpreted as being controlled by the subject of the matrix clause. In (43a), only the main clause subject 'mother' can be interpreted as the controller of the adverbial subject. Notice in particular that the dative-marked secondary object 'father' cannot function as the controller. Example (43b) is ungrammatical, because the controllee in the adverbial clause would be the secondary object rather than the subject. The generalization concerning this construction, then, is that both controller and controllee must be grammatical subjects.

(43) a   [__ kaṭṭil-il kiṭannu-koṇṭə] acchanə   amma   kaašə koṭuṭṭu.
            bed-LOC lay-while   father-DAT mother-NOM money gave
          'Mother gave the money to Father while she/*he lay on the bed.'

     b   *[__ amma   kaašə koṭuṭṭu-koṇṭə] acchan   sukhamaayi iṟunnu.
            mother-NOM money gave-while   father-NOM happily   sat
          (for: 'Father lived happily, while Mother gave him money.')

Now let us apply this test to a simple dative experiencer clause like (44a). In sentence (44b) the dative experiencer of 'hungry' functions as the controllee, while in (44c) the dative experiencer of 'want to sleep' functions as the controller (cf. [39a–b]). The fact that both of these sentences are grammatical shows that dative experiencers can be both the controller and the controllee in this construction, in contrast to dative secondary objects which (as we saw in [43]) can be neither. So these examples provide additional evidence that "dative subjects" really are grammatical subjects.

(44) a   kuṭṭikkə wišannu.
          child-DAT hungered
          'The child was hungry.'

     b   [__ wišannu-koṇṭə] kuṭṭi   pusṭakam waayiccu.
            hungered-while child-NOM book-NOM read-PAST
          'The child read the book while feeling hungry.'

c   [__ pustakam   waayiccu-koṇṭə]   kuṭṭikkə   uraṇṇ-aṇam.
          book-NOM   read-while   child-DAT sleep-want
          'The child wants to sleep while reading the book.'

10.2.3   Subjecthood tests in Hindi

Tara Mohanan (1994:148–150) discusses several different tests for subjecthood in Hindi. We will consider just two of them here. The first involves restrictions on the interpretation of regular (non-reflexive) pronouns. The general rule in Hindi is that a (non-reflexive) pronoun may not take the subject of its minimal clause as its antecedent.

The genitive pronoun in examples (45a–b) must take a discourse antecedent, i.e., must refer to some person not mentioned in that sentence. The crucial point here is that the dative NP cannot be interpreted as the antecedent, even though there is no other potential antecedent within the sentence. This fact is immediately explained if the dative NP is the grammatical subject of the sentence, but very hard to explain otherwise.

(45) a   vijay-ko   uskii   kʰiḍkii-se   caand   dikʰaa.
          Vijay$_i$-DAT pro$_{j/*i}$-GEN window-INSTR moon(NOM) see-PERF
          'Vijay saw the moon from his/her (i.e., someone else's) window.'

     b   vijay-ko   kitaab   uske   gʰar-mā   milii.
          Vijay$_i$-DAT book(NOM)   pro$_{j/*i}$-GEN home-LOC   get-PERF
          'Vijay found a book at his/her (i.e., someone else's) home.'

The second test for subjecthood is control of a participial adjunct clause. The subject of a participial clause like that in (46) is obligatorily controlled (i.e., cannot be expressed by an overt NP, even a pronoun), and only the matrix subject can be the controller. In (46a), only the matrix subject *Ravi* can be interpreted as the controller, i.e., the one who is smiling; the matrix object *Vijay* is not eligible for this interpretation.[13] In (46b) the matrix verb is passivized, leaving the semantic roles unchanged but reversing the grammatical relations. As the gloss indicates, the possible interpretations are also reversed: now the controller cannot be *Ravi*, but must be *Vijay* (the passive subject). This clearly shows that the controller must be the grammatical subject of the matrix clause. The same pattern of grammaticality holds when the adverbial clause contains a past participle (*Having done X, . . .*); see Mohanan (1994:129) for examples.

(46) a   ravii-ne   vijay-ko   [__ muskuraate   hue] biṭʰaayaa.
          Ravi$_i$-ERG   Vijay$_j$-ACC   smile-IMPERF   be   sit-CAUS-PERF
          'Ravi$_i$ seated Vijay$_j$ while __$_{i/*j}$ smiling.'

     b   ravii-se   vijay   [__ muskuraate   hue] biṭʰaayaa   gayaa.
          Ravi$_i$-INSTR Vijay$_j$-NOM   smile-IMPERF   be   sit-CAUS-PERF go-PERF
          'Vijay$_j$ was seated by Ravi$_i$ while __$_{*i/j}$ smiling.'

In (47) we see two examples involving the same kinds of adverbial clause, but this time embedded in a matrix clause of the "dative subject" type. In both sentences, the dative argument of the matrix clause is interpreted as the controller, indicating that it is indeed the grammatical subject. (Note that the controllee in [47b] is also a dative subject.)

(47) a   vijay-ko   apne bʰaayii-se   [__ muskuraate   hue] milnaa hai.
          Vijay_i-DAT self's brother_j-INSTR   smile-IMPERF be   meet be
          'Vijay_i must meet his brother_j while ___i/*j smiling.'

     b   ravii-ko   [__ kitaab   paa kar] baɖii kʰušii huii.
          Ravi_i-DAT   book-NOM get do   much joy   happen-PERF
          '___i having got the book, Ravi_i was very happy.'

10.3   Quirky non-subjects in German

Constructions like those discussed in section 10.2.1 are found in a wide range of languages. Some examples are presented in (48):

(48) a   **Korean** (Shibatani, 1999:64)
          Inho-eykey(-nun) ton-i   mahni iss-ta.
          Inho-DAT(-TOP) money-NOM much exist-INDIC
          'Inho has a lot of money.'

     b   **Japanese** (Shibatani, 1999:64)
          Ken-ni(-wa)   nihongo-ga   hanas-e-ru.
          Ken-DAT(-TOP) Japanese-NOM speak-POTENT-PRES
          'Ken can speak Japanese.'

     c   **Latin** "dative of possession" (Allen and Greenough, 1931:232)
          est mihi   domī   pater   (Vergil, Ecl. iii.33)
          is me(DAT) at.home father(NOM)
          'I have a father at home.' (lit.: 'There is to me a father at home.')

As we have seen, there is fairly strong evidence for recognizing the existence of dative subjects in Malayalam and Hindi. Can we therefore conclude that the dative NPs in (48) are also grammatical subjects? Obviously not. Superficial similarities between languages in terms of case, word order, etc. do not necessarily indicate similarity in the underlying grammatical relations. Even closely related languages may differ in this respect. To illustrate this point, let us return to some of the German data we discussed in section 10.1.2.

Example (6) above illustrated the fact that some verbs in German assign dative case to their objects. As in Icelandic, this lexically specified case is preserved under passivization:

(49) a   Ich   habe   ihm   geholfen.
          I(NOM) have-1sg him(DAT) helped
          'I helped him.'

b   Ihm   wurde geholfen.
         him(DAT) was   helped
         'He was helped.'

Example (49b) looks very much like the Icelandic sentence (19a); but there is an important difference. Zaenen, Maling, and Thráinsson (1985) argue that in the German sentence (49b), the preverbal dative NP 'him' is not a grammatical subject, unlike its Icelandic counterpart. They present several different kinds of evidence to support this statement. For example, German has a rule of subject ellipsis very similar to that of Icelandic. As (50b) shows, this rule can apply to normal passive subjects; but if we try to omit the dative NP of (49b) in the same context, the result is ungrammatical (50c).

(50) a   Er   kam und (er)   besuchte die.Kinder.
          he(NOM) came and he(NOM) visited   the.children(ACC)
          'He came and (he) visited the children.'

    b   Er   kam und (er)   wurde verhaftet.
          he(NOM) came and he(NOM) was   arrested
          'He came and (he) was arrested.'

    c   *Er   kam und __   wurde geholfen.
          he(NOM) came and (DAT) was   helped
          (for: 'He came and was helped.')

A second unique property of grammatical subjects in German is that only subjects can be the controllee (or "target") in an Equi construction. Again, this test does not distinguish between normal active and passive subjects (51a–b). But the passivized dative object of (49b) cannot be an Equi target, as illustrated in (51c).

(51) a   Er   hofft, wegzugehen.
          he(NOM) hopes to.go.away
          'He hopes to go away.'

    b   Er   hofft, aufgenommen zu werden.
          he(NOM) hopes admitted   to be
          'He hopes to be admitted.'

    c   *Ihm/*Er   hofft, geholfen zu werden.
          him(DAT)/he(NOM) hopes helped   to be
          (for: 'He hopes to be helped.')

In a related construction, when the subject of an infinitive is omitted it can be understood to have arbitrary reference. This usage is possible for both active subjects (52a) and normal passive subjects (52b); but not for a passivized dative object (52c).

(52) a   Im Sommer zu reisen, ist angenehm.
          In summer to travel is agreeable
          'To travel in the summer is agreeable.'

    b   Aufgenommen zu werden, ist angenehm.
              admitted   to be   is agreeable
              'To be admitted is agreeable.'

    c   *Geholfen zu werden, ist angenehm.
              helped   to be   is agreeable
              (for: 'To be helped is agreeable.')

These three tests, together with other similar evidence, clearly indicate that passivized dative objects in German are not grammatical subjects. We must conclude that sentence (49b) is an IMPERSONAL (i.e., subjectless) passive (see chapter 3, section 3.2.1).

Zaenen *et al.* suggest that German systematically prohibits arguments whose case is lexically specified from appearing as subjects. This hypothesis is supported by the existence of non-passive predicates which take a single non-nominative NP argument. An example is given in (53). All of the subjecthood tests mentioned above show that the preverbal NP in this sentence is not a grammatical subject, which is just what Zaenen *et al.*'s hypothesis would lead us to predict.

(53)   Mir   ist übel.
           me(DAT) is nasty
           'I am nauseated.'

To sum up, we have seen that Icelandic, Malayalam, and Hindi allow subjects with non-canonical case marking. In German, however, we find patterns of case marking and word order that seem identical to Icelandic, but which involve very different assignments of grammatical relations. The moral of the story is that morphological features such as case, agreement, or even word order by themselves do not provide sufficient evidence for determining grammatical relations. As stated at the beginning of this chapter, grammatical relations must be identified on the basis of syntactic properties.

Notes

1. Dorothee Beerman (p.c.) points out that the semantic distinction signaled by this alternation is actually somewhat more complex. However, the simplified characterization presented here (and in most textbooks for learners of German) will be sufficient for present purposes.
2. Verbs of this type ('follow,' 'visit,' 'meet,' etc.) are special in other languages as well. In certain Malayo-Polynesian languages, they function as "semi-transitive" verbs (Chung, 1978; Kroeger, 1996).
3. As suggested by the glosses in (9a–b), non-nominative subjects do not trigger normal subject agreement marking on the verb. A similar pattern is found in many South Asian languages, as discussed in section 10.2.
4. Zaenen, Maling, and Thráinsson (1985) state that this pattern is true for "many" Icelandic speakers, and in fact this appears to be the majority dialect (Maling, 1982).

For other speakers, the reflexive pronoun is obligatory if the antecedent is a subject, but optional if the antecedent is an object.

5. Zaenen, Maling, and Thráinsson (1985) state that (11c–d) could be grammatical if the verb is interpreted as an intransitive 'dig' rather than the intended transitive 'bury.' But under the intransitive reading, there is no ellipsis in the second clause. They also provide additional data to show that subject ellipsis cannot apply under identity with a preceding object.

6. The adjunct phrase 'in his foolishness' is a constituent of the matrix clause. This shows that the raised argument 'me,' which precedes it, must also be a constituent of the matrix clause. The presence of the adjunct phrase thus rules out the possibility that this construction is not really an example of raising an element from the lower clause into the higher, but simply a re-ordering of elements within the complement clause.

7. As noted in section 10.3, Zaenen, Maling, and Thráinsson (1985) demonstrate that this is not true in the corresponding German constructions, e.g., *Ihm wurde geholfen*.

8. Kiparsky (1973); Aronoff (1976:43).

9. Andrews points out that some speakers find examples like (23c) and (24c), involving anaphoric control of an argument which takes quirky case, unnatural; but for speakers who do accept such constructions, the preference for nominative case is clear.

10. Mohanan (1994) points out that inanimate objects in Hindi may optionally take accusative case, but only if they are definite. Nominative case marking allows either a definite or indefinite interpretation.

11. As noted in n. 3, a very similar pattern holds in Icelandic: the verb does not agree with quirky case subjects, but does agree with nominative objects when the subject is non-nominative.

12. This third singular neuter form represents the default agreement category.

13. Note that the accusative case marker in Hindi is homophonous with the dative.

11 Syntactic ergativity

In chapter 10 we saw that case and agreement markers are not always in a one-to-one correspondence with grammatical relations. For example, we discussed a number of languages in which certain verbs require special case marking for their subjects or objects. In other languages, the marking of subjects depends on the transitivity of the clause: transitive subjects are marked one way, while intransitive subjects are marked another way. When, as is frequently true for such languages, intransitive subjects are marked in the same way as transitive objects, we say that the language is ERGATIVE.

Ergativity in case or agreement systems is not uncommon among the world's languages. More rarely, however, we encounter languages in which the kind of subjecthood tests discussed in chapter 10 reveal an "ergative" pattern in the syntax. This "syntactic ergativity" will be the main focus of this chapter. We will suggest that syntactically ergative languages differ from other, more familiar, languages in their pattern of linking grammatical relations to semantic roles. But first, let us review the properties of a simple ergative case system.

11.1 Morphological ergativity

As we saw in the preceding chapter, the subject of a German clause normally takes nominative case. This is true whether the clause is transitive, as in (1a), or intransitive, as in (1b). Direct objects take a different case marker, namely the accusative (1c).

(1) a Der   Hund hat mich   gebissen.
        the(MASC.NOM) dog   has me(ACC) bitten
        'The dog bit me.'

    b   Der   Hund schläft.
        the(MASC.NOM) dog   sleeps
        'The dog is sleeping.'

    c   Ich   sah den   Hund.
        I(NOM) saw the(MASC.ACC) dog
        'I saw the dog.'

The case-marking pattern for masculine singular definite subject and object NPs in German is displayed in (2). We are primarily interested in the fact that intransitive subjects take the same marker (*der*) as transitive agents, while transitive patients take a distinct marker (*den*). This kind of pattern is cross-linguistically the most common among case-marking languages. It is referred to as a NOMINATIVE-ACCUSATIVE (or sometimes just "accusative") system, because these are the names which are normally used for the two cases involved.

(2)   INTRANSITIVE   │SUBJECT: *der*│
        TRANSITIVE   │AGENT: *der*│   PATIENT: *den*

A different case-marking pattern, which is found in a smaller but still significant number of languages, is illustrated in the following data:

(3)   **Walmatjari** (Australia; adapted from Healey, 1990; data from Hudson, 1978)
    a   parri pa   laparni.
        boy AUX run
        'The boy ran.'

    b   manga pa   laparni.
        girl   AUX run
        'The girl ran.'

    c   wirlka pa   laparni.
        lizard AUX run
        'The lizard ran.'

    d   parri pa   pinya manga-ngu.
        boy AUX hit   girl
        'The girl hit the boy.'

    e   wirlka pa   nyanya parri-ngu.
        lizard AUX see   boy
        'The boy saw the lizard.'

    f   ngapa pa   nyanya manga-ngu.
        water AUX see   girl
        'The girl saw the water.'

These examples show that in Walmatjari, patients of transitive clauses get the same case marking as subjects of intransitive clauses, namely -Ø. Agents of transitive clauses get a special case marker (-*ngu*). This pattern is displayed in (4).

(4)   INTRANSITIVE   │SUBJECT: -Ø│
        TRANSITIVE   AGENT: -*ngu* │PATIENT: -Ø│

This kind of case-marking pattern, in which transitive agents take a unique marker, is referred to as an ERGATIVE system. The case marker used for transitive agents is called ERGATIVE case, while the case marker (often zero, as in Walmatjari) used for transitive patients and intransitive subjects is called ABSOLUTIVE case. The ergative and accusative patterns are compared in the following diagram, using "S" for the subject of an intransitive clause, "A" for the agent of a transitive clause, and "P" for the patient of a transitive clause.

(5)

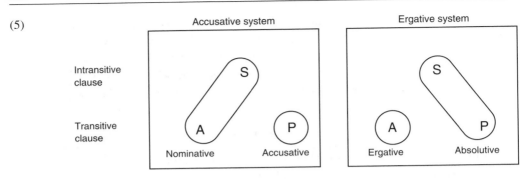

11.2   Ergativity and grammatical relations

In an ergative system like (4), the relationship between case marking and grammatical relations is not immediately obvious. In an intransitive clause like (3a–c), the absolutive argument is clearly the subject. But in a transitive clause like (3d–f), this same case is used for the patient, while the agent takes a different case marker (ergative). This pattern raises an obvious question: which argument of the transitive clause is the grammatical subject, the ergative agent or the absolutive patient? The answer is: it depends. We cannot tell without more information about the syntactic behavior of each argument.

As we emphasized in the preceding chapter, grammatical relations like SUBJ and OBJ are syntactic concepts. The subject of a sentence must be identified on the basis of its syntactic properties. In many languages there is a tendency for the subject to bear the semantic role of agent (or Actor) and to function as a discourse topic, but these factors in themselves do not determine subjecthood. Case marking, on the other hand, is a purely morphological device. Case assignment may be determined on the basis of grammatical relations or semantic roles, or some combination of the two. In addition, we have seen that case assignment can be determined by a special feature in the lexical entry of a particular verb or preposition. Thus we cannot identify the grammatical relations of the arguments in a clause simply by looking at the case-marking patterns.

It turns out that ergative languages differ in their syntactic properties. Warlpiri is another Australian language (related to Walmatjari) with an ergative case-marking pattern, as the following examples demonstrate:

(6)   **Warlpiri** (Simpson, 1991:155ff.)

a   Ngaju-Ø ka-rna   parnka-mi.
       I-ABS   PRES-1sg.SUBJ run-NONPAST
       'I am running.'

b   Ngarrka-Ø ka-Ø   parnka-mi.
       man-ABS   PRES-3sg.SUBJ run-NONPAST
       'A man is running.'

c   Ngajulu-rlu ka-rna-Ø   ngarrka-Ø nya-nyi.
        I-ERG   PRES-1sg.SUBJ-3sg.OBJ man-ABS see-NONPAST
        'I see the man.'

d   Ngarrka-ngku ka-Ø-ju   ngaju-Ø nya-nyi.[1]
        man-ERG   PRES-3sg.SUBJ-1sg.OBJ me-ABS see-NONPAST
        'A/the man sees me.'

On the other hand, the pattern of verbal agreement follows a NOM–ACC pattern. As the examples in (6) illustrate, the same subject-agreement clitics are used for both the absolutive argument of an intransitive clause and the ergative argument of a transitive clause, e.g., first person singular -*rna* in (6a) and (6c). A distinct object-agreement clitic is used for the patient of a transitive clause, e.g., -*ju* in (6d). Where more than one overt agreement clitic occurs, as in (7), the subject agreement marker normally comes first:

(7)   **Warlpiri** (Simpson, 1991:161)
a   luwa-rnu-rna-ngku.
        shoot-PAST-1sg.SUBJ-2sg.OBJ
        'I shot you.'

b   luwa-rnu-npa-ju.
        shoot-PAST-2sg.SUBJ-1sg.OBJ
        'You shot me.'

So the morphological evidence is mixed: case marking is ergative, while agreement is accusative. We will need to appeal to syntactic evidence to determine which argument is the subject.

The clearest tests for grammatical subjecthood in Warlpiri involve the control relation (see Hale, 1982, 1983; Simpson and Bresnan, 1983).[2] For example, in adverbial clauses formed with the complementizer =*karra*, both controller and controllee must be the grammatical subjects of their respective clauses. As the examples in (8) illustrate, the controller may be either the absolutive argument of an intransitive clause (8a) or the ergative argument of a transitive clause (8b–c). Similarly, the controllee may be either the absolutive argument of an intransitive clause (8b) or the ergative argument of a transitive clause (8a,c,d). So this control pattern groups transitive agents with intransitive subjects. In spite of the difference in case marking (absolutive vs. ergative), both types of arguments bear the same grammatical relation, namely subject.

(8)   **Warlpiri** (Hale, 1982; Simpson, 1991:310)
a   Ngarrka   ka   wirnpirli-mi,   karli   jarnti-rninja=karra.
        man(ABS) PRES whistle-NONPAST boomerang(ABS) trim-PURP=COMP
        'The man is whistling, while trimming the boomerang.'

b   Wati-ngki marlu   nya-ngu   jarnti-rninja=karra-rlu.[3]
        man-ERG kangaroo(ABS) see-PAST run-PURP=COMP-ERG
        'The man saw the kangaroo while he (the man) was running.'

c   Ngarrka-ngku ka   purlapa   yunpa-rni,
     man-ERG   PRES corroboree(ABS) sing-NONPAST
     karli   jarnti-rninja=karra-rlu.
     boomerang trim-PURP=COMP-ERG
     'The man is singing a corroboree, while trimming the boomerang.'

d   Napurrula   ka-ju   ngaju-ku wangka-mi,
     Napurrula(ABS) PRES-1sg.OBJ me-DAT   speak-NONPAST
     ngurlu kipi-rninja=karra.
     seed   winnow-PURP=COMP
     'Napurrula is speaking to me, while winnowing seed.'

Example (8d) illustrates the fact that it is grammatical relations, and not case marking, which determine the control pattern in this construction. The verb *wangka* 'speak' is one of a restricted class of verbs that takes a special, lexically determined, case-marking pattern, in this instance an absolutive agent and a dative goal. As (8d) shows, the absolutive agent of this verb can also function as the controller of the =*karra* clause, because it is the grammatical subject of its clause.

Hale (1982, 1983), Simpson (1983, 1991), Laughren (1989, 1992), and Levin (1983) discuss several other kinds of evidence which can be used to identify grammatical subjects in Warlpiri. In each case, the evidence identifies the agent of a transitive clause as the subject, and not the patient. In other words, the ergative case-marking pattern in Warlpiri is purely morphological. The assignment of grammatical relations follows a nominative–accusative pattern: transitive agents (A) and intransitive absolutive arguments (S) are both realized as grammatical subjects; transitive patients (P) bear a distinct relation, namely object.

In some other languages, however, syntactic properties themselves follow an ergative pattern: subjecthood tests pick out the patient of a transitive verb and the single argument of an intransitive verb. The best known example of this type is Dyirbal, another language of Australia.

11.3   Subjecthood tests in Dyirbal

The term SYNTACTIC ERGATIVITY refers to a situation in which the syntactic system of a language, and in particular the properties which provide tests for subjecthood, follow an ergative pattern. That is, in a syntactically ergative language like Dyirbal, the grammatical subject of a basic transitive clause like (9) is in fact the patient ('the woman'). This statement may seem hard to accept, because such a pattern is quite unfamiliar to speakers of most other languages. Let us therefore examine some of the syntactic tests which support this claim.[4]

(9)   balan dʸugumbil baŋgul yaṟaŋgu balga-n.
       DET-woman-ABS DET-man-ERG hit-REAL[5]
       'The man hit the woman.' (Dixon 1972:130)

Morphologically, Dyirbal exhibits a "split-ergative" case-marking system. This term means that some NPs follow the ergative pattern, while others do not. In Dyirbal, first and second person pronouns follow the NOM–ACC pattern, while all other NPs follow the ergative pattern. The basic distribution of case markers is summarized in (10); but note that these markers have a number of different allomorphs.

(10)   **Dyirbal case markers** (Dixon, 1979:87)

	1st and 2nd person pronouns	**3rd person pronouns**	**common nouns/ proper names**
intransitive subjects	-Ø	-Ø	-Ø
transitive agents	-Ø	-ŋgu	-ŋgu
transitive patients	-nʸa	-Ø	-Ø

Dyirbal has four genders, or noun classes. The gender of a common noun is reflected in the form of the determiner, which also indicates the case of the NP and the degree of proximity to the speaker ('here,' 'there but visible,' or 'there and not visible'). The various case and gender forms of the medial demonstrative, which signals 'there but visible,' are listed in (11). These are the determiners used in the examples below.

(11)   **Dyirbal medial demonstratives** (Dixon, 1972:44–47, 306–311)

	ABSOLUTIVE	ERG/INSTR	DATIVE	GENITIVE
Class I	bayi	baŋgul	bagul	baŋul
Class II	balan	baŋgun	bagun	baŋun
Class III	balam	baŋgum	bagum	—
Class IV	bala	baŋgu	bagu	baŋu

However, the difference in case marking between first and second person pronouns vs. all other NPs is irrelevant to the syntax. In all of the constructions discussed below, subjects of intransitive verbs (S) and patients of transitive verbs (P) play a unique role, no matter whether they are morphologically marked for absolutive, nominative, or accusative case. In the discussion that follows, we will use the term ABSOLUTIVE ARGUMENT to refer to the union of these two classes, S and P, regardless of case marking.

11.3.1   Relativization

In Dyirbal relative clauses, the modifying clause follows the head noun and is marked by adding the suffix -ŋu to the verb. Example (12b) shows a relative clause based on the simple intransitive clause in (12a). The relativized function in (12b) corresponds to the intransitive subject, i.e., the absolutive argument of the basic clause. Example (12c) shows a relative clause based on a simple transitive clause meaning 'I saw the woman.' The relativized function in (12c) corresponds to the transitive patient, once again the absolutive argument of the basic clause. As example (12d) demonstrates, the relativized verb agrees with the case marking of the head noun, which in this sentence is ergative.

The example in (12e) is ungrammatical. In this case, the relativized argument is the ergative, i.e., the transitive agent, which is not allowed. Relativization of instrumental, dative, or other oblique arguments is also ungrammatical. So relativization in Dyirbal is constrained by the following generalization: the relativized function must correspond to the absolutive argument of the basic clause.

(12) a   bayi yaṛa bani-nʸu.
           man-ABS come.here-REAL
           'The man came here.' (Dixon, 1972:59)

     b   ŋadʸa   bayi yaṛa [__   bani-ŋu]   buṛa-n.
           1sg.NOM man-ABS (ABS) come-REL see-REAL
           'I saw the man who came.' (Foley and Van Valin, 1984:112)

     c   balan dʸugumbil [ŋadʸa   __   buṛa-ŋu] nʸina-nʸu.
           woman-ABS   1sg-NOM (ABS) see-REL sit-REAL
           'The woman that I saw is sitting down.' (Dixon, 1972:100)

     d   bayi yaṛa baŋgun dʸugumbiṛu [__   waynʸdʸi-ŋu-ru]   buṛa-n.
           man-ABS woman-ERG   (ABS) go.uphill-ERG-REL see-REAL
           'The woman who was going uphill saw a man.' (Dixon, 1972:101)

     e   *bayi yaṛa [__   balan dʸugumbil buṛa-ŋu] bani-nʸu.
           man-ABS (ERG) woman-ABS   see-REL come-REAL
           (for: 'The man who saw the woman came here.') (Foley and Van Valin, 1984:112)

As we saw in chapter 7, Keenan and Comrie's cross-linguistic study of relativization predicts that, if only a single class of arguments can be relativized in a particular language, that argument will be the grammatical subject. Thus the fact that only the absolutive argument can be relativized in Dyirbal strongly suggests that it is the grammatical subject.

11.3.2   Coordination reduction

When two clauses which contain coreferential arguments are conjoined, the common argument may be deleted in the second clause provided that it is the absolutive argument of both clauses. This is illustrated in the following examples.

In (13a), the absolutive argument (i.e., the transitive patient) of the second clause is missing; it is interpreted as being coreferential with the absolutive argument of the first clause ('man'). In (13b) the omitted absolutive argument of the second clause can only be interpreted as being coreferential with the absolutive argument (i.e., the patient 'woman') of the first clause, and not with the ergative agent 'man.' But (13c) is ungrammatical, because the omitted argument in the second clause is the agent of a transitive verb, which is not the absolutive argument.

(13) a   bayi yaṛa bani-nʸu,   baŋgun dʸugumbiṛu __   balga-n.
          man-ABS come-REAL woman-ERG   (ABS) hit-REAL
          'The man came and was hit by the woman.' (Dixon, 1972:130)

   b   balan dʸugumbil baŋgul yaṛaŋgu balga-n,   __   bani-nʸu.
        woman-ABS   man-ERG   hit-REAL (ABS) come-REAL
        'The woman was hit by the man and came here.'
        (*'The man hit the woman and came here.') (adapted from Dixon, 1972:131)

   c   *bayi yaṛa bani-nʸu,   balan dʸugumbil __   balga-n.
        man-ABS come-REAL, woman-ABS   (ERG) hit-REAL
        (for: 'The man came and hit the woman.')

So this construction too reveals a syntactic property which is uniquely shared
by the intransitive subject (S) and transitive patient (P).

11.3.3   Non-finite purpose clauses

   A non-finite verb form bearing the suffix $-i \sim -gu$ is used in Dyirbal
adverbial clauses which express purpose (Dixon, 1972:146). In this construction,
the absolutive argument of the purpose clause must be omitted (understood), and
must be controlled by the absolutive argument of the matrix verb.

   In (14a), both controller and controllee are intransitive subjects (S). In (14b), the
controllee is an intransitive subject (S). The only possible choice for controller is
the matrix patient (P); the matrix agent cannot be interpreted as controller. In (14c)
and (14d), both controller and controllee are transitive patients (P). But sentence
(14e) is ungrammatical, because the controllee is a transitive agent (A). These
examples are especially significant, because there is a strong cross-linguistic
tendency for controllees to be grammatical subjects. This evidence provides strong
support for the claim that the absolutive argument in Dyirbal is the grammatical
subject.

(14) a   bayi yaṛa walma-nʸu   waynʸdʸil-i.
          man-ABS get.up-REAL go.downhill-PURP
          'The man got up in order to go downhill.' (Dixon, 1972:68)

   b   balan dʸugumbil baŋgul yaṛaŋgu balga-n   badʸi-gu.
        woman-ABS   man-ERG   hit-REAL fall-PURP
        'The man hit the woman to (make her/*himself) fall.' (Dixon, 1972:68)

   c   balam miranʸ baŋgul yaṛaŋgu dimba-nʸu   ŋinda   babil-i.
        beans-ABS   man-ERG   carry-REAL 2sg.NOM peel-PURP
        'The man brought beans so that you could scrape them.' (Dixon, 1972:68)

   d   bayi yaṛa baŋgul gubi-ŋgu munda-n   baŋgun dʸugumbiṛu balgal-i.
        man-ABS shaman-ERG   lead-REAL woman-ERG   hit-PURP
        'The shaman brought the man to be hit by the woman.' (Dixon, 1972:159)

e   *balan dʸugumbil baŋgul yaṟaŋgu wawu-n   balan nayinba walmbil-i.
         woman-ABS   man-ERG   fetch-REAL girl-ABS   awaken-PURP
         (for: 'The man fetched the woman to wake up the girls.')
         (Foley and Van Valin, 1984:113)

11.3.4   Equi constructions

Dixon (1979:128–129) describes a pattern found in Dyirbal which he labels the "jussive" construction. This construction involves Equi verbs such as *giga-l* 'tell to do.' Dixon shows that the controllee must be the absolutive argument of the complement clause. (Notice that the verb of the complement clause bears the purposive suffix.) Thus (15), where the controllee is an intransitive subject (S), and (16), where the controllee is a transitive patient (P), are both fine. Example (17), however, is ungrammatical because the controllee is a transitive agent (A). Once again, in light of the cross-linguistic tendency for controllees to be grammatical subjects, this evidence supports the claim that the absolutive argument in Dyirbal is the grammatical subject.

(15)   ŋana   yabu   giga-n   banagay-gu.
           1pl.NOM mother-ABS tell-REAL return-PURP
           'We told mother to return.' (Dixon, 1979:129)

(16)   ŋadya   bayi yaṟa giga-n   gubi-ŋgu   mawal-i
           1sg.NOM man-ABS tell-REAL shaman-ERG examine-PURP
           'I told the man to be examined by the doctor.' (Comrie, 1981:112)

(17)   *ŋana   yabu   giga-n   ŋuma   buṟal-i.
           we-NOM mother-ABS tell-REAL father-ABS see-PURP
           (for: 'We told mother to watch father.')

11.3.5   Plural agreement[6]

The suffix *-dʸay* 'many' can be added to the verb to indicate that the absolutive argument is plural. It cannot be used to indicate plurality of the transitive agent, as illustrated in (18). Cross-linguistically, if the verb agrees with only one argument in a transitive clause, that argument is normally the subject. So this evidence too is consistent with the hypothesis which we are considering.

(18) a   bayi yaṟa nʸinan-dʸa-nʸu.
           man-ABS sit-PLURAL-REAL
           'Many men are sitting down.' (Dixon, 1972:249)

      b   balam miranʸ   baŋgul yaṟaŋgu gundal-dʸa-nʸu.
           black.bean-ABS man-ERG   put.in-PLURAL-REAL
           'The man gathered many beans.'
           (Not: *'Many men gathered beans.') (Dixon, 1972:249)

11.3.6   Scope of adverbial modifiers

The adverbial particle *wara* 'wrongly, badly' always modifies the absolute argument of its clause. The results of this constraint are clearly seen in sentence (20), where the particle cannot be interpreted as modifying either the transitive agent ('man') or the action itself ('cut'), but only the patient ('tree'). This particle creates another context in which S and P share a unique syntactic property which A lacks.

(19)   bayi yaṛa wara   bani-n^{y}u.
         man-ABS wrongly come-REAL
         'The wrong man came.' (Mel'čuk, 1979:42)

(20)   bala yugu baŋgul yaṛaŋgu wara   nudi-n.
         tree-ABS   man-ERG   wrongly cut-REAL
         'The man cut the wrong tree.' (Mel'čuk, 1979:42; cf. Dixon, 1972:118)
         (Not: *'The wrong man cut the tree'; *'The man cut the tree in the wrong way.')

To summarize the results of this section, we have examined a wide variety of syntactic constructions in which the absolute argument plays a unique and pivotal role. Some of the syntactic properties we have discussed are associated cross-linguistically with grammatical subjects, while others seem to be language-specific features. But the special status of the absolute argument in Dyirbal syntax seems best explained by assuming that Dyirbal is syntactically ergative, i.e., that the absolute argument is the grammatical subject.

We should point out that the term "syntactic ergativity" is used by some linguists in a slightly different way. Dyirbal syntax is striking in the uniformity of its orientation toward the patient, rather than the agent, in basic transitive clauses. Some other languages seem to exhibit a "mixed" orientation: some syntactic properties follow the ergative pattern, grouping S and P, while others follow the nominative–accusative pattern, grouping S and A. Some linguists apply the term "syntactic ergativity" to individual constructions, rather than to languages as a whole, identifying those syntactic properties which group S with P but exclude A as being syntactically ergative.

11.4   Antipassive

11.4.1   Antipassive in Dyirbal

There is an interesting construction in Dyirbal, which is formed by adding the suffix *-ŋay* (∼ *-nay*) to a transitive verb. This construction is called the ANTIPASSIVE, for reasons to be discussed below. The most obvious effect of adding this suffix is a change in the case-marking pattern of the transitive clause: the agent of the antipassive takes absolute case, rather than ergative, and the patient takes dative case, rather than absolute.[7] Notice the contrast between the basic transitive clause in (21a) and the corresponding antipassive in (21b).

(21) a   bayi bargan baŋgul yaṛa-ŋgu dʸurga-nʸu.
        wallaby-ABS man-ERG   spear-REAL
        'The man is spearing a wallaby.' (Dixon, 1972:65)

     b   bayi yaṛa bagul bargan-gu dʸurga-na-nʸu.
        man-ABS wallaby-DAT   spear-ANTIPASS-REAL
        'The man is spearing a wallaby.' (Dixon, 1972:66)

Besides the difference in case marking, there is also a striking difference with regard to the subjecthood tests which we discussed in the previous section. If (and only if) the verb carries the antipassive suffix, the agent can be relativized, deleted in coordinate clauses, or function as the controllee in purpose clauses and Equi constructions.

We saw in example (12) that the agent of a basic transitive clause cannot be relativized; that is why (22a) is ungrammatical. But the example becomes completely grammatical when the antipassive suffix is added to the verb of the modifying clause, as in (22b). This contrast suggests that, in addition to bearing absolutive case marking, the agent of the antipassive is functioning syntactically as the absolutive argument, i.e., the grammatical subject.

(22)   **Relativization**
    a   *bayi yaṛa [__   bayi yuṛi   bagal-ŋu] banaga-nʸu.
       man-ABS (ERG) kangaroo-ABS spear-REL return-REAL
       (for: 'The man who speared the kangaroo is returning.')

    b   bayi yaṛa [bagal-ŋa-ŋu   __   bagul yuṛi-gu] banaga-nʸu.
       man-ABS spear-ANTIPASS-REL (ABS) kangaroo-DAT return-REAL
       'The man who speared the kangaroo is returning.' (Dixon, 1972:101)

The examples in (13) illustrated the fact that, in a coordinate sentence, the absolutive argument of the second clause may be deleted if and only if it is coreferential with the absolutive argument of the first clause. Sentence (13c), repeated below as (23a), is ungrammatical because the deleted NP is not the absolutive argument but the ergative agent of the second clause. But the sentence becomes grammatical when the antipassive suffix is added to the verb of the second clause, as in (23b). Again, this contrast suggests that the agent of the antipassive is functioning syntactically as the absolutive argument.

(23)   **Coordination reduction**
    a   *bayi yaṛa bani-nʸu,   balan dʸugumbil __   balga-n.
       man-ABS come-REAL, woman-ABS   (ERG) hit-REAL
       (for: 'The man came and hit the woman.')

    b   bayi yaṛa bani-nʸu,   bagun dʸugumbil-gu __   balgal-ŋa-nʸu.
       man-ABS come-REAL, woman-DAT   (ABS) hit-ANTIPASS-REAL
       'The man came and hit the woman.' (Dixon, 1972:130)

In section 11.3.3 we saw that in a purpose clause, both controller and controllee must be the absolute arguments of their respective clauses. Sentence (14e), repeated below as (24a), is ungrammatical because the controllee is an ergative agent. But when the antipassive suffix is added to the verb of the subordinate clause, as in (24b), the sentence becomes grammatical. Sentence (25) provides a similar example, with the agent of the antipassive functioning as controllee.

(24)   **Purpose clauses**
    a   *balan dʸugumbil baŋgul yaṛa-ŋgu wawu-n   balan nayinba walmbil-i.
         woman-ABS   man-ERG   fetch-REAL girl-ABS   awaken-PURP
         (for: 'The man fetched the woman to wake up the girls.')

    b   balan dʸugumbil baŋgul yaṛa-ŋgu wawu-n,
         woman-ABS   man-ERG   fetch-REAL
         bagun nayinba-gu walmbil-ŋay-gu.
         girl-DAT   awaken-ANTIPASS-PURP
         'The man fetched the woman to wake up the girls.'(Dixon, 1972:74)

(25)   ŋuma   banaga-nʸu   yabu-gu   buṛal-ŋay-gu.
        father-ABS return-REAL mother-DAT see-ANTIPASS-PURP
        'Father returned to watch mother.' (Dixon, 1979:128)

Similarly, only the absolutive argument of the complement clause can function as controllee of the Equi (or "jussive") construction; this was illustrated in (15–17). Example (26a), in which the controllee is an ergative agent, is ungrammatical; but the sentence becomes grammatical when the antipassive suffix is added to the complement verb (26b). A second example of this pattern is seen in (27). Thus the control facts in purpose clauses and Equi complements support the conclusion that the agent of the antipassive clause is functioning syntactically as the absolutive argument, i.e., the grammatical subject.

(26)   **Equi ("jussive") constructions**
    a   *ŋana   yabu   giga-n   nguma   buṛal-i.
         we-NOM mother-ABS tell-REAL father-ABS see-PURP
         (for: 'We told mother to watch father.')

    b   ŋana   yabu   giga-n   ŋuma-gu   buṛal-ŋay-gu.
         we-NOM mother-ABS tell-REAL father-DAT see-ANTIPASS-PURP
         'We told mother to watch father.' (Dixon, 1979:129)

(27)   balan dʸugumbil baŋgul yaṛa-ŋgu giga-n   bagun buni-gu mabal-ŋay-gu.
        woman-ABS   man-ERG   tell-REAL fire-DAT   light-ANTIPASS-PURP
        'The man told the woman to light a fire.'(Dixon, 1972:76)

All of the evidence we have considered in this section indicates that the antipassive construction involves more than just a change in case marking. The syntactic properties of both agent and patient are affected by this process, with the agent taking on the properties associated with absolutive arguments in basic clauses. Thus the change in case marking seems to reflect a change in grammatical relations.

Since we have argued that the absolutive argument in Dyirbal is the grammatical subject of its clause, we must conclude that in the antipassive construction the agent replaces the patient as grammatical subject. How exactly does this change take place?

Recall that we defined the "absolutive argument" as being the patient of a transitive clause or the single direct argument (i.e., term) of an intransitive clause. Dative case in Dyirbal is normally used for oblique arguments, so the fact that the patient takes dative case in the antipassive construction suggests that it has been demoted to oblique status. But if this is true, then the antipassive clause contains only one direct argument, namely the agent. It is therefore syntactically intransitive; the agent is the sole direct argument, and therefore an absolutive according to our definition of the term. The absolutive case marking on the agent follows the regular rules of morphological case assignment in the language; and as absolutive argument, the agent bears the grammatical subject relation in the antipassive clause.

So the crucial effect of the antipassive morpheme is to demote the patient from term (direct argument) to oblique, creating an intransitive clause. Compare this process with passivization. As we saw in chapter 3, passivization always involves the demotion of the agent to oblique (or adjunct) status. Some languages allow impersonal passives, in which no argument is promoted to subject; but all passives involve the demotion of the agent. Thus passive and antipassive are strongly parallel in their effects. Both processes are referred to as DETRANSITIVIZING operations, because both reduce the number of direct arguments in the clause: passive by demoting the agent; antipassive by demoting the patient.

11.4.2   Uses of the antipassive construction in other languages

In Dyirbal, as we have seen, the antipassive is obligatory whenever a transitive agent is relativized, deleted under identity in a coordinate clause, functions as a controllee, etc. But in addition to these syntactically motivated uses, there may be semantic or pragmatic factors which cause speakers to choose the antipassive form in particular contexts. Some of these uses are particularly common among languages that have an antipassive.

Because the antipassive always demotes the patient, it tends to be used when the patient is less prominent than the agent. For example, in many ergative languages the antipassive is preferred or even required when the patient is indefinite. In the Eskimo example (28a), the verb appears in its basic transitive form, agreeing with both agent and patient. The agent takes ergative case and the patient absolutive, as expected; and the patient, although expressed as a bare common noun, is interpreted as being definite. Compare this pattern with the corresponding antipassive in (28b). In this example, the patient takes instrumental case, suggesting that it has been demoted to oblique status; the verb agrees only with the agent; and the agent, as the only direct argument in its clause, takes absolutive case. Once again the patient is expressed as an unmodified common noun, but in this construction it is interpreted as being indefinite. The same contrast occurs in Chukchee, as exemplified in (29a–b).

(28)   **Greenlandic Eskimo** (Sadock, 1980:306; Baker, 1988:131)

    a   Angut-ip   arnaq   unatar-paa.
          man-ERG woman(ABS) beat-3sgA/3sgP
          'The man beat the woman.'

    b   Angut   arna-mik   unata-a-voq.
          man(ABS) woman-INSTR beat-ANTIPASS-3sgS
          'The man beat a woman.'

    c   Angut   unata-a-voq.
          man(ABS) beat-ANTIPASS-3sgS
          'The man beat someone.'

(29)   **Chukchee** (Siberia; Kozinsky, Nedjalkov, and Polinskaja, 1988)

    a   ʔaaček-a   kimitʔ-ən ne-nlʔetet-ən.
          youth-ERG load-ABS 3plA-carry-3sgP
          'The young men carried away the load.'

    b   ʔaaček-ət   ine-nlʔetet-gʔe-t   kimitʔ-e.
          youth-ABS ANTIPASS-carry-3plS load-INSTR
          'The young men carried away a load.'

Another context where the antipassive is frequently preferred or required is when the patient is unspecified, i.e., omitted entirely. This pattern was illustrated for Eskimo in (28c); a similar Chukchee example is seen in (30b).

(30)   **Chukchee** (Kozinsky, Nedjalkov, and Polinskaja, 1988)

    a   ətləg-e   qora-ŋə   qərir-nin.
          father-ERG deer-ABS look.for-3sgA/3sgP
          'The father looked for the deer.'

    b   ətləg-ən   ena-rer-gʔe.
          father-ABS ANTIPASS-look.for-3sgS
          'The father did some searching.' (i.e., searched for something)

The antipassive may also be required when the patient is incorporated into the verb. In (31a), the patient is expressed by an independent absolutive NP *qaa-t* 'deer'. In (31b), however, the patient is expressed by a noun stem which is morphologically affixed to the antipassive verb.

(31)   **Chukchee** (Kozinsky, Nedjalkov, and Polinskaja, 1988)

    a   ənan   qaa-t   qərir-nin-et.
          he(ERG) deer-ABS.PL look.for-3sgA/3plP
          'He looked for the deer (pl.).'

    b   ətlon   qaa-Ø-rer-gʔe.[8]
          he(ABS) deer-ANTIPASS-look.for-3sgS
          'He was looking for deer.'

The antipassive is frequently used to indicate that the patient is unaffected or only partially affected by the action. In (32b), the antipassive is used to produce a partitive interpretation, meaning that only part of the meat was eaten, in contrast to the ergative (32a), which implies that all of the meat was eaten. In (33b), the antipassive is used to indicate that the action was directed toward the patient but did not necessarily affect the patient, in contrast to the ergative (33a).

(32)   **Eskimo** (Foley and Van Valin, 1985)

    a   Arna-p   niqi   niri-vaa.
         woman-ERG meat(ABS) eat-3sgA/3sgP
         'The woman ate the meat.'

    b   Arnaq   niqi-mik   niri-NNig-puq.
         woman(ABS) meat-INSTR eat-ANTIPASS-3sgS
         'The woman ate some of the meat.'

(33)   **Chukchee** (Kozinsky, Nedjalkov, and Polinskaja, 1988)

    a   ətləg-e   keyŋ-ən   penrə-nen.
         father-ERG bear-ABS attack-3sgA/3sgP
         'The father attacked the bear.'

    b   ətləg-ən   penrə-tko-gʔe   kayŋ-etə.
         father-ABS attack-ANTIPASS-3sgS bear-DAT
         'The father rushed at the bear.'

Hopper and Thompson (1980) point out that these kinds of semantic contrasts are correlated with transitivity in many languages. The antipassive construction is a paradigm example of this correlation. Syntactically, it creates an intransitive clause by demoting the patient. Semantically, it often marks the patient as being indefinite, partially affected, etc.

11.5   Syntactic ergativity in Western Austronesian

Several Western Austronesian languages have been described as syntactically ergative in the sense that the patient, rather than the agent, is the grammatical subject of a basic transitive clause. What makes these Austronesian examples especially interesting is that they tend to exhibit NON-DEMOTING voice alternations. This means that a typical transitive verb will appear in two different forms, one taking the patient as subject and the other taking the agent as subject; but both forms are syntactically transitive. Both agent and patient are terms (non-oblique arguments) no matter which one is selected as subject. In other words, the alternation in subject selection in these languages does not involve the demotion of a core argument, unlike the passive or antipassive constructions we have discussed thus far.

Rather than speaking of "agents" and "patients" in this section, I will (following Foley and Van Valin, 1984) use the more general terms ACTOR and UNDER-GOER. The Actor is, roughly speaking, the most agent-like semantic role in the clause, whether that is an experiencer, inanimate force, instrument, or even recipient (e.g., with *get* or *receive*). The Undergoer is the argument which the speaker views as being most directly affected by the action, or toward which the action is directed. I will refer to the construction in which the Actor is selected as grammatical subject as the ACTOR VOICE (AV), and the construction in which the Undergoer is selected as grammatical subject as the UNDERGOER VOICE (UV).

We have defined a syntactically ergative language as being one in which the patient, rather than the agent, is the grammatical subject of a basic transitive clause. Thus if there are two different transitive clause types, we cannot evaluate the claim of syntactic ergativity until we know which one is more "basic." In the languages we will consider here there are several reasons to believe that the basic transitive clause is the UV form, in which the Undergoer is selected as grammatical subject. One piece of evidence comes from morphological markedness: the UV form of the verb is generally unmarked (i.e., expressed as a bare stem), while the AV form of the verb bears an overt affix. Another kind of evidence has to do with text frequency: the Undergoer Voice tends to be used more frequently in transitive clauses than the Actor Voice. (This tendency stands in strong contrast to languages like English, in which active verbs far outnumber passive verbs in most contexts.) Both of these facts support the claim that the UV form is more basic than the AV form. We will discuss this issue in more detail, bringing in other kinds of evidence, in section 11.5.3.

It is certainly not the case that all Western Austronesian languages are syntactically ergative, but this pattern has been reported in a number of languages which are geographically widely scattered and genetically not closely related. In this section we will examine some of the relevant data in two relatively well-documented cases: Balinese (spoken in south central Indonesia) based on the analysis and data of Arka (1998) and Wechsler and Arka (1998); and Pangutaran Sama (spoken in the southern Philippines) with data taken from Walton (1986).

11.5.1   Balinese

In Balinese, the UV form of a transitive verb is unmarked, as illustrated in (34a). The AV form is marked by an underspecified nasal prefix which merges with or assimilates to a following obstruent; this is illustrated in (34b), where *N-* + *tumbas* > *numbas*. The AV prefix *N-* is realized as a velar nasal when the stem does not begin with an obstruent. (Note: Balinese has two registers, or speech varieties. Choice of register depends on the relative age, social status, etc. of the speaker and hearer, and also the identity of the person or thing being talked about. Unless otherwise marked, the following examples represent the low/common register.)

(34)   **Balinese** (high register; Wechsler and Arka, 1998:388)
   a   Bawi-ne punika Ø-tumbas tiang.
          pig-DEF that   UV-buy   1sg
          'I bought the pig.'

b   Tiang numbas bawi-ne punika.
        1sg AV.buy pig-DEF that
        'I bought the pig.'

As these examples illustrate, the Undergoer appears in pre-verbal position in UV clauses while the Actor appears in pre-verbal position in AV clauses. Wechsler and Arka (1998) present several independent pieces of evidence to support their analysis of the pre-verbal NP as grammatical subject.

The first piece of evidence comes from relativization. In Balinese, the only positions which can be relativized are subjects (using a gapping strategy) and possessors of subjects (using a resumptive pronoun strategy). Thus the Undergoer can be relativized only when the subordinate verb is marked for UV; note the contrast in (35a–b). The Actor can be relativized only when the subordinate verb is marked for AV, as illustrated in (35c–d).

(35)   **Balinese relativization** (Wechsler and Arka, 1998:390)

    a   anak-e   cenik [ane Ø-gugut cicing] ento
            person-DEF small REL UV-bite dog   that
            'the child whom the dog bit'

    b   *anak-e   cenik [ane ngugut cicing] ento
            person-DEF small REL AV.bite dog   that
            (for: 'the child whom the dog bit')

    c   cicing [ane ngugut anak-e   cenik] ento
            dog   REL AV.bite person-DEF small that
            'the dog that bit the child'

    d   *cicing [ane anak-e   cenik Ø-gugut] ento
            dog   REL person-DEF small UV-bite that
            (for: 'the dog that bit the child')

Second, only grammatical subjects can undergo Raising. Examples (36–37) illustrate this using the intransitive Raising predicate *ngenah* 'seem.' When this predicate appears with a full sentential complement, i.e., when no Raising is involved, the complement verb may appear in either the UV (36a) or AV (37a) form. When the complement verb takes UV marking, only the Undergoer can be raised (36b–c); and when the complement verb takes AV marking, only the Actor can be raised (37b–c).

(36)   **Balinese** (Wechsler and Arka, 1998:391)

    a   Ngenah sajan [kapelihan-ne   Ø-engkebang ci].
          seem   much mistake-3sg.POSS UV-hide   2sg
          'It is very apparent that you are hiding his/her wrongdoing.'

    b   Kapelihan-ne   ngenah sajan Ø-engkebang ci.
          mistake-3sg.POSS seem   much UV-hide   2sg
          'It is very apparent that you are hiding his/her wrongdoing.'

c   *Ci ngenah sajan kapelihan-ne   Ø-engkebang.
    2sg seem   much mistake-3sg.POSS UV-hide

(37)   **Balinese** (Wechsler and Arka, 1998:392)

    a   Ngenah sajan [ci ngengkebang kapelihan-ne].
    seem   much 2sg AV.hide   mistake-3sg.POSS
    'It is very apparent that you are hiding his/her wrongdoing.'

    b   Ci ngenah sajan ngengkebang kapelihan-ne.
    2sg seem   much AV.hide   mistake-3sg.POSS
    'It is very apparent that you are hiding his/her wrongdoing.'

    c   ?*Kapelihan-ne   ngenah sajan ci ngengkebang.
    mistake-3sg.POSS seem   much 2sg AV.hide

The same restrictions apply in the case of "Subject to Object Raising." The examples in (38) involve the transitive Raising predicate *tawang* 'know.' When the complement verb is a UV form, only the Undergoer can be raised (38a–b); and when the complement verb takes AV marking, only the Actor can be raised (38c–d). (For simplicity the UV form of the matrix verb is used in all of these examples, but the same pattern holds when the matrix verb is marked for AV.)

(38)   **Balinese** (Wechsler and Arka, 1998:397)

    a   Wayan Ø-tawang-a   lakar Ø-tangkep polisi.
    Wayan UV-know-3sg FUT UV-arrest police
    'He knew that the police would arrest Wayan.'

    b   *Polisi Ø-tawang-a   Wayan lakar Ø-tangkep.
    police UV-know-3sg Wayan FUT UV-arrest

    c   Polisi Ø-tawang-a   lakar nangkep Wayan.
    police UV-know-3sg FUT AV.arrest Wayan
    'He knew that the police would arrest Wayan.'

    d   *Wayan Ø-tawang-a   polisi lakar nangkep.
    Wayan UV-know-3sg police FUT AV.arrest

There is a very strong cross-linguistic tendency for Raising to target only subjects, so these facts provide strong support for the claim that AV verbs select the Actor as grammatical subject, while UV verbs select the Undergoer as grammatical subject.

Similarly, the controllee in Equi constructions and adverbial clauses must be the grammatical subject. Thus in (39), when the complement verb appears in the UV form (39a), the controllee must be the Undergoer; and when the complement verb appears in the AV form (39b), the controllee must be the Actor. The examples in (40) involve an adverbial purpose clause. Once again, the controllee must be the Undergoer when the subordinate clause contains a UV verb (40a), but the controllee must be the Actor when the subordinate clause contains an AV verb (40b).

(39)   **Balinese** (Artawa, 1998:134)

a   Tiang edot [__ Ø-tangkep polisi].
1sg want   UV-arrest police
'I want the police to arrest me.'

b   Tiang edot [__ nangkep polisi].
1sg want   AV.arrest police
'I want to arrest the police.'

(40)   **Balinese** (adapted from Artawa, 1998:91)

a   Cai teka mai [apang __ bisa Ø-tulung-in   cang].[9]
2sg come here so.that can UV-help-APPL 1sg
'You came here so that I could help you.'

b   Cai teka mai [apang __ bisa nulung-in   cang].
2sg come here so.that can AV.help-APPL 1sg
'You came here so that you could help me.'

The examples in (41) show that non-subjects cannot be controllees in an Equi construction. (Notice that in these examples, apparently involving a father speaking to his child, the speaker uses the term 'father' in place of a first person pronoun.) When the complement verb appears in the AV form, the controllee must be the Actor as in (41a); it cannot be the Undergoer (41c). Similarly, when the complement verb appears in the UV form, the controllee must be the Undergoer (41b); it cannot be the Actor (41d).

(41)   **Balinese** (Arka, 1998, chapter 2; Artawa, 1998)

a   Cai edot [__ nyakitin bapa]?
2 want   AV.hurt father
'Do you want to hurt me (=Father)?'

b   Cai edot [__ sakitin bapa]?
2 want   UV.hurt father
'Do you want me (=Father) to hurt you?'

c   *Bapa sing edot [cai nyakitin __].
father NEG want 2 AV.hurt
'I (=Father) do not want you to hurt me.'

d   *Bapa sing edot [cai sakitin __].
father NEG want 2 UV.hurt
'I (=Father) do not want to hurt you.'

All of this evidence confirms the fact that the alternation between AV and UV involves a change in the grammatical subject of the clause. This in itself is not surprising, of course, since many languages have superficially similar voice systems. What is surprising is our earlier claim that both AV and UV clauses are syntactically transitive, containing two direct (term) arguments; neither construction involves the demotion of a core argument. We will now look at some of the evidence which supports this claim.

Wechsler and Arka (1998) state that terms in Balinese (as in English) are always NPs, while oblique arguments are always expressed as PPs. Thus the fact that both Actor and Undergoer appear as bare NPs in AV and UV clauses suggests that they are both terms. This conclusion is supported by the behavior of "floating quantifiers."

Balinese has several quantifiers meaning 'all.' These quantifiers normally occur within the NP which they modify, but they may also appear in sentence-final position. When this happens, the quantifier may be interpreted as modifying any NP argument of the sentence; but it cannot modify a PP argument, as illustrated in the following examples. (All the arguments in these examples are pronouns, which take on a plural interpretation when modified by the quantifier. The complex quantifier *ajak makejang* 'all' is used only for animate NPs.)

(42)   **Balinese** (Wechsler and Arka, 1998:404)

a   Ia matakon [teken tiang] ibi   ajak.makejang.
     3 ask   to   1   yesterday all
     (i) 'They all asked me yesterday.'
     but not: (ii)?*'He asked us all yesterday.'

b   Ia nakon-in   tiang ibi   ajak.makejang.
     3 AV.ask-APPL 1   yesterday all
     (i) 'They all asked me yesterday.'
     or: (ii) 'He asked us all yesterday.'

c   Ia dengok-in   tiang ibi   ajak.makejang.
     3 UV.visit-APPL 1   yesterday all
     (i) 'We all visited him yesterday.'
     or: (ii) 'I visited all of them yesterday.'

Sentence (42a) is an intransitive sentence containing a third person subject and a first person oblique argument. The floated quantifier 'all' can only be interpreted as modifying the subject NP, and not the oblique PP. But in (42b) the verb takes an applicative suffix which creates an AV transitive clause. Both Actor and Undergoer appear as bare NPs, and both can be interpreted as being modified by the floated quantifier. The same is true of the UV clause in (42c).

Wechsler and Arka (1998) state that floating quantifiers in Balinese may modify any term (direct argument) but no non-term. Thus the examples in (42) provide evidence that both AV and UV clauses contain two direct arguments; both are syntactically transitive.

Further support for this claim comes from the contrast between the UV construction and the Balinese passive, which is illustrated in (43). We are interested primarily in comparing the status of the Actor phrase within the two constructions. Notice that the Actor of the passive is marked with a preposition *antuk*, whereas the UV Actor appears as a bare NP. The Actor of the passive is optional, as indicated by the parentheses in (43a), but the Actor phrase is obligatory in the UV construction.[10]

(43)   **Balinese Passive** (high register; Wechsler and Arka, 1998:429; Wayan Arka, p.c.)

    a   Buku-ne   ka-ambil   (antuk i   guru).
              book-DEF PASS-take by   ART teacher
              'The book has been taken (by the teacher).'

    b   Buku-ne   ka-ambil   antuk i   guru   sami(an).
              book-DEF PASS-take by   ART teacher all
              'The books have all been taken by the teachers.'
              (not: *'The books have been taken by all the teachers.')

In (43b) the floating quantifier *sami(an)* 'all' (high form) can only be interpreted as modifying the patient 'books,' and not as modifying the passive Actor 'teachers.' This fact provides additional evidence for the claim that passive Actors, unlike UV Actors, are oblique arguments.

Possessor topicalization provides another test for termhood. As in Indonesian (see chapter 7), certain possessors in Balinese can be topicalized using a resumptive pronoun strategy. Arka (1998) shows that this is possible only for possessors of term NPs, but not for possessors of obliques. The construction is illustrated in (44b), where the topicalized NP corresponds to the possessor of the subject; and (45b), where the topicalized NP corresponds to the possessor of the direct object. Note the use of the resumptive pronoun =*ne*.

(44) a   Ibi   [*panak I Ketut=e*]_{SUBJ} gugut   cicing.
        yesterday child   I Ketut=DEF UV.bite dog
        'Yesterday a dog bit I Ketut's child'

    b   *I Ketut* ibi   *panak=ne* gugut   cicing.
        I Ketut yesterday child=3   UV.bite dog
        'As for I Ketut, a dog bit his child yesterday.'

(45) a   Dibi   tiang nulungin [*pianak I Ketut=e*]_{OBJ}. (high reg.)
        yesterday 1   AV.help child   I Ketut =DEF
        'I helped I Ketut's child yesterday'.

    b   *I Ketut* dibi   tiang nulungin *pianak=ne*. (high reg.)
        I Ketut yesterday 1   AV.help child=3
        'As for I Ketut, I helped his child yesterday.'

The examples in (46) show that, in a ditransitive clause, the topicalized element may be the possessor of either the primary object (46a) or the secondary object (46b).

(46) a   *I Ketut*, ci maang *adin=ne* jam.
        I Ketut 2 AV.give sibling=3 watch
        'As for I Ketut, you gave his younger sibling a watch.'

    b   *I Ketut*, ci maang   cang *jam=ne*.
        I Ketut 2 AV.give 1   watch=3sg
        'As for I Ketut, you gave me his watch.'

The critical example is (47b), which shows that the possessor of an oblique argument cannot be topicalized. In other words, this construction is a valid test for termhood. Thus (45) and (46) provide clear evidence for the transitivity of the AV construction.

(47) a   Ibi   cai ngejang nasi [*di bodag I Ketut=e*]$_{\text{OBL}}$.
           yesterday 2   AV.put rice in basket I Ketut=DEF
           'You put rice in I Ketut's basket yesterday.'

    b   *I Ketut* ibi   cai ngejang nasi *di bodag=ne*.
           I Ketut yesterday 2   AV.put rice in basket=3
           (for: 'As for I Ketut, you put rice in his basket yesterday.')

Unfortunately this test cannot be applied to possessors of Actors in the UV construction, because UV Actors are normally indefinite while possessed NPs are normally definite. However, additional evidence for the termhood of these arguments (and hence the transitivity of the UV clause) comes from reflexive binding. The Actor of a UV clause can function as the antecedent of a reflexive pronoun within that clause, as in (48a). (The Actor in this example is the clitic pronoun =*a*; the Undergoer *awakne* 'himself' is the grammatical subject, but occurs in final position in this sentence.) But the passive Actor cannot be the antecedent of a reflexive, as illustrated in (48b).[11] Wechsler and Arka (1998) argue that this contrast is explained by the difference in syntactic status between UV Actors, which are terms, and passive Actors, which are oblique arguments.

(48) a   **UV form**:
        Bambang-e ento Ø-pulang-in=a   awakne.
        hole-DEF   that UV-drop-APPL=3$_i$ himself$_i$
        'Into the hole he dumped himself.'

    b   **Passive form** (high register):
        ?*Bambang-e ento ka-pulang-in   ragan idane antuk ida.
        hole-DEF   that PASS-drop-APPL himself$_i$ by   3$_i$
        (*'Into the hole himself was dumped by him.')

We conclude, then, that Balinese has two different transitive clause types. We will refer to the UV construction as an ERGATIVE clause, because the Undergoer is the grammatical subject. It contrasts with the AV construction, in which the Actor is the grammatical subject, which we will refer to as an ACTIVE clause. Let us now turn to another language which exhibits a very similar pattern.

11.5.2   Pangutaran Sama

The contrast between Actor Voice and Undergoer Voice in Pangutaran Sama is illustrated in examples (49–51). Walton (1986:2) states that the basic word-order pattern in a transitive clause, regardless of voice marking, is Verb–Actor–Undergoer–other. As these examples show, UV verbs are morphologically unmarked (i.e., expressed as a bare stem). The AV form for most transitive verbs is marked by an underspecified nasal prefix, similar to the Balinese AV marker, as seen in (50b) and (51b). A few verbs take a different prefix *mag-*, as in (49b).

(49) a   Ø-tigad onde' so.
          UV-cut child snake
          'The child cut the snake.'

     b   mag-tigad onde' so.
          AV-cut   child snake
          'The child cut a snake.'

(50) a   Ø-bəlli ku   taumpa'.
          UV-buy 1sg.GEN   shoe
          'I bought the shoes.'

     b   N-bəlli aku   taumpa'.
          AV-buy 1sg.NOM   shoe
          'I bought some shoes.'

(51) a   Ø-kəllo' nu   aku.
          UV-fetch 2sg.GEN 1sg.NOM
          'You fetch me.'

     b   N-kəllo' ka'u   ma=aku.
          AV-fetch 2sg.NOM DAT=1sg
          'You fetch me.'   (Walton, 1986:107, 109)

As examples (50–51) illustrate, pronouns are inflected for case, with subjects taking nominative case and non-subject Actors taking genitive case. Other NPs are unmarked for case. As in Balinese, both Actor and Undergoer are generally expressed as bare NPs in both AV and UV clauses. But if the Undergoer of an AV clause is definite and human (or personal), as in (51b), it is often marked with the prepositional clitic *ma=*.[12] This marker has both dative and locative uses; I will gloss it as a dative case marker.

Notice that the Undergoer NP in (49) and (50) consists of a bare common noun. In the UV sentences (49a) and (50a) the Undergoer is interpreted as being definite, while in the corresponding AV sentences (49b) and (50b) it is interpreted as being indefinite. This is not accidental, but reflects an important constraint on the choice of voice marking. Gault (1999:8–9) states that in Sama Bangingi', a language very closely related to Pangutaran, grammatical subjects are nearly always definite; and if the Undergoer is definite, it will normally be chosen as grammatical subject, i.e., the verb will normally appear in the UV form. This generalization holds true for Tagalog and a large number of other Philippine languages as well.

Like Balinese, Pangutaran Sama has an applicative suffix which can promote an oblique argument (e.g., benefactive) to Undergoer. Verbs that carry this applicative suffix can appear in both voices, UV (52b) and AV (52c), like any other transitive stem.

(52) a   Ø-bəlli ku   taumpa' ma si   Andi.
        UV-buy 1sg.GEN shoe   DAT PERS Andy
        'I bought the shoes for Andy.'

    b   Ø-bəlli-an   ku   si   Andi taumpa'.
        UV-buy-APPL 1sg.GEN PERS Andy shoe
        'I bought Andy some shoes.'

    c   N-bəlli-an   aku   si   Andi taumpa'.
        AV-buy-APPL 1sg.NOM PERS Andy shoe
        'I bought Andy some shoes.'

Let us now consider some of the evidence which shows that the Actor is the grammatical subject of an AV clause, while the Undergoer is the grammatical subject of a UV clause. As in Balinese, an important piece of evidence comes from relativization: only grammatical subjects can be relativized. Thus when the Undergoer is relativized, the embedded clause must contain a UV verb (53a–b), but when the Actor is relativized the embedded clause must contain an AV verb (53c–d).

(53) a   pəddi na tangan ku   [bay Ø-pəppōk mastal].
        painful now hand   1sg.GEN PAST UV-strike teacher
        'My hand which the teacher beat is painful.'

    b   *pəddi na tangan ku   [bay N-pəppōk mastal].
        painful now hand   1sg.GEN PAST AV-strike teacher

    c   tətto na mastal [bay N-pəppōk tangan ku].
        laugh now teacher PAST AV-strike hand   1sg.GEN
        'the teacher who beat my hand is laughing.'

    d   *tətto na mastal [bay Ø-pəppōk tangan ku].
        laugh now teacher PAST UV-strike hand   1sg.GEN

Walton (1986:123–128) shows that the same constraint applies to other "filler–gap" constructions, specifically Clefts, Wh- questions, and topicalization. In each case the "gap" must be the grammatical subject of its clause, i.e., the Actor in AV clauses and the Undergoer in UV clauses.

Another test for subjecthood in Sama involves a class of Raising predicates meaning 'easy,' 'difficult,' 'likely,' 'almost,' etc. Walton states that only the grammatical subject of the complement clause can be raised to preverbal position following these predicates.[13] Thus only the Actor can be raised when the complement verb is marked for AV as in (54), and only the Undergoer can be raised when the complement verb is marked for UV as in (55a). When the Undergoer is raised in this construction, it seems to be more common for the Actor to be supressed (i.e., omitted entirely) through the use of the passive (see below), as in (55b), or the abilitative/non-volitional form of the verb.[14]

(54) a   alōd   du   aku   N-apas   manuk.
             difficult indeed 1sg.NOM AV-chase chicken
             'It is difficult for me to chase chickens.'

     b   luhay aku   N-daog   atu   ku.
             easily 1sg.NOM AV-defeat enemy 1sg.GEN
             'I will easily defeat my opponent.'

(55) a   alōd   du   so-sandu'   Ø-bono'   ku.
             difficult indeed cobra   UV-kill 1sg.GEN
             'It was difficult for me to kill the cobra.'

     b   alōd   du   so-sandu'   b-i-ono'.
             difficult indeed cobra   PASS-kill
             'It is difficult to kill a cobra.'

As in Balinese, there is a clear contrast in Sama between the UV construction and a true passive. As illustrated in (56), the passive in Pangutaran Sama is marked by an infix -i- which immediately follows the first consonant of the stem. In addition to this difference in verbal morphology, the passive Actor is marked by a preposition uk, while the UV Actor is (as we have seen) a bare NP.

(56) a   Ø-bəlla   dənda kiyakan kami.
             UV-cook girl   food   1pl.GEN
             'The girl cooked our food.'

     b   b-i-lla   uk dənda kiyakan kami.
             PASS-cook by girl   food   1pl.GEN
             'Our food was cooked by the girl.'

Further differences between UV and passive Actors are illustrated in (57) and (58). First, passive Actors are optional; they can be freely omitted, as in (57b). UV Actors, in contrast, cannot be omitted except under coreference with a definite antecedent; this is shown in (57a). Second, passive Actors may be displaced from their normal post-verbal position to appear at the end of the sentence, as in (58c); but this is not possible with UV Actors, as seen in (58b).

(57) a   *Ø-bəlla   kiyakan kami.
             UV-cook food   1pl.GEN
             (for: 'Someone cooked our food.')

     b   b-i-lla   na   kiyakan kami.
             PASS-cook now food   1pl.GEN
             'Our food is already cooked.'

(58) a   Ø-kulamas Putli'   həlla   na   maka jaum.
             UV-scratch princess husband 3sg.GEN with needle
             'The princess scratched her husband with a needle.'

b   *Ø-kulamas həlla   na   maka jaum Putli'.
     UV-scratch husband 3sg.GEN with needle princess
     (for: 'The princess scratched her husband with a needle.')

c   k-i-ulamas   həlla   na   maka jaum   uk Putli'.
     PASS-scratch husband 3sg.GEN with needle by princess
     'Her husband was scratched with a needle by the princess.'

Walton cites these differences as evidence that the passive Actor is an oblique argument, whereas the UV Actor is a term. So the alternation between Actor Voice vs. Undergoer Voice in Pangutaran Sama, as in Balinese, does not involve the demotion of a core argument.[15]

11.5.3   "Patient preference" and markedness

Non-demoting voice systems are found in a number of other Western Austronesian languages as well. Schachter (1984) presents a clear analysis of such a system in Toba Batak, spoken on the island of Sumatra in northwestern Indonesia. Kroeger (1993) proposes a non-demoting analysis for the more complex voice system of Tagalog, and this analysis could be readily extended to many other languages of the central Philippines and northeastern Borneo.

The existence of such systems was, until relatively recently, a controversial issue. Most generative theories of syntax in the 1970s and 1980s predicted that voice alternations could only occur through the demotion of the underlying subject, normally the agent.

Another somewhat controversial feature of these languages is the ergative "slant" to the syntax, i.e., the apparent preference for selecting Undergoers rather than Actors as grammatical subjects. Many theories predicted that the Actor must universally be selected as subject in the most basic transitive construction. Languages like Dyirbal were thought to be exceedingly rare, and were handled by some exceptional means. But linguists are discovering that syntactic ergativity is more common than we once thought.

We suggested in the introduction to section 11.5 that the basic transitive construction in Sama and Balinese was the UV form. What we mean by "basic" in this sense can be more precisely expressed in terms of MARKEDNESS.

The concept of markedness expresses the tendency for one member of a set of opposing values to be "preferred" over the others. In any paradigm or set of linguistic elements which may contrast with each other, the most basic or preferred element is called the UNMARKED member of the set. Some of the criteria which can be used to identify this element include the following:[16]

a   MORPHOLOGICAL MARKEDNESS:
        the element which is morphologically simpler (e.g., bears fewer affixes) is likely to be the most basic (unmarked) alternative. In particular, zero morphemes tend to be associated with the unmarked alternative.

b   FREQUENCY:

the unmarked alternative tends to occur more frequently, e.g., in text counts, than its marked counterparts.

c   DISTRIBUTION:

the unmarked alternative is generally less restricted in its distribution; it tends to occur in a broader range of environments than its marked counterparts. In contexts where the opposition is neutralized, i.e., where only one of the competing forms may occur, the unmarked form is more likely to be chosen.

d   ACQUISITION:

children tend to acquire the unmarked form earlier than its marked counterparts.

Let us try to use these criteria to evaluate the claim that Undergoer Voice is the unmarked voice category in the languages we have been discussing. First, in terms of morphological markedness, we have already seen that the UV form in both Balinese and Sama bears a zero morpheme, in contrast to the nasal prefix which marks the corresponding AV form.

Second, with respect to text frequency, we have mentioned that UV tends to occur more frequently than AV. Let us look at some of the numbers which support this claim:

Sama Bangingi':

Gault (1999:61) did an analysis of voice selection in Sama Bangingi' narratives. She reports that, out of 246 transitive clauses in 7 texts, only 25 percent were AV forms, 75 percent UV (or other minor types).

Toba Batak:

Wouk (1984) carried out a study of Toba Batak texts. Out of 312 transitive clauses in her sample, only 108 (roughly 35 percent) were active (AV) while 204 (roughly 65 percent) were non-active.

Tagalog:

Cooreman, Fox, and Givón (1984) report on a similar study of Tagalog, based on a number of texts taken from Bloomfield's corpus. They report that 166 out of the 203 verb-initial (i.e., basic word order) transitive clauses in their sample were in non-active voice. That is, the Actor was selected as subject in only 18.2 percent of the transitive clauses with basic word order.

These figures stand in sharp contrast to the pattern observed in languages like English. In most English texts, the active voice is far more frequent than the passive. Svartvik (1966) analyzed extracts from two English novels and found that the passive voice was used in only 8 percent of the transitive clauses; 92 percent of the transitive clauses were active. However, in a sample of scientific writing the ratio was nearly even: 51 percent active, 49 percent passive.[17] So the relative frequency is clearly influenced by factors like "register," degree of formality, etc.; but in most everyday contexts, English speakers use the active voice far more often than the passive.

The ratio of AV to UV in Balinese seems to fall somewhere between the figures for English and those for the other Austronesian languages mentioned above. Wayan Pastika (1999) carried out a very detailed study on the voice category of transitive verbs in Balinese narrative discourse. He found that in spoken narrative, the ratio of AV to UV in main clauses was 50:50, whereas in written narrative the ratio of AV to UV was around 70:30. AV was used more frequently in subordinate clauses in both genres, but the difference in frequency was more pronounced in written narrative.[18]

A third kind of evidence that UV is more basic than AV relates to occurrence in particular environments. As mentioned in the previous section, the rule of subject selection for Sama, Tagalog, and other Philippine languages favors the UV form. If there is only one definite argument in a clause, that argument will normally be selected as subject. But if both the Actor and Undergoer are definite, the Undergoer will normally be selected as subject (i.e., the UV form will be used).[19] Thus in environments where the Actor and Undergoer are equally "available" for subject selection, the Undergoer is strongly preferred.

Finally, the available evidence on child language acquisition leads to the same conclusion. Studies on the acquisition of Tagalog verbs (Tucker, 1971; Segalowitz and Galang, 1978; Galang, 1982) indicate that Tagalog-speaking children learn UV forms earlier than the corresponding AV forms. We would normally expect children to learn the most basic form first. For example, in English (and most other languages for which data are available) children acquire the active voice before the passive. So the developmental evidence cited above supports the claim that UV is more basic than AV, at least in Tagalog.[20]

11.6   Conclusion

The crucial difference between a syntactically ergative language like Dyirbal and a language of the more familiar (nominative–accusative) type (e.g., English) has to do with the alignment of semantic roles to grammatical relations. A basic transitive clause in an accusative language has the agent as subject (59a), while a basic transitive clause in an ergative language has the patient as subject (59b). We have argued that some languages, like Balinese and Sama, have transitive constructions of both types. (We follow Wechsler and Arka [1998] here in identifying the agent of an ergative clause as a kind of semantically restricted object; cf. Marantz [1984].)

(59) a   *cut* < agent, patient > **Active**
              | |
            SUBJ OBJ

    b   *cut* < agent, patient > **Ergative**
              | |
            OBJ SUBJ

In chapter 3 we saw that the passive rule demotes the agent to oblique status, and typically promotes the patient to subject. As we have seen in this chapter, the antipassive rule in ergative languages has the opposite effect, demoting the patient to the status of an oblique. The alignments which these processes create are shown in (60).

(60) a   *cut* < agent, patient > **Passive**
              | |
          (OBL) SUBJ

    b   *cut* < agent, patient > **Antipassive**
              | |
         SUBJ (OBL)

One difficulty in recognizing syntactic ergativity is that certain properties which are often assumed to be tests for subjecthood may actually, at least in some languages, be determined on the basis of semantic roles. Since the agent is not the same as the grammatical subject in the ergative construction, there is a potential for a "split" pattern in the syntax between agent properties and subject properties. Reflexive binding and certain types of Equi construction are frequently associated with agents, while Raising and relativization are more likely to be restricted to grammatical subjects. See Manning (1996) for a detailed discussion of these issues and a cross-linguistic survey of syntactic ergativity.

Notes

1. The use of the overt pronoun in this example produces an emphatic reading.
2. Reflexive binding is another very helpful test, since the antecedent of a reflexive must always be the subject. But since there is no passive alternation in Warlpiri, this test does not distinguish grammatical subjects from Actors.
3. The adverbial clause in (8b–c) agrees in case marking with its controller.
4. Most of the examples in this section were originally taken from Dixon (1972). The Dyirbal data have been widely discussed by a number of authors, including Dixon (1979), Mel'čuk (1979), Foley and Van Valin (1984), Comrie (1981), and Levin (1983).
5. Dixon (1972:55) states that two tenses are morphologically distinguished in Dyirbal: future vs. "unmarked" (i.e., non-future). In the examples that follow the future tense is labeled IRREALIS, and the non-future tense is labeled REALIS. The realis suffix has two allomorphs, *-n* and *–nʸu*.
6. Dixon (1972:249) identifies this suffix as an aspect marker; it can also be used to mark repeated actions.

7. Dixon (1972:65) states that it is also possible for the demoted patient of the antipassive to take instrumental/ergative case marking.

8. The antipassive morpheme in Chukchee appears in a number of different allomorphs; here it is marked by zero.

9. Wayan Arka (p.c.) states that *tiang* is the formal (high register) first person pronoun, while *(i)cang* is the corresponding informal (low register) form. *Cai* and *ci* are variant forms of the informal second person pronoun.

10. The Actor can only be omitted from a UV clause under identity with some other NP in its immediate context, i.e., as an instance of zero anaphora with a definite antecedent.

11. Balinese reflexives may take discourse antecedents, if the clause contains no term argument which is higher on the Thematic Hierarchy. This can produce apparent binding by passive agents, as in Wechsler and Arka (1998), ex. (95).

12. The use of dative case for definite animate direct objects is widespread in the Philippines. These dative objects are clearly terms, rather than obliques, at least in Tagalog. The use of *ma* to mark objects in Sama requires further study; it appears to be more restricted than the corresponding Tagalog pattern, and may even be lexically specified.

13. Walton, following the terminology of Foley and Van Valin (1984), uses the term "Pragmatic Pivot" instead of grammatical subject.

14. The Actor cannot be suppressed when the complement verb is a normal UV form, as discussed immediately below. The primary uses of the abilitative/non-volitional mood in Sama seem quite parallel to the use of the non-volitional mood in Tagalog and other Philippine languages, though the specific affix involved in the non-volitional UV form is not cognate.

15. Walton (1986) identifies the AV form as an "antipassive," partly on the basis of the dative marking on definite human objects. But, as Foley and Van Valin (1984:177) point out, there is no evidence that these objects have been demoted to oblique status; see n. 12 above.

16. Adapted from Greenberg (1966); Croft (1990).

17. These figures are taken from Svartvik (1966:62), table 4.13.

18. Passives are excluded from these figures. Passive forms accounted for 6.4 percent of all transitive clauses in spoken narrative, and for 9.8 percent in written narrative. If passive and UV forms were counted together in opposition to the active (AV) form, non-active forms would account for a majority of main clauses in spoken narrative, but would still (almost certainly) represent a minority in written narrative, and in subordinate transitive clauses of both genres.

19. Of course, this rule can be overridden in sentences where some other argument is "extracted" (i.e., questioned, clefted, relativized, etc.), since these operations apply only to subjects.

20. I do not know of any similar studies in the other languages discussed here.

References

Abbreviations

BLS *Proceedings of the nth annual meeting of the Berkeley Linguistics Society* (Berkeley: University of California)

CLS *Papers from the nth regional meeting of the Chicago Linguistic Society* (University of Chicago)

Abasheikh, M. 1979. The grammar of Chimwi:ni causatives. Ph.D. dissertation, University of Illinois, Urbana.

Abbott, Barbara. 1976. Right node raising as a test for constituenthood. *Linguistic Inquiry* 7.4:639–642.

Agbedor, Paul. 1993. Verb serialization in Ewe. *Studies in the Linguistic Sciences* 23.1:21–42.

Aikhenvald, Alexandra. 1999. Serial constructions and verb compounding: evidence from Tariana (North Arawak). *Studies in Language* 23.3:469–498.

Aissen, Judith. 1974. Verb raising. *Linguistic Inquiry* 5:325–366.

1992. Topic and focus in Mayan. *Language* 68.1:43–80.

Akmajian, Adrian, Susan Steele, and Thomas Wasow. 1979. The category AUX in universal grammar. *Linguistic Inquiry* 10.1:1–64.

Allen, J. H., and J. B. Greenough. 1931. *New Latin Grammar*. New Rochelle, NY: Aristide D. Caratzas (repr. 1992).

Alsagoff, Lubna. 1991. Topic in Malay: the other subject. Ph.D. dissertation, Stanford University.

Alsina, Alex. 1992. The argument structure of causatives. *Linguistic Inquiry* 23:517–555.

Alsina, Alex, and Smita Joshi. 1991. Parameters in causative constructions. *CLS* 27.1:1–15.

Alsina, Alex, and Sam A. Mchombo. 1993. Object asymmetries and the Chichewa applicative construction. In Sam Mchombo, ed., *Theoretical aspects of Bantu grammar*. Stanford, CA: CSLI Publications.

Andrews, Avery. 1982. The representation of case in Modern Icelandic. In Bresnan, ed., ch. 7.

1985. The major functions of the noun phrase. In Shopen, ed., vol. 1, 62–154.

1990. Case structures and control. In Maling and Zaenen, eds., *Modern Icelandic syntax*. New York: Academic Press, 187–234.

Andrianierenana, Clement-Luc. 1996. Morphological causatives in Malagasy. *UCLA Occasional Papers in Linguistics* 17:58–75.

Arka, I Wayan. 1998. From morphosyntax to pragmatics in Balinese: a lexical-functional approach. Ph.D. dissertation, University of Sydney.

Aronoff, Mark. 1976. *Word formation in generative grammar*. Cambridge, MA: MIT Press.

Artawa, Ketut. 1998. *Ergativity and Balinese syntax*. NUSA: Linguistic Studies of Indonesian and Other Languages in Indonesia, vol. 42, parts 1–3. Jakarta: Universitas Katolik Indonesia Atma Jaya. (Revised version of 1994 Ph.D. dissertation, La Trobe University.)

Asher, R. E. 1985. *Tamil*. London, Sydney & Dover: Croom Helm.

Asmah Hj. Omar, and Rama Subbiah. 1968. *An introduction to Malay grammar*. Kuala Lumpur: Dewan Bahasa dan Pustaka.

Baker, Mark. 1985. The Mirror Principle and morphosyntactic explanation. *Linguistic Inquiry* 16:373–416.

1988. *Incorporation: a theory of grammatical function changing*. University of Chicago Press.

1989. Object-sharing and projection in serial verb constructions. *Linguistic Inquiry* 20:513–553.

Bamgboṣe, Ayọ. 1974. On serial verbs and verbal status. *Journal of West African Languages* 9.1:17–48.

Banfield, Ann. 1973. Narrative style and the grammar of direct and indirect speech. *Foundations of Language* 10:1–39.

Bell, Sarah J. 1979 (1976). *Cebuano subjects in two frameworks*. Indiana University Linguistics Club.

Bendix, Edward. 1972 (MS). Serial verbs in the Caribbean and West Africa: their semantic analysis in Papiamento. mimeo, Hunter College of the City University of New York.

Bickford, J. Albert. 1998. *Tools for analyzing the world's languages: morphology and syntax*. Dallas: Summer Institute of Linguistics.

Blood, Cindy. 1992. Subject–verb agreement in Kisar. In D. Burquest and W. Laidig, eds., *Descriptive studies in languages of Maluku*, 1–21. NUSA: Linguistic Studies of Indonesian and Other Languages in Indonesia, vol. 34. Jakarta: Universitas Katolik Indonesia Atma Jaya.

Borer, Hagit. 1984. Restrictive relatives in Modern Hebrew. *Natural Language and Linguistic Theory* 2:219–260.

Bradshaw, Joel. 1993. Subject relationships within serial verb constructions in Numbami and Jabêm. *Oceanic Linguistics* 32:133–161.

1999. Null subjects, switch-reference, and serialization in Jabêm and Numbami. *Oceanic Linguistics* 38.2:270–296.

Bresnan, Joan. 1982a. The passive in lexical theory. In Bresnan, ed., ch. 1.

1982b. Control and complementation. In Bresnan, ed., ch. 5.

ed. 1982c. *The mental representation of grammatical relations*. Cambridge, MA: MIT Press.

1997. Mixed Categories as Head Sharing Constructions. Proceedings of the LFG97 Conference, University of California, San Diego, ed. by Miriam Butt and Tracy Holloway King. On-line, Stanford University: http://www-csli.stanford.edu/publications/LFG2/lfg97.html

2001. *Lexical-Functional Syntax*. Oxford: Blackwell.

Bresnan, Joan, and Jonni M. Kanerva. 1989. Locative inversion in Chichewa: a case study of factorization in grammar. *Linguistic Inquiry* 20.1:1–50.

Bresnan, Joan, and Sam A. Mchombo. 1987. Topic, pronoun and agreement in Chichewa. *Language* 63:741–782.

Bruce, Les. 1988. Serialization: from syntax to lexicon. *Studies in Language* 12.1:19–49.

Butt, Miriam. 1995. *The structure of complex predicates in Urdu*. Stanford, CA: CSLI Publications.

Byrne, Francis. 1987. *Grammatical relations in a radical creole: verb complementation in Saramaccan*. Amsterdam: John Benjamins.

1990. Tense marking in serial structures. In Joseph and Zwicky, eds.

Cann, Ronnie, Tami Kaplan, and Ruth Kempson. In press. Data at the grammar–pragmatics interface: the case of English resumptive pronouns. To appear in *Lingua*.

Chen, Ping. 1996. Pragmatic interpretations of structural topics and relativization in Chinese. *Journal of Pragmatics* 20:389–406.

Chomsky, Noam. 1957. *Syntactic structures*. The Hague: Mouton.

1965. *Aspects of the theory of syntax*. Cambridge, MA: MIT Press.

1981. *Lectures on government and binding*. Dordrecht: Foris.

Chung, Sandra. 1976. On the subject of two passives in Indonesian. In Li, ed., 57–98.

1978. *Case marking and grammatical relations in Polynesian*. Austin: University of Texas Press.

Cohen, Nancy. 1976. Some interclausal relations in Jeh. *Mon-Khmer Studies* 5:153–164.

Cole, Peter. 1976. A causative construction in Modern Hebrew: theoretical implications. In Peter Cole, ed., *Studies in modern Hebrew syntax and semantics*. The Hague: North-Holland Publishing Company, 99–128.

Cole, Peter, and Jerrold M. Saddock, eds. 1977. *Grammatical relations. Syntax and Semantics 8*. New York: Academic Press.

Cole, Peter, and Li-May Sung. 1994. Head movement and long-distance reflexives. *Linguistic Inquiry* 25.3:335–406.

Collins, Christopher. 1997. Argument sharing in serial verb constructions. *Linguistic Inquiry* 28:461–497.

Comrie, Bernard. 1976. The syntax of causative constructions: cross-language similarities and divergences. In Shibatani, ed., 1976c, 261–312.

1977. In defense of spontaneous demotion: the impersonal passive. In Cole and Saddock, eds., 47–58.

1981. *Language universals and linguistic typology*. University of Chicago Press.

Comrie, B., and E. L. Keenan. 1979. Noun Phrase Accessibility Revisited. *Language* 55.3:649–664.

Cooreman, Ann. 1988. The antipassive in Chamorro: variations on the theme of transitivity. In Shibatani, ed. 1988. 561–593.

Cooreman, A., B. Fox, and T. Givón. 1984. The discourse definition of ergativity. *Studies in Language* 8:1–34.

Creissels, Denis. 2000. Typology. In B. Heine and D. Nurse, eds., *African languages: an introduction*. Cambridge and New York: Cambridge University Press, 231–258.

Croft, William. 1990. *Typology and universals*. Cambridge and New York: Cambridge University Press.

Crowley, Terry. 1987. Serial verbs in Paamese. *Studies in Language* 11:35–84.

Culy, Christopher. 1990. Syntax and semantics of internally headed relative clauses. Ph.D. dissertation, Stanford University.

Dalrymple, Mary. 1993. *The syntax of anaphoric binding*. Stanford, CA: CSLI Publications.

2001. *Lexical-Functional grammar. Syntax and semantics*, vol. 34. New York: Academic Press.

Davies, William D., and Carol Rosen. 1988. Unions as multi-predicate clauses. *Language* 64.1.52–88.

Déchaine, Rose-Marie. 1993. Serial verb constructions. In *Syntax; ein Internationales Handbuch zeitgenössischer Forschung, 1.Halbband*, ed. by J. Jacobs *et al*. Berlin: De Gruyter, 799–825.

Dik, Simon C. 1978. *Functional grammar*. Amsterdam and New York: North-Holland.

Dixon, R. M. W. 1972. *The Dyirbal language of north Queensland*. Cambridge University Press.

1979. Ergativity. *Language* 55.1:59–138.

Dryer, Matthew S. 1986. Primary objects, secondary objects, and antidative. *Language* 62.4:808–845.

Dubinsky, Stanley. 1990. Light verbs and predicate demotion in Japanese. In K. Dziwirek, P. Farrell, and E. Mejías-Bikandi, eds., *Grammatical relations: a cross-theoretical perspective*. Stanford, CA: CSLI Publications.

Dukes, Michael. 1998. Evidence for grammatical functions in Tongan. In M. Butt and T. King, eds., Proceedings of the LFG98 Conference. CSLI On-Line Publications: http://www-csli.stanford.edu/pubs/

Durie, Mark. 1997. Grammatical structures in verb serialization. In A. Alsina, J. Bresnan, and P. Sells, eds., Complex predicates. Stanford, CA: CSLI Publications.

Falk, Yehuda N. 1984. The English auxiliary system: a Lexical-Functional analysis. Language 60.3:483–509.

———. 2001. Lexical-Functional Grammar: an introduction to parallel constraint-based syntax. Stanford, CA: CSLI Publications.

Foley, William, and Mike Olson. 1985. Clausehood and verb serialization. In J. Nichols and A. C. Woodbury, eds., Grammar inside and outside the clause: some approaches to theory from the field. Cambridge: Cambridge University Press.

Foley, William A., and Robert D. Van Valin. 1984. Functional syntax and universal grammar. New York: Cambridge University Press.

———. 1985. Information packaging in the clause. In Shopen, ed., vol. 1, 282–364.

Galang, Rosita G. 1982. Acquisition of Tagalog verb morphology: linguistic and cognitive factors. Philippine Journal of Linguistics 13.2:1–15.

Gault, JoAnn Marie. 1999. An ergative description of Sama Bangingi'. Philippine Journal of Linguistics special monograph issue no. 46. Manila: Linguistic Society of the Philippines.

Geluykens, Ronald. 1992. From discourse process to grammatical construction: on left-dislocation in English. Amsterdam: John Benjamins.

Gibson, Jeanne. 1978. Surface and derived structure in Indonesian. In Wurm and Carrington, eds., Second international conference on Austronesian linguistics: proceedings, fascicle 1. Pacific Linguistics C-61. Canberra: Research School of Pacific and Asian Studies, Australian National University, 537–557.

———. 1980. Clause union in Chamorro and in universal grammar. Ph.D. dissertation, University of California, San Diego.

Gibson, Jeanne, and Inci Özkaragöz. 1981. The syntactic nature of the Turkish causative construction. CLS 17:83–98.

Gibson, Jeanne, and Eduardo Rapposo. 1986. Clause union, the Stratal Uniqueness Law, and the chômeur relation. Natural Language and Linguistic Theory 4.2:295–331.

Givón, Talmy. 1973. Complex NPs, word order and resumptive pronouns in Hebrew. In Corum, Smith-Stark, and Weiser, eds. You take the high node and I'll take the low node: papers from the comparative syntax festival. Chicago: Chicago Linguistic Society, 135–146.

Givón, Talmy. 1984. Syntax: a functional-typological introduction, vol. 1. Amsterdam and Philadelphia: John Benjamins.

Gradin, Dwight. 1976. The verb in Jeh. Mon-Khmer Studies 5:43–75.

Greenberg, Joseph H. 1966. Language universals, with special reference to feature hierarchies. Janua Linguarum, Series Minor 59. The Hague: Mouton.

Grosu, Alexander. 1976. A note on subject raising to object and Right Node Raising. Linguistic Inquiry 7.4:642–645.

Guo Wu. 1995. The teaching of Chinese and the Chinese way of thinking. Australian Review of Applied Linguistics Series S, 12:131–152.

Haegeman, Liliane. 1991. Introduction to Government and Binding Theory. Oxford, and Cambridge, MA: Blackwell.

Hale, Kenneth. 1981. On the position of Walbiri in a typology of the base. Indiana University Linguistics Club.

———. 1982. Some essential features of Warlpiri verbal clauses. In Swartz, ed., Papers in Warlpiri grammar. Berrimah, NT: Summer Institute of Linguistics.

———. 1983. Warlpiri and the grammar of non-configurational languages. Natural Language and Linguistic Theory 1:5–47.

1991. Misumalpan verb sequencing constructions. In Claire Lefebvre, ed., *Serial verbs: grammatical, comparative and cognitive approaches*. Amsterdam: John Benjamins.

Hall, Fitzedward. 1882. On the separation, by a word or words, of *to* and the infinitive mood. *The American Journal of Philology* 3:17–24.

Hamel, Patricia J. 1993. Serial verbs in Loniu and an evolving preposition. *Oceanic Linguistics* 32.1:111–132.

Haspelmath, Martin. 1996. Word-class-changing inflection and morphological theory. In Booij and van Marle, eds., *Yearbook of Morphology 1995*. Dordrecht: Kluwer Academic Publishers, 43–66.

Healey, Joan. 1990. *Grammar exercises*. Kangaroo Ground, Victoria: Summer Institute of Linguistics.

Hewitt, B. G. 1979. *Abkhaz*. Lingua descriptive studies, vol. 2. Amsterdam: North-Holland Pub.

Hopper, Paul. 1979. Some observations on the typology of focus and aspect in narrative language. *Studies in Language* 3:37–64.

1983. Ergative, passive, and active in Malay narrative. In F. Klein-Andreu, ed., *Discourse perspectives in syntax*. New York: Academic Press, 67–88.

Hopper, Paul, and Sandra A. Thompson. 1980. Transitivity in grammar and discourse. *Language* 56:251–299.

Huddleston, Rodney. 1984. *Introduction to the grammar of English*. Cambridge University Press.

Hudson, Joyce. 1978. *The core of Walmatjari grammar*. Canberra: Australian Institute for Aboriginal Studies.

Hyman, Larry. 1971. Consecutivisation in Fe?Fe?. *Journal of African Languages* 10.2:29–42.

1975. On the change from SOV to SVO: evidence from Niger-Congo. In C. N. Li, ed., *Word order and word order change*. Austin: University of Texas Press, 113–47.

Hyman, Larry, and Karl Zimmer. 1976. Embedded topic in French. In Li, ed., 189–211.

Ishikawa, Akira. 1985. Complex predicates and lexical operations in Japanese. Ph.D. dissertation, Stanford University.

Jackendoff, Ray S. 1990. *Semantic structures*. Cambridge, MA: MIT Press.

Jansen, V., H. J. Koopman, and P. Muysken. 1978. Serial verbs in the creole languages. *Amsterdam Creole Studies* 2:125–159.

Jarkey, N. 1991. Serial verbs in White Hmong: a functional approach. Ph.D. dissertation, University of Sydney.

Joseph, Brian D., and Arnold M. Zwicky, eds. 1990. *When verbs collide: papers from the 1990 Ohio state mini-conference on serial verbs*. Ohio State University Working Papers in Linguistics 39.

Kaplan, Ronald M., and Joan Bresnan. 1982. Lexical-Functional Grammar: a formal system for grammatical representation. In Bresnan, ed., ch. 4.

Keenan, Edward L. 1985a. Passive in the world's languages. In Shopen, ed., vol. 1, 243–281.

1985b. Relative clauses. In Shopen, ed., vol. 2, 141–170.

Keenan, Edward L., and Bernard Comrie. 1977. NP accessibility and universal grammar. *Linguistic Inquiry* 8:63–100.

1979. Data on the noun phrase accessibility hierarchy. *Language* 55:333–351.

Kim, Kyu-hyun. 1995. WH-clefts and left-dislocation in English conversation: cases of topicalization. In P. Downing and M. Noonan, eds., *Word order in discourse*. Amsterdam: John Benjamins, 247–296.

Kimenyi, Alexandre. 1980. *A relational grammar of Kinyarwanda*. Berkeley, CA: University of California Press.

King, Tracy Holloway. 1995. *Configuring topic and focus in Russian*. Stanford, CA: CSLI Publications.

Kiparsky, Paul. 1973. "Elsewhere" in phonology. In Anderson and Kiparsky, eds., *A festschrift for Morris Halle*. New York: Holt, Rinehart and Winston, 93–106.

——— 1997. The rise of positional licensing. In A. Van Kemenade and N. Vincent, eds., *Parameters of morphosyntactic change*. London: Cambridge University Press, 460–494.

Kisseberth, C., and M. Abasheikh. 1977. The object relationship in Chi-Mwi:ni, a Bantu language. In Cole and Saddock, eds., 179–218.

Koopman, Hilda. 1983. Control from COMP and comparative syntax. *The Linguistic Review* 2:365–391.

——— 1984. *The syntax of verbs: from verb movement rules in the Kru languages to universal grammar*. Studies in generative grammar 15. Dordrecht and Cinnaminson, NJ: Foris Publications.

Koshimizu, Masaru. 1985. *Chugokugo no goho no hanashi: Chugokugo bunpo gairon*. Chugokugo kenkyu gakushu sosho. [Lectures on Chinese usage: introduction to Chinese grammar. Studies in Chinese Language Series.] Tokyo: Koseikan.

Kozinsky, I. Š., V. P. Nedjalkov, and M. S. Polinskaja. 1988. Antipassive in Chukchee: oblique object, object incorporation, zero object. In Shibatani, ed., 1988. 651–706.

Kroch, Anthony. 1981. On the role of resumptive pronouns in amnestying island constraint violations. *CLS* 17:125–135.

Kroeger, Paul R. 1993. *Phrase structure and grammatical relations in Tagalog*. Stanford, CA: CSLI Publications.

——— 1996. The morphology of affectedness in Kimaragang Dusun. In H. Steinhauer, ed., *Papers in Austronesian Linguistics No. 3*. Pacific Linguistics A-84. Canberra: Research School of Pacific and Asian Studies, Australian National University.

——— in press. Kimaragang. In S. Adelaar and N. Himmelmann, eds., *The Austronesian languages of Asia and Madagascar*. London: Routledge-Curzon.

Kuno, Susumu. 1972. Functional sentence perspective. *Linguistic Inquiry* 3:269–320.

——— 1973. *The structure of the Japanese language*. Cambridge, MA: MIT Press.

Lane, J. 1991. Kalam serial verb constructions. M.A. thesis, University of Auckland.

Laniran, Y., and O. Sonaiya. 1987. Problems in the syntax and semantics of serial verb constructions in Niger-Congo: the Yoruba example. Paper presented at the 1st Niger-Congo Syntax and Semantics Workshop, Boston University, April 1987.

Laughren, Mary. 1989. The Configurationality Parameter and Warlpiri. In L. K. Maracz and P. Muysken, eds., *Configurationality: the typology of asymmetries*. Dordrecht: Foris Publications, 319–353.

——— 1992. Secondary predication as a diagnostic of underlying structure in Pama-Nyungan languages. In I. M. Roca, ed., *Thematic structure: its role in grammar*. Linguistic Models Series. Berlin and New York: Foris Publications, 199–246.

Levin, Beth. 1983. On the nature of ergativity. Ph.D. dissertation, Massachusetts Institute of Technology.

Li, Charles N., ed. 1976. *Subject and topic*. New York: Academic Press.

Li, Charles, and Sandra Thompson. 1976. Subject and topic: a new typology of language. In Li, ed., 457–489.

——— 1981. *Mandarin Chinese: a functional reference grammar*. Berkeley, CA: University of California Press.

Longacre, Robert E. 1983. Switch reference systems from two distinct linguistic areas: Wojokeso (Papua New Guinea) and Guanano (northern South America). In John Haiman and Pamela Munro, eds., *Switch-reference and universal grammar: proceedings of a symposium on switch reference and universal grammar, Winnipeg, May 1981*. vol. 2. Typological Studies in Language 2. Philadelphia: John Benjamins, 185–207.

——— 1985. Sentences as combinations of clauses. In Shopen, ed., vol. 2, 235–286.

——— 1996. *The grammar of discourse*, 2nd edn. New York and London: Plenum Press.

Lord, Carol. 1974. Causative constructions in Yoruba. *Studies in African Linguistics*, Supplement 5:195–204.

———. 1975. Igbo verb compounding and the lexicon. *Studies in African Linguistics* 6:23–47.

Lyons, John. 1966. Towards a "notional" theory of the "parts of speech." *Journal of Linguistics* 2:209–236.

Macdonald, R. Ross (with Soenjono Darjowidjojo). 1976. *Indonesian reference grammar*. Washington, DC: Georgetown University Press.

Makino, Seiichi. 1982. Japanese grammar and functional grammar. *Lingua* 57:125–173.

Maling, Joan. 1982. Clause-bounded reflexives in Modern Icelandic. In L. Hellan and K. Christensen, eds., *Topics in Scandinavian syntax*. Boston: Reidel, 53–63.

Manning, Christopher. 1996. *Ergativity: argument structure and grammatical relations*. Stanford, CA: CSLI Publications.

Marantz, Alec. 1984. *On the nature of grammatical relations*. Linguistic Inquiry Monographs, no. 10. Cambridge, MA: MIT Press.

Martin, J. R. 1990. Interpersonal grammatization: mood and modality in Tagalog. *Philippine Journal of Linguistics* 21.1:2–50.

Mashudi B. H. Kader. 1981. *The syntax of Malay interrogatives*. Kuala Lumpur: Dewan Bahasa dan Pustaka.

Masica, C. 1976. *Defining a linguistic area: South Asia*. Chicago: University of Chicago Press.

Matthews, P. H. 1981. *Syntax*. Cambridge and New York: Cambridge University Press.

Matsumoto, Yo. 1996. *Complex predicates in Japanese: a syntactic and semantic study of the notion "word."* Stanford, CA: CSLI Publications.

———. 1998. A re-examination of the cross-linguistic parameterization of causative predicates: Japanese perspectives. In M. Butt and T. King, eds., The Proceedings of the LFG '98 Conference. University of Queensland, Brisbane. CSLI On-Line Publications. ISSN 1098–6782. Available at: http://www-csli.stanford.edu/pubs/

Matsumoto, Yoshiko. 1997. *Noun-modifying constructions in Japanese: a frame semantic approach*. Studies in Language Companion Series 35. Amsterdam and Philadelphia: John Benjamins.

McCawley, James D. 1988. *The syntactic phenomena of English*. Chicago: University of Chicago Press.

Mel'čuk, Igor. 1979. The predicative construction in Dyirbal. In *Studies in dependency syntax. Linguistica extranea: Studia 2*. (Ed. by Paul T. Roberge.) Ann Arbor: Karoma Publishers, 23–90.

Merrifield, William *et al.* 1987. *Laboratory manual for morphology and syntax*. Dallas: Summer Institute of Linguistics.

Mohanan, K. P. 1982. Grammatical relations and clause structure in Malayalam. In J. Bresnan, ed., ch. 8.

———. 1983a. Move NP or lexical rules? Evidence from Malayalam causativisation. In L. Levin, M. Rappaport, and A. Zaenen, eds., *Papers in LFG*. Indiana University Linguistic Club.

———. 1983b. Functional and anaphoric control. *Linguistic Inquiry* 14:641–674.

Mohanan, K. P., and Tara Mohanan. 1990. Dative subjects in Malayalam: semantic information in syntax. In M. Verma and K. P. Mohanan, eds., *Experiencer subjects in South Asian languages*. Stanford, CA: CSLI Publications, 43–57.

Mohanan, Tara. 1988. Causatives in Malayalam. Unpublished MS. Department of Linguistics, Stanford University.

———. 1994. *Argument structure in Hindi*. Stanford, CA: CSLI Publications.

Nevis, Joel. 1988 (1985). *Finnish particle clitics and general clitic theory*. Outstanding dissertations in linguistics. New York: Garland.

O'Grady, William. 1987. The interpretation of Korean anaphora. *Language* 63:251–277.

Olson, Michael L. 1981. Barai clause junctures: toward a functional theory of interclausal relations. Ph.D. dissertation, Australian National University.

Pastika, I Wayan. 1999. Voice selection in Balinese narrative discourse. Ph.D. dissertation, Australian National University.

Payne, Thomas. 1997. *Describing morphosyntax: a guide for field linguists*. Cambridge: Cambridge University Press.

Perlmutter, David, ed. 1983. *Studies in relational grammar I*. Chicago: University of Chicago Press.

Pike, Kenneth L. 1966. *Tagmemic and matrix linguistics applied to selected African languages*. Ann Arbor, MI: University of Michigan Center for Research on Language and Language Behavior; Office of Education, U.S. Dept. of Health, Education and Welfare.

Pinker, Stephen. 1989. *Learnability and cognition*. Cambridge, MA: MIT Press.

Prince, Ellen. 1990. Syntax and discourse: a look at resumptive pronouns. *BLS* 16:482–497.

1997. On the functions of left-dislocation in English discourse. In A. Kamio, ed., *Directions in functional linguistics*. Amsterdam: John Benjamins, 117–143.

Pullum, Geoffrey K. 1990. Constraints on intransitive quasi-serial verb constructions in modern colloquial English. In Joseph and Zwicky, eds., 218–239.

1997. The morpholexical nature of *to*-contraction. *Language* 73:79–102.

Radford, Andrew. 1988. *Transformational grammar: a first course*. Cambridge: Cambridge University Press.

Ramli Hj. Salleh. 1989. *Fronted constituents in Malay: base structures and move alpha in a configurational non-Indo-European language*. Kuala Lumpur: Dewan Bahasa dan Pustaka.

Ramos, Teresita V. 1971. *Tagalog Structures*. PALI Language Texts. Honolulu: University of Hawaii Press.

Rao, M., and E. Bashir. 1985. On the semantics and pragmatics of Telugu causatives. *CLS* 21.2:228–240.

Reesink, Ger P. 1987. *Structures and their functions in Usan: a Papuan language of Papua New Guinea*. Studies in language companion series, vol. 13. Amsterdam and Philadelphia: John Benjamins.

Roberts, John R. 1988. Amele switch reference and the theory of grammar. *Linguistic Inquiry* 19:45–63.

Ross, John Robert. 1967. Constraints on variables in syntax. Ph.D. dissertation, Massachusetts Institute of Technology.

1986. *Infinite syntax*. Norwood, NJ: ABLEX.

Rouveret, Alain, and Jean-Roger Vergnaud. 1980. Specifying reference to the subject: French causatives and conditions on representations. *Linguistic Inquiry* 11:97–202.

Sadock, Jerrold M. 1980. Noun incorporation in Greenlandic: a case of syntactic word-formation. *Language* 57:300–319.

Sag, Ivan A., and Janet Dean Fodor. 1994. Extraction without traces. WCCFL 13. Stanford, CA: CSLI Publications, 365–84.

Saksena, Anuradha. 1980. The affected agent. *Language* 56.4:812–826.

Sayers, Dorothy. 1936. *Gaudy night*. New York: Harper & Row.

Schachter, Paul. 1974. A non-transformational account of serial verbs. *Studies in African Linguistics*, Supplement 5:253–270.

1976. The subject in Philippine languages: topic, actor, actor-topic, or none of the above. In Li, ed., 491–518.

1977. Reference-related and role-related properties of subjects. In Cole and Saddock, eds., 279–306.

1984. Semantic-role-based syntax in Toba Batak. In Schachter, ed., 122–149.

ed. 1984. *Studies in the structure of Toba Batak*. UCLA Occasional Papers in Linguistics No. 5. Los Angeles: Department of Linguistics, UCLA.

1985. Parts-of-speech systems. In Shopen, ed., vol. 1, 3–61.

Schiller, Eric. 1990a. On the definition and distribution of serial verb constructions. In Joseph and Zwicky, eds., 34–64.

1990b. The typology of serial verb constructions. *CLS* 26:393–406.

Sebba, Mark. 1987 (1983). *The syntax of serial verbs*. Amsterdam: John Benjamins.

Segalowitz, Norman, and Rosita G. Galang. 1978. Agent–patient word order preference in the acquisition of Tagalog. *Journal of Child Language* 5:47–64.

Sells, Peter. 1990. Is there Subject-to-Object Raising in Japanese? In K. Dziwirek, P. Farrell, and E. Mejías-Bikandi, eds., *Grammatical relations: a cross-theoretical perspective*. Stanford, CA: CSLI Publications.

Seuren, Pieter. 1990. Serial Verb Constructions. In Joseph and Zwicky, eds., 14–33.

Shi, Dingxu. 2000. Topic and topic-comment constructions in Mandarin Chinese. *Language* 76.2:383–408.

Shibatani, Masayoshi. 1976a. The grammar of causative constructions: a conspectus. In Shibatani, ed., 1976c, 1–40.

1976b. Causativization. In Shibatani, ed., 1976d, 239–294.

ed. 1976c. *The grammar of causative constructions. Syntax and semantics*, vol. 6. New York: Academic Press.

ed. 1976d. *Japanese generative grammar. Syntax and Semantics*, vol. 5. New York: Academic Press.

ed. 1988. *Passive and voice*. Typological studies in language 16. Amsterdam and Philadelphia: John Benjamins.

1999. Dative subject constructions twenty-two years later. *Studies in the linguistic sciences* 29.2:45–76.

Shopen, Timothy, ed. 1985. *Language typology and syntactic description*, vols. 1–3. Cambridge University Press.

Simpson, Jane H. 1983. Aspects of Warlpiri morphology and syntax. Ph.D. dissertation, Massachusetts Institute of Technology.

1991. *Warlpiri morpho-syntax: a lexicalist approach*. Dordrecht: Kluwer Academic.

Simpson, Jane, and Joan Bresnan. 1983. Control and obviation in Warlpiri. *Natural Language and Linguistic Theory* 1:49–64.

Sneddon, James. 1996. *Indonesian reference grammar*. London and New York: Routledge; and St. Leonards, NSW: Allen & Unwin.

Song, Jae Jung. 1991. Causatives and universal grammar: an alternative interpretation. *Transactions of the Philological Society* 89.1:65–94.

Sridhar, S. N. 1979. Dative subjects and the notion of subject. *Lingua* 49:99–125.

Stageberg, Norman C. 1971. *An introductory English grammar* (second edn.). New York: Holt, Rinehart & Winston.

Stahlke, Herbert. 1970. Serial verbs. *Studies in African Linguistics* 1.1:60–99.

Steele, Susan. 1978. The category AUX as a language universal. In Greenberg et al., eds., *Universals of human language: word structure*. Stanford, CA: Stanford University Press, vol. 3, 7–45.

Stern, Guy, and Everett F. Bleiler. 1961. *Teach yourself essential German grammar*. New York: Dover Publications.

Svartvik, Jan. 1966. *On voice in the English verb*. Janua Linguarum, Series Practica 63. The Hague: Mouton.

Tallerman, Maggie. 1998. *Understanding syntax*. London and New York: Arnold.

Tan Fu. 1991. Notion of subject in Chinese. Ph.D. dissertation, Stanford University.

Thomas, David. 1971. *Chrau grammar*. Oceanic Linguistics Special Publication 7. Honolulu: University Press of Hawaii.

Topping, Donald M. 1973. *Chamorro reference grammar*. Honolulu: University of Hawaii Press.

Tsujimura, Natsuko. 1996. *An introduction to Japanese linguistics*. Cambridge, MA, and Oxford: Basil Blackwell.

Tsutsui, Michio. 1981. Ellipsis of *wa* in Japanese. In S. Makino, ed., *Papers from the Middlebury symposium on Japanese discourse analysis*. Urbana, IL: University of Illinois, 295–319.

Tucker, G. Richard. 1971. Focus acquisition by Filipino children. *Philippine Journal of Psychology* 4.1:21–24.

Underhill, Robert. 1976. *Turkish grammar*. Cambridge, MA: MIT Press.

Vamarasi, Marit Kana. 1999. *Grammatical relations in Bahasa Indonesia*. Pacific Linguistics, Series D, vol. 93. Canberra: Research School of Pacific and Asian Studies, The Australian National University.

Van Leynseele, H. 1975. Restrictions on serial verbs in Anyi. *Journal of West African Languages* 16:189–218.

Vitale, Anthony J. 1981. *Swahili syntax*. Publications in language sciences, no. 5. Dordrecht and Cinnaminson, NJ: Foris Publications.

Walton, Charles. 1986. *Sama verbal semantics: classification, derivation and inflection*. Linguistic Society of the Philippines, Special Monograph Issue, 25. Manila: Linguistic Society of the Philippines.

Wasow, Thomas. 1977. Transformations and the lexicon. In P. Culicover, T. Wasow, and A. Akmajian, eds., *Formal syntax*. New York: Academic Press, 327–60.

Wasow, Thomas, and T. Roeper. 1972. On the subject of gerunds. *Foundations of Language* 8:4–61.

Wechsler, Stephen, and I Wayan Arka. 1998. Syntactic ergativity in Balinese: an argument structure based theory. *Natural Language and Linguistic Theory* 16.2:387–441.

Williamson, Kay. 1965. *A grammar of the Kolokuma dialect of Ịọ*. West African Language Monographs 2. Cambridge: Cambridge University Press.

Woodbury, Anthony C. 1977. Greenlandic Eskimo, ergativity, and relational grammar. In Cole and Saddock, eds., 307–336.

Wouk, Fay. 1984. Scalar transitivity and trigger choice in Toba Batak. In Schachter, ed., 195–219.

Xu, Liejiong, and D. Terrence Langendoen. 1985. Topic structures in Chinese. *Language* 61.1:1–27.

Zaenen, Annie, Joan Maling, and Höskuldur Thráinsson. 1985. Case and grammatical functions: the Icelandic passive. *Natural Language and Linguistic Theory* 3:441–483.

Zimmer, Karl E. 1976. Some constraints on Turkish causativization. In Shibatani, ed., 1976c, 399–412.

General index

Language index